Identification for Prediction and Decision

Identification *for* Prediction *and* Decision

Charles F. Manski

Harvard University Press   *Cambridge, Massachusetts, and London, England*
2007

Library of Congress Cataloging-in-Publication Data

Manski, Charles F.
  Identification for prediction and decision / Charles F. Manski.
      p.   cm.
  Includes bibliographical references and index.
  ISBN-13: 978-0-674-02653-7 (alk. paper)
  ISBN-10: 0-674-02653-5 (alk. paper)
 1. Forecasting—Methodology.   2. Social prediction.   3. Decision making.   I. Title.
  H61.4.M36 2007
    303.49—dc22   2007006086

*To Chris, Jeff, John, Phil, Elie, Arie, Francesca,
Adeline, Jörg, Adam, and Alex.*

With Appreciation.

Contents

Preface

My 1995 book, *Identification Problems in the Social Sciences* (IPSS), put forward a fresh worldview to guide empirical research in the social sciences and worked out the implications in selected settings. I recommended that researchers first ask what can be learned from data using knowledge of the sampling process alone, then ask what more can be learned when data are combined with weak but widely credible distributional assumptions, and finally ask what further can be learned when the data are combined with stronger, less credible assumptions. I reasoned that inferences predicated on weak assumptions can achieve wide consensus, while ones that require strong assumptions almost inevitably are subject to sharp disagreements. Hence beginning with the data alone establishes a "domain of consensus" among researchers and serves to bound their disagreements.

I have found that my reasoning arouses strong reactions. Some think it natural and compelling, while others see it as unnecessarily conservative. The flashpoint of controversy has been the fact that empirical analysis with weak assumptions typically yields bounds on parameters of interest rather than point inferences. Some researchers are comfortable reporting findings in the form of bounds and appreciate the inherent trade-off between strength of assumptions and strength of findings that the bounds make plain. Others hold firm to the traditional practice of reporting point estimates of parameters, even though these estimates may rest on fragile foundations. I do not expect a consensus to emerge soon in favor of my worldview, but I do perceive that social scientists are increasingly aware of the basic issues and increasingly take them seriously.

I believe that the most effective way to build the case for a general point of view is to develop its implications as deeply and widely as possible. When I completed work on IPSS in June 1994, I could see many directions to deepen and broaden the analysis presented in the book, but I did not anticipate all of the domains in which important new findings would emerge. Now, more than twelve years later, I can with satisfaction point to significant advances in multiple directions.

I have increasingly felt that it would be valuable to write a *next-generation* monograph that presents the important new themes opened and findings achieved since publication of IPSS, while retaining most of the material that appeared there. I delayed for several years because I knew from experience how enveloping the task of book writing could be. Mike Aronson at Harvard University Press gently encouraged me from time to time, until finally I was ready to begin. It has been a pleasure to work with Mike, as it was when preparing IPSS. I am grateful to Alex Tetenov and to two reviewers for their comments on a draft of the manuscript. I am also grateful to the National Science Foundation for its financial support through grant SES-0549544.

The dedication at the front of the book is to a sequence of Ph.D. students whose dissertation research I have been privileged to advise since the early 1990s, first at the University of Wisconsin–Madison and then at Northwestern. The persons named have made their own contributions to the study of identification for prediction and decision. And they have become valued colleagues and friends.

December 2006

Identification for Prediction and Decision

Introduction

The Reflection Problem

Here is an identification problem from everyday life: Suppose that you observe the almost simultaneous movements of a person and of his image in a mirror. Does the mirror image induce the person's movements, does the image reflect the person's movements, or do the person and image move together in response to a common external stimulus? Data alone cannot answer this question. Even if you were able to observe innumerable instances in which persons and their mirror images move together, you would not be able to logically deduce the process at work. To reach a conclusion requires that you understand something of optics and of human behavior.

A related identification problem, which I have called the *reflection problem* (Manski, 1993), arises if you try to interpret the common observation that individuals belonging to the same group tend to behave similarly. Three hypotheses often advanced to explain this phenomenon are

endogenous effects, where the propensity of an individual to behave in some way varies with the prevalence of the behavior in the group;

contextual effects, where the propensity of an individual to behave in some way varies with the distribution of background characteristics in the group;

correlated effects, where individuals in the same group tend to behave similarly because they face similar environments or have similar individual characteristics.

Similar behavior within groups could stem from endogenous effects; for example, group members could experience pressure to conform to group norms. Or group similarities might reflect correlated effects; for example, persons with similar characteristics might choose to associate with one another. Data on the behavior of individuals in groups, even innumerable observations, cannot per se distinguish between these hypotheses. To draw conclusions requires that empirical evidence be combined with sufficiently strong maintained assumptions about the nature of individual behavior and social interactions.

Why might you care whether observed patterns of group behavior are generated by endogenous effects, contextual effects, correlated effects, or in some other way? A good practical reason is that different processes have different implications for public policy. For example, understanding how students interact in classrooms is critical to the evaluation of many aspects of educational policy, from ability tracking to class size standards to racial integration programs.

Suppose that, unable to interpret observed patterns of behavior, you seek the expert advice of several social scientists. One asserts that pressure to conform to group norms makes the individuals in a group tend to behave similarly (an endogenous effect). Another states that behavior depends on the demographic composition of the group (a contextual effect). A third maintains that persons with similar characteristics choose to associate with one another (a correlated effect). All of these assertions may be consistent with the empirical evidence. The data alone cannot reveal which is correct. Perhaps all are. This is an identification problem.

The Law of Decreasing Credibility

The reflection problem illustrates that data alone do not suffice to draw conclusions about a population of interest. Inference always requires assumptions about the population and the sampling process generating the available data. Methodological research aims to illuminate the logic of inference by showing how data and assumptions combine to yield conclusions.

Empirical researchers usually enjoy learning of positive methodological findings. Particularly pleasing are results showing that available data and credible assumptions permit one to draw strong conclusions. Negative findings are less welcome. Researchers are especially reluctant to learn that, given the available data, some desirable conclusion cannot be drawn unless untenable assumptions are invoked. Be this as it may, both positive and negative findings are important.

Empirical researchers should be concerned with both the logic and the credibility of their inferences. Credibility is a subjective matter, yet I take there to be wide agreement on a principle (Manski, 2003) that I have called

The Law of Decreasing Credibility The credibility of inference decreases with the strength of the assumptions maintained.

This principle implies that empirical researchers face a dilemma as they decide what assumptions to maintain. Stronger assumptions yield inferences that may be tighter but less credible. Methodological research cannot resolve the dilemma but can clarify its nature.

Identification and Statistical Inference

For over a century, the study of inferential methods has made productive use of probability and statistics. One supposes that the problem is to learn about a population described by a probability distribution and that the available data are observations drawn from the population by some sampling process. One combines the data with assumptions to draw statistical conclusions about the population.

Working within this framework, it is useful to separate the inferential problem into statistical and identification components. Studies of identification seek to characterize the conclusions that could be drawn if one could use the sampling process to obtain an unlimited number of observations. Studies of statistical inference seek to characterize the generally weaker conclusions that can be drawn from a finite number of observations. The study of identification logically comes first. Negative identification findings imply that statistical inference is fruitless: it makes no sense to try to use a sample of finite size to infer something that could not be learned even if a sample of infinite size were available. Positive identification findings imply that one should go on to study statistical inference.

Koopmans (1949, p. 132) put it this way in the article that introduced the term *identification* into the literature:

> In our discussion we have used the phrase "a parameter that can be determined from a sufficient number of observations." We shall now define this concept more sharply, and give it the name *identifiability* of a parameter. Instead of reasoning, as before, from "a sufficiently large number of observations" we shall base our discussion on a hypothetical knowledge of the probability distribution of the observations, as defined more fully below. It is clear that exact knowledge of this probability distribution cannot be derived from any finite number of observations. Such knowledge is the limit approachable but not attainable by extended observation. By hypothesizing nevertheless the full availability of such knowledge, we obtain a clear separation between problems of statistical inference arising from the variability of finite samples, and problems of identification in which we explore the limits to which inference even from an infinite number of observations is suspect.

As Koopmans recognized, statistical and identification problems limit in distinct ways the conclusions that may be drawn in empirical research. Statistical problems may be severe in small samples but diminish in importance as the sampling process generates more observations. Identification problems cannot be solved by gathering more of the same kind of data. These inferential difficulties can be alleviated only by invoking stronger assumptions or by initiating new sampling processes that yield different kinds of data.

Extrapolation To illustrate the distinction, consider Figures I.1 and I.2. Both figures concern a researcher who wants to predict a random variable y conditional on a specified value for some other variable x. The available data are a random sample of observations of (y, x) drawn from a population in which x takes values only at the integer values $[0, 4]$ and $[6, 8]$. In Figure I.1, the researcher has 100 observations of (y, x) and uses these data to draw a confidence interval for the mean of y conditional on x at each integer value of x. In Figure I.2, the researcher has 1000 observations and similarly draws a confidence interval.

Inspect the integers [0, 4] and [6, 8]. The wide confidence intervals of Figure I.1 are a statistical problem. Gathering more data permits one to estimate the conditional mean of y more precisely and so narrows the confidence intervals, as shown in Figure I.2. Now inspect the value $x = 5$. The confidence interval is infinitely wide in Figure I.1 and remains so in Figure I.2. This is an identification problem. The sampling process never generates observations at $x = 5$, so the data reveal nothing about the mean of y there. ❏

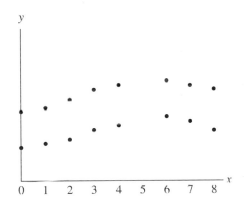

Figure I.1   Confidence interval based on 100 observations.

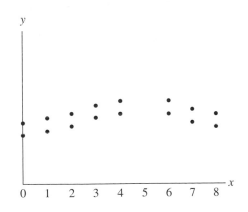

Figure I.2   Confidence interval based on 1000 observations.

Prediction and Decisions

This book studies identification problems that arise in prediction and decision making. The basic prediction problem will be to learn the probability distribution of an outcome y conditional on a covariate x. We will study decision problems in which the relative merits of alternative actions depend on the outcome distribution $P(y \mid x)$. In particular, we will ask how a decision maker might reasonably choose an action when the available data and credible assumptions only partially identify this distribution.

It may be self-evident that central objectives of empirical research should be to make predictions and inform decision making. However, it is necessary to observe that much research does not have these objectives in mind. Scientists sometimes motivate research as an effort to improve our "understanding" of a subject, and argue that this is a worthwhile objective even if there are no further implications. For example, in a text on statistical methods in epidemiology, Fleiss (1981, p. 92) states that the retrospective studies of disease that are a staple of medical research do not yield policy-relevant predictions and so are "necessarily useless from the point of view of public health." Nevertheless, the author goes on to say that "retrospective studies are eminently valid from the more general point of view of the advancement of knowledge." Justifications of this sort will not be found in this book.

Coping with Ambiguity

Beyond its study of specific identification problems, this book develops a general theme. Available data and credible assumptions often yield only partial conclusions about a population of interest. Hence decision makers often have only part of the information they need to choose unambiguously best actions. I will stress that researchers and decision makers need to cope with ambiguity. We need to face up to the fact that we cannot answer all of the questions that we ask.

Some scientific conventions, notably the reporting of sampling confidence intervals in statistical analysis, promote the expression of uncertainty. But other scientific practices encourage misplaced certainty.

One problem has been the fixation of research on point identification of parameters. Empirical studies have typically sought to learn the value of some parameter characterizing a population of interest. The conventional practice has been to invoke assumptions strong enough to identify the exact value of this parameter. Even if these assumptions are implausible, they are defended as necessary for inference to proceed. In fact, identification is not an all-or-nothing proposition. We will see that weaker and more plausible assumptions often partially identify parameters, bounding them in informative ways.

A related problem has been the common view that a scientist should choose one hypothesis to maintain, even if that means discarding others that are a priori plausible and consistent with the available empirical evidence. This view was expressed in an influential methodological essay written by Milton Friedman. Friedman (1953) placed prediction as the central objective of science, writing (p. 5): "The ultimate goal of a positive science is the development of a 'theory' or 'hypothesis' that yields valid and meaningful (i.e., not truistic) predictions about phenomena not yet observed." He went on to say (p. 10): "The choice among alternative hypotheses equally consistent with the available evidence must to some extent be arbitrary, though there is general agreement that relevant considerations are suggested by the criteria 'simplicity' and 'fruitfulness,' themselves notions that defy completely objective specification."

I do not see why a scientist must choose one hypothesis to hold, especially when this requires the use of "to some extent . . . arbitrary" criteria. Indeed, using arbitrary criteria to choose a single hypothesis has an obvious drawback in predicting phenomena not yet observed: one may have made a wrong choice. The credibility of scientists would be higher if we would strive to offer predictions under the range of plausible hypotheses that are consistent with the available evidence.

Forthright acknowledgment of ambiguity should be the norm, but it is distressingly rare. The scientific community rewards those who produce strong novel findings. The public, impatient for solutions to its pressing concerns, rewards those who offer simple analyses leading to unequivocal policy recommendations. These incentives make it tempting for researchers to maintain assumptions far stronger than they can persuasively defend, in order to draw strong conclusions.

The pressure to produce an answer, without qualifications, seems particularly intense in the environs of Washington, D.C. A perhaps apocryphal, but quite believable, story circulates about an economist's attempt to describe his uncertainty about a forecast to President

Lyndon B. Johnson. The economist presented his forecast as a likely range of values for the quantity under discussion. Johnson is said to have replied, "Ranges are for cattle. Give me a number."

Organization of the Book

This book builds on the foundation laid in my earlier *Identification Problems in the Social Sciences* (Manski, 1995). There I put forward the theme of "coping with ambiguity" and showed some implications for prediction with incomplete data and for the analysis of treatment response.

The present book might aptly be described as *Identification Problems in the Social Sciences, The Next Generation*. The ideas on prediction discussed in the 1995 book have subsequently spawned an expanding literature that now embraces not only prediction per se but also the role of prediction in decision making. At the end of this introduction, I discuss the development of this literature and give references to original sources. I have collected many findings in two technical monographs, *Partial Identification of Probability Distributions* (Manski, 2003) and *Social Choice with Partial Knowledge of Treatment Response* (Manski, 2005), that cover the material in a rigorous and thorough manner meant to facilitate further study by econometricians and statisticians. However, these monographs and the journal articles on which they are based are not intended to be broadly accessible to students and researchers in the social sciences. This book, like the 1995 one, is meant to reach the broader audience.

Here, as in the earlier book, each chapter juxtaposes developments of methodology with empirical or numerical illustrations. Here, as there, I maintain a relatively simple notation and mathematical apparatus, with occasional elaboration as warranted. By and large, the book uses only the most basic elements of probability theory taught in undergraduate courses in mathematical statistics. As will become evident, an enormous amount about identification can be learned from transparent applications of the Law of Total Probability, the Law of Iterated Expectations, and Bayes Theorem.

I sometimes think it important to report findings whose proof requires more technical derivation than seems prudent to place directly in the text. When this is the case, I usually isolate the proof in a separate subsection or place it in a Complement at the end of the relevant chapter. In some cases I do not provide the proof and instead cite the source where the finding originally appeared.

Several chapters have Complements containing word problems that I have used as exam questions when teaching the subject to first-year Ph.D. students and advanced undergraduates. These problems apply and elaborate on the ideas developed in the text.

This book is about identification and does not aim to give equal time to statistical inference. Nevertheless, it would be remiss to ignore statistics entirely. Chapters 1 and 2 discuss the basic statistical ideas that enable consistent estimation of identifiable features of probability distributions. After that, I largely ignore statistics until Chapter 12, which applies elements of statistical decision theory to the normative question of treatment choice.

The book has fifteen chapters organized into three parts. Here is a synopsis.

Part I. The six chapters of Part I study prediction with incomplete data. Chapter 1 lays out the classical problem of prediction with complete population data. It also discusses statistical inference from random samples.

Chapters 2 through 4 form a unit on prediction when some outcome data are missing, a perennial problem in survey research with item or interview nonresponse. Chapter 2 studies prediction using the empirical evidence alone. Chapter 3 shows the identifying power of various assumptions using instrumental variables. Chapter 4 discusses prediction with parametric models.

Chapter 5 studies the decomposition of mixtures, an abstract problem that manifests itself in the ecological inference problem of political science as well as in prediction with contaminated data. Chapter 6 covers response-based sampling, also known as choice-based sampling in econometrics and as case-control sampling in epidemiology.

In addition to their particular content, Chapters 1 through 3 develop concepts and notation that are used and elaborated on throughout the book. Hence all readers should pay close attention to these chapters. Chapters 4 through 6 can be read in isolation from one another.

Part II. The six chapters of Part II concern analysis of treatment response. Studies of treatment response aim to predict the outcomes that would occur if alternative treatment rules were applied to a population. A fundamental problem is that one cannot observe the outcomes that a person would experience under all treatments. At most, one can observe the outcome that a person experiences under the treatment he actually receives. The counterfactual outcomes that a person would have experienced under other treatments are logically unobservable.

Chapters 7 through 9 form a unit on the selection problem; that is, prediction of the outcomes that would occur if all persons with specified covariates were to receive the same treatment, using data on a study population where treatments vary across persons. Chapter 7 studies the selection problem using the empirical evidence alone, explains the appeal and limitations of randomized experiments, and discusses inference with various other assumptions. Chapter 8, on linear simultaneous equations, covers linear models of treatment response that have long been used to study supply and demand in competitive markets, behavior in noncooperative games, and the reflection problem. Chapter 9 shows the identifying power of the assumption of monotone treatment response, which supposes that outcomes increase with the intensity of treatment.

Chapter 10 studies the mixing problem; that is, the use of data from randomized experiments to predict the outcomes that would occur under treatment rules that make treatment vary across persons with the same covariates. The mixing problem is an interesting converse to the selection problem. It also serves as a bridge to the subject of treatment choice.

Chapters 11 and 12 consider a social planner who, having only partial knowledge of treatment response, must choose treatments for a heterogeneous population. Chapter 11 first lays out the general problem of choice under ambiguity and then examines treatment choice when the distribution of treatment response is partially identified. Chapter 12 uses Wald's statistical decision theory to frame the problem of treatment with sample data. This chapter differs from the rest of the book because it fully integrates the study of identification and statistical inference.

Part III. The three chapters of Part III study prediction of choice behavior as a problem of predicting treatment response. Here a treatment is a choice set—a set of feasible actions among which a person must choose. The response of interest is the action that a person would choose if he were to face a specified choice set.

Chapter 13 examines how economists practice revealed preference analysis, which combines choice data and rationality assumptions to infer decision rules and predict counterfactual choices. Chapter 14 considers how measurement of expectations can help to predict choice behavior. The concluding Chapter 15 discusses the continuing controversy about the realism of rationality assumptions and briefly describes how experimental psychologists and neuroscientists study behavior.

The Developing Literature on Partial Identification

For most of the twentieth century, econometricians and statisticians commonly thought of identification as a binary event—a parameter is either identified or it is not. Empirical researchers combined available data with assumptions that yield point identification and they reported point estimates of parameters. Many researchers recognized with discomfort that point identification often requires strong assumptions that are difficult to motivate. However, they saw no other way to perform inference.

We will see in this book that there is enormous scope for fruitful inference using weaker and more credible assumptions that partially identify population parameters. Yet, until recently, study of partial identification was rare and fragmented. Frisch (1934) and Reiersol (1941) developed sharp bounds on the slope parameter of a linear regression with errors-in-variables, with later refinement by Klepper and Leamer (1984). Fréchet (1951) studied the conclusions about a joint probability distribution that may be drawn given knowledge of its marginals; see Ruschendorf (1981) for subsequent findings. Duncan and Davis (1953) used a numerical example to show that the ecological inference of political science is a problem of partial identification. Cochran, Mosteller, and Tukey (1954) suggested conservative analysis of surveys with missing outcome data due to nonresponse by sample members, although Cochran (1977) subsequently downplayed the idea. Peterson (1976) initiated study of partial identification of the competing risks model of survival analysis; Crowder (1991) and Bedford and Meilijson (1997) have carried this work further.

For whatever reason, these scattered contributions long remained at the fringes of professional consciousness and did not spawn systematic study of partial identification. However, a coherent body of research on the subject took shape in the 1990s and has grown rapidly. The new literature on partial identification emerged out of concern with traditional approaches to inference with missing outcome data. As will be discussed in Chapters 2 and 3, empirical researchers have commonly assumed that missingness is random, in the sense that the observability of an outcome is statistically independent of its value. Yet this and other point-identifying assumptions have regularly been criticized as implausible. So it was natural to ask what random sampling with partial observability of outcomes reveals about outcome distributions if nothing is known about the missingness process or if assumptions weak enough to be widely credible are imposed. This question was posed and partially answered in Manski (1989), with subsequent development in Manski (1994, 2003, chaps. 1 and 2), Blundell et al. (2007), and Stoye (2004).

Study of inference with missing outcome data led naturally to consideration of conditional prediction and analysis of treatment response. A common objective of empirical research is to predict an outcome conditional on given covariates, using data from a random sample of the population. Often, sample realizations of outcomes and/or covariates are missing. Horowitz and Manski (1998, 2000) and Zaffalon (2002) study nonparametric prediction when nothing is known about the missingness process; Horowitz et al. (2003) and Horowitz and Manski (2006) consider the computationally challenging problem of parametric prediction. Missing data on outcomes and covariates is the extreme case of interval measurement of these variables. Manski and Tamer (2002) study conditional prediction with interval data on outcomes or covariates, while Haile and Tamer (2003) analyze an interesting problem of interval data that arises in econometric analysis of auctions.

Analysis of treatment response must contend with the fundamental problem that counterfactual outcomes are not observable; hence, findings on partial identification with missing outcome data are directly applicable. Yet analysis of treatment response poses much more than a generic missing data problem. One reason is that observations of realized outcomes, when combined with suitable assumptions, can provide information about counterfactual ones. Another is that practical problems of treatment choice as well as other concerns motivate research on treatment response and thereby determine what population parameters are of interest. For these reasons, it has been productive to study partial identification of treatment response as a subject in its own right. This stream of research was initiated independently in Robins (1989) and Manski (1990a). Subsequent contributions include Manski (1995, 1997a, 1997b), Balke and Pearl (1997), Heckman, Smith, and Clements (1997), Hotz, Mullin, and Sanders (1997), Manski and Nagin (1998), Manski and Pepper (2000), Heckman and Vytlacil (2001), Molinari (2002), Pepper (2003), and Shaikh and Vytlacil (2005). The normative problem of treatment choice when treatment response is partially identified is studied in Manski (2000, 2002a, 2004a, 2005, 2006, 2007) and Brock (2006).

Readers who prefer to learn about methodology through the study of empirical applications will find diverse case studies on partial identification of treatment response. Manski et al. (1992) investigate the effect of family structure on children's outcomes, and Hotz, Mullin, and Sanders (1997) analyze the effect of teenage childbearing. Manski and Nagin (1998) study the effect of judicial sentencing on criminal recidivism. Pepper (2000) examines the intergenerational effects of welfare receipt. Manski and Pepper (2000) and Ginther (2002) analyze the returns to schooling. Horowitz and Manski (2000) study a medical clinical trial with missing data on outcomes and covariates. Pepper (2003) asks what welfare-to-work experiments reveal about the operation of welfare policy when case workers have discretion in treatment assignment. Scharfstein, Manski, and Anthony (2004) analyze an educational experiment with randomized assignment to treatment but nonrandom attrition of subjects. Bhattacharya, Shaikh, and Vytlacil (2005) evaluate the effectiveness of a specific medical treatment, while Honoré and Lleras-Muney (2006) assess progress in the "War on Cancer."

Another broad subject of study has been inference on the components of finite probability mixtures. The mathematical problem of decomposition of mixtures arises in many substantively distinct settings, including contaminated sampling, ecological inference, and conditional prediction with missing or misclassified covariate data. Findings on partial identification of mixtures have application to all of these subjects and more. Research on this subject includes Horowitz and Manski (1995), Bollinger (1996), Cross and Manski (2002), Dominitz and Sherman (2004, 2006), Kreider and Pepper (2007), and Molinari (2007).

There has been other research as well. In discrete response analysis, response-based sampling poses a "reverse regression" problem in which one seeks to learn the distribution of outcomes given covariates but the sampling process reveals the distribution of covariates given outcomes.

This problem has been studied in Manski (1995, chap. 4, 2001, 2003, chap. 6) and King and Zeng (2002). In econometric analysis of multiplayer games, a long-standing problem has been to infer behavior from outcome data when the game being studied may have multiple equilibria. Ciliberto and Tamer (2004) address this problem. And Honoré and Tamer (2006) address another long-standing problem of econometrics, this being the *initial conditions* problem of dynamic discrete choice analysis.

All of the above concerns the study of identification per se. In addition, there is much recent and ongoing research on associated issues of statistical inference. There has been particular interest in the construction of confidence sets for partially identified parameters, which has been studied by Horowitz and Manski (2000), Imbens and Manski (2004), Chernozhukov, Hong, and Tamer (2007), Andrews, Berry, and Jia (2004), Shaikh (2005), Beresteanu and Molinari (2006), Galichon and Henry (2006), and Rosen (2006).

I

Prediction with Incomplete Data

1

Conditional Prediction

1.1 Predicting Criminality

In 1982, the RAND Corporation released a study of criminal behavior as reported in 1978 by a sample of 2200 prison and jail inmates in California, Michigan, and Texas (Chaiken and Chaiken, 1982; Greenwood and Abrahamse, 1982). Most respondents reported that they had committed five or fewer crimes per year in the period before their current arrest and conviction. A small group reported much higher rates of crime commission, in some cases more than one hundred per year.

The researchers found that, using information on a person's past convictions, drug use, and employment, they could predict well whether that person had been a high-rate offender. This finding suggested to at least part of the research team that *selective incapacitation* should be encouraged as a crime-fighting tool (Greenwood and Abrahamse, 1982). Selective incapacitation calls for the sentencing of convicted criminals to be tied to predictions of their future criminality. Those with backgrounds that predict high rates of offenses would receive longer prison terms than those with other backgrounds.

The RAND study generated much controversy, especially when a prediction approach devised by Greenwood and Abrahamse found its way into legislative proposals for selective incapacitation (see Blackmore and Welsh, 1983, and Blumstein et al., 1986). Some of the controversy concerned the normative acceptability of selective incapacitation, but much of it concerned the validity of extrapolations from the RAND findings.

The findings characterize the empirical association between background and reported crime commission within one cohort of inmates imprisoned in three states under the sentencing policies then in effect. Would this association continue to hold when applied to other cohorts of inmates in other states? Would it hold when applied to convicted criminals who are not imprisoned under existing sentencing policies? Would it hold if sentencing policy were to change? In particular, would it hold if selective incapacitation were to be implemented?

The RAND study did not address these questions. Greenwood and Abrahamse's approach to prediction of criminality simply presumed that the empirical association between background and reported crime commission would remain approximately the same when extrapolated to other times, places, and sentencing policies.

1.2 Probabilistic Prediction

To move beyond a loose discussion of prediction, we need to be familiar with the standard probabilistic framework that social scientists and statisticians use to describe prediction problems. This framework will be used throughout the book.

Conditional Distributions

Consider a population of interest, whose members are characterized by random variables y and x, which take values in a set $Y \times X$. The joint probability (or frequency) distribution of (y, x) across this population is $P(y, x)$. A person is drawn at random from the subpopulation of persons with a specified value of x. The problem is to predict his value of y.

For example, the RAND study of criminal behavior had x include a person's past convictions, drug use, and employment. The variable y was the number of crimes of a particular type that a person commits in a specified time period. Criminologists treat the rate of crime commission as a random variable to express the idea that criminal behavior may be heterogeneous among persons with the same observed attributes.

Treating crime commission as random does not require one to imagine that an actual randomizing device, such as a lottery, determines criminal behavior.

Given a value for x, the most that one can do to predict y is to determine its conditional probability distribution $P(y \mid x)$. Empirical research aims to learn such conditional probability distributions.

Notation and Terminology The notation $P(y \mid x)$ is variously used in this book to denote

(i) the distribution of y conditional on x, viewed as a function of x;
(ii) the distribution of y conditional on x, evaluated at a specified value of x;
(iii) the probability that y takes a given value conditional on x, viewed as a function of x;
(iv) the probability that y takes a given value conditional on x, evaluated at a specified value of x.

The correct interpretation is usually clear from the context. Where there seems some chance of ambiguity, I make the correct interpretation explicit. In any case, y is called the outcome and x are covariates.

To simplify the notation, I occasionally shorten $P(y \mid x)$ to $P(y)$, leaving the conditioning on x implicit. I usually do not do this, because I want the reader to keep in mind that description of the covariates is as essential to the definition of a prediction problem as is description of the outcome to be predicted. The inferential problems examined in this book can be addressed for any choice of y and x, but are well defined only once these variables are specified. ❑

Best Predictors

One needs to know the entire distribution $P(y \mid x)$ to characterize fully the population behavior of y given x, but one can make some useful predictions with more limited information. One might be asked to select a single number as a *best predictor* of y conditional on x. Choosing a best predictor is a decision problem, whose solution depends on the objective.

The conventional way to choose a best predictor is to minimize expected loss with respect to a specified loss function. Let y be real-valued. Then a best predictor solves a minimization problem

(1.1) $\min\limits_{p} E[L(y-p) \mid x].$

Here p is a predictor value and $L(\cdot)$ is the loss function. That is, $L(\cdot)$ is a function that takes the value zero when p equals y and increases in value as the distance between p and y grows. One might want to choose p to minimize loss, but this objective is not well defined, y being a random variable rather than a single number. A sensible objective that is well defined is minimization of expected loss. The expression $E[L(y-p) \mid x]$ is expected loss when p is used to predict y, given knowledge of x.

A solution to problem (1.1) is called a best predictor of y conditional on x. If the minimization problem has multiple solutions, then these are all best predictors. It is sometimes convenient, although not necessary, to use an auxiliary rule to pick out one solution.

Note Although choosing a best predictor to minimize expected loss is the convention in the literature, it is not the only reasonable prediction objective. The qualitative idea of a best predictor is retained if one minimizes another locational feature of the loss distribution, such as the median. Then a best predictor solves the problem $\min_{p} M[L(y-p) \mid x]$, where M denotes the median of a probability distribution. See Manski (1988a). ❏

Best predictors are determined by the loss function $L(\cdot)$ and by the probability distribution $P(y \mid x)$. Two prominent loss functions, which treat under- and overpredictions of y symmetrically, are square loss and absolute loss; that is, $L(u) = u^2$ and $L(u) = |u|$, where $u \equiv y - p$ denotes the prediction error. Complement 1A shows that the mean (or expected value) of y conditional on x and the median of y conditional on x, denoted $E(y \mid x)$ and $M(y \mid x)$, are best predictors under these loss functions. When considered as functions of x, features of conditional probability distributions are known as *regressions*. The mean and median of y conditional on x are the mean and median regressions of y on x.

A useful generalization of absolute loss, treating under- and overpredictions of y asymmetrically, is the asymmetric α-absolute loss function

$$L(u) = (1 - \alpha)|u| \quad \text{if } u \leq 0$$
$$ = \quad\;\; \alpha|u| \quad \text{if } u \geq 0,$$

where α is a specified constant in the interval $(0, 1)$. It can be shown that a best predictor under this loss function is the α-quantile of y conditional on x, denoted $Q_\alpha(y \mid x)$. By definition, the α-quantile is the smallest number t such that $P(y \leq t \mid x) \geq \alpha$. This somewhat cumbersome definition simplifies if y has a smoothly increasing distribution function. Then the α-quantile is the unique value t that solves the equation $P(y < t \mid x) = \alpha$. The median is the name given to the 0.5-quantile.

Definition of a Quantile Throughout this book, I use the definition of a quantile given above. Some authors, such as Koenker and Bassett (1978), define the α-quantile of y conditional on x to be any solution to the problem of best prediction under asymmetric α-absolute loss. This best prediction problem can have multiple solutions so, under the Koenker and Bassett definition, a quantile can be set-valued. ❏

Specifying a Loss Function

One does not need to know the entire distribution $P(y \mid x)$ to determine a best predictor. One need only know its mean, a quantile, or another feature depending on the loss function. It is essential to understand that the various best predictors are not the same. When one specifies a loss function and minimizes expected loss, one attempts to summarize the entire conditional probability distribution $P(y \mid x)$ by a single number. In general, different loss functions generate distinct summary statistics.

For example, if one changes from square loss to absolute loss, the best predictor changes from the mean to the median. Laypeople and researchers alike sometimes act as if the mean and the median are interchangeable statistics. That is incorrect. In fact, Chapter 2 will examine an important situation with missing data in which one can bound the median of a distribution yet learn nothing at all about its mean.

The need for care in specifying a loss function lessens only in some special cases where one can bring to bear credible assumptions about $P(y \mid x)$. Suppose, in particular, that $P(y \mid x)$ is known to be symmetric.

Then the best predictors associated with all convex, symmetric loss functions coincide; see Ferguson (1967). Square loss and absolute loss are convex, so the mean and the median coincide when $P(y \mid x)$ is symmetric.

1.3 Estimation of Best Predictors from Random Samples

How might one learn the conditional distribution $P(y \mid x)$, or at least the value of a best predictor of y given x? This question has been studied extensively when one can draw observations of (y, x) at random from the population of interest.

Random sampling reveals $P(y, x)$ even if one assumes nothing about the form of this distribution. Suppose that one has a sample of size N. Then a natural estimate of $P(y, x)$ is its sample analog, the *empirical distribution* $P_N(y, x)$. The empirical distribution is the multinomial distribution that places mass $1/N$ on each of the N observations $[(y_i, x_i), i = 1, \ldots, N]$. If a particular value of (y, x) recurs in the data, it receives multiple $1/N$ weights.

To see why it is natural to use $P_N(y, x)$ to estimate $P(y, x)$, consider estimation of the probability $P[(y, x) \in A]$ that (y, x) falls in some set A. The empirical distribution estimates this by the fraction of observations of (y, x) that fall in the set A. This is the empirical probability

$$(1.2) \qquad P_N[(y, x) \in A] = \frac{1}{N} \sum_{i=1}^{N} 1[(y_i, x_i) \in A],$$

where the indicator function $1[\cdot]$ takes the value one if the bracketed logical condition holds and zero otherwise. The Strong Law of Large Numbers shows that, as the sample size N increases, the right-hand side of (1.2) almost surely converges to $P[(y, x) \in A]$. So, with random sampling, one can learn $P[(y, x) \in A]$ even if one knew nothing a priori about its value. This holds for every set A. So one can learn the distribution $P(y, x)$.

To make conditional predictions, we are interested not in $P(y, x)$ but in $P(y \mid x)$ at a specified value of x, say, x_0. There are several cases to consider, distinguished by the status of the value x_0 in the population. To present these cases, we need the concept of the *support* of a probability distribution. A covariate value x_0 is said to be on the support of the distribution $P(x)$ if there is positive probability of observing x arbitrarily close to x_0. A value x_0 is said to be off the support of $P(x)$ if there is zero probability of observing x within some neighborhood of x_0.

Covariates with Positive Probability

Suppose first that the value x_0 occurs with positive probability; that is, $P(x = x_0) > 0$. Then no assumptions are needed to learn the conditional distribution $P(y \mid x = x_0)$. A natural estimate is the conditional empirical distribution $P_N(y \mid x = x_0)$, which gives the empirical distribution of y within the subsample of observations where x takes the value x_0.

   To see this, consider the problem of estimating the probability $P(y \in B \mid x - x_0)$ that y falls in some set B, conditional on x taking the value x_0. The conditional empirical distribution estimates this by the fraction of observations of y falling in the set B, among those for which $x_i = x_0$. This is the conditional empirical probability

(1.3)

$$P_N(y \in B \mid x = x_0) = \frac{\sum\limits_{i-1}^{N} 1[y_i \in B, x_i = x_0]}{\sum\limits_{i=1}^{N} 1[x_i = x_0]}$$

$$= \frac{\dfrac{1}{N} \sum\limits_{i=1}^{N} 1[y_i \in B, x_i - x_0]}{\dfrac{1}{N} \sum\limits_{i=1}^{N} 1[x_i = x_0]}.$$

The Strong Law of Large Numbers shows that, as N increases, the numerator on the right-hand side of (1.3) almost surely converges to the joint probability $P(y \in B, x = x_0)$ and the denominator converges to the marginal probability $P(x = x_0)$. Given that $P(x = x_0)$ is positive, the ratio of the numerator to denominator converges to the ratio of probabilities $P(y \in B, x = x_0)/P(x = x_0)$, which equals $P(y \in B \mid x = x_0)$ by Bayes Theorem. This holds for every set B. So one can learn the conditional distribution $P(y \mid x = x_0)$.

   Corresponding estimates of the conditional mean and median $E(y \mid x)$ and $M(y \mid x)$ are the conditional empirical mean and median $E_N(y \mid x)$

and $M_N(y \mid x)$, which give the sample mean and median value of y among those observations for which $x_i = x_0$. The former quantity has a simple expression that we can analyze readily, this being

$$(1.4) \qquad E_N(y \mid x = x_0) = \frac{\displaystyle\sum_{i=1}^{N} y_i \cdot 1[x_i = x_0]}{\displaystyle\sum_{i=1}^{N} 1[x_i = x_0]} = \frac{\dfrac{1}{N}\displaystyle\sum_{i=1}^{N} y_i \cdot 1[x_i = x_0]}{\dfrac{1}{N}\displaystyle\sum_{i=1}^{N} 1[x_i = x_0]}.$$

The Strong Law of Large Numbers shows that as N increases, the numerator on the right-hand side of (1.4) almost surely converges to $E(y \cdot 1[x = x_0])$, which equals $E(y \mid x = x_0)P(x = x_0)$. As before, the denominator converges to $P(x = x_0)$. Given that $P(x = x_0)$ is positive, the ratio of the numerator to denominator converges to $E(y \mid x = x_0)$.

Covariates with Zero Probability but On the Support

Now suppose that $P(x = x_0) = 0$, but x_0 is on the support of $P(x)$. Thus there is positive probability that x falls arbitrarily close to x_0. This is the situation when x has a continuous distribution with positive density at x_0; for example, when x is normally distributed. The conditional empirical distribution no longer works as an estimate for $P(y \mid x = x_0)$; with probability one, no sample observations of x equal x_0. On the other hand, values of x close to x_0 are likely to appear in the sample. This suggests that $P(y \mid x = x_0)$ might be estimated by the empirical distribution of y among those observations for which x_i is suitably near x_0.

This idea works for estimation of most any feature of $P(y \mid x = x_0)$. For specificity, consider the conditional mean. Let $\rho(x_i, x_0)$ measure the distance between the covariate value of interest x_0 and an observed value x_i. When x is scalar, $\rho(x_i, x_0)$ would usually be the absolute value $|x_i - x_0|$. When x is a vector, $\rho(x_i, x_0)$ can be any reasonable measure of the distance between x_i and x_0; for example, the Euclidean distance between these vectors. Let the parameter d_N be a sample-size dependent *bandwidth* chosen by the researcher to operationalize the idea that one wishes to confine attention to those observations for which x_i is near x_0. Then we might estimate $E(y \mid x = x_0)$ by the sample mean of y among the observations for which $\rho(x_i, x_0) < d_N$. This is the *local average* (or *uniform kernel*) estimate

$$(1.5) \qquad \theta_N(x_0, d_N) \equiv \frac{\displaystyle\sum_{i=1}^{N} y_i \cdot 1[\rho(x_i, x_0) < d_N]}{\displaystyle\sum_{i=1}^{N} 1[\rho(x_i, x_0) < d_N]}.$$

A basic finding of the modern statistical literature on *nonparametric regression* analysis is that estimate (1.5) converges in large samples to $E(y \mid x = x_0)$, provided that these conditions hold:

(i) $E(y \mid x)$ varies continuously with x, for x near x_0.
(ii) The conditional variance $V(y \mid x)$ is bounded for x near x_0.
(iii) One tightens the bandwidth as the sample size increases.
(iv) One does not tighten the bandwidth too rapidly as the sample size increases.

Conditions (i) and (ii) are minimal regularity assumptions. One can always choose bandwidths so that conditions (iii) and (iv) hold. Complement 1B elaborates on nonparametric regression analysis.

Covariates Off the Support

Finally, suppose that x_0 is off the support of $P(x)$. Thus, there is some positive value d_0 such that $P[\rho(x, x_0) < d_0] = 0$. For example, this was the situation at the value $x_0 = 5$ in Figure I.1 of the Introduction. Then the local average estimate (1.5) no longer works; the estimate ceases to exist when one attempts to reduce the bandwidth d_N below d_0.

This failure is symptomatic of a fundamental problem. If there is zero probability of observing x near x_0, then the conditional distribution $P(y \mid x = x_0)$ can be varied arbitrarily without changing the joint distribution $P(y, x)$. Thus the data alone reveal nothing about $P(y \mid x = x_0)$. Prediction of y when x_0 is off the support is a problem of extrapolation.

1.4 Extrapolation

Suppose that distribution $P(y, x)$ is known, perhaps from data generated by random sampling. The only way to infer $P(y \mid x = x_0)$ at x_0 off the support of $P(x)$ is to impose assumptions enabling one to deduce $P(y \mid x = x_0)$ from $P(y, x)$. What kinds of assumptions do and do not have identifying power?

For specificity, consider the conditional mean $E(y \mid x = x_0)$. An important negative fact is that the continuity assumption (condition (i) near the end of Section 1.3) that enabled nonparametric estimation of $E(y \mid x = x_0)$ on the support of $P(x)$ reveals nothing about $E(y \mid x = x_0)$ off the support. To understand why, let x_1 be the point on the support that is closest to x_0. Continuity of $E(y \mid x)$ in x implies that $E(y \mid x)$ is near $E(y \mid x = x_1)$ when x is near x_1, but it does not tell us how to interpret the two uses of the word "near" as magnitudes. In particular, we do not know whether the distance separating x_0 and x_1 should be interpreted as large or small.

This reasoning applies not only to continuity but to any smoothness assumption that only restricts the behavior of $E(y \mid x)$ locally around the point x_1. For example, differentiability conveys a stronger sense of smoothness than does continuity, but this assumption too only restricts the behavior of $E(y \mid x)$ near x_1. Thus, extrapolation requires an assumption that restricts $E(y \mid x)$ globally. In other words, it requires information that enables one to deduce $E(y \mid x = x_0)$ from knowledge of $E(y \mid x)$ at x-values that are not necessarily "near" x_0.

Invariance Assumptions and Shape Restrictions

Perhaps the most common practice is to assume that y behaves in the same way at x_0 as it does at some specified x_1 on the support of $P(x)$. That is, assume

(1.6) $P(y \mid x = x_0) = P(y \mid x = x_1).$

Such an *invariance* assumption was implicitly invoked by Greenwood and Abrahamse when they recommended that their predictor of criminality be applied to times, places, and sentencing policies other than those observed in the RAND study.

An invariance assumption is often applied when the outcomes of social experiments with randomized assignment of treatments are used to predict the outcomes of actual social programs. An experiment is said to have *external validity* if the distribution of outcomes realized by a treatment group is the same as the distribution of outcomes that would be realized in an actual program. Campbell and Stanley (1963, p. 5) put it this way: "*External validity* asks the question of *generalizability:* To what populations, settings, treatment variables, and measurement variables can this effect be generalized?"

Invariance assumptions are special cases of the general idea of *shape restrictions,* which make assumptions about how the conditional distribution $P(y \mid x)$ varies with x. Consider the conditional mean $E(y \mid x)$. A familiar shape restriction is the linear regression assumption that $E(y \mid x)$ varies linearly with x. Another is the monotone regression assumption that $E(y \mid x)$ is an increasing function of x. These and other shape restrictions may enable extrapolation off the support of $P(x)$.

Testing and Using Theories

From the perspective of prediction, the primary function of scientific theory is to justify the imposition of shape restrictions and other global assumptions that enable extrapolation. A secondary function is to justify imposing assumptions that improve the sampling precision with which probability distributions may be estimated on their supports. The latter function of theory is secondary because assumptions are not essential to estimate $P(y \mid x)$ on the support but are essential to extrapolation.

Scientists and philosophers sometimes say that a function of theory is to explain "why" observed outcomes are what they are; that is, to establish some sense of causation. This function of theory is connected to prediction only to the extent that causal explanations help motivate assumptions with predictive power. To put the matter starkly, consider Greenwood and Abrahamse's approach to predicting criminality. A jurisdiction contemplating using the approach to make selective incapacitation decisions does not need to ask why the association between background and criminality found in the RAND study was what it was. It needs only to ask whether it is reasonable to assume that this association holds in its own circumstances.

Various chapters in this book examine how social science theories have been used to motivate assumptions that enable extrapolation. I shall defer discussion of these theories until then, but a general comment about the empirical testing of theories is warranted here.

Theories are testable where they are least needed, and are not testable where they are most needed. Theories are least needed to learn conditional distributions $P(y \mid x)$ on the support of $P(x)$. They are most needed to determine these distributions off the support.

The restrictions on $P(y \mid x)$ implied by a theory may fail to hold either on or off the support of $P(x)$. Failures of a theory on the support are detectable; statisticians have developed methods of hypothesis testing for this purpose. Failures off the support are inherently not detectable. Scientific controversies arise when researchers hypothesize different theories whose implied restrictions on $P(y \mid x)$ hold on the support of $P(x)$ but differ off the support. There is no objective way to distinguish among theories that "fit the data" but imply different extrapolations.

1.5 Predicting High School Graduation

Predicting children's outcomes conditional on family attributes is a long-standing substantive concern of the social sciences. A collaborative study illustrates the methodological concerns of this chapter.

Manski, Sandefur, McLanahan, and Powers (1992) used data from the National Longitudinal Study of Youth (NLSY) to estimate the probability that an American child graduates from high school, conditional on race, sex, family structure during adolescence, and father's and mother's years of schooling. Thus we estimated $P(y = 1 \mid x)$, where $y = 1$ indicates high school graduation and where $x = $ (race, sex, family structure, parents' schooling). As in the prediction of criminality, our treatment of high school graduation as a random variable expresses the idea that outcomes may be heterogeneous among persons with the same observed covariates.

The surveyed population consists of persons born between January 1, 1957, and December 31, 1964, who resided in the United States in 1979. From 1979 on, the NLSY has periodically sought to interview a random sample of this population and supplemental samples of some subpopulations (Center for Human Resource Research, 1992). The random sample data are used here.

Our measure of family structure was a binary variable, taken from the 1979 survey, indicating whether the respondent resided in an intact or nonintact family at age 14. A nonintact family was defined to be one that does not include both biological or adoptive parents; that is, a family with one parent, with a parent and stepparent, or with no parents. High school graduation was a binary variable, taken from the 1985 survey, indicating whether a respondent received a high school diploma or GED certificate by age 20. The findings discussed here concern the samples of respondents who were ages 14 to 17 in 1979 and for whom complete data were available.

The covariates in this study were all discrete, so the conditional empirical probability (1.3) could have been used to estimate the conditional probabilities of high school graduation. We thought it reasonable to assume, however, that among children with the same race, sex, and family structure, the probability of high school graduation should vary smoothly with parents' years of schooling. So, within each (race, sex, family structure) cell, we used a local average similar to (1.5) to estimate graduation probabilities as a function of parents' schooling.

Table 1.1 presents the findings for children whose parents have both completed twelve years of schooling. Similar estimates may be computed for children whose parents have other levels of schooling.

Inspection of the table indicates several patterns. Conditioning on (sex, family structure, parents' schooling), the estimated graduation probabilities of black and white children are pretty much identical, except that a black female in a nonintact family is more likely to graduate than is a white female in a nonintact family. Conditioning on (race, family structure, parents' schooling), a female is more likely to graduate than is a male. Conditioning on (race, sex, parents' schooling), a child in an intact family is more likely to graduate than is a child in a nonintact family.

The entries in Table 1.1, and analogous estimates computed for other levels of parents' schooling, enable one to predict high school graduation outcomes conditional on specified family attributes in the American environment of the 1980s. The NLSY data suffice to make these predictions. No theory of family dynamics, intergenerational mobility, gender

Table 1.1 Estimated high school graduation probabilities for children whose parents have completed twelve years of schooling

	Intact family	Nonintact family
White male	0.89	0.77
White female	0.94	0.79
Black male	0.87	0.78
Black female	0.95	0.88

Source: Manski et al. (1992), table 4.

roles, or race is needed. Nor need one know the graduation requirements, attendance policies, or educational philosophies of American
schools.

Suppose, however, that one wishes to predict the outcomes that would
occur if the American environment of the 1980s were to change. For
example, what would graduation probabilities be if American schools
were to modify the graduation requirements, attendance policies, or educational philosophies that were in effect in the 1980s? What would
they be if employers and postsecondary institutions were to become
unwilling to accept the GED certificate as an educational creden-
tial? What would they be if social welfare agencies were to implement proposed "family-preservation" programs aimed at increasing
the fraction of intact families in the population? These questions call
for extrapolations and so cannot be answered using the NLSY data
alone.

Complement 1A. Best Predictors under Square and Absolute Loss

This complement proves that the conditional mean and median are best
predictors under square and absolute loss. To simplify the notation, I
consider a problem of unconditional prediction in which the decision
maker does not observe any covariates x. If covariates are observed,
everything that follows can be interpreted as conditioning on a specified
value of x.

Square Loss

Let $L(\cdot)$ be the square loss function $L(u) = u^2$. Let $\mu \equiv E(y)$ and let θ
be any real number distinct from μ. Then

$$E(y - \theta)^2 = E[(y - \mu) + (\mu - \theta)]^2$$
$$= E(y - \mu)^2 + (\mu - \theta)^2 + 2(\mu - \theta)E(y - \mu)$$
$$= E(y - \mu)^2 + (\mu - \theta)^2 > E(y - \mu)^2.$$

Thus μ uniquely minimizes expected loss.

Absolute Loss

Let $L(\cdot)$ be the absolute loss function $L(u) = |u|$. By definition, the median of y is the real number $m \equiv \min \theta : P(y \le \theta) \ge \frac{1}{2}$. To prove that the median is a best predictor under absolute loss, first compare the expected loss at m with that at any $\theta < m$. We find

$$
\begin{aligned}
E[|y - \theta|] - E[|y - m|] &= E[|y - \theta| - |y - m|] \\
&= (\theta - m) P(y \le \theta) \\
&\quad + E[2y - (\theta + m) \mid \theta < y < m] P(\theta < y < m) \\
&\quad + (m - \theta) P(y \ge m) \\
&\ge (\theta - m) P(y \le \theta) + (\theta - m) P(\theta < y < m) \\
&\quad + (m - \theta) P(y \ge m) \\
&= -(m - \theta) P(y < m) + (m - \theta) P(y \ge m) \\
&= (m - \theta)[P(y \ge m) - P(y < m)].
\end{aligned}
$$

By the definition of the median, $P(y < m) \le \frac{1}{2}$. So the final expression is nonnegative.

Now compare the expected loss at m with that at any $\theta > m$.

$$
\begin{aligned}
E[|y - \theta|] - E[|y - m|] &= E[|y - \theta| - |y - m|] \\
&= (\theta - m) P(y \le m) \\
&\quad + E[(\theta + m) - 2y \mid m < y < \theta] P(m < y < \theta) \\
&\quad + (m - \theta) P(y \ge \theta) \\
&\ge (\theta - m) P(y \le m) + (m - \theta) P(m < y < \theta) \\
&\quad + (m - \theta) P(y \ge \theta) \\
&= (\theta - m) P(y \le m) - (\theta - m) P(m < y) \\
&= (\theta - m)[P(y \le m) - P(m < y)].
\end{aligned}
$$

By the definition of the median, $P(y \le m) \ge \frac{1}{2}$. So the final expression is nonnegative.

Complement 1B. Nonparametric Regression Analysis

This complement first explains why the local average estimate (1.5) discussed in Section 1.3 is consistent. It then elaborates further on nonparametric regression analysis. The reader interested in a comprehensive treatment of the subject should see Härdle (1990).

Consistency of the Local Average Estimate

Consider how the local average estimate behaves if the bandwidth d_N is kept fixed at some value d. As N increases, the Strong Law of Large Numbers implies that the estimate converges to $E[y \mid \rho(x, x_0) < d]$, the mean of y conditional on x being within d of x_0. If $E(y \mid x)$ is continuous at $x = x_0$, then as d approaches zero, $E[y \mid \rho(x, x_0) < d]$ approaches $E(y \mid x = x_0)$. These two facts suggest that an estimate converging to $E(y \mid x = x_0)$ can be obtained by adopting a bandwidth selection rule that makes d_N approach zero as N increases. This works, provided that d_N does not approach zero too quickly. The rate of approach must be slower than $1/N^{1/k}$, where k is the dimension of the vector x. The last proviso is needed to make the number of observations used to calculate the estimate increase adequately with N.

To understand this, assume that x has positive, continuous density at the point x_0. Continuity implies that the density of x is approximately constant in a neighborhood of x_0. It follows that, for small d_N, the probability that a realization of x is within d_N of x_0 is approximately proportional to the volume of a neighborhood of radius d_N. This volume is proportional to $(d_N)^k$. Hence the expected number of observations with x_i within d_N of x_0 is approximately proportional to $N(d_N)^k$. Consistent estimation of $E(y \mid x = x_0)$ requires that $N(d_N)^k$ should approach infinity as N increases. To achieve this, d_N must approach zero at a rate slower than $1/N^{1/k}$.

Choosing an Estimate

Many local average estimates of regressions are available. Different metrics can be chosen to define the distance between x_0 and x. Different bandwidth selection rules can be applied to determine how near x_i should be to x_0 for observation i to be used in estimating $E(y \mid x = x_0)$.

Indeed, the class of methods can be enlarged by loosening the sharp line delineating observations used in estimation from those not used.

The logic of local average estimation holds if all observations are used, those with x_i near x_0 being given the most weight. Thus $E(y \mid x = x_0)$ can be estimated by a local weighted average (or kernel) estimate

$$\frac{\sum_{i=1}^{N} y_i \cdot K[\rho(x_i, x_0)/d_N]}{\sum_{i=1}^{N} K[\rho(x_i, x_0)/d_N]},$$

where $K(\cdot)$ is a nonnegative weight (or kernel) function that decreases as $\rho(x_i, x_0)/d_N$ increases. In practice, unimodal symmetric probability density functions with mode zero are often used as weighting functions. The estimate (1.5) is the special case in which $K[\rho(x_i, x_0)/d_N] = 1$ if $\rho(x_i, x_0)/d_N < 1$ and $K[\rho(x_i, x_0)/d_N] = 0$ otherwise.

A major problem confronting empirical researchers wanting to estimate regressions nonparametrically is that the available statistical theory offers too little guidance on choosing a criterion for "nearness." Many rules for choosing the bandwidth yield consistent estimates with limiting normal distributions. Asymptotic theory explains how to control the rate at which the bandwidth approaches zero so as to optimize the estimate's rate of convergence. But it does not prescribe how best to select the bandwidth, given a sample of fixed size and composition.

The absence of theoretical guidance on setting the bandwidth, and more generally on defining nearness, leaves the empirical researcher with enormous discretion. This discretion gives applied nonparametric regression analysis a subjective flavor. As the selected bandwidth approaches zero, the estimated regression curve fits the data increasingly well but becomes increasingly jagged. As the bandwidth approaches infinity, the estimated curve becomes smoother and flatter. Thus the researcher can, through the choice of bandwidth, influence some properties of the estimate.

Attempting to reduce the degree of subjectivity in their analyses, researchers sometimes report multiple estimates computed using different nearness criteria. This practice has an analog in parametric regression analysis, where researchers sometimes report multiple estimates computed using different consistent estimation methods.

Researchers may also seek to reduce subjectivity by using data-dependent, automated rules to choose the bandwidth. A prominent

automated rule is *cross-validation*. Here one fixes the bandwidth, estimates the regression on each of the N possible subsamples of size $N - 1$,
and, in each case, uses the estimate to predict y conditional on x for the
left-out observation. The cross-validated bandwidth is that yielding the
best predictions of the left-out values of y.

Complement 1C. Word Problems

Problem 1.1

A researcher observes the scores of the population of foreign Ph.D. students who take and pass the composition part of the TOEFL examination.
For each student, the researcher observes the following:

$y =$ the TOEFL composition score (the passing scores are 4, 5, 6)
$x = 1$ if the student has a mathematics or science bachelor's degree,
        0 otherwise

The population distribution $P(y, x)$ is shown below.

		Test score		
Degree	$y = 4$	$y = 5$	$y = 6$	Totals
$x = 0$	0.20	0.40	0.15	0.75
$x = 1$	0.05	0.10	0.10	0.25
Total	0.25	0.50	0.25	1.00

a. Find a best predictor of y conditional on $x = 0$, under absolute loss.

b. Find a best predictor of y conditional on $x = 1$, under square loss.

c. Find a best predictor of x conditional on $y = (4$ or $5)$, under square
   loss.

d. Find a best predictor of x conditional on $y = 6$, under absolute loss.

e. Observing that $P(y = 6 \mid x = 0) = 0.2$ and $P(y = 6 \mid x = 1) = 0.4$,
   a researcher states the following:

   The data indicate that receiving a mathematics or science bachelor's
   degree substantially increases the chance that a student obtains the

highest test score. The estimated effect of a math/science degree is to increase the probability of scoring 6 from 0.2 to 0.4.

Does this statement accurately describe the empirical finding? Explain.

Problem 1.2

An election official wants to make a point prediction of the number of persons in a tiny village who will vote in an election. The village has two eligible voters, denoted $j = 1$ and 2. Let $y_j = 1$ if person j will vote and $y_j = 0$ otherwise. The official knows that the voting probabilities for the two voters are

$$P(y_1 = 1) = P(y_2 = 1) = 0.5.$$

a. Assume that $P(y_1, y_2) = P(y_1)P(y_2)$. Find a best predictor of $y_1 + y_2$ under square loss. Under absolute loss.

b. Assume instead that $P(y_1 = y_2) = 1$. Now find a best predictor of $y_1 + y_2$ under square loss. Under absolute loss.

2

Missing Outcomes

Nonresponse is a perennial concern in the collection of survey data. Some persons are not interviewed, and some who are interviewed do not answer some of the questions posed. For example, the U.S. Bureau of the Census (1991, pp. 387–388) reported that in the March 1990 administration of the Current Population Survey (CPS), approximately 4.5 percent of the 60,000 households in the targeted sample were not interviewed. Incomplete income data were obtained from approximately 8 percent of the persons in the households that were interviewed.

Longitudinal surveys experience nonresponse in the form of sample attrition. Piliavin and Sosin (1988) interviewed a sample of 137 individuals who were homeless in Minneapolis in late December 1985. Six months later, the researchers attempted to reinterview these respondents but succeeded in locating only 78.

Chapters 2 through 4 study inference on conditional probability distributions from random sample data when some data are missing. I focus on the important and relatively simple case of missing outcomes, but also cover the case of interval measurement of outcomes in Complement 2A and that of jointly missing outcomes and covariates in Complement 2B. Whereas Chapters 2 and 3 maintain a nonparametric perspective on the inferential problem, Chapter 4 considers parametric prediction with missing data.

2.1 Anatomy of the Problem

Basically, inference with missing outcome data is a matter of contemplating all the values that the missing data might take. The set of feasible outcome distributions is determined by considering all logically possible configurations of the missing data. I first consider the problem in generality and then give several applications.

To formalize the inferential problem, we need to expand the description of the population in Chapter 1 to include a binary variable indicating when outcomes are observed. Thus let each member of the population be characterized by a triple (y, z, x). As before, y is the outcome to be predicted and x are the covariates. The new variable z takes the value one if y is observed and the value zero otherwise. As in Section 1.3, let a sampling process draw N persons at random from the population. For each $i = 1, \ldots, N$, outcome y_i is observable if $z_i = 1$ and missing if $z_i = 0$.

The objective is to use the available data to learn about $P(y \mid x)$ at a specified value of x on the support of $P(x)$. The structure of the inferential problem is displayed by the Law of Total Probability:

$$(2.1) \quad \begin{aligned} P(y \mid x) &= P(y \mid x, z = 1)\, P(z = 1 \mid x) \\ &\quad + P(y \mid x, z = 0)\, P(z = 0 \mid x). \end{aligned}$$

The sampling process asymptotically reveals $P(z = 1 \mid x)$ and $P(z = 0 \mid x)$, the probabilities that an outcome is observable or missing. It also reveals the distribution $P(y \mid x, z = 1)$ of observable outcomes when $P(z = 1 \mid x) > 0$. The sampling process is uninformative regarding the distribution $P(y \mid x, z = 0)$ of missing outcomes, which may be any probability distribution on Y. Hence the empirical evidence reveals that $P(y \mid x)$ lies in the *identification region*

$$(2.2) \quad \begin{aligned} H[P(y \mid x)] &\equiv [P(y \mid x, z = 1)\, P(z = 1 \mid x) \\ &\quad + \gamma P(z = 0 \mid x), \gamma \in \Gamma_Y], \end{aligned}$$

where Γ_Y denotes the set of all probability distributions on the set Y. The identification region is a proper subset of Γ_Y whenever the probability $P(z = 0 \mid x)$ of missing data is less than one, and is the single distribution $P(y \mid x, z = 1)$ when $P(z = 0 \mid x) = 0$. Hence $P(y \mid x)$

is *partially identified* when $0 < P(z = 0 \mid x) < 1$ and is *point-identified* when $P(z = 0 \mid x) = 0$.

Notation and Terminology The Greek letter H[·] is used throughout this book to denote the identification region for the quantity in brackets. The identification region is the set of feasible values for this quantity, given the maintained assumptions and the sampling process generating data. The quantity in brackets is point-identified if the identification region contains a single element. It is partially identified if the identification region contains multiple elements but is smaller than the universe of logically possible values. ❏

The description given above concerns identification of the entire outcome distribution. A common objective of empirical research is to infer a parameter of this distribution; for example, one may want to learn the conditional mean $E(y \mid x)$. Viewing this in abstraction, let $\theta(\cdot)$ be a function mapping probability distributions on Y into the real line and consider inference on the parameter $\theta[P(y \mid x)]$. The identification region for this parameter is the set of all the values it can take when $P(y \mid x)$ ranges over all of its feasible values. Thus $H\{\theta[P(y \mid x)]\} = \{\theta(\eta), \eta \in H[P(y \mid x)]\}$.

Identification of Event Probabilities

The above derivation is simple but abstract. To begin to show its practical implications, I now suppose that one wants to learn the probability $P(y \in B \mid x)$ that y falls in a specified set B.

By the Law of Total Probability, we may write $P(y \in B \mid x)$ as

(2.3)
$$P(y \in B \mid x) = P(y \in B \mid x, z = 1)\,P(z = 1 \mid x)$$
$$+ P(y \in B \mid x, z = 0)\,P(z = 0 \mid x).$$

The random sampling process reveals $P(y \in B \mid x, z = 1)$, $P(z = 1 \mid x)$, and $P(z = 0 \mid x)$, but provides no information on $P(y \in B \mid x, z = 0)$. The last quantity necessarily lies between zero and one. This yields the following "worst-case" bound on $P(y \in B \mid x)$:

(2.4)
$$P(y \in B \mid x, z = 1)\,P(z = 1 \mid x) \leq P(y \in B \mid x)$$
$$\leq P(y \in B \mid x, z = 1)\,P(z = 1 \mid x) + P(z = 0 \mid x).$$

The lower bound is the value $P(y \in B \mid x)$ takes if the missing values of y never fall in B, while the upper bound is the value $P(y \in B \mid x)$ takes if all the missing values of y fall in B.

Bound (2.4) is *sharp*. That is, the lower and upper bounds are the smallest and largest feasible values of $P(y \in B \mid x)$. The identification region for $P(y \in B \mid x)$ is the entire interval connecting the bounds. The width of this interval is the probability $P(z = 0 \mid x)$ of missing data. Thus the empirical evidence is informative unless y is always missing. Observe that the width of the interval may vary with x, but it does not vary with the set B.

Bound (2.4) has many important applications. One is the bound that it implies on the distribution function of a real-valued outcome. Suppose that y is real-valued. Then the distribution function for $P(y \mid x)$ is the function $F(\cdot)$ such that $F(t) = P(y \leq t \mid x)$ for all real numbers t. Application of (2.4) to $P(y \leq t \mid x)$ gives

(2.5)
$$P(y \leq t \mid x, z = 1)\, P(z = 1 \mid x) \leq P(y \leq t \mid x)$$
$$\leq P(y \leq t \mid x, z = 1)\, P(z = 1 \mid x) + P(z = 0 \mid x).$$

The feasible distribution functions are all increasing functions of t that take values between the lower and upper bounds in (2.5) for all values of t.

Identification of Quantiles

Bound (2.5) can be inverted to obtain sharp bounds on quantiles of $P(y \mid x)$. Consider the α-quantile. The bounds on $Q_\alpha(y \mid x)$ are easy to derive when the probability of missing data is sufficiently small and the distribution function $P(y \leq t \mid x, z = 1)$ for the observable outcomes is continuous and strictly increasing in t.

If $P(z = 0 \mid x) < \alpha$, the smallest feasible value of $Q_\alpha(y \mid x)$ is the value of t that solves the equation

(2.6) $$P(y \leq t \mid x, z = 1)\, P(z = 1 \mid x) + P(z = 0 \mid x) = \alpha.$$

This value of t makes the upper bound on $P(y \leq t \mid x)$ equal α, and any smaller value implies that $P(y \leq t \mid x) < \alpha$. The solution to (2.6) is the $[\alpha - P(z = 0 \mid x)]/P(z = 1 \mid x)$-quantile of $P(y \mid x, z = 1)$.

If $P(z = 0 \mid x) < 1 - \alpha$, the largest feasible value of $Q_\alpha(y \mid x)$ is the value of t that solves the equation

$$(2.7) \qquad P(y \leq t \mid x, z = 1) \, P(z = 1 \mid x) = \alpha.$$

This value of t makes the lower bound on $P(y \leq t \mid x)$ equal α, and any larger value implies that $P(y \leq t \mid x) > \alpha$. The solution to (2.7) is the $\alpha / P(z = 1 \mid x)$-quantile of $P(y \mid x, z = 1)$.

It takes more work to derive the bound in the general case where $P(y \mid x, z = 1)$ may have discontinuities or flat segments, or where the probability of missing data is too large for (2.6) or (2.7) to have a solution. Let y_0 and y_1 denote the smallest and largest logically possible values of y; thus, $y_0 \equiv \min_{y \in Y}$ and $y_1 \equiv \max_{y \in Y}$. Manski (1994) shows that the sharp lower and upper bounds on $Q_\alpha(y \mid x)$ are $r(\alpha, x)$ and $s(\alpha, x)$, where

$$r(\alpha, x) \equiv [\alpha - P(z = 0 \mid x)] / P(z = 1 \mid x)\text{-quantile}$$
$$\text{of } P(y \mid x, z = 1) \text{ if } P(z = 0 \mid x) < \alpha,$$
$$\equiv y_0 \text{ otherwise;}$$
$$s(\alpha, x) \equiv \alpha / P(z = 1 \mid x)\text{-quantile of } P(y \mid x, z = 1)$$
$$\text{if } P(z = 0 \mid x) \leq 1 - \alpha,$$
$$\equiv y_1 \text{ otherwise.}$$

The lower bound is generally informative if $P(z = 0 \mid x) < \alpha$, and the upper bound if $P(z = 0 \mid x) \leq 1 - \alpha$. In the case of the median, where $\alpha = \frac{1}{2}$, both bounds are informative if $P(z = 0 \mid x) < \frac{1}{2}$.

Although $r(\alpha, x)$ and $s(\alpha, x)$ are the sharp bounds on $Q_\alpha(y \mid x)$, the identification region need not be the entire interval connecting these bounds. Suppose that y is discrete. Quantiles must be elements of the set Y of logically possible values of y. Hence the identification region for $Q_\alpha(y \mid x)$ can only include the elements of the interval $[r(\alpha, x), s(\alpha, x)]$ that belong to Y.

2.2 Bounding the Probability of Exiting Homelessness

To illustrate the bound on conditional probabilities given in (2.4), consider the attrition problem that arose in the study of homelessness undertaken by Piliavin and Sosin (1988). These researchers wished to learn the probability that an individual who is homeless at a given date has a home six months later. Thus the population of interest is the set of people who are homeless at the initial date. The outcome variable y is binary, with $y = 1$ if the individual has a home six months later and $y = 0$ if the person remains homeless. The covariates x are individual background attributes. The objective is to learn $P(y = 1 \mid x)$. The missing data problem is that only a subset of the people in the original sample could be located six months later. So $z = 1$ if a respondent was located for reinterview, $z = 0$ otherwise.

Suppose that the only covariate is a respondent's sex. Consider the males. Initial interview data were obtained from 106 men, of whom 64 were located six months later. Of the latter group, 21 had exited from homelessness. So the empirical probability estimate of $P(y = 1 \mid \text{male}, z = 1)$ is 21/64 and that of $P(z = 1 \mid \text{male})$ is 64/106. The resulting estimate of the bound on $P(y = 1 \mid \text{male})$ is [21/106, 63/106] or approximately [0.20, 0.59].

Consider the females. Data were obtained from 31 women, of whom 14 were located six months later. Of these, 3 had exited from homelessness. So the estimate of $P(y = 1 \mid \text{female}, z = 1)$ is 3/14 and the estimate of $P(z = 1 \mid \text{female})$ is 14/31. The estimate of the bound on $P(y = 1 \mid \text{female})$ is [3/31, 20/31], or approximately [0.10, 0.65].

Interpretation of these estimates should be cautious, given the small sample sizes. Taking the results at face value, we have a tighter bound on $P(y = 1 \mid \text{male})$ than on $P(y = 1 \mid \text{female})$ because the attrition rate for men is lower than that for women. The attrition rates, hence the widths of the bounds, are 0.39 for men and 0.55 for women. The important point is that both bounds are informative. Having imposed no assumptions on the attrition process, we are nevertheless able to place meaningful bounds on the probability that a person who is homeless on a given date is no longer homeless six months later.

Is the Cup Part Empty or Part Full?

Consider the estimated bound for the probability that a male exits homelessness; that is, [0.20, 0.59]. Even ignoring sampling variability in the estimate, this may seem a modest finding. After all, $P(y = 1 \mid \text{male})$ could take any value in an interval of width 0.39. Surely, we would like to pin the value down more tightly than that. One might be tempted to use the midpoint of the interval [0.20, 0.59] as a point estimate of $P(y = 1 \mid \text{male})$, but there is no empirical justification for doing so.

The bound appears more useful when one focuses on the fact that it establishes a domain of consensus about the value of $P(y = 1 \mid \text{male})$. Researchers making different assumptions about the attrition process may logically reach different conclusions about the location of the exit probability within the interval $[0.20, 0.59]$. But all researchers who accept the Piliavin and Sosin data as a random sample from the population of interest must agree that, abstracting from sampling error, the exit probability is neither less than 0.20 nor greater than 0.59. It is valuable to be able to narrow the region of potential dispute from the interval $[0, 1]$ to the interval $[0.20, 0.59]$.

For a very long time, the attention of social scientists was so focused on point estimation that researchers did not appreciate the usefulness of simple bounds such as those reported here. When the idea was suggested, it was not pursued. For example, in a study of the statistical problems of the Kinsey report on sexual behavior, Cochran, Mosteller, and Tukey (1954, pp. 274–282) used bounds of the form (2.4) to express the possible effects of nonresponse to the Kinsey survey. Unfortunately, the subsequent literature did not follow up on the idea. In fact, Cochran (1977) dismissed bounding the effects of survey nonresponse. Using the symbol W_2 to denote the probability of missing data, he stated (p. 362): "The limits are distressingly wide unless W_2 is very small."

Although bounds using the empirical evidence alone sometimes are "distressingly wide," I feel that this fact should not dissuade researchers from reporting them. Even when wide, these bounds are valuable for two reasons. First, they establish a domain of consensus among researchers who may disagree about the precise value of a population parameter. Second, they make explicit the fundamental role that credible assumptions play in inferential methods that yield tighter findings. Wide bounds reflect real uncertainties that cannot be washed away by assumptions lacking credibility.

2.3 Means of Functions of the Outcome

This section and the next continue our study of inference using the data alone, without accompanying distributional assumptions. Here we consider inference on the conditional mean $E[g(y) \mid x]$, where $g(\cdot)$ is a specified function of y.

Bounded Random Variables

Suppose that $g(\cdot)$ has bounded range. Let the lower and upper bounds be called g_0 and g_1; thus, $g_0 \equiv \min_{y \in Y} g(y)$ and $g_1 \equiv \max_{y \in Y} g(y)$. I shall suppose for simplicity that $g(\cdot)$ attains its bounds. Thus there exists a $y_{0g} \in Y$ such that $g(y_{0g}) = g_0$ and a $y_{1g} \in Y$ such that $g(y_{1g}) = g_1$. If $g(\cdot)$ does not attain its lower or upper bound, result (2.9) below remains valid with the closed interval on the right-hand side replaced by one that is open from below or above.

Let the objective be to infer the expectation $E[g(y) \mid x]$ using the empirical evidence alone. The Law of Iterated Expectations gives

$$
(2.8) \quad
\begin{aligned}
E[g(y) \mid x] = {} & E[g(y) \mid x, z = 1] P(z = 1 \mid x) \\
& + E[g(y) \mid x, z = 0] P(z = 0 \mid x).
\end{aligned}
$$

The sampling process asymptotically reveals $E[g(y) \mid x, z = 1]$ and $P(z \mid x)$. However, the available data reveal nothing about $E[g(y) \mid x, z = 0]$, which can take any value in the interval $[g_0, g_1]$. Hence the identification region for $E[g(y) \mid x]$ is the interval

$$
(2.9) \quad
\begin{aligned}
& H\{E[g(y) \mid x]\} \\
& = \big[E[g(y) \mid x, z = 1] P(z = 1 \mid x) + g_0 P(z = 0 \mid x), \\
& \qquad E[g(y) \mid x, z = 1] P(z = 1 \mid x) + g_1 P(z = 0 \mid x) \big].
\end{aligned}
$$

This interval is a proper subset of $[g_0, g_1]$, hence informative, whenever $P(z = 0 \mid x) < 1$. Its width is $(g_1 - g_0) P(z = 0 \mid x)$. Thus the severity of the identification problem varies directly with the probability of missing data.

To illustrate application of (2.9), let B be any subset of Y and let $g(y) = 1[y \in B]$. Then $g_0 = 0$, $g_1 = 1$, $E[g(y) \mid x] = P(y \in B \mid x)$, and $E[g(y) \mid x, z = 1] = P(y \in B \mid x, z = 1)$. Thus (2.9) provides an alternative derivation of the bound on $P(y \in B \mid x)$ given earlier in (2.4).

Unbounded Random Variables

The situation changes if $g(\cdot)$ is unbounded from below or above; that is, if $g_0 = -\infty$ or $g_1 = \infty$. In such cases, result (2.9) still holds but has different implications whenever $P(z = 0 \mid x) > 0$.

Inspection of (2.9) shows that the lower bound on $E[g(y) \mid x]$ is $-\infty$ if $g_0 = -\infty$ and is ∞ if $g_1 = \infty$. The identification region has infinite width but remains informative if $g(\cdot)$ is bounded from at least one side. However, it is the entire real line if $g(\cdot)$ is unbounded from both below and above. Thus the presence of missing data makes credible assumptions a prerequisite for inference on the mean of an unbounded random variable.

Suppose that y itself is unbounded. Recall the result (2.5) giving an informative bound on the distribution function for $P(y \mid x)$. It may seem surprising that one should be able to bound the distribution function of y but not its mean. The explanation is a fact central to the field of robust statistics: the mean of a random variable is not a continuous function of its distribution function. Hence small perturbations in the distribution function can generate large movements in the mean. See Huber (1981).

To obtain some intuition for this fact, consider a thought experiment. Let t_0 and t_1 be real numbers, with $t_1 > t_0$. Let δ be a number between zero and one. Let w be a random variable with $P(w \leq t_0) = 1 - \delta$ and $P(w = t_1) = \delta$. Suppose w is perturbed by moving the mass at t_1 to some $t_2 > t_1$. Then $P(w \leq t)$ remains unchanged for $t < t_1$ and $t \geq t_2$, and decreases by δ in the interval $t \in [t_1, t_2)$. But $E(w)$ increases by the amount $\delta(t_2 - t_1)$. Now let t_2 increase to infinity. The perturbed distribution function remains within a δ-bound of the original one, but the perturbed mean increases to infinity.

2.4 Parameters That Respect Stochastic Dominance

The sharp bounds on event probabilities, quantiles, and means presented in Sections 2.1 and 2.3 were all obtained by the same simple argument. Wherever outcome data were missing, we inserted the values of y that yield the smallest and largest values of the parameter of interest to obtain the lower and upper bounds. This idea can be applied more generally to all parameters that respect stochastic dominance.

Stochastic dominance formalizes the idea that one distribution tends to yield larger outcomes than another. Consider two probability distributions on the real line, say, Q and Q'. Distribution Q is said to stochastically dominate distribution Q' if $Q(y \leq t) \leq Q'(y \leq t)$ for all values of t.

Let Γ_R denote the space of all distributions on the real line. A real-valued parameter $D(\cdot) : \Gamma_R \to R$ is said to *respect stochastic dominance* if $D(Q) \geq D(Q')$ whenever Q stochastically dominates Q'. Leading examples of parameters that respect stochastic dominance are quantiles and the means of increasing functions of y. Spread parameters such as the variance or interquartile range do not respect stochastic dominance.

As earlier, let y_0 and y_1 denote the smallest and largest logically possible values of y. The minimum value of any parameter $D(\cdot)$ that respects stochastic dominance is obtained by supposing that all missing values of y equal y_0. Similarly, the maximum value is obtained by supposing that all missing values equal y_1.

Estimation of the sharp bounds on $D[P(y)]$ is easy. To estimate the lower bound, one supposes that $y_i = y_0$ for every observation i with missing data. One then computes the usual point estimate of the parameter of interest, whether it be a mean or a quantile. To estimate the upper bound, one likewise supposes that $y_i = y_1$ whenever observation i is missing.

I have written above that spread parameters such as the variance and interquartile range do not respect stochastic dominance. Analysis of identification of such parameters when outcome data are missing is not nearly as simple and will not be addressed here. The interested reader should see Blundell et al. (2007) and Stoye (2004).

2.5 Distributional Assumptions

The preceding shows some of what can be learned about $P(y \mid x)$ using the data alone, without assumptions about the distribution of $P(y, z, x)$. Performing inference in the absence of distributional assumptions provides a natural starting point for empirical analysis but ordinarily will not be the ending point. Having determined what can be learned without assumptions, one should then ask what more can be learned if plausible assumptions are imposed.

Ideally, we would like to learn the identifying power of all distributional assumptions, so as to characterize the entire spectrum of inferential possibilities. But there does not appear to be any effective way to conduct an exhaustive identification analysis. So we will focus on assumptions that are often asserted in empirical studies and that have identifying power. Our study of inference using distributional assumptions begins here and will continue in Chapters 3 and 4.

Missingness at Random

Certainly, the most common practice in empirical studies has been to assume that data are missing at random. Formally, the assumption is that the missing outcomes have the same distribution as the observed ones, conditional on x:

(2.10) $P(y \mid x, z = 0) = P(y \mid x, z = 1).$

This is an invariance assumption of the kind discussed in Section 1.4. Assumption (2.10) point-identifies $P(y \mid x)$ when combined with the empirical evidence. In particular, it implies that $P(y \mid x)$ coincides with the observable distribution $P(y \mid x, z = 1)$.

Although commonly invoked in empirical research, the assumption of missingness at random is often criticized as implausible, especially in settings where data are missing by choice. Consider, for example, the reporting of income and wealth in surveys. Many persons regard their income and wealth as private information and choose not to respond to survey questions on these subjects. A widespread concern is that persons with higher income and wealth may tend to have higher nonresponse rates. Section 2.6 discusses other situations in which data are missing by choice.

As much as missingness at random may be criticized, the assumption cannot be proved wrong using the data alone. The reason is simple. The available data reveal nothing about the distribution of missing data $P(y \mid x, z = 0)$. Hence it is logically possible that this distribution is the same as the distribution of observed data $P(y \mid x, z = 1)$.

Refutable and Nonrefutable Assumptions

Missingness at random is a leading case of a class of assumptions that are not refutable using the data alone. Any assumption that directly restricts the distribution $P(y \mid x, z = 0)$ of missing data is nonrefutable.

Let us consider such assumptions in abstraction. One may assert that $P(y \mid x, z = 0)$ lies in a specified set of distributions, say, Γ_{0Y}. Recall the reasoning that led from the Law of Total Probability (2.1) to the identification region (2.2) using the data alone. The same reasoning now yields this smaller identification region for $P(y \mid x)$:

(2.11)
$$H_0[P(y \mid x)] \equiv [P(y \mid x, z = 1) P(z = 1 \mid x)$$
$$+ \gamma P(z = 0 \mid x), \gamma \in \Gamma_{0Y}].$$

Missingness at random is the special case in which Γ_{0Y} contains just one element, $P(y \mid x, z = 1)$.

Different researchers can invoke different nonrefutable assumptions, and there is no way to use the available data to decide who, if anyone, is correct. After all, one does not observe the missing data. Hence one cannot prove empirically that $P(y \mid x, z = 0)$ does not lie in the set Γ_{0Y}. All one might do is argue that, for whatever reasons, it is not plausible that $P(y \mid x, z = 0)$ lies in Γ_{0Y}.

Other distributional assumptions are refutable. Of particular interest are assumptions asserting that the distribution of interest, $P(y \mid x)$, lies in a specified set of distributions, say, Γ_{1Y}. For example, one might assert that $P(y \mid x)$ is a symmetric distribution or, more narrowly, a normal distribution. The data alone reveal that $P(y \mid x)$ lies in the set of distributions $H[P(y \mid x)]$ given in (2.2). Hence $P(y \mid x)$ must lie in the intersection of Γ_{1Y} and $H[P(y \mid x)]$. Thus the identification region now is

$$(2.12) \quad H_1[P(y \mid x)] \equiv H[P(y \mid x)] \cap \Gamma_{1Y}.$$

Suppose that the set $H_1[P(y \mid x)]$ turns out to be empty. Then the assumption that $P(y \mid x) \in \Gamma_{1Y}$ is inconsistent with the empirical evidence. Hence one should conclude that $P(y \mid x)$ does not lie in Γ_{1Y}.

The converse does not hold. Suppose that $P(y \mid x)$ does not lie in Γ_{1Y}. The intersection of $H[P(y \mid x)]$ and Γ_{1Y} could nonetheless be non-empty, depending on the specifics of the case. A finding that $H_1[P(y \mid x)]$ is nonempty means only that one cannot refute the assumption that $P(y \mid x) \in \Gamma_{1Y}$. It does not mean that the assumption is correct.

The above reasoning applies to assumptions regarding parameters of $P(y \mid x)$. Consider the conditional mean $E[g(y) \mid x]$. One may assert that $E[g(y) \mid x]$ lies in a specified subset of the real line, say, R_1. Then the identification region for $E[g(y) \mid x]$ is

$$(2.13) \quad H_1\{E[g(y) \mid x)]\} \equiv H\{E[g(y) \mid x)]\} \cap R_1,$$

where $H\{E[g(y) \mid x)]\}$ is the identification region (2.9) using the data alone. The assumption is inconsistent with the empirical evidence if $H_1\{E[g(y) \mid x)]\}$ turns out to be empty.

Refutability and Credibility

It is important not to confuse the refutability of an assumption with its credibility. Refutability is a matter of logic, and credibility is a subjective matter.

Refutability is a property of an assumption and the available empirical evidence. An assumption is refutable if it is inconsistent with some possible configuration of the empirical evidence. It is nonrefutable otherwise.

Credibility is a property of an assumption and the person contemplating it. An assumption is credible to the degree that someone thinks it so.

2.6 Wage Regressions and the Reservation-Wage Model of Labor Supply

Return now to the question of how data come to be missing. In Section 2.5 we considered the assumption that data are missing at random, and I noted that this assumption is suspect when data are missing by choice. This section gives a classic illustration, due to Gronau (1974), of how choice can make missingness at random implausible.

A major problem of missing data in labor economics occurs in efforts to estimate wage regressions, which measure how market wages vary with schooling, work experience, and demographic background. Available surveys such as the CPS provide background data for each respondent and wage data for those respondents who work. Even if all subjects respond fully to the questions posed, there remains a missing data problem in that the surveys do not provide market-wage data for respondents who do not work. Economists consider these wages to be well defined but unobserved—they are the wages that nonworkers could have earned had they chosen to work.

Consider the process determining whether wages are observed in surveys. Gronau reasoned as follows:

(i) Wage data are available for respondents who work.
(ii) Respondents work when they choose to do so.
(iii) The wage one would be paid influences the decision to work.
(iv) Hence the distributions of observed and unobserved wages may differ.

A simple model often used to express this reasoning supposes that each individual knows the wage y that would be paid if he or she were to work. The individual chooses to work if y is greater than some lowest acceptable wage R, called the person's *reservation wage*, and chooses not to work if y is below the reservation wage. So wages are observed when $y > R$ and are missing when $y < R$.

The reservation-wage model does not predict whether a person works if $y = R$, but it is conventionally assumed that this event occurs with probability zero in the population. Hence the borderline case may be ignored. With this caveat, the reservation-wage model implies that

$$(2.14) \quad P(y \mid x, z = 1) = P(y \mid x, y > R),$$

$$(2.15) \quad P(y \mid x, z = 0) = P(y \mid x, y < R),$$

and

$$(2.16) \quad P(z = 1 \mid x) - P(y > R \mid x).$$

If the reservation-wage model accurately describes the decision to work, then it is correct to assume that wage data are missing at random if and only if

$$(2.17) \quad P(y \mid x, y > R) = P(y \mid x, y < R),$$

or equivalently,

$$(2.18) \quad P(y \mid x, r > 0) = P(y \mid x, r < 0),$$

where $r \equiv y - R$ denotes the difference between the market and reservation wage. Condition (2.17) holds if persons with high market wages also tend to have high reservation wages. In particular, it holds if the difference r between market and reservation wages is statistically independent of the market wage y. The condition generally does not hold otherwise.

Homogeneous Reservation Wages

A particularly stark case where wage data are not missing at random occurs when all persons with covariates x have the same reservation wage, say, $R(x)$. Then all missing wages are smaller than all observed wages, conditional on x.

The homogeneous-reservation-wage assumption has considerable identifying power. Let $y^*(x)$ denote the smallest observed wage for persons with covariates x. The value of $y^*(x)$ is an upper bound on $R(x)$. Hence, for all $t \geq y^*(x)$,

$$(2.19) \quad P(y \leq t \mid x, z = 0) = P[y \leq t \mid x, y < R(x)] = 1.$$

It follows that for all such t,

$$
\begin{aligned}
P(y \leq t \mid x) &= P(y \leq t \mid x, z = 1)\, P(z = 1 \mid x) \\
(2.20) \quad & \quad + P(y \leq t \mid x, z = 0)\, P(z = 0 \mid x) \\
&= P(y \leq t \mid x, z = 1)\, P(z = 1 \mid x) + P(z = 0 \mid x).
\end{aligned}
$$

Thus $P(y \leq t \mid x)$ is point-identified for $t \geq y^*(x)$.

Result (2.20) implies that the α-quantile $Q_\alpha(y \mid x)$ is point-identified for all $\alpha > P(z = 0 \mid x)$. In particular,

$$
\begin{aligned}
Q_\alpha(y \mid x) &\equiv \min t : P(y \leq t \mid x) \geq \alpha \\
&= \min t\colon P(y \leq t \mid x, z = 1)\, P(z = 1 \mid x) \\
& \quad + P(z = 0 \mid x) \geq \alpha \\
(2.21) \quad &= \min t\colon P(y \leq t \mid x, z = 1) \\
& \quad \geq [\alpha - P(z = 0 \mid x)]/P(z = 1 \mid x) \\
&\equiv Q_a(y \mid x, z = 1),
\end{aligned}
$$

where $a \equiv [\alpha - P(z = 0 \mid x)]/P(z = 1 \mid x)$. Recall from Section 2.1 that $Q_a(y \mid x, z = 1)$ is the sharp lower bound on $Q_\alpha(y \mid x)$ using the empirical evidence alone.

It is interesting to compare inference on $Q_\alpha(y \mid x)$ under the homogeneous-reservation-wage assumption and under the assumption that wages are missing at random. These two assumptions are mutually inconsistent, but neither is refutable. Whereas the former assumption implies that $Q_\alpha(y \mid x) = Q_a(y \mid x, z = 1)$, the latter implies that $Q_\alpha(y \mid x) = Q_\alpha(y \mid x, z = 1)$. Observe that $a \leq \alpha$ for all values of α and $P(z = 0 \mid x)$. Hence researchers who perform inference under the two assumptions reach systematically different nonrefutable conclusions about quantiles of the wage distribution.

Other Cases of Missingness by Choice

The reservation-wage model of labor supply provides a nice illustration of missingness by choice. As another example, suppose one wishes to predict the outcomes a high school graduate would experience if he or she were to enroll in college (see Willis and Rosen, 1979). The outcomes of college enrollment are observable only for those high school graduates who actually enroll. The persons who enroll presumably are those who anticipate college to have favorable outcomes for them, relative to nonenrollment. If anticipated outcomes are related to realized ones, then the distribution of outcomes experienced by those who actually enroll may differ from the distribution of outcomes that nonenrollees would have experienced had they enrolled. We will see many similar examples in Part II, when we study analysis of treatment response.

The message is that choice behavior may make the observability of a behavioral outcome depend partly on the value of the outcome. Choice does not imply that the assumption of missingness at random is necessarily wrong, but it does cast much doubt on the assumption. Anyone concerned with prediction of y conditional on x must take notice. Using the observed distribution of outcomes to predict y conditional on x leads one astray to the extent that $P(y \mid x, z = 1)$ differs from $P(y \mid x)$.

2.7 Statistical Inference

Sample Analogs of Identification Regions

The fundamental inferential problem created by missing data is a failure of identification. To keep attention focused on identification, I have thus far treated as known the conditional distributions identified by the sampling process. Thus the identification regions that we have derived are functions of $P(y \mid x, z = 1)$ and $P(z \mid x)$.

In practice, one can estimate $P(y \mid x, z = 1)$ and $P(z \mid x)$ by their sample analogs, the empirical distributions $P_N(y \mid x, z = 1)$ and $P_N(z \mid x)$. Hence a natural estimate of the identification region for $P(y \mid x)$ is its sample analog

(2.22)
$$H_N[P(y \mid x)] \equiv [P_N(y \mid x, z = 1) P_N(z = 1 \mid x)$$
$$+ \gamma P_N(z = 0 \mid x), \gamma \in \Gamma_Y].$$

Correspondingly, a natural estimate of the identification region for a parameter $\theta[P(y \mid x)]$ is $\{\theta(\eta), \eta \in H_N[P(y \mid x)]\}$. In any case, the sample analog of an identification region is a function of the sample data and, hence, is a random variable—or more precisely, a random set.

Consider, for example, the conditional mean $E[g(y) \mid x]$. Its identification region (2.9) is a population concept, expressing what can be learned about the parameter given knowledge of $E[g(y) \mid x, z = 1]$ and $P(z \mid x)$. A natural estimate of this region is its sample analog

$$
\begin{aligned}
&H_N\{E[g(y) \mid x]\} \\
(2.23) \qquad &= \big[E_N[g(y) \mid x, z = 1]P_N(z = 1 \mid x) + g_0 P_N(z = 0 \mid x), \\
&\quad E_N[g(y) \mid x, z = 1]P_N(z = 1 \mid x) + g_1 P_N(z = 0 \mid x)\big].
\end{aligned}
$$

The conditional empirical means in (2.23) converge to their population counterparts in (2.9) as N increases. Hence the interval $H_N\{E[g(y) \mid x]\}$ is a consistent estimate of $H\{E[g(y) \mid x]\}$.

It is transparent that $H_N\{E[g(y) \mid x]\}$ is a consistent estimate of $H\{E[g(y) \mid x]\}$. Many of the problems that we will study in this book are similarly simple, but we will occasionally discuss ones in which the identification region is an abstract set and its estimate is the sample analog of this set. The standard definition of consistency used in statistics and econometrics concerns a sequence of point estimates that converges to a point as sample size increases. The standard definition can be extended to cover cases in which a sequence of set-valued estimates converges to a set. Complement 2C shows how to do this.

Confidence Sets

The statistics literature on point estimation of population parameters uses confidence sets to measure the uncertainty created by sampling variation. Recall the standard definition of a confidence set for a real parameter θ. One first specifies a *coverage probability* α, where $0 < \alpha < 1$. One next considers alternative ways to use the sample data to form sets on the real line. Let $C(\cdot)$ be a set-valued function that maps the data into a set on the real line; thus, for each possible value ψ of the sample data, $C(\psi)$ is the set that results when the data are ψ. Then $C(\cdot)$ gives an α-confidence set for θ if $\text{Prob}[\psi : \theta \in C(\psi)] = \alpha$. In words, an α-confidence set contains the true value of θ with probability α as the sampling process is engaged repeatedly to draw independent data samples.

It typically is not possible to determine the exact coverage probability of a confidence set. Hence statisticians seek asymptotically valid confidence sets, whose coverage probabilities can be shown to converge to α as the sample size grows. A common practice begins with a consistent estimate of θ, say, $\theta_N(\psi)$, and constructs an interval of the form $[\theta_N(\psi) - \delta_{0N}(\psi), \theta_N(\psi) + \delta_{1N}(\psi)]$, where $\delta_{0N}(\psi) > 0$ and $\delta_{1N}(\psi) > 0$ are chosen so that $\mathrm{Prob}\{\psi: \theta \in [\theta_N(\psi) - \delta_{0N}(\psi), \theta_N(\psi) + \delta_{1N}(\psi)]\}$ converges to α as N increases.

Although the statistics literature has focused on parameters that are point-identified, the standard definition of a confidence set also applies to parameters that are partially identified. In addition, one can define confidence sets for identification regions. Let $H(\theta)$ be the identification region for θ. Then $C(\cdot)$ gives an α-confidence set for $H(\theta)$ if $\mathrm{Prob}[\psi: H(\theta) \subset C(\psi)] = \alpha$. An α-confidence set for $H(\theta)$ necessarily covers θ with probability at least α. This holds because the true value of θ lies in $H(\theta)$; hence, $\mathrm{Prob}[\psi: \theta \in C(\psi)] \geq \mathrm{Prob}[\psi: H(\theta) \subset C(\psi)]$.

Consider the conditional mean $E[g(y) \mid x]$ of a bounded function $g(\cdot)$. A consistent estimate of the identification region was given in (2.16). A confidence set can be constructed by widening this estimate suitably, to have the form

(2.24)
$$C(\psi) = \big[E_N[g(y) \mid x, z = 1] P_N(z = 1 \mid x)$$
$$+ g_0 P_N(z = 0 \mid x) - \delta_{0N}(\psi),$$
$$E_N[g(y) \mid x, z = 1] P_N(z = 1 \mid x)$$
$$+ g_1 P_N(z = 0 \mid x) + \delta_{1N}(\psi) \big].$$

Horowitz and Manski (2000) show how $\delta_{0N}(\psi)$ and $\delta_{1N}(\psi)$ may be chosen so the coverage probability for $H\{E[g(y) \mid x]\}$ converges to α as N increases. Imbens and Manski (2004) show how they may be chosen so the coverage probability for $E[g(y) \mid x]$ converges to α. In both cases, $\delta_{0N}(\psi)$ and $\delta_{1N}(\psi)$ converge to zero as N increases. Thus the confidence set asymptotically shrinks to the identification region for $E[g(y) \mid x]$.

Testing Refutable Assumptions

Finally, recall the distinction made in Section 2.5 between refutable and nonrefutable assumptions. Nonrefutable assumptions cannot be disproved when the distributions $P(y \mid x, z = 1)$ and $P(z \mid x)$ are known. Hence they cannot be tested statistically when sample data are used to estimate these distributions.

Refutable assumptions generally are statistically testable using random sample data. To illustrate, consider again the assumption that $E[g(y) \mid x]$ lies in a specified subset of the real line, say, R_1. The identification region for $E[g(y) \mid x)]$ using the data alone is estimated consistently by its sample analog $H_N\{E[g(y) \mid x)]\}$, stated in (2.23). This suggests a statistical test of the hypothesis that $E[g(y) \mid x] \in R_1$: Reject the hypothesis if $H_N\{E[g(y) \mid x)]\}$ is sufficiently distant from R_1.

Complement 2A. Interval Measurement of Outcomes

The phenomenon of missing outcomes juxtaposes extreme observational states: each realization of y is observed either completely or not at all. Empirical researchers sometimes encounter intermediate observational states, in which realizations of y are observed to lie in proper but nonunitary subsets of the outcome space Y. A common intermediate state is interval measurement of real-valued outcomes.

Consider, for example, the question about annual household income posed in the Current Population Survey. Respondents are not asked to give their exact income. Instead, they are read a list of categories and are asked to state the category in which their income falls. Thus we may learn from the CPS that annual household income is in the range [$20,000–$24,999], [$60,000–$74,999], or [$200,000 or more].

To formalize interval measurement, let each member of the population have values for variables y_- and y_+, where $y_- \leq y \leq y_+$. We have interval measurement of outcomes if realizations of (y_-, y_+) are observable but realizations of y are not directly observable. I say that y is not "directly" observable to cover the possibility that $y_- = y_+$, in which case observation of (y_-, y_+) implies observation of y.

Sampling with missing outcomes is a special case of interval measurement. As earlier, let y_0 and y_1 be the smallest and largest logically possible values of y. A realization of y is effectively observed when $(y_- = y_+)$ and missing when $(y_- = y_0, y_+ = y_1)$.

Interval measurement yields simple lower and upper bounds on any parameter of $P(y \mid x)$ that respects stochastic dominance. The minimum value of any parameter $D(\cdot)$ that respects stochastic dominance is obtained by supposing that y always equals y_-. Similarly, the maximum value is obtained by supposing that y always equals y_+.

Formally, distribution $P(y_- \mid x)$ is a feasible value of $P(y \mid x)$ and is stochastically dominated by all other feasible values of $P(y \mid x)$. Hence $D[P(y_- \mid x)]$ is the smallest feasible value of $D[P(y \mid x)]$. Similarly, $P(y_+ \mid x)$ is a feasible value of $P(y \mid x)$ and stochastically dominates all other feasible values of $P(y \mid x)$. Hence $D[P(y_+ \mid x)]$ is the largest feasible value of $D[P(y \mid x)]$.

Estimation of the bounds $D[P(y_-)]$ and $D[P(y_+)]$ is easy. To estimate the lower bound, one supposes that $y_j = y_{j-}$ for every sample member j. One then computes the usual point estimate of the parameter of interest, whether it be a mean or a quantile. To estimate the upper bound, one likewise supposes that $y_j = y_{j+}$.

Measurement Devices with Bounded Range

A common source of interval data is use of a measurement device with a bounded range of sensitivity, say, (L, U). For example, a scale for weighing persons may report weights only in the range 20–300 pounds. A tire pressure gauge may report pressure only in the range 10–100 pounds per square inch. An earthquake monitoring device may report quake intensity only in the range 3–8 of the Richter scale. In each case, the device provides an accurate measurement of the outcome when it falls within the range of sensitivity. When the outcome is below the lower bound, the device reveals that the outcome takes a value in the interval $[0, L]$. When the outcome is above the upper bound, it reveals that the outcome lies in the interval $[U, \infty)$.

The inferential consequences of a bounded range of sensitivity depend on the distribution of outcomes and on the parameter of interest. It is particularly interesting to consider quantiles of the distribution. Suppose that application of the measurement device to the population of interest yields an interval measurement $[0, L]$ in a fraction λ_L of the cases, an interval measurement $[U, \infty)$ in a fraction λ_U of the cases, and a point measurement within the range (L, U) in the remaining fraction $1 - \lambda_L - \lambda_U$ of the cases. Then the α-quantile of y is point-identified when $\lambda_L < \alpha < 1 - \lambda_U$ and is partially identified otherwise. The identification region for $Q_\alpha(y)$ is $[0, L]$ when $\alpha \le \lambda_L$ and is $[U, \infty)$ when $\alpha \ge 1 - \lambda_U$.

Complement 2B. Jointly Missing Outcomes and Covariates

Empirical researchers may face complex patterns of missing data. Some sample members may have missing outcomes, others may have missing covariates, and others may have jointly missing outcomes and covariates. Nevertheless, it is instructive to study the polar cases in which all missing data are of the same type. When these polar cases are understood, it is not hard to combine the lessons learned to characterize inference with multiple types of missing data.

We have thus far studied the polar case where only outcome data are missing. This complement analyzes the case where outcomes and covariates are jointly missing; that is, one observes a realization of (y, x) either in its entirety or not at all. We will not consider the third polar case, where only covariate data are missing, because it is qualitatively different and considerably more difficult to analyze. The interested reader should see Horowitz and Manski (1998, 2000) and Manski (2003, chap. 3).

Jointly missing outcomes and covariates are a regular occurrence in survey research. Realizations of (y, x) may be missing in their entirety when sample members refuse to be interviewed or cannot be contacted by survey administrators.

To study inference with joint missingness, let the binary indicator z now take the value one when (y, x) is observed and the value zero otherwise. Let ξ denote a specified value of x. We will show that the identification region for $P(y \mid x = \xi)$ using the data alone is

$$\text{(2B.1)} \qquad H[P(y \mid x = \xi)] = \{ P(y \mid x = \xi, z = 1) r(\xi) \\ + \gamma [1 - r(\xi)], \gamma \in \Gamma_Y \},$$

where

$$r(\xi) \equiv \frac{P(x = \xi \mid z = 1) \, P(z = 1)}{P(x = \xi \mid z = 1) \, P(z = 1) + P(z = 0)}.$$

Proof of (2B.1) We begin again with the Law of Total Probability:

(2B.2)
$$P(y \mid x = \xi) = P(y \mid x = \xi, z = 1) \, P(z = 1 \mid x = \xi)$$
$$+ P(y \mid x = \xi, z = 0) \, P(z = 0 \mid x = \xi).$$

As in the case of missing outcomes, the sampling process reveals $P(y \mid x = \xi, z = 1)$ and is uninformative about $P(y \mid x = \xi, z = 0)$. The difference from the case of missing outcomes is that the sampling process only partially reveals $P(z \mid x = \xi)$.

For $i = 0$ or 1, Bayes Theorem gives

(2B.3)
$$P(z = i \mid x = \xi)$$
$$= \frac{P(x = \xi \mid z = i) \, P(z = i)}{P(x = \xi \mid z = 1) \, P(z = 1) + P(x = \xi \mid z = 0) \, P(z = 0)}.$$

Inserting (2B.3) into (2B.2) yields

(2B.4)
$$P(y \mid x = \xi)$$
$$= \frac{P(y \mid x = \xi, z = 1) \, P(x = \xi \mid z = 1) \, P(z = 1)}{P(x = \xi \mid z = 1) \, P(z = 1) + P(x = \xi \mid z = 0) \, P(z = 0)}$$
$$+ \frac{P(y \mid x = \xi, z = 0) \, P(x = \xi \mid z = 0) \, P(z = 0)}{P(x = \xi \mid z = 1) \, P(z = 1) + P(x = \xi \mid z = 0) \, P(z = 0)}.$$

Consider the right-hand side of equation (2B.4). The sampling process reveals $P(z)$, $P(x = \xi \mid z = 1)$, and $P(y \mid x = \xi, z = 1)$. It is uninformative about $P(x = \xi \mid z = 0)$ and $P(y \mid x = \xi, z = 0)$. Hence the identification region for $P(y \mid x = \xi)$ is

(2B.5)
$$H[P(y \mid x = \xi)]$$
$$= \bigcup_{p \in [0, 1]} \left\{ P(y \mid x = \xi, z = 1) \frac{P(x = \xi \mid z = 1) \, P(z = 1)}{P(x = \xi \mid z = 1) \, P(z = 1) + pP(z = 0)} \right.$$
$$\left. + \gamma \frac{pP(z = 0)}{P(x = \xi \mid z = 1) \, P(z = 1) + pP(z = 0)}, \gamma \in \Gamma_Y \right\}.$$

For each $p \in [0, 1]$, the distributions in brackets are mixtures of $P(y \mid x = \xi, z = 1)$ and arbitrary distributions on Y. The set of mixtures enlarges as p increases from 0 to 1. Hence it suffices to set $p = 1$. This yields (2B.1). ❑

It is interesting to compare the present identification region for $P(y \mid x = \xi)$ with the region obtained when only outcomes are missing. The two regions have the same form, with $r(\xi)$ here replacing $P(z = 1 \mid x = \xi)$ there. The quantity $r(\xi)$ is the smallest feasible value of $P(z = 1 \mid x = \xi)$ and is obtained by conjecturing that all missing covariates have the value ξ. Thus joint missingness of (y, x) exacerbates the identification problem produced by missingness of y alone.

The degree to which joint missingness exacerbates the identification problem depends on the prevalence of the value ξ among the observable realizations of x. Inspection of (2B.1) shows that $r(\xi) = P(z = 1)$ when $P(x = \xi \mid z = 1) = 1$ and decreases to zero as $P(x = \xi \mid z = 1)$ falls to zero. Thus, region (2B.1) is uninformative if the observable covariate distribution $P(x = \xi \mid z = 1)$ places zero mass on the value ξ.

Conditioning on a Subset of the Outcomes

A type of joint missingness occurs when outcomes are missing, and the objective is to learn a conditional distribution of the form $P(y \mid y \in B)$, where B is a specified subset of Y. If the outcome y is not observed, then the conditioning event $\{y \in B\}$ is not observed either.

This type of joint missingness differs a bit from that discussed above. Whereas the conditioning event $\{y \in B\}$ constrains the feasible values of y, the conditioning event $\{x = \xi\}$ does not. Nevertheless, a result similar to (2B.1) holds. The identification region is

$$\mathrm{H}[P(y \mid y \in B)] = \big\{ P(y \mid y \in B, z = 1)r(\xi)$$
(2B.6)
$$+ \gamma[1 - r(\xi)], \gamma \in \Gamma_B \big\},$$

where Γ_B is the space of all probability distributions on the set B. The proof of (2B.6) is analogous to that of (2B.1).

Illustration: Bounding the Probability of Employment and the Unemployment Rate

Horowitz and Manski (1998) used data from the National Longitudinal Survey of Youth (NLSY) to estimate the probability that a member of

Table 2B.1   Employment status of NLSY respondents, 1991

Employment status	Number of respondents
Employed ($y = 2$)	4332
Unemployed ($y = 1$)	297
Out of labor force ($y = 0$)	927
Ever-interviewed nonrespondents	555
Never-interviewed nonrespondents	701
Total	6812

Source: Horowitz and Manski (1998), Table 1.

the surveyed population is employed in 1991, as well as the unemployment rate for this population. The NLSY was previously described in Section 1.5.

In this illustration, the outcome y indicates an individual's employment status at the time of the 1991 interview. In the 1979 base year, the NLSY sought to interview a random sample of 6812 individuals and succeeded in obtaining interviews from 6111 of the sample members. Data on employment status in 1991 are available for 5556 of the 6111 individuals interviewed in the base year. The remaining 555 are nonrespondents, some because they were not interviewed in 1991 and some because they did not answer the employment-status question in their 1991 interviews. Table 2B.1 presents these response statistics and the frequencies with which different outcome values are reported.

The empirical nonresponse rate, which takes account of sample members who were never interviewed, is $P(z = 0) = 1256/6812 = 0.184$. The empirical probability of employment for the 5556 individuals who responded to the 1991 employment-status question is $P(y = 2 \mid z = 1) = 4332/5556 = 0.780$. The probability of employment among nonrespondents can take any value in the interval [0, 1]. Hence the identification region for the employment probability $P(y = 2)$ is

$$P(y = 2) \in [(0.780)(0.816), (0.780)(0.816) + (0.184)]$$
$$= [0.636, 0.820].$$

Now consider inference on the official unemployment rate as measured in the United States by the Bureau of Labor Statistics. This rate is the probability of unemployment within the subpopulation of persons who are in the labor force. When the 1991 employment status of an NLSY sample member is not reported, data are missing not only on that person's unemployment outcome but also on his or her membership in the labor force. Thus inference on the official unemployment rate poses a problem of jointly missing outcome and covariate data.

The quantity of interest is $P[y = 1 \mid y \in \{1, 2\}]$. The data show that the empirical unemployment rate among the individuals who responded to the 1991 employment-status question and who reported that they were in the labor force is $P[y = 1 \mid y \in \{1, 2\}, z = 1] = 297/4629 = 0.064$. In addition, $P(z = 1) = 5556/6812 = 0.816$ and $P[y \in \{1, 2\} \mid z = 1] = (4332 + 297)/5556 = 0.833$. Hence $r(\xi)$ defined in equation (2B.1) has the value 0.787; here ξ is the event $\{y \in \{1, 2\}\}$. Thus the identification region for the official unemployment rate is

$$P[y = 1 \mid y \in \{1, 2\}] \in [(0.064)(0.787), (0.064)(0.787) + 0.213]$$
$$= [0.050, 0.263].$$

Complement 2C. Convergence of Sets to Sets

To define consistency of estimates of set-valued identification regions, we need to define convergence of sets to sets. A natural way to do this begins with the ordinary idea of convergence of points to points. Let Θ denote a set, let θ^* be an element of Θ, and let $\theta_N, N = 1, \ldots, \infty$ be a sequence of elements of Θ. The sequence converges to θ^* if $\lim_{N \to \infty} \rho(\theta_N, \theta^*) = 0$, where $\rho(\cdot, \cdot)$ is a specified metric on Θ.

Now let Θ^* be some closed subset of Θ and let $\Theta_N, N = 1, \ldots, \infty$ be a sequence of closed subsets of Θ. Let $\rho(\Theta_N, \Theta^*)$ measure the distance from Θ_N to Θ^*, and $\rho(\Theta^*, \Theta_N)$ measure the distance from Θ^* to Θ_N, as follows:

(2C.1a) $\rho(\Theta_N, \Theta^*) \equiv \max\limits_{\theta_N \in \Theta_N} \min\limits_{\theta^* \in \Theta^*} \rho(\theta_N, \theta^*)$

(2C.1b) $\rho(\Theta^*, \Theta_N) \equiv \max\limits_{\theta^* \in \Theta^*} \min\limits_{\theta_N \in \Theta_N} \rho(\theta_N, \theta^*)$.

The function $\rho(\cdot, \cdot)$ defined in (2C.1) is the ordinary metric of the last paragraph when applied to sets containing one element each; if $\Theta_N = \theta_N$ and $\Theta^* = \theta^*$, then $\rho(\Theta_N, \Theta^*) = \rho(\Theta^*, \Theta_N) = \rho(\theta_N, \theta^*)$. In general, however, the generalized distance function $\rho(\cdot, \cdot)$ is asymmetric in its arguments. The quantity $\rho(\Theta_N, \Theta^*)$ is small if every element of Θ_N is close to some element of Θ^*, while $\rho(\Theta^*, \Theta_N)$ is small if every element of Θ^* is close to some element of Θ_N.

Finally, consider $\max\{\rho(\Theta_N, \Theta^*), \rho(\Theta^*, \Theta_N)\}$, which is called the *Hausdorff distance* between the sets Θ_N and Θ^*. With this definition, it is clear how we should define convergence of sets. We shall say that the sequence Θ_N, $N = 1, \ldots, \infty$ converges to Θ^* if

$$(2C.2) \quad \lim_{N \to \infty} \max\{\rho(\Theta_N, \Theta^*), \rho(\Theta^*, \Theta_N)\} - 0.$$

Thus the sequence converges if both $\rho(\Theta_N, \Theta^*)$ and $\rho(\Theta^*, \Theta_N)$ converge to zero.

A statistical estimate is said to be strongly consistent if it converges with probability one. This idea applies equally well to sets as to points. If Θ_N, $N - 1, \ldots, \infty$ is a sequence of estimates of Θ^*, the estimate is strongly consistent if (2C.2) holds with probability one.

3

Instrumental Variables

3.1 Distributional Assumptions and Credible Inference

Distributional assumptions combined with data may yield stronger conclusions than are possible using data alone. To cope with missing outcomes, researchers have traditionally imposed assumptions that point-identify outcome distributions. It has been particularly common to assert that data are missing at random.

Researchers who assert that data are missing at random almost inevitably find this assumption difficult to justify. Analysts who pose other point-identifying assumptions regularly encounter the same difficulty. This should not be surprising. The empirical evidence reveals nothing about the distribution of missing data. An assumption must be quite strong to pick out one among all possible distributions.

The Law of Decreasing Credibility calls attention to the fundamental tension between the credibility and strength of conclusions. Inference using the empirical evidence alone sacrifices strength of conclusions in order to maximize credibility. Inference with point-identifying assumptions sacrifices credibility in order to achieve strong conclusions. Between these poles, there is a vast middle ground of assumptions that have some identifying power.

Assumptions Using Instrumental Variables

This chapter studies assumptions that use instrumental variables. Some such assumptions imply point identification. Others have less power but, perhaps, more credibility. Some assumptions using instrumental variables are refutable and others are not.

What is an instrumental variable? As in Chapter 2, suppose that each member of the population has values for (y, z, x), where x and z are observable covariates and y is an outcome that is observable if $z = 1$. In addition, suppose that each person has a value for an observable covariate v taking values in a space V. The covariates v may be entirely distinct from (x, z), may partially overlap with (x, z), or may even be identical to (x, z). In any event, we will say that v is an instrumental variable if one poses an assumption that somehow connects the conditional distributions $P(y \mid v)$ across different values of v.

The term *instrumental variable* is due to Reiersol (1945), who thought of v as an instrument or tool that may help to identify an object of interest. Reiersol, along with other econometricians of his time, used instrumental variables to help identify linear simultaneous equation systems. Goldberger (1972), in a review of the literature, dates this use of instrumental variables back to Wright (1928). This classical application of instrumental variables will be described in Chapter 8.

Modern econometric research uses instrumental variables to help cope with many identification problems, including missing outcomes. Whatever the application may be, it is important to understand that observation of covariate v does not per se carry any implications for inference. Observation of v is useful only when combined with an assumption that has identifying power. Empirical researchers often ask whether some covariate is or is not a "valid instrument" in an application of interest. The expression "valid instrument" is imprecise because it focuses attention on the covariate used in the role of v, without reference to the accompanying assumption. It would be more precise to ask whether an assumption using an instrumental variable is credible.

There are many ways to define the covariates v and to form assumptions that connect the conditional distributions $P(y \mid v)$ across different values of v. Hence there are many ways to use instrumental variables to help identify outcome distributions when some outcome data are missing. This chapter covers several possibilities, but cannot be exhaustive.

Section 3.2 considers assumptions that assert some form of missingness at random. Section 3.3 assumes that the outcome y is statistically independent of some covariates. Section 3.4 weakens these assumptions to ones asserting equality of certain conditional means. Section 3.5

studies monotone instrumental variables, which weaken the equalities defining the above assumptions to weak inequalities.

To simplify the presentation, I shall suppose that the space V of possible values for v has finitely many values, each of which occurs with positive probability. If this is not the case, then substantially the same findings hold under regularity conditions for nonparametric regression analysis such as those discussed in Section 1.3 and Complement 1B.

3.2 Missingness at Random

Consider again the assumption that data are missing at random: $P(y \mid x, z = 0) = P(y \mid x, z = 1)$. This assumption uses an instrumental variable, with $v = z$. Conditioning on x, the assumption asserts equality of outcome distributions across values of z.

Researchers who feel that missingness at random is implausible when conditioning only on x sometimes feel that the assumption is plausible when conditioning on x and other observable covariates. That is, researchers who are unwilling to assume that $P(y \mid x, z = 0) = P(y \mid x, z = 1)$ sometimes are willing to assume that

$$(3.1) \quad P(y \mid x, w, z = 0) = P(y \mid x, w, z = 1),$$

where w is an observable covariate taking values in a space W.

Equation (3.1) poses a nonrefutable assumption that point-identifies $P(y \mid x)$. It is nonrefutable because it directly restricts the distribution of missing data. To show that it is point-identifying, use the Law of Total Probability to write

$$(3.2) \quad P(y \mid x) = \sum_{k \in W} P(y \mid x, w = k) P(w = k \mid x).$$

For each $k \in W$, assumption (3.1) implies that $P(y \mid x, w = k) = P(y \mid x, w = k, z = 1)$. Hence (3.2) becomes

$$(3.3) \quad P(y \mid x) = \sum_{k \in W} P(y \mid x, w = k, z = 1) P(w = k \mid x).$$

The sampling process asymptotically reveals the right-hand side of (3.3). Hence $P(y \mid x)$ is point-identified.

This result has long been well known, so much so that it is unclear when the idea originated. In the survey sampling literature, the result provides the basis for construction of sampling weights that aim to enable population inference in the presence of missing data; see Complement 3A. Rubin (1976) used the term *missing at random* to describe assumption (3.1). In applied econometric research, the assumption is sometimes called *selection on observables*; see Fitzgerald, Gottschalk, and Moffitt (1998, section IIIA) for discussion of the history.

Assumption (3.1) is sometimes posed in the alternate form

$$(3.4) \qquad P(z = 1 \mid x, w, y) = P(z = 1 \mid x, w).$$

When y has a discrete distribution or is continuous with a density, Bayes Theorem shows that (3.4) is equivalent to (3.1). Suppose that y is discrete. Applying Bayes Theorem to the left-hand side of (3.4) gives

$$(3.5) \qquad \frac{P(y = j \mid x, w, z = 1)\, P(z = 1 \mid x, w)}{P(y = j \mid x, w)} = P(z = 1 \mid x, w)$$

for each $j \in Y$. Solving (3.5) yields $P(y = j \mid x, w, z = 1) = P(y = j \mid x, w)$, which is the same as (3.1). The analogous derivation holds if y is continuous, with the density for y replacing the probability masses in (3.5). See Complement 3B for further discussion.

Conditioning Is Not Controlling

Researchers often assert that missingness at random conditional on (x, w) is more credible than is missingness at random conditional on x alone. To justify this, they say that (x, w) "controls for" more determinants of missing data than does x alone. Unfortunately, the term "controls for" is a vague expression with no formal standing in probability theory. When researchers say that conditioning on certain covariates "controls for" the determinants of missing data, they rarely give even a verbal explanation of what they have in mind, never mind a mathematical explanation.

There is no general foundation to the assertion that missingness at random becomes a better assumption as one conditions on more covariates. The assertion may be well grounded in some settings, but it is not self-evident. Indeed, outcomes may be missing at random conditional on x but not conditional on the longer covariate vector (x, w).

An example was given in Section 2.6, where we discussed the reservation-wage model of labor supply. We saw there that wage data are missing at random conditional on x if equation (2.17) holds. However, wages are not missing at random conditional on (x, R), where R is a person's reservation wage.

3.3 Statistical Independence

Missingness at random assumes a particular form of statistical independence: y is independent of the missingness indicator z, conditional on the covariates (x, w). We now consider more general forms of statistical independence: y is independent of some observed covariates v, conditional on other observed covariates u. That is,

$$(3.6) \quad P(y \mid u, v) = P(y \mid u).$$

Here u is an observable covariate taking values in a space U. There is no need to specify how the covariates (u, v) may relate to the covariates (x, z). The result to be shown here holds, whatever u and v may be.

Consider $P(y \mid u, v = k)$, where $k \in V$ is any specified value of v. Using the data alone, application of (2.2) shows that the identification region for $P(y \mid u, v = k)$ is

$$(3.7) \quad \mathrm{H}[P(y \mid u, v = k)] = \{ P(y \mid u, v = k, z = 1) \, P(z = 1 \mid u, v = k) \\ + \gamma_k \cdot P(z = 0 \mid u, v = k), \, \gamma_k \in \Gamma_Y \}.$$

The statistical independence assumption (3.6) states that $P(y \mid u) = P(y \mid u, v = k)$ for all values of k. Hence $P(y \mid u)$ must lie within all of the identification regions $\mathrm{H}[P(y \mid u, v = k)]$, $k \in V$. Moreover, any distribution that lies within all of these k-specific regions is a feasible value for $P(y \mid u)$. Thus the identification region for $P(y \mid u)$ is the intersection of these regions, namely,

$$(3.8) \quad \mathrm{H}_1[P(y \mid u)] = \bigcap_{k \in V} \{ P(y \mid u, v = k, z = 1) \, P(z = 1 \mid u, v = k) \\ + \gamma_k \cdot P(z = 0 \mid u, v = k), \, \gamma_k \in \Gamma_Y \}.$$

The structure of $H_1[P(y \mid u)]$ shows that assumption (3.6) may be refutable. Suppose that the intersection of sets on the right-hand side of (3.8) turns out to be empty. Then there exists no value of $P(y \mid u)$ that lies within all of the identification regions $H[P(y \mid u, v = k)]$, $k \in V$. Hence the assumption must be incorrect.

Binary Outcomes

The derivation of (3.8) from assumption (3.6) is straightforward, but the resulting identification region $H_1[P(y \mid u)]$ has a rather abstract form. Manski (2003, chap. 2) shows that the region has a tractable characterization when the outcome y is discrete. The region has a particularly simple form if y is binary, taking values 0 and 1. Then the real number $P(y = 1 \mid u)$ fully characterizes the distribution $P(y \mid u)$ and $H_1[P(y = 1 \mid u)]$ is the interval

(3.9)
$$
\begin{aligned}
& H_1[P(y = 1 \mid u)] \\
&= \Big[\max_{k \in V} P(y = 1 \mid u, v = k, z = 1)\, P(z = 1 \mid u, v = k), \\
&\quad \min_{k \in V} P(y = 1 \mid u, v = k, z = 1)\, P(z = 1 \mid u, v = k) \\
&\quad + P(z = 0 \mid u, v = k) \Big].
\end{aligned}
$$

To see this, consider $P(y = 1 \mid u, v = k)$, where $k \in V$ is any specified value of v. Using the data alone, equation (2.4) shows that the identification region for $P(y = 1 \mid u, v = k)$ is the interval

(3.10)
$$
\begin{aligned}
& H[P(y = 1 \mid u, v = k)] \\
&= \big[P(y = 1 \mid u, v = k, z = 1)\, P(z = 1 \mid u, v = k), \\
&\quad P(y = 1 \mid u, v = k, z = 1)\, P(z = 1 \mid u, v = k) \\
&\quad + P(z = 0 \mid u, v = k) \big].
\end{aligned}
$$

The statistical independence assumption states that $P(y = 1 \mid u) = P(y = 1 \mid u, v = k)$ for all values of k. Hence $P(y = 1 \mid u)$ must lie within all of the intervals $H[P(y = 1 \mid u, v = k)]$, $k \in V$. The identification region for $P(y = 1 \mid u)$ is the intersection of these k-specific intervals, namely, (3.9).

Identifying Power

The identifying power of assumption (3.6) can range from point identification of $P(y \mid u)$ to no power at all, depending on the nature of the instrumental variable.

A sufficient condition for point identification is that, for some $k \in V$, one of the sets whose intersection is taken in (3.8) contains a single distribution. This happens when v is the missingness indicator z. Then $H[P(y \mid u, v = 1)]$ contains a single distribution and $H[P(y \mid u, v = 0)]$ contains all distributions.

Assumption (3.6) has no identifying power if v is statistically independent of the pair (y, z), conditional on u. Then the sets $H[P(y \mid u, v = k)]$, $k \in V$ are all the same. Hence their intersection is the same as the identification region obtained using the data alone. This happens when one uses a random number generator to assign a value of v to each member of the population. A covariate generated by drawing random numbers is necessarily statistically independent of (y, z) and, thus, has no identifying power.

Intermediate findings occur when v is statistically related to missingness but is not a perfect predictor of missingness. Then the sets $H[P(y \mid u, v = k)]$, $k \in V$ overlap but are not the same. The size and shape of their intersection depends on the specifics of the case.

It is interesting to observe that, under assumption (3.6), observation of an instrumental variable is useful for prediction of y only because outcome data are missing. The assumption states that $P(y \mid u, v) = P(y \mid u)$ for all values of v. Hence observation of v is useless for prediction of y when the sampling process reveals $P(y \mid u)$, as it does in the absence of missing data.

Combining Multiple Surveys

When is a statistical independence assumption plausible? The assumption is often apt when a researcher is able to combine data from multiple surveys. These may be multiple surveys of a single population or surveys of different populations that can credibly be assumed to have the same outcome distribution.

The possibility of combining multiple surveys of a single population arises regularly. One survey may attempt to interview respondents face-to-face, another by telephone, and another by mail or over the Internet. Each interview mode may yield its own pattern of nonresponse. Persons may vary in their willingness to be interviewed face-to-face, over the phone, or in an Internet survey. When they do agree to be interviewed, the survey mode may affect their willingness to answer questions that may be sensitive or that require careful thought.

Or surveys may be undertaken at different points in time. One survey may interview respondents in a given geographic area in March of a given year and another in June or September. Formally, these are surveys of different populations, as the residents of an area may change over time. However, the surveys may be combined if one thinks it credible to assume that the relevant outcome distribution is time-invariant.

In both of these cases, (3.8) gives the identification region for the outcome distribution, with v indexing the surveys undertaken with different interview modes or at different points in time. If the various surveys have different patterns of missingness, region (3.8) may be smaller than that obtained using only one survey.

3.4 Equality of Means

The assumptions studied in Sections 3.2 and 3.3 assert the equality of entire conditional distributions across different values of the instrumental variable. Analogous assumptions assert equality only of specified distributional parameters. Parameter-specific assumptions are logically weaker than the corresponding distributional ones; hence, they may be more credible. For this reason, researchers who want to infer a particular parameter often maintain assumptions of parameter equality rather than distributional equality. We consider here cases in which the parameter of interest is a conditional mean $E[g(y) \mid x]$.

Means Missing at Random

The mean independence version of the missingness-at-random assumption studied in Section 3.2 is

$$(3.11) \quad E[g(y) \mid x, w, z = 0] = E[g(y) \mid x, w, z = 1].$$

This nonrefutable assumption point-identifies $E[g(y) \mid x]$. To prove this, use the Law of Iterated Expectations to write

$$(3.12) \quad E[g(y) \mid x] = \sum_{k \in W} E[g(y) \mid x, w = k] P(w = k \mid x).$$

For each value $k \in W$, assumption (3.11) implies that $E[g(y) \mid x, w = k] = E[g(y) \mid x, w = k, z = 1]$. Hence (3.12) becomes

$$(3.13) \quad E[g(y) \mid x] = \sum_{k \in W} E[g(y) \mid x, w = k, z = 1] P(w = k \mid x).$$

The sampling process reveals the right-hand side of (3.13). Hence $E[g(y) \mid x]$ is point-identified.

Mean Independence

The mean independence version of the statistical independence assumption studied in Section 3.3 is

$$(3.14) \quad E[g(y) \mid u, v] = E[g(y) \mid u].$$

To derive the identification region, consider $E[g(y) \mid u, v = k]$, where $k \in V$ is any specified value of v. Using the data alone, equation (2.9) shows that the identification region for $E[g(y) \mid u, v = k]$ is the interval

$$\begin{aligned}
\mathrm{H}&\{E[g(y) \mid u, v = k]\} \\
&= \big[E[g(y) \mid u, v = k, z = 1] P(z = 1 \mid u, v = k) \\
&\quad + g_0 P(z = 0 \mid u, v = k), \\
&\quad E[g(y) \mid u, v = k, z = 1] P(z = 1 \mid u, v = k) \\
&\quad + g_1 P(z = 0 \mid u, v = k) \big].
\end{aligned}$$

(3.15)

Assumption (3.14) states that $E[g(y) \mid u] = E[g(y) \mid u, v = k]$ for all values of k. Hence $E[g(y) \mid u]$ must lie within all of the intervals

$H\{[E[g(y) \mid u, v = k]\}, k \in V$. Thus the identification region for $E[g(y) \mid u]$ is the intersection of these intervals, namely,

$$H_1\{E[g(y) \mid u]\}$$

(3.16)
$$= \Big[\max_{k \in V} E[g(y) \mid u, v = k, z = 1] P(z = 1 \mid u, v = k)$$
$$+ g_0 P(z = 0 \mid u, v = k),$$
$$\min_{k \in V} E[g(y) \mid u, v = k, z = 1] P(z = 1 \mid u, v = k)$$
$$+ g_1 P(z = 0 \mid u, v = k)\Big].$$

This result generalizes the finding (3.9) for binary outcomes shown in Section 3.3; simply set $g(y) = 1[y = 1]$ to obtain that finding.

Assumption (3.14) is refutable if it is logically possible for the right-hand side of (3.16) to be empty. Then there exists no value of $E[g(y) \mid u]$ that lies within all of the identification regions $H\{E[g(y) \mid u, v = k]\}$, $k \in V$. Hence the assumption must be incorrect.

3.5 Inequality of Means

The assumptions studied so far have asserted equality of distributions or parameters across different values of the instrumental variable. Empirical researchers often find these equalities too strong to be credible. There is therefore reason to consider weakening them in ways that may enhance credibility while preserving some identifying power. One way to do this is to change the equalities into weak inequalities.

When considering entire probability distributions for a real-valued outcome, stochastic dominance provides a natural way to define inequalities between distributions; see the definition of stochastic dominance in Section 2.4. When considering a real-valued parameter of a distribution, one replaces equalities with ordinary inequalities. This section shows how, focusing on the equalities of means studied in Section 3.4.

Means Missing Monotonically

Weakening assumption (3.11) from an equality to a weak inequality gives

(3.17) $E[g(y) \mid x, w, z = 1] \geq E[g(y) \mid x, w, z = 0]$.

This asserts that, for each realization of w, the mean value of $g(y)$ when y is observed is greater than or equal to the mean value of $g(y)$ when y is missing. An analogous assumption would reverse the direction of the inequality.

To illustrate, let $g(y) = y$ and consider inference on a wage regression, discussed earlier in Section 2.6. Then assumption (3.17) states that, among persons with a specified value of (x, w), those who work have at least as high a mean market wage as those who do not work. This is weaker than (3.11), which asserts that the mean market wage is the same for those who do and do not work.

Assumption (3.17) is too weak to point-identify $E[g(y) \mid x]$, but it does have identifying power. To determine its implications, use the Law of Iterated Expectations to write

$$E[g(y) \mid x]$$

$$(3.18) \qquad = \sum_{k \in W} E[g(y) \mid x, w = k, z = 1] P(w = k, z = 1 \mid x)$$

$$+ E[g(y) \mid x, w = k, z = 0] P(w = k, z = 0 \mid x).$$

The sampling process asymptotically reveals all of the quantities on the right-hand side of (3.18) except for $E[g(y) \mid x, w = k, z = 0]$. By assumption (3.17), this quantity can take any value between g_0 and $E[g(y) \mid x, w = k, z = 1]$. Hence the identification region for $E[g(y) \mid x]$ is the interval

$$H_1\{E[g(y) \mid x]\}$$

$$(3.19) \qquad = \Big[E[g(y) \mid x, z = 1] P(z = 1 \mid x) + g_0 P(z = 0 \mid x),$$

$$\sum_{k \in W} E[g(y) \mid x, w = k, z = 1] P(w = k \mid x) \Big].$$

This identification region is a right-truncated subset of the region obtained using the data alone. The smallest feasible value of $E[g(y) \mid x]$ is the same as when using the data alone. The largest is the value that $E[g(y) \mid x]$ would take under assumption (3.11).

Monotone Regressions

To weaken assumption (3.14), let the set V be ordered. The weakened assumption is

(3.20)
$$E[g(y) \mid u, v = k] \geq E[g(y) \mid u, v = k']$$
$$\text{for all } (k, k') \in V \times V \text{ such that } k \geq k'.$$

In words, the mean regression of $g(y)$ on (u, v) weakly increases with v, holding u fixed.

Empirical researchers often conjecture that regressions are increasing in some covariate, but they rarely perform inference with this as a maintained assumption. Consider again the case of wage regressions. In that setting, u might be a set of demographic variables and v might be realized years of schooling. Then the assumption states that, among persons with the same demographic covariates u, mean wage weakly increases with realized years of schooling.

Manski and Pepper (2000) show that the identification region for $E[g(y) \mid u]$ under assumption (3.20) is the interval

(3.21)
$$H_1\{E[g(y) \mid u]\}$$
$$= \left[\sum_{k \in V} P(v = k) \{ \max_{k' \leq k} E[g(y)z + g_0(1 - z) \mid u, v = k'] \}, \right.$$
$$\left. \sum_{k \in V} P(v = k) \{ \min_{k' \geq k} E[g(y)z + g_1(1 - z) \mid u, v = k'] \} \right].$$

This identification region is a subset of the region obtained using the data alone and is a superset of the one obtained under assumption (3.14).

Complement 3A. Imputations and Nonresponse Weights

Organizations conducting major surveys commonly release public data files that provide imputations for missing data or nonresponse weights to be used for estimating distributional parameters when data are missing. This complement discusses how imputations and nonresponse weights are used to estimate the mean $E[g(y)]$ of a function of y.

Imputations

Imputation methods assign to each sample member with a missing realization of y some logically possible value, say, y^*. This done, $E[g(y)]$ is estimated by the sample average

$$(3A.1) \quad \theta_N = \frac{1}{N} \sum_{i=1}^{N} g(y_i)z_i + g(y_i^*)(1 - z_i),$$

which uses the actual value of y when available and the imputation otherwise. By the Strong Law of Large Numbers, the estimate θ_N converges to

$$(3A.2) \quad \theta \equiv E[g(y) \mid z = 1] P(z = 1) + E[g(y^*) \mid z = 0] P(z = 0)$$

as the sample size increases.

A common imputation practice is to assign each respondent i with missing outcome data a value y_i^* drawn from the distribution $P(y \mid z = 1)$. Then θ of (3A.2) equals $E[g(y)]$ if outcomes are missing at random. Variations on the theme assume that outcomes are missing at random conditional on an instrumental variable v, and draw y_i^* from $P(y \mid v = v_i, z = 1)$. See Rubin (1987).

Whatever imputation method is used, θ necessarily lies in the identification region for $E[g(y)]$. This is so because imputations are logically possible values of the missing data. Hence $E[g(y^*) \mid z = 0]$ is a possible value for the mean $E[g(y) \mid z = 0]$ of the missing outcomes. However, θ does not generally equal $E[g(y)]$. Equality holds only if $E[g(y^*) \mid z = 0]$ equals the unknown $E[g(y) \mid z = 0]$.

Nonresponse Weights

Suppose that a random sample of size N has been drawn from the population of interest. Let $N(1)$ denote the sample members for whom $z = 1$, and let N_1 be the size of this subsample. The standard construction of nonresponse weights uses an observable covariate v to construct a weighting function $s(\cdot)$. The mean $E[g(y)]$ is estimated by the weighted sample average

$$(3A.3) \quad \theta_N \equiv \frac{1}{N_1} \sum_{i \in N(1)} s(v_i)g(y_i).$$

By the Strong Law of Large Numbers, the estimate θ_N converges to $E[s(v)g(y) \mid z = 1]$. The standard weights provided by survey organizations are constructed so that $E[s(v)g(y) \mid z = 1]$ equals $E[g(y)]$ when the data are missing at random conditional on v. The standard weights have the form

$$(3\text{A}.4) \quad s(v) = \frac{P(v = k)}{P(v = k \mid z = 1)}, \quad k \in V.$$

The Law of Iterated Expectations shows that, with these weights,

$$
\begin{aligned}
E[s(v)g(y) \mid z = 1] \\
(3\text{A}.5) \qquad &= \sum_{k \subset V} E[s(v)g(y) \mid v = k, z = 1] P(v = k \mid z = 1) \\
&= \sum_{k \in V} E[g(y) \mid v = k, z = 1] P(v = k).
\end{aligned}
$$

The right-hand side of this equation equals $E[g(y)]$ if $E[g(y) \mid v, z = 1] = E[g(y) \mid v]$.

Complement 3B. Conditioning on the Propensity Score

Recall the form (3.4) given for the assumption of missingness at random conditional on (x, w), repeated here as

$$(3\text{B}.1) \quad P(z = 1 \mid x, w, y) = P(z = 1 \mid x, w).$$

The probability $e(x, w) \equiv P(z = 1 \mid x, w)$ of observing y conditional on (x, w) is sometimes called the *propensity score*. Rosenbaum and Rubin (1983) show that if (3B.1) holds, then outcomes are also missing at random conditional on $[x, e(x, w)]$. This complement presents and discusses their result.

To show the result, observe that (3B.1) is the same as

$$(3\text{B}.2) \quad P[z = 1 \mid x, w, e(x, w), y] = e(x, w).$$

Let $\delta \in [0, 1]$. Integrating both sides of (3B.2) with respect to the distribution $P[w \mid x, e(x, w) = \delta, y]$ yields

(3B.3) $P[z = 1 \mid x, e(x, w) = \delta, y] = \delta$.

Thus outcomes are missing at random conditional on x and the propensity score.

Based on the above derivation, Rosenbaum and Rubin argue that conditioning on the propensity score rather than on w is valuable when w is multidimensional, in which case the real-valued $e(x, w)$ has lower dimension than w. In particular, they assert that dimension reduction simplifies statistical analysis with sample data.

Curiously, their argument neglects the fact that propensity scores are not known with sample data—they are regressions that must be estimated. Thus conditioning on the propensity score does not really reduce the dimensionality of the conditioning variables. Rather, it transfers the multidimensional inference problem to estimation of the propensity score. See Imbens (2004) for a comprehensive discussion of this matter.

Whatever merits conditioning on the propensity score may have for statistical inference, the idea is unrelated to identification. Rosenbaum and Rubin begin by assuming that outcomes are missing at random conditional on (x, w). They derive from this assumption the fact the outcomes are missing at random conditional on x and the propensity score.

Complement 3C. Word Problems

Problem 3.1
A public health researcher wants to learn the fraction of adult Americans who have received a dose of the smallpox vaccine. Let $y = 1$ if a person received the vaccine and $y = 0$ otherwise. The researcher wants to learn $P(y = 1)$, the probability that an adult American received the vaccine.

The researcher draws a very large random sample of adult Americans and asks the sample members if they have received the vaccine. All persons drawn into the sample agree to be interviewed and to answer the question truthfully. However, some persons do not recall if they have received the vaccine and so do not respond. Thus let $z = 1$ if a person recalls whether he or she received the vaccine and $z = 0$ otherwise. The researcher observes y for persons with $z = 1$, but does not observe y for persons with $z = 0$. Suppose that the researcher also learns the sex (w = male or female) of each sample member.

Let $P(y, z, w)$ denote the population distribution and suppose that the sample evidence reveals the following:

$P(y = 1, z = 1, w = \text{male}) = 0.3$ $P(y = 1, z = 1, w = \text{female}) = 0.28$

$P(y = 0, z = 1, w = \text{male}) = 0.1$ $P(y = 0, z = 1, w = \text{female}) = 0.16$

$P(z = 0, w = \text{male})$ $= 0.1$ $P(z = 0, w = \text{female})$ $= 0.06$

(Interpret the sample frequencies as if they are population probabilities.)

    a. Using the sample evidence alone, what can the researcher conclude about $P(y = 1)$?

    b. Assume that the fraction of males who received the vaccine equals the fraction of females who received the vaccine. That is, $P(y = 1 \mid w = \text{male}) = P(y = 1 \mid w = \text{female})$. Now what can the researcher conclude about $P(y = 1)$?

    c. Assume that among persons of each sex, those who recall whether they received the vaccine are more likely to have received it than are those who do not recall. That is,

$$P(y = 1 \mid w = \text{male}, z = 1) > P(y = 1 \mid w = \text{male}, z = 0)$$
$$P(y = 1 \mid w = \text{female}, z = 1) > P(y = 1 \mid w = \text{female}, z = 0).$$

Now what can the researcher conclude about $P(y = 1)$?

    d. Assume that persons who received the vaccine are more likely to recall than are those who did not receive the vaccine. That is, suppose that $P(z = 1 \mid y = 1) \geq P(z = 1 \mid y = 0)$. Now what can the researcher conclude about $P(y = 1)$? (*Note:* This assumption does not condition on w.)

Problem 3.2

A health researcher uses a scale to measure the weight of each student in the population of Northwestern undergraduates. Let y be a student's true weight and let y^* be weight as measured on the scale. Let $x = 1$ if a person is vegetarian and $x = 0$ otherwise.

The researcher finds it credible to assume the following:

Assumption 1. The scale is accurate in the range [100, 240] pounds but
   is inaccurate outside this range. Thus $y = y^*$ when $y^* \in [100, 240]$,
   $y < 100$ when $y^* < 100$, and $y > 240$ when $y^* > 240$.
Assumption 2. True weight in the population is never below 80 pounds
   and never above 300 pounds.

The researcher weighs each member of the population and reports
these findings:

$$P(y^* < 100 \mid x = 0) = 0.05, \qquad E(y^* \mid x = 0) = 180,$$
$$M(y^* \mid x = 0) = 160, \qquad P(y^* > 240 \mid x = 0) = 0.10.$$
$$P(y^* < 100 \mid x = 1) = 0.10, \qquad E(y^* \mid x = 1) = 160,$$
$$M(y^* \mid x = 1) = 150, \qquad P(y^* > 240 \mid x = 1) = 0.$$

a. What can you conclude about $E(y \mid x = 0)$?

b. What can you conclude about $M(y \mid x = 0)$?

c. The NU nutritionist uses the findings to support a proposal that NU
   dining halls henceforth should serve entirely vegetarian meals. The
   nutritionist states:

   > The data indicate that being a vegetarian substantially decreases
   > the chance that a student is severely overweight. The effect of a
   > vegetarian diet is to decrease the probability of weighing more than
   > 240 pounds from 0.10 to 0.

   Does this statement accurately describe the empirical finding?
   Explain.

Problem 3.3

This question concerns survey research performed by a sports sociol-
ogist on the baseball perspectives of American married couples as the
2006 World Series between the Detroit Tigers and St. Louis Cardinals is
about to begin. The researcher draws a random sample of couples and in-
quires about their preference for the winning team. However, the survey
has some nonresponse.

Let the population of married couples be described by the distribution $P(z_t, y_t, t = 0, 1)$. Here

$t = 0$ denotes the wife and $t = 1$ denotes the husband.

$y_t = 1$ if person t prefers that the Tigers win the 2006 World Series, $y_t = 0$ otherwise.

$z_t = 1$ if person t reports his/her preference on the survey, $z_t = 0$ if t does not respond.

The survey findings are given in the table below.

Wife response	Husband response		
	$z_1 = 1, y_1 = 0$	$z_1 = 1, y_1 = 1$	$z_1 = 0$
$z_0 = 1, y_0 = 0$	0.20	0.05	0.05
$z_0 = 1, y_0 = 1$	0.05	0.30	0.05
$z_0 = 0$	0.10	0.10	0.10

Assume that persons who respond to the question always do so truthfully. Assume that the response frequencies in the table are population probabilities, not just sample estimates of those probabilities. When answering the questions below, use the empirical evidence alone.

a. What can the researcher infer about $P(y_0 = y_1)$, the probability that a (wife, husband) couple share the same preference?

b. What can the researcher infer about $E(y_1 - y_0)$, the mean difference in the preference of husbands and wives?

c. What can the researcher infer about $M(y_1 - y_0)$, the median difference in the preference of husbands and wives?

d. What can the researcher infer about $M(y_1) - M(y_0)$, the difference between the median preference of husbands and wives?

Problem 3.4
Let $P(y, z, x)$ be the population distribution of (y, z, x). All three variables are binary, taking the value 0 or 1. All population realizations of (z, x) are observed. Realizations of y are observed when $z = 1$.

Several assumptions are given below. Take each in turn and determine (i) whether the assumption is refutable and (ii) the identification region for $P(y = 1)$ under the assumption. In each case explain your answer.

   a. Assume that $P(y \mid x = 1, z = 1)$ stochastically dominates $P(y \mid x = 0, z = 1)$.

   b. Assume that $P(y \mid x = 1)$ stochastically dominates $P(y \mid x = 0)$.

   c. Assume that the *linear probability model* $P(y = 1 \mid x) = \alpha + \beta x$ holds, where (α, β) are parameters.

Problem 3.5

The Illinois State Police monitors driving on the interstate highways that pass through Illinois. A lawsuit has been filed asserting that the State Police discriminates against out-of-state drivers when officers stop vehicles for speeding on the part of the Northwest Tollway (I-90) near the Wisconsin border. The plaintiff asserts that discrimination against out-of-state drivers exists if

$$\alpha \equiv P(y = 1 \mid z = 0) - P(y = 1 \mid z = 1) > 0.$$

These probabilities pertain to the population of vehicles that cross the Illinois-Wisconsin border on I-90. Here $y = 1$ if the Illinois State Police stopped a vehicle for speeding and $y = 0$ otherwise. The variable $z = 1$ if the vehicle had an Illinois license plate and $z = 0$ otherwise. As evidence of discrimination, the plaintiff in the lawsuit has provided this empirical evidence:

$$P(y = 1 \mid z = 0) = 0.02, \qquad P(y = 1 \mid z = 1) = 0.01.$$

In defense, the State Police has asserted that the above inequality does not imply discrimination. The State Police asserts that discrimination exists if

$$\beta \equiv P(y = 1 \mid s > 65, z = 0) - P(y = 1 \mid s > 65, z = 1) > 0,$$

where s is vehicle speed and where 65 miles per hour is the posted speed limit.

Questions a–c ask what one can learn about β when empirical knowledge of $P(y \mid z)$ is combined with certain assumptions. Thus suppose that $P(y = 1 \mid z = 0) = 0.02$ and $P(y = 1 \mid z = 1) = 0.01$ when answering these questions.

a. Assume that the police are more likely to stop vehicles that exceed the speed limit than ones that do not exceed the speed limit, whether the vehicle belongs to a resident or not. Thus assume that

$$P(y = 1 \mid s > 65, z = j) > P(y = 1 \mid s \leq 65, z = j), \quad j = 0, 1.$$

Given this assumption, what can one learn about β?

b. Assume that the police never stop vehicles driven at or below the speed limit. Also, more than half of all vehicles exceed the speed limit, whether the vehicle belongs to a resident or not. Thus assume that

$$P(y = 1 \mid s \leq 65, z = j) - 0, \quad j = 0, 1;$$
$$P(s > 65 \mid z = j) > 0.5, \quad j = 0, 1.$$

Given these assumptions, what can one learn about β?

c. Assume that the police follow a strict rule when deciding whether to stop a vehicle, this being to stop the vehicle if and only if its speed exceeds 80 miles per hour. Thus assume that

$$y = 1 \Leftrightarrow s > 80.$$

Given this assumption, what can one learn about β?

d. Now suppose that $P(y \mid z = 0)$ and $P(y \mid z = 1)$ are not known. However, someone has been able to learn the conditional probabilities $P(y = 1 \mid s, z)$ for all values of (s, z). Given knowledge of $P(y = 1 \mid s, z)$, what can one learn about β?

e. Suppose that a researcher is able to learn the distributions $P(s \mid z = 0)$ and $P(s \mid z = 1)$ of vehicle speeds of nonresidents and residents.

The researcher reports these distributional statistics:

$$E(s \mid z = 0) = 70, \quad E(s^2 \mid z = 0) = 4925.$$
$$E(s \mid z = 1) = 75, \quad E(s^2 \mid z = 1) = 5629.$$

Given this information, what can one learn about $P(s > 80 \mid z = 0)$ and $P(s > 80 \mid z = 1)$?

4

Parametric Prediction

Thus far, our study of prediction with missing data has been entirely nonparametric. This chapter considers parametric prediction models. Such models assume that the population distribution of outcomes and covariates, or at least some features of this distribution, lies in a specified parametric family. Conventional parametric assumptions have strong identifying power but weak substantive foundations. Hence they illustrate well the Law of Decreasing Credibility.

Section 4.1 considers a point-identifying model of market and reservation wages that has often been used by labor economists to estimate wage regressions. Section 4.2 discusses a broader class of "selection models," which jointly describe the determination of outcomes and their observability. Section 4.3 studies the identifying power of parametric models for best predictors, with no assumptions on the missingness process.

4.1 The Normal-Linear Model of Market and Reservation Wages

Labor economists have widely used the reservation-wage model to explain labor supply and, hence, the observability of market wages. Recall the version of the model discussed in Section 2.6. Each individual knows the wage y that would be paid if he were to work. The individual chooses to work if y is greater than his reservation wage R, and chooses not to work if y is below the reservation wage. So wages are observed when $y > R$ and are missing when $y < R$.

The reservation-wage model per se has no identifying power. The model implies that the distribution of missing wages has the form $P(y \mid x, y < R)$, but it imposes no restrictions on the form of this distribution. To have identifying power, the model must be augmented by assumptions on the distribution $P(y, R \mid x)$ of market and reservation wages.

A common practice has been to restrict $P(y, R \mid x)$ to a family of distributions specified up to some parameters. One specification, the *normal-linear model*, has received considerable attention. This model assumes that, conditional on x, the distribution of $(\log y, \log R)$ is bivariate normal with mean $(x\beta_1, x\beta_2)$ and variance matrix Σ. This assumption reduces the problem of inference on $P(y \mid x)$ to that of identifying the parameters $(\beta_1, \beta_2, \Sigma)$. These parameters are point-identified if, under the maintained assumptions, there is exactly one value of $(\beta_1, \beta_2, \Sigma)$ that implies the observable distributions $P(y \mid x, z = 1)$ and $P(z \mid x)$. If the assumptions are incorrect, it may be that no value of the parameters generates these observable distributions.

The normal-linear model of market and reservation wages was introduced by Gronau (1974), who used it to illustrate the general problem of missingness by choice in labor supply. Gronau cautioned that the model imposes strong assumptions, and he did not endorse it as a tool for empirical research. Nevertheless, many researchers subsequently chose to apply the model, especially after the introduction of a computationally simple "two-step" estimation method by Heckman (1976).

In the late 1970s, the normal-linear model was greeted with much enthusiasm by labor economists. This enthusiasm was based partly on its ease of estimation using the two-step method and partly on a misconception that the model offers a credible solution to the problem of missing wage data. Researchers of the time did not always appreciate that solutions to missing data problems are only as good as the assumptions imposed. However, enthusiasm eventually waned with recognition that the model achieves point identification through assumptions that have no substantive grounding in labor economics.

The Two-Step Method

Consideration of the two-step method shows much about how the normal-linear model achieves point identification. The present discussion focuses on the problem of inference on β_1. This is the quantity of interest in the many studies that seek to learn the wage regression $E(\log y \mid x)$, which equals $x\beta_1$ under the normal-linear model.

To begin, write the model in the form

(4.1a) $\log y = x\beta_1 + \epsilon_1,$

(4.1b) $\log R = x\beta_2 + \epsilon_2,$

(4.1c) $P(\epsilon_1, \epsilon_2 \mid x) \sim N(0, \Sigma).$

Here $N(0, \Sigma)$ denotes the bivariate normal distribution with mean zero and variance matrix Σ. In what follows, σ_{11} and σ_{22} denote the variances of ϵ_1 and ϵ_2, σ_{12} is their covariance, $\Phi(\cdot)$ denotes the standard normal distribution function, and $\phi(\cdot)$ is the standard normal density function.

The data reveal the probability $P(z - 1 \mid x)$ of observing y and the conditional expectation $E(\log y \mid x, z = 1)$. The quantity $P(z = 1 \mid x)$ is related to the parameters $(\beta_1, \beta_2, \Sigma)$ as follows:

(4.2)
$$
\begin{aligned}
P(z = 1 \mid x) &= P(\log y > \log R \mid x) \\
&= P(x\beta_1 + \epsilon_1 > x\beta_2 + \epsilon_2 \mid x) \\
&= P[\epsilon_2 - \epsilon_1 < x(\beta_1 - \beta_2)] \\
&= \Psi[x(\beta_1 - \beta_2)/\sigma],
\end{aligned}
$$

where $\sigma^2 \equiv \sigma_{11} + \sigma_{22} - 2\sigma_{12}$ is the variance of $\epsilon_2 - \epsilon_1$. It can be shown that $E(\log y \mid x, z = 1)$ is related to the parameters as follows:

(4.3)
$$
\begin{aligned}
E(\log y \mid x, z = 1) &= E(\log y \mid x, \log y > \log R) \\
&= E(\log y \mid x, x\beta_1 + \epsilon_1 > x\beta_2 + \epsilon_2) \\
&= x\beta_1 + E(\epsilon_1 \mid x, x\beta_1 + \epsilon_1 > x\beta_2 + \epsilon_2) \\
&= x\beta_1 - \sigma_{1u}m[x(\beta_1 - \beta_2)/\sigma],
\end{aligned}
$$

where σ_{1u} is the covariance of ϵ_1 and $(\epsilon_2 - \epsilon_1)/\sigma$ and where

(4.4) $m[x(\beta_1 - \beta_2)/\sigma] \equiv \dfrac{\phi[x(\beta_1 - \beta_2)/\sigma]}{\Phi[x(\beta_1 - \beta_2)/\sigma]}.$

The function $m(\cdot)$ is called the *inverse Mills ratio*. See, for example, Maddala (1983, sec. 8.4).

Assume that the support of distribution $P(x)$ is not concentrated on a linear subspace of the covariate space. Then solution of equation (4.2) for different values of x reveals the value of the composite parameter $(\beta_1 - \beta_2)/\sigma$. Hence we may consider $m[x(\beta_1 - \beta_2)/\sigma]$ to be a known function of x. This done, solution of equation (4.3) for different values of x reveals the values of β_1 and σ_{1u}.

The two-step method applies the above reasoning to the sample data. The first step estimates $(\beta_1 - \beta_2)/\sigma$ and, hence, $m[x(\beta_1 - \beta_2)/\sigma]$. This is usually accomplished by applying the maximum-likelihood method to the probit model in (4.2). The second step estimates β_1 and σ_{1u}. This is usually accomplished by performing the least-squares fit of $\log y$ to the covariates x and the estimate of $m[x(\beta_1 - \beta_2)/\sigma]$.

The fragility of two-step inference is evident from equation (4.3). The equation states that $E(\log y \mid x, z = 1)$ is the sum of two functions of x, the linear function $x\beta_1$ and the nonlinear function $\sigma_{1u} m[x(\beta_1 - \beta_2)/\sigma]$. The linearity of the first function rests on the assumption that $E(\log y \mid x)$ is linear in x. The particular nonlinear form of the second function rests on the entire complex of assumptions that comprise the normal-linear model. Any deviation from these assumptions alters how $E(\log y \mid x, z = 1)$ varies with x and, hence, affects the least-squares fit performed in the second of the two steps.

To illustrate, let us maintain all assumptions except for the homoscedasticity assumption that the variance of (ϵ_1, ϵ_2) is the same for all values of x. Instead, let the variance be permitted to change with x, so the constant matrix Σ becomes a function $\Sigma(x)$. Then (4.2) and (4.3) become

$$(4.5) \qquad P(z = 1 \mid x) = \Phi[x(\beta_1 - \beta_2)/\sigma(x)]$$

and

$$(4.6) \qquad E(\log y \mid x, z = 1) = x\beta_1 - \sigma_{1u}(x)m[x(\beta_1 - \beta_2)/\sigma(x)].$$

In the absence of assumptions restricting how $\Sigma(x)$ varies with x, the right-hand side of each equation is an unknown function of x. Hence the equations no longer reveal β_1. To achieve identification requires supplementation of equations (4.5) and (4.6) with information on how $\Sigma(x)$ varies with x. But what might be the source of such information? Even if one accepts the overall structure of the normal-linear model, labor economics provides no basis for assumptions of homoscedasticity or particular forms of heteroscedasticity.

4.2 Selection Models

The normal-linear model of market and reservation wages exemplifies a class of parametric selection models that describe how outcomes and missingness vary with observed and unobserved covariates. The expression "selection model" is used because these models aim to explain missingness as the result of a choice, such as the choice to work in the reservation-wage model.

The selection models used in empirical research generally have the form

(4.7a) $y = f(x, b) + \delta,$

(4.7b) $z = 1[g(x, c) + \epsilon > 0],$

(4.7c) $P(\delta, \epsilon \mid x) = F(x, d).$

Thus outcome y is observed if the quantity $g(x, c) + \epsilon$ exceeds the threshold zero. The functions f and g are prespecified up to the values of the parameters b and c, which are to be inferred from the data. The quantities δ and ϵ are unobserved covariates whose distribution $P(\delta, \epsilon \mid x)$ is assumed to have the form $F(x, d)$, where the parameters d are to be inferred from the data. Maddala (1983) discusses such models, with explanation of conditions that are necessary and sufficient for point identification and consistent estimation of the parameters.

In applications, researchers usually give f and g the linear forms $f(x, b) = xb$ and $g(x, c) = xc$. They usually assume that (δ, ϵ) is statistically independent of x. Moreover, they usually assume that the distribution $P(\delta, \epsilon)$ is bivariate normal with mean zero and an unknown variance matrix Σ. They usually do not require that δ and ϵ be statistically independent of one another. Permitting dependence is important because, in the context of (4.7), statistical independence of δ and ϵ is equivalent to the assumption that data are missing at random conditional on x.

A Semiparametric Model

Selection models point-identify their parameters through a complex of assumptions that usually have little if any substantive foundation. Seeking to strengthen the credibility of these models, econometricians have sought ways to weaken or modify the assumptions and yet retain point identification. To give a sense of the possibilities, I briefly sketch a semiparametric two-step idea that has been explored by various authors; see, for example, Ahn and Powell (1993).

Consider the model

(4.8a) $y = xb + \delta,$

(4.8b) $z = 1[xc + \epsilon > 0],$

(4.8c) (δ, ϵ) statistically independent of x, with $E(\delta) = E(\epsilon) = 0.$

This is a conventional normal-linear model, except that the shape of $P(\delta, \epsilon)$ is left unspecified rather than assumed to be normal. It follows from (4.8) that

(4.9) $P(z = 1 \mid x) = P(xc + \epsilon > 0 \mid x) = h_1(xc)$

and

(4.10) $E(y \mid x, z = 1) = xb + E(\delta \mid x, xc + \epsilon > 0) = xb + h_2(xc),$

where h_1 and h_2 are unknown functions. It can be shown that equation (4.9) identifies c up to normalizations of intercept and scale if x has continuous support and other regularity conditions hold. Given this, equation (4.9) point-identifies b up to a normalization of intercept if it is known that b does not equal c up to scale.

The above result shows that some progress can be made toward improving the credibility of selection models by weakening their traditional parametric assumptions. However, one should not expect too much. The semiparametric two-step approach discards only the assumption that (δ, ϵ) is bivariate normal, retaining the rest of the traditional structure of the model. And even this modest weakening of the model has a price. One requires assumptions on the support of $P(x)$ and on the relationship between b and c that are not necessary in the traditional setup. Even then, one cannot infer the intercept component of b.

4.3 Parametric Models for Best Predictors

Suppose that one knows nothing about the process that makes some outcomes observable and others missing. Then one can neither assume that outcomes are missing at random nor pose any meaningful selection model. So the main routes to point identification promoted in statistical and econometric research are closed.

In this setting, one may still bring to bear assumptions that restrict the conditional outcome distribution $P(y \mid x)$. We have already shown in Chapter 3 that such assumptions can have identifying power. Section 3.3 studied statistical independence assumptions that assert y to be statistically independent of some covariates, conditional on the others. Section 3.5 discussed monotone regression assumptions that assert $E(y \mid x)$ to be increasing in one component of x, conditional on the other components.

Empirical researchers often assert a parametric model for $E(y \mid x)$, $M(y \mid x)$, or another best predictor of y given x. I will show that such models generally have identifying power but that they typically do not yield point identification. The ideas discussed here apply to prediction under any loss function, but I focus on square loss for specificity. Thus the best predictor is $E(y \mid x)$, and the parametric model assumes that

(4.11) $E(y \mid x) = f(x, b).$

Here b is a parameter taking values in a parameter space B and $f(\cdot, \cdot)$ is a specified real-valued function.

Identification of the Parameters and of the Best Predictor

It is simple to determine the identifying power of a parametric model. Consider the joint identification region for $[E(y \mid x = \xi), \xi \in X]$ using the empirical evidence alone. A parameter value $b \in B$ is feasible if and only if the implied values of $[f(\xi, b), \xi \in X]$ lie within this region; that is, if

(4.12) $[f(\xi, b), \xi \in X] \in H[E(y \mid x = \xi), \xi \in X].$

The region $H[E(y \mid x = \xi), \xi \in X]$ has the Cartesian product form

(4.13) $H[E(y \mid x = \xi), \xi \in X] = \underset{\xi \in X}{\times} H[E(y \mid x = \xi)],$

where

$$H[E(y \mid x = \xi)]$$
$$= \big[E(y \mid x = \xi, z = 1) P(z = 1 \mid x = \xi)$$
(4.14)
$$+ y_0 P(z = 0 \mid x = \xi),$$
$$E(y \mid x = \xi, z = 1) P(z = 1 \mid x = \xi)$$
$$+ y_1 P(z = 0 \mid x = \xi) \big]$$

and where y_0 and y_1 are the smallest and largest logically possible values of y. Thus b is feasible if and only if

$$E(y \mid x = \xi, z = 1) P(z = 1 \mid x = \xi)$$
$$+ y_0 P(z = 0 \mid x = \xi) \leq f(\xi, b)$$
(4.15)
$$\leq E(y \mid x = \xi, z = 1) P(z = 1 \mid x = \xi)$$
$$+ y_1 P(z = 0 \mid x = \xi)$$

for all $\xi \in X$.

Let B_0 denote the subset of B for which (4.15) holds. Then B_0 is the identification region for b and $[f(\xi, b), \xi \in X]$, $b \in B_0$ is the identification region for $[E(y \mid x = \xi), \xi \in X]$ using the empirical evidence and model (4.11).

What if B_0 turns out to be empty? Then no value of b yields a function $f(x, b)$ that equals a feasible value of $E(y \mid x)$. So the parametric model must be incorrect. Thus parametric models are refutable assumptions whenever it is logically possible for B_0 to be empty.

Linear Index Models

Identification region B_0 is particularly simple to describe when the parametric model has the linear index form

(4.16) $E(y \mid x) = f(xb),$

where $f(\cdot)$ is a strictly increasing function of xb. Here b is a vector of the same length as x, and xb is the scalar product of x and b.

When $f(\cdot)$ has the linear index form, inequality (4.15) yields linear inequalities on the parameters b. Let $f^{-1}(\cdot)$ denote the inverse of $f(\cdot)$.

Then (4.15) is equivalent to

$$f^{-1}\big[E(y \mid x = \xi, z = 1)\, P(z = 1 \mid x = \xi)$$
$$+ y_0 P(z = 0 \mid x = \xi)\big] \le \xi b$$

(4.17)

$$\le f^{-1}\big[E(y \mid x = \xi, z = 1)\, P(z = 1 \mid x = \xi)$$
$$+ y_1 P(z = 0 \mid x = \xi)\big]$$

for all $\xi \in X$. B_0 is the set of values of b that satisfy these linear inequalities.

Statistical Inference

It is natural to estimate B_0 by its sample analog B_{0N}. When $f(\cdot)$ is a linear index model, B_{0N} is the set of parameter values that satisfy the linear equalities

$$f^{-1}\big[E_N(y \mid x = \xi, z = 1)\, P_N(z = 1 \mid x = \xi)$$
$$+ y_0 P_N(z = 0 \mid x = \xi)\big] \le \xi b$$

(4.18)

$$\le f^{-1}[E_N(y \mid x = \xi, z = 1)\, P_N(z = 1 \mid x = \xi)$$
$$+ y_1 P_N(z = 0 \mid x = \xi)\big]$$

for all $\xi \in X$.

A possible complication is that B_{0N} may be empty even though B_0 is nonempty. This can happen because the empirical distribution of the data obtained in a random sample generally differs from the population distribution generating the sample. It is desirable to have methods for estimating B_0 that yield B_{0N} when this set is nonempty and that also deliver reasonable estimates when B_{0N} is empty. Complement 4A shows how this may be accomplished.

Complement 4A. Minimum-Distance Estimation of Partially Identified Models

The reasoning used in Section 4.3 is not specific to inference with missing outcome data. It applies to whatever inferential problem may prevent point identification of $E(y \mid x)$ and whatever form the identification region $H[E(y \mid x = \xi), \xi \in X]$ may take. Moreover, it applies when considering inference on any parameter of $P(y \mid x)$, not only the conditional expectation $E(y \mid x)$.

Let $\theta(x)$ be any parameter of $P(y \mid x)$ and let $H[\theta(\xi), \xi \in X]$ be the identification region for $[\theta(\xi), \xi \in X]$ using the data alone. Consider the model

(4A.1) $\theta(x) = f(x, b)$.

A parameter value $b \in B$ is feasible if and only if

(4A.2) $[f(\xi, b), \xi \in X] \in H[\theta(\xi), \xi \in X]$.

The identification region is the set B_0 of parameter values for which (4A.2) holds. It is natural to estimate B_0 by its sample analog B_{0N},

(4A.3) $B_{0N} = \{b \in B : [f(\xi, b), \xi \in X] \in H_N[\theta(\xi), \xi \in X]\}$,

where $H_N[\theta(\xi), \xi \in X]$ is the sample analog of $H[\theta(\xi), \xi \in X]$. However, as noted at the end of Section 4.3, B_{0N} may turn out to be empty even though B_0 is nonempty.

This complement describes a *minimum-distance* approach to estimation that yields B_{0N} when this set is nonempty and that also delivers reasonable estimates when B_{0N} is empty. The approach was originally proposed and studied by Manski and Tamer (2002) in the specific setting of parametric best prediction with missing or interval data. The present discussion makes plain that the idea has general applicability. To simplify the presentation, I shall suppose that the space X of possible values for x has finitely many values, each of which occurs with positive probability.

Consider $b \in B$. Observe that $[f(\xi, b), \xi \in X]$ is a point in $R^{|X|}$, where $|X|$ is the number of elements in X. Let $\rho(\cdot, \cdot)$ be a metric measuring the distance between any two elements of $R^{|X|}$; for example, ρ might be the usual Euclidean distance. Given any point $\theta \in R^{|X|}$ and any closed set $\Theta \subset R^{|X|}$, let

(4A.4) $\rho(\theta, \Theta) \equiv \min_{\psi \in \Theta} \rho(\theta, \psi)$

measure the distance from point θ to set Θ. This definition, which is a special case of the set-to-set distance defined in equation (2C.1a), says that the distance from a point to a set is the distance from the point to the closest element of the set.

Suppose that the set $H[\theta(\xi), \xi \in X]$ is closed. Then, by the definition of B_0, the distance from $[f(\xi, b), \xi \in X]$ to $H[\theta(\xi), \xi \in X]$ is zero if $b \in B_0$ and is positive if $b \notin B_0$. Thus B_0 is the set of parameter values that minimize the distance from $[f(\xi, b), \xi \in X]$ to $H[\theta(\xi), \xi \in X]$. Formally,

(4A.5) $B_0 = \underset{b \in B}{\operatorname{argmin}}\ \rho\big\{[f(\xi, b), \xi \in X], H[\theta(\xi), \xi \in X]\big\}.$

Now consider estimation with sample data. Replace $H[\theta(\xi), \xi \in X]$ with its sample analog $H_N[\theta(\xi), \xi \in X]$ and reconsider (4A.5). This yields the minimum-distance estimate

(4A.6) $B_{0N\rho} \equiv \underset{b \in B}{\operatorname{argmin}}\ \rho\big\{[f(\xi, b), \xi \in X], H_N[\theta(\xi), \xi \in X]\big\}.$

This estimate coincides with B_{0N} when the latter is nonempty; that is, when there exist parameter values b such that the distance from $[f(\xi, b), \xi \subset X]$ to $H_N[\theta(\xi), \xi \in X]$ is zero. Then the metric ρ used to measure distance is immaterial. The rationale for $B_{0N\rho}$ is that this estimate remains well defined and sensible when B_{0N} is empty. Then $B_{0N\rho}$ is the set of parameter values that minimizes the everywhere positive distance from $[f(\xi, b), \xi \in X]$ to $H_N[\theta(\xi), \xi \in X]$, with distance measured by ρ.

The minimum-distance estimate studied in Manski and Tamer (2002) applied this approach to parametric best prediction with missing or interval data. We showed that a slightly enlarged version of $B_{0N\rho}$ is consistent in the sense of Complement 2C. The enlargement of $B_{0N\rho}$, motivated by technical subtleties in the proof of consistency, defines the estimate to be all parameter values that come sufficiently close to minimizing the objective function, not just those that exactly minimize the objective function.

5

Decomposition of Mixtures

5.1 The Inferential Problem and Some Manifestations

This chapter studies the decomposition of mixtures, a problem of incomplete data that arises in varied settings. Stripped to its algebraic essentials, the simplest problem of mixture decomposition concerns a linear equation of the form $A = BC + D(1 - C)$. You know that all of the quantities (A, B, C, D) lie in the unit interval, and you know the values of A and C. Your problem is to determine the feasible values of (B, D). This opening section states the abstract inferential problem and discusses two prominent manifestations.

The Problem in Abstraction

Consider a population with members characterized by random variables (y, x, w). Here y is a real outcome taking values in an outcome space Y and (x, w) are covariates taking values in a space $X \times W$. I will suppose throughout that w takes finitely many values, with $P(x = \xi, w = \omega) > 0$ for each $(\xi, \omega) \in X \times W$. Much of this chapter concerns the relatively simple case in which w takes only two values. In any case, the objective is to learn about $P(y \mid x, w)$.

The problem is identification of $P(y \mid x, w)$ when the empirical evidence only reveals the distributions $P(y \mid x)$ and $P(w \mid x)$. The nature of the problem is revealed by the Law of Total Probability. For each covariate value $\xi \in X$,

$$(5.1) \quad P(y \mid x = \xi) = \sum_{\omega \in W} P(y \mid x = \xi, w = \omega) P(w = \omega \mid x = \xi).$$

Knowledge of $P(y \mid x)$ and $P(w \mid x)$ restricts $[P(y \mid x = \xi, w = \omega), \omega \in W]$ to vectors of distributions that solve (5.1). In the absence of distributional assumptions, all such vectors are feasible. Hence the identification region for $[P(y \mid x = \xi, w = \omega), \omega \in W]$ using the empirical evidence alone is

$$\mathrm{H}\{[P(y \mid x = \xi, w = \omega), \omega \in W]\}$$

$$(5.2) \qquad = \left[\gamma_\omega \in \Gamma_Y, \omega \in W: \right.$$

$$\left. P(y \mid x = \xi) = \sum_{\omega \in W} \gamma_\omega P(w = \omega \mid x = \xi) \right].$$

Identification region (5.2) is always nonempty. In particular, letting $P(y \mid x = \xi, w = \omega) = P(y \mid x = \xi)$ for all $\omega \in W$ solves (5.1). Beginning in Section 5.2, we will characterize the region more fully and study the identifying power of various assumptions that may be combined with the empirical evidence.

In the language of probability theory, the inferential problem is to decompose a mixture with known mixing probabilities into its component distributions. Distribution $P(y \mid x = \xi)$ is said to be a *mixture* of the distributions $[P(y \mid x = \xi, w = \omega), \omega \in W]$. The latter distributions are called the *components of the mixture,* and $[P(w = \omega \mid x = \xi), \omega \in W]$ are the *mixing probabilities.* Covariates x and w play different roles in the mixture decomposition problem, the former being used only as a conditioning variable and the latter also being used to form the mixture. To distinguish x and w, I shall refer to w as the *mixing covariate.*

Mixture decomposition problems arise in many applied literatures with differing concerns and terminology. I discuss here two manifestations, ecological inference and contaminated sampling. Another will be discussed in Chapter 10.

Ecological Inference

Suppose that data are available from two sampling processes, each of which has a severe missing data problem. One sampling process draws persons at random from the population and yields observable realizations of (y, x), but the corresponding realizations of w are not recorded. The other sampling process draws persons at random and yields observable realizations of (w, x), but the realizations of y are not recorded. These two sampling processes reveal the distributions $P(y \mid x)$ and $P(w \mid x)$. Political scientists and sociologists use the term *ecological inference* to describe the resulting problem of inference on $P(y \mid x, w)$ given knowledge of $P(y \mid x)$ and $P(w \mid x)$; important early contributions include Robinson (1950), Duncan and Davis (1953), and Goodman (1953). Although this term is not especially evocative, I will follow tradition and use it here.

A prominent instance of ecological inference arises in the analysis of voting behavior. Social scientists have long been interested in the geographic and demographic variation in voting across the population. Surveys yielding information on individual attributes and voting behavior are not always available, and, when they are, the credibility of self-reports of voting behavior may be open to question. Hence social scientists have often sought to infer voting patterns from two data sources that are readily available and credible: (a) administrative records on voting by electoral district and (b) census data on the attributes of persons in each district.

Let y denote the voting outcome of interest. Let x denote an electoral district. Let w denote personal attributes thought to be related to voting behavior. The objective is to learn $P(y \mid x, w)$, the distribution of voting outcomes among persons in district x with attributes w. Voting records may reveal $P(y \mid x)$, and census data may reveal $P(w \mid x)$. The problem is to use knowledge of $P(y \mid x)$ and $P(w \mid x)$ to learn $P(y \mid x, w)$.

Contaminated and Corrupted Sampling

Suppose that each member of the population is characterized by two real-valued outcomes, say, y_a and y_b. Variable y_b is the outcome of interest, while y_a is not of interest. A random sample is drawn from the population, and the realizations of covariate x are always observed.

However, the realizations of y_a and y_b are not directly observable. Instead, one observes

(5.3) $y \equiv y_a(1 - w) + y_b w,$

where w is an unobserved binary random variable taking the values 0 and 1. Thus one observes y_b when $w = 1$ and observes y_a when $w = 0$.

The variable y is said to be a contaminated measure of y_b. The term *contaminated sampling* is used to describe this observational problem when it is assumed that w is statistically independent of y_b. The term *corrupted sampling* is used when this assumption is not maintained.

The researcher's objective is to learn $P(y_b \mid x)$. By the Law of Total Probability,

(5.4)
$$P(y_b \mid x) = P(y_b \mid x, w = 0)\, P(w = 0 \mid x)$$
$$+ P(y_b \mid x, w = 1)\, P(w = 1 \mid x).$$

In some applications, auxiliary data sources reveal $P(w = 0 \mid x)$, which measures the prevalence of contamination; Section 5.3 gives an illustration. The empirical evidence reveals nothing about $P(y_b \mid x, w = 0)$, because $y = y_a$ when $w = 0$.

It remains to consider $P(y_b \mid x, w = 1)$. This distribution equals $P(y \mid x, w = 1)$ because $y = y_b$ when $w = 1$. The Law of Total Probability gives

(5.5)
$$P(y \mid x = \xi) = P(y \mid x = \xi, w = 0)\, P(w = 0 \mid x = \xi)$$
$$+ P(y \mid x = \xi, w = 1)\, P(w = 1 \mid x = \xi).$$

With $P(y \mid x)$ and $P(w \mid x)$ known, inference on $P(y \mid x, w = 1)$ is a mixture decomposition problem.

Inference on $P(y_b \mid x)$ would be less difficult if the realizations of w were observed. Then the sampling process would reveal $P(y \mid x, w = 1)$, and the only problem would be that the data are uninformative about $P(y_b \mid x, w = 0)$. Thus corrupted sampling would become inference with missing outcomes using the empirical evidence alone, and contaminated sampling would become inference under the assumption that outcomes are missing at random.

Errors-in-Variables Contaminated/corrupted sampling is one of two prominent conceptualizations of data errors. The other supposes that an observed outcome y is the sum of an unobserved outcome of interest y^* and another unobserved random variable u; that is, $y = y^* + u$. The observable y is said to measure the unobservable y^* with *errors-in-variables*. The problem of inference on $P(y^*)$ given knowledge of $P(y)$ is said to be a *deconvolution problem*. Researchers studying inference on $P(y^*)$ usually maintain the assumption that u is statistically independent of y^* and that $P(u)$ is centered at zero in some specified sense. ❏

The Task Ahead

The task ahead is to characterize identification region (5.2) using the data alone and to determine the identifying power of assumptions that may shrink the region. Sections 5.2 and 5.3 address inference using the data alone, focusing on the relatively simple case where the mixing covariate w is binary. Section 5.4 shows how an assumption using instrumental variables can achieve point identification.

This chapter focuses entirely on the identification problem confronted in the decomposition of mixtures, without explicit reference to statistical inference. As in previous chapters, the identification findings to be described here can be used to form corresponding finite-sample estimates. A simple way to accomplish this is to replace distributions $P(y \mid x)$ and $P(w \mid x)$ with their sample analogs.

5.2 Binary Mixing Covariates

In this section and the next, I suppose that the mixing covariate w is binary, taking the values 0 and 1. This case suffices to cover applications to contaminated sampling. It is also an important special case for ecological inference. Cross and Manski (2002) analyze the more complex problem of inference when the mixing covariate is multinomial.

To simplify the notation, I now shorten $P(y \mid x)$ and $P(w \mid x)$ to $P(y)$ and $P(w)$, leaving the conditioning on x implicit. This done, I also let $p \equiv P(w = 0)$. With this shorthand, the Law of Total Probability in equation (5.1) or (5.5) becomes

$$(5.6) \qquad P(y) = pP(y \mid w = 0) + (1 - p)P(y \mid w = 1).$$

The identification region for $[P(y \mid w = 0), P(y \mid w = 1)]$ is

(5.7)
$$H[P(y \mid w = 0), P(y \mid w = 1)]$$
$$= \{(\gamma_0, \gamma_1) \in \Gamma_Y \times \Gamma_Y : P(y) = p\gamma_0 + (1 - p)\gamma_1\}.$$

Inference on One Component Distribution

Result (5.7) is simple but a bit abstract. The first step in developing its practical implications is to observe that it is enough to study identification of one of the two distributions $P(y \mid w = 0)$ or $P(y \mid w = 1)$. This is so because, by (5.6), specification of one of these distributions implies a unique value for the other. Hence determination of either $H[P(y \mid w = 0)]$ or $H[P(y \mid w = 1)]$ suffices to determine the joint identification region $H[P(y \mid w = 0), P(y \mid w = 1)]$.

For specificity, consider $P(y \mid w = 1)$. Manipulation of (5.6) yields

(5.8) $\quad P(y \mid w = 1) = [P(y) - pP(y \mid w = 0)]/(1 - p).$

Letting $P(y \mid w = 0)$ range over all elements of Γ_Y yields a tentative identification region for $P(y \mid w - 1)$, this being the set $\{[P(y) - p\gamma_0]/(1 - p), \gamma_0 \in \Gamma_Y\}$. However, some elements of this set may not be proper probability distributions—they may yield probabilities that lie outside the interval $[0, 1]$. Eliminating these elements yields the identification region

(5.9) $\quad H[P(y \mid w = 1)] = \Gamma_Y \cap \{[P(y) - p\gamma_0]/(1 - p), \gamma_0 \in \Gamma_Y\}.$

Event Probabilities

Next, let B be any subset of Y and consider the event probability $P(y \in B \mid w = 1)$. We will show that the identification region for $P(y \in B \mid w = 1)$ is the interval

(5.10)
$$H[P(y \in B \mid w = 1)]$$
$$= [0, 1] \cap \big[[P(y \in B) - p]/(1 - p), P(y \in B)/(1 - p)\big].$$

Observe that the lower bound is greater than zero, hence informative, when $p < P(y \in B)$. The upper bound is less than one, hence informative, when $p < 1 - P(y \in B)$. When both conditions hold, which requires that p be less than $\frac{1}{2}$, the interval has width $p/(1-p)$.

It is unclear when result (5.10) first appeared. It was sketched by Duncan and Davis (1953) in their concise seminal study of ecological inference. They attributed it to the early statistician Yule. I give the main elements of a formal proof by Horowitz and Manski (1995, corollary 1.2) in their study of identification under contaminated sampling.

Proof of (5.10) We first use the Law of Total Probability to write

$$(5.11) \quad P(y \in B) = pP(y \in B \mid w = 0) + (1 - p) P(y \in B \mid w = 1).$$

Solving this linear equation for $P(y \in B \mid w = 1)$ yields

$$(5.12) \quad P(y \in B \mid w = 1) = [P(y \in B) - pP(y \in B \mid w = 0)]/(1 - p).$$

Letting $P(y \in B \mid w = 0)$ take all values in the interval $[0, 1]$ yields a tentative identification region for $P(y \in B \mid w = 1)$, this being the interval

$$\big[[P(y \in B) - p]/(1 - p), \, P(y \in B)/(1 - p) \big].$$

However, not all values of $P(y \in B \mid w = 0)$ may be feasible; some values may make the lower bound of the above interval less than zero or the upper bound greater than one. Shrinking the interval to include only proper probabilities yields the interval on the right-hand side of (5.10).

The above argument constitutes the entire proof when the outcome y is binary. When y takes more than two values, further work is necessary to show that all elements of the interval in (5.10) are feasible values of $P(y \in B \mid w = 1)$. This is so if, for each point $c \in H[P(y \in B \mid w = 1)]$, there exist distributions $(\gamma_0, \gamma_1) \in \Gamma_Y \times \Gamma_Y$ such that $\gamma_1(B) = c$ and $P(y) = p\gamma_0 + (1 - p)\gamma_1$. To complete the proof, Horowitz and Manski (1995) show by construction that such distributions exist. For the details, see Horowitz and Manski (1995, corollary 1.2) or Manski (2003, proposition 4.2). ❑

Parameters That Respect Stochastic Dominance

Now consider inference on the conditional mean $E(y \mid w = 1)$ or the α-quantile $Q_\alpha(y \mid w = 1)$, where $\alpha \in (0, 1)$. Identification of these parameters can be addressed directly, but it is easier to prove a general result for the class of parameters that respect stochastic dominance and then apply this result to the mean and quantiles. Recall that we previously defined this class of parameters in Section 2.4.

It can be shown that the identification region $H[P(y \mid w = 1)]$ contains a "smallest" member L_p that is stochastically dominated by all feasible values of $P(y \mid w = 1)$ and a "largest" member U_p that stochastically dominates all feasible values of $P(y \mid w = 1)$. These smallest and largest distributions are truncated versions of the distribution $P(y)$ of observed outcomes: L_p right-truncates $P(y)$ at its $(1 - p)$-quantile, and U_p left-truncates $P(y)$ at its p-quantile. Formally, L_p and U_p are defined as follows:

(5.13a)
$$L_p[-\infty, t] \equiv P(y \le t)/(1 - p) \qquad \text{for } t < Q_{(1-p)}(y)$$
$$= 1 \qquad \text{for } t \ge Q_{(1-p)}(y).$$

(5.13b)
$$U_p[-\infty, t] \equiv 0 \qquad \text{for } t < Q_p(y)$$
$$\equiv [P(y \le t) - p]/(1 - p) \qquad \text{for } t \ge Q_p(y).$$

Complement 5A proves that L_p and U_p are the smallest and largest members of $H[P(y \mid w = 1)]$.

With this as background, it follows immediately that if $D(\cdot)$ is a parameter that respects stochastic dominance, the smallest feasible value of $D[P(y \mid w = 1)]$ is $D(L_p)$ and the largest feasible value is $D(U_p)$. Thus sharp bounds on $E(y \mid w = 1)$ are the means of L_p and U_p. Sharp bounds on $Q_\alpha(y \mid w = 1)$ are the α-quantiles of L_p and U_p. By (5.13), the α-quantile of L_p is the $\alpha(1 - p)$-quantile of $P(y)$, and the α-quantile of U_p is the $[\alpha(1 - p) + p]$-quantile of $P(y)$.

The above result determines sharp lower and upper bounds on $D[P(y \mid w = 1)]$, but it does not assert that the identification region is the entire interval connecting these bounds. It can be shown that the identification region is the entire interval if $D(\cdot)$ is the expectation parameter. However, the interior of the interval may contain nonfeasible values if $D(\cdot)$ is another parameter that respects stochastic dominance.

Suppose, for example, that y is discrete and $D(\cdot)$ is a quantile. As previously discussed in Section 2.4, quantiles must be elements of the set Y of logically possible values of y. Hence the identification region for $D[P(y \mid w = 1)]$ can only include the elements of the interval $[D(L_p), D(U_p)]$ that belong to Y.

5.3 Contamination through Imputation

Organizations conducting major surveys often impute values for missing data and report statistics that mix real and imputed data. Consider an observer who sees the reported statistics but who does not see the raw survey data and does not know the imputation rule used when data are missing. The observer may apply the findings of Section 5.2 to analyze the available data. I use income statistics published by the U.S. Bureau of the Census to illustrate. This illustration originally appeared in Horowitz and Manski (1995).

Income Distribution in the United States

Data on the household income distribution in the United States are collected annually in the Current Population Survey (CPS). Summary statistics are published by the U.S. Bureau of the Census (the Bureau) in Series P-60 of its Current Population Reports. Two sampling problems identified by the Bureau are interview nonresponse, where some households in the CPS sampling frame are not interviewed, and item nonresponse, where some of those interviewed do not provide complete income responses. Faced with these nonresponse problems, the Bureau uses available information to impute missing income data. The Bureau mixes actual and imputed data to produce the household income statistics reported in its Series P-60 publications.

From the perspective of contaminated sampling, y_b is the income a household selected for interview in the CPS would report if it were to complete the survey, y_a is the income the Bureau would impute to the household if the household were not to complete the survey, and $w = 1$ if a CPS household actually completes the survey. Then $P(y \mid w = 1)$ is the distribution of income reported by those CPS households who complete the survey, $P(y_b)$ is the distribution of income that would be obtained if all CPS households were to complete the survey, and $P(y)$ is the distribution of household income found in the Series P-60 publications. The error probability p is the probability that a CPS household does not complete the survey.

The Bureau's imputation practice is valid if the distribution $P(y \mid w = 0)$ of incomes imputed for persons who do not complete the survey coincides with the distribution $P(y_b \mid w = 0)$ that these persons would report if they were to complete the survey; then $P(y) = P(y_b)$. However,

$P(y \mid w = 0)$ and $P(y_b \mid w = 0)$ could differ markedly. The identification regions developed in Section 5.2 are agnostic about the quality of the Bureau's imputation practice.

Consider the year 1989. U.S. Bureau of the Census (1991, pp. 387–388) states that in the March 1990 CPS, which provided data on incomes during 1989, approximately 4.5 percent of the 60,000 households in the sampling frame were not interviewed and that incomplete income data were obtained from approximately 8 percent of the persons in interviewed households. The Bureau's publication does not report how the latter group is spread across households, but we can be sure that no more than $(0.08)(0.955) = 0.076$ of the households have item nonresponse. Hence 0.121 provides an upper bound on p. The calculations below use this as the value of p.

Now consider $P(y)$. U.S. Bureau of the Census (1991, table 5, p. 17) reports findings for each of twenty-one income intervals (in thousands of dollars):

$P[0, 5)\ = 0.053$	$P[35, 40) = 0.066$	$P[70, 75) =\ 0.018$
$P[5, 10)\ = 0.103$	$P[40, 45) - 0.060$	$P[75, 80) -\ 0.015$
$P[10, 15) = 0.097$	$P[45, 50) = 0.048$	$P[80, 85) =\ 0.013$
$P[15, 20) = 0.092$	$P[50, 55) - 0.043$	$P[85, 90) =\ 0.009$
$P[20, 25) = 0.087$	$P[55, 60) = 0.032$	$P[90, 95) =\ 0.008$
$P[25, 30) = 0.083$	$P[60, 65) - 0.028$	$P[95, 100) - 0.006$
$P[30, 35) = 0.076$	$P[65, 70) = 0.023$	$P[100, \infty) = 0.039$

Let us "fill out" $P(y)$ by imposing the auxiliary assumption that income is distributed uniformly within each interval except the last. We may now obtain bounds on features of $P(y \mid w = 1)$.

Consider, for example, the probability that household income is below $30,000. We have $P[0, 30) = 0.515$ and $p = 0.121$. By (5.10), the bound on $P(y \leq 30 \mid w = 1)$ is [0.448, 0.586].

Now consider median household income. The median of $P(y \mid w = 1)$ must lie between the $0.5(1 - p)$- and $[0.5(1 - p) + p]$-quantiles of $P(y)$. Invoking the auxiliary assumption that $P(y)$ is uniform within $5000 intervals, the sharp lower and upper bounds on the median of $P(y \mid w = 1)$ are [$25,482, $33,026].

These bounds show some of what one can learn about $P(y \mid w = 1)$ using the statistics reported in the Series P-60 publications. Stronger conclusions could be drawn if one were to have access to the raw CPS survey data, which flags the cases in which income data are imputed. The raw data enable one to isolate the respondents for whom $w = 1$ and, thus, to point-identify $P(y \mid w = 1)$.

Corrupted Sampling

Suppose that the objective is to learn $P(y_b)$, the distribution of income that would be obtained if all CPS households were to complete the survey. This distribution equals $P(y \mid w = 1)$ under the contaminated sampling assumption that data are missing at random. What can we conclude about $P(y_b)$ without imposing this assumption?

By the Law of Total Probability,

$$
\begin{aligned}
P(y_b) &= pP(y_b \mid w = 0) + (1 - p)\, P(y_b \mid w = 1) \\
       &= pP(y_b \mid w = 0) + (1 - p)\, P(y \mid w = 1).
\end{aligned}
$$
(5.14)

The sampling process reveals that $P(y \mid w = 1)$ lies in the set $H[P(y \mid w = 1)]$ given in (5.9). It reveals nothing about $P(y_b \mid w = 0)$. Hence the identification region for $P(y_b)$ is

$$
(5.15) \quad H[P(y_b)] = \{p\gamma_0 + (1 - p)\gamma_1, \ (\gamma_0, \gamma_1) \in \Gamma_Y \times H[P(y \mid w = 1)]\}.
$$

Consider event probabilities. It follows from (5.10) and (5.15) that

$$
(5.16) \quad H[P(y_b \in B)] = [0,\, 1] \cap [P(y \in B) - p,\ P(y \in B) + p].
$$

Consider a parameter $D(\cdot)$ that respects stochastic dominance. Let η_0 and η_1 be the degenerate distributions placing all mass on the minimal and maximal values of y. The "smallest" and "largest" (in the sense of stochastic dominance) feasible values of distribution $P(y_b)$ are $p\eta_0 + (1 - p)L_p$ and $p\eta_1 + (1 - p)U_p$. Hence the smallest and largest feasible values of $D[P(y_b)]$ are $D[p\eta_0 + (1 - p)L_p]$ and $D[p\eta_1 + (1 - p)U_p]$. When $D(\cdot)$ is the α-quantile, the lower bound is the $(\alpha - p)$-quantile of $P(y)$ and the upper bound is the $(\alpha + p)$-quantile of $P(y)$.

In the context of the CPS, consider again the probability that household income is below \$30,000. We have $P[0, 30) = 0.515$ and $p = 0.121$, so the bound on $P(y_b \le 30)$ is $[0.394, 0.636]$. Consider again median household income. The median of $P(y_b)$ must lie between the $(0.5 - p)$- and $(0.5 + p)$-quantiles of $P(y)$. Invoking the auxiliary assumption that $P(y)$ is uniform within \$5000 intervals, the bound on the median of $P(y_b)$ is $[\$21,954, \$37,273]$.

5.4 Instrumental Variables

We have so far studied inference on $P(y \mid x, w)$ using only knowledge of $P(y \mid x)$ and $P(w \mid x)$. Tighter inferences may be feasible if distributional assumptions are imposed. Whereas the notation of Sections 5.2 and 5.3 suppressed the conditioning variable x, we now make x explicit again. Whereas the mixing covariate w was binary in Sections 5.2 and 5.3, it may be multinomial here.

This section considers an assumption first studied by Goodman (1953) in the context of ecological inference. The objective is inference on the conditional means $E(y \mid x, w)$. The assumption uses x as an instrumental variable and asserts mean independence of y from x, conditional on w; that is,

$$(5.17) \quad E(y \mid x = \xi, w = \omega) = E(y \mid w = \omega), \quad \text{all } (\xi, \omega) \in X \times W.$$

In a voting application, this says that persons who have the same demographic attributes but who reside in different districts vote the same way, on average.

To begin, Goodman observed that the Law of Iterated Expectations gives

$$(5.18) \quad \begin{aligned} &E(y \mid x = \xi) \\ &= \sum_{\omega \in W} E(y \mid x = \xi, w = \omega) P(w = \omega \mid x = \xi), \quad \xi \in X. \end{aligned}$$

For each $\xi \in X$, the data reveal $E(y \mid x = \xi)$ and $[P(w = \omega \mid x = \xi), \omega \in W]$, but not $[E(y \mid x = \xi, w = \omega), \omega \in W]$. Thus (5.18) is a system of

$|X|$ linear equations with the $|X| \times |W|$ unknowns $E(y \mid x = \xi, w = \omega)$, $(\xi, \omega) \in X \times W$.

Now impose assumption (5.17). Then equation (5.18) becomes

$$(5.19) \quad E(y \mid x = \xi) = \sum_{\omega \in W} E(y \mid w = \omega) \, P(w = \omega \mid x = \xi), \quad \xi \in X.$$

This is a system of $|X|$ equations with the $|W|$ unknowns $E(y \mid w = \omega)$, $\omega \in W$. Applying elementary linear algebra, Goodman concluded that these equations have a unique solution if $|X| \geq |W|$ and if the $|X| \times |W|$ dimensional matrix of mixing probabilities $[P(w = \omega \mid x = \xi), (\xi, \omega) \in X \times W]$ has full rank $|W|$. Then assumption (5.17) point-identifies $E(y \mid w = \omega)$, $\omega \in W$.

Goodman also observed that assumption (5.17) is refutable. Equation system (5.19) may have no solution, or its solution may lie outside the logical range of y. In both cases, one should conclude that (5.17) is incorrect.

The Identification Region

Goodman's remarkably simple analysis fully resolves the inference problem when equation system (5.19) has one solution or no solution. It does not, however, show how to use assumption (5.17) when (5.19) has multiple solutions, as is generically the case when $|X| < |W|$.

Cross and Manski (2002) show that the identification region for $[E(y \mid w = \omega), \omega \in W]$ under assumption (5.17) is

$$
(5.20) \quad
\begin{aligned}
&H_0[E(y \mid w = \omega), \omega \in W] \\
&\equiv \bigcap_{\xi \in X} H[E(y \mid x = \xi, w = \omega), \omega \in W].
\end{aligned}
$$

The reasoning is similar to that applied in Chapter 3, where we studied the identifying power of statistical independence and mean independence assumptions for inference with missing data. Under assumption (5.17), a conjectured value for $[E(y \mid w = \omega), \omega \in W]$ is feasible if and only if it is a feasible value of $[E(y \mid x = \xi, w = \omega), \omega \in W]$ for all $\xi \in X$. Hence the identification region for $[E(y \mid w = \omega), \omega \in W]$ is the intersection across $\xi \in X$ of the regions $H[E(y \mid x = \xi, w = \omega), \omega \in W]$ obtained using the empirical evidence alone.

Complement 5A. Sharp Bounds on Parameters That Respect Stochastic Dominance

Recall the distributions L_p and U_p defined in Section 5.2. Let $D(\cdot)$ be a parameter that respects stochastic dominance. This complement shows that, using the data alone, $D(L_p)$ and $D(U_p)$ are sharp bounds on $D[P(y \mid w = 1)]$. The proof is a paraphrase of Horowitz and Manski (1995, proposition 4).

I first show that $D(L_p)$ is the sharp lower bound on $D[P(y \mid w = 1)]$. $D(L_p)$ is a feasible value for $D[P(y \mid w = 1)]$ because

$$P(y \leq t) = (1 - p)L_p[-\infty, t] + pU_{(1-p)}[-\infty, t], \ \forall t \in R.$$

Thus $(L_p, U_{(1-p)}) \in H[P(y \mid w = 1), P(y \mid w = 0)]$. $D(L_p)$ is the smallest feasible value for $D[P(y \mid w = 1)]$ because L_p is stochastically dominated by every member of $H[P(y \mid w = 1)]$. To prove this, one needs to show that $L_p[-\infty, t] \geq \eta[-\infty, t]$ for all $\eta \in H[P(y \mid w = 1)]$ and all $t \in R$.

Fix η. If $t \geq Q_{(1-p)}(y)$, then

$$L_p[-\infty, t] - \eta[-\infty, t] = 1 - \eta[-\infty, t] \geq 0.$$

If $t < Q_{(1-p)}(y)$, then

$$\eta[-\infty, t] > L_p[-\infty, t] \Rightarrow (1 - p)\eta[-\infty, t] > P(y \leq t)$$
$$\Rightarrow (1 - p)\eta[-\infty, t] + p\gamma[-\infty, t] > P(y < t)$$

for $\gamma \in \Gamma_Y$. This contradicts the supposition that $\eta \in H_p[P(y \mid w = 1)]$. Hence $\eta[-\infty, t] \leq L_p[-\infty, t]$ for all t.

Now consider $D(U_p)$. This is a feasible value for $D[P(y \mid w = 1)]$ because

$$P(y \leq t) = (1 - p)U_p[-\infty, t] + pL_{(1-p)}[-\infty, t], \ \forall t \in R.$$

Thus $(U_p, L_{(1-p)}) \in H[P(y \mid w = 1), P(y \mid w = 0)]$. $D(U_p)$ is the largest feasible value for $D[P(y \mid w = 1)]$ because U_p stochastically dominates every member of $H_p[P(y \mid w = 1)]$. To prove this, one needs to show that $U_p[-\infty, t] \leq \eta[-\infty, t]$ for all $\eta \in H[P(y \mid w = 1)]$ and all $t \in R$.

Fix η. If $t < Q_p(y)$, then

$$U_p[-\infty, t] - \eta[-\infty, t] = 0 - \eta[-\infty, t] \leq 0.$$

If $t \geq Q_p(y)$, then

$$\eta[-\infty, t] < U_p[-\infty, t]$$
$$\Rightarrow (1-p)\eta[-\infty, t] < P(y \leq t) - p$$
$$\Rightarrow (1-p)\eta[-\infty, t] + p\gamma[-\infty, t] < P(y \leq t)$$

for $\gamma \in \Gamma_Y$. This contradicts the supposition that $\eta \in H_p[P(y \mid w = 1)]$. Hence $U_p[-\infty, t] \leq \eta[-\infty, t]$ for all t.

Response-Based Sampling

In the Introduction to this book, I quoted a text on epidemiology as stating that retrospective studies of disease are "useless from the point of view of public health," but "valid from the more general point of view of the advancement of knowledge" (Fleiss, 1981, p. 92). The term *retrospective studies* refers to a sampling process also known to epidemiologists as *case-control* sampling. This sampling process is known to economists studying individual behavior as *choice-based* sampling. I shall use the discipline-neutral term *response-based* sampling here.

Consider a population each of whose members is described by some covariates x and by a response (or outcome) y. A common problem of empirical research in epidemiology, economics, and elsewhere is to infer the response probabilities $P(y \mid x)$ when the population is divided into response strata and random samples are drawn from some or all strata. This is response-based sampling.

For each $j \in Y$, sampling from the stratum with $y = j$ reveals the distribution $P(x \mid y = j)$ of covariates within this stratum. So response-based sampling raises this inferential question: What does knowledge of $P(x \mid y = j)$ for some or all $j \in Y$ reveal about $P(y \mid x)$?

This chapter studies inference from response-based samples and then uses the findings to examine more general forms of stratified sampling. I restrict attention to the simple but important special case where the response y is binary, taking the values 0 and 1. I begin by describing the epidemiological research practices that motivate Fleiss's curious statement.

6.1 The Odds Ratio and Public Health

Relative and Attributable Risk

Let $x = (w, r)$, where w denotes some covariates and r denotes other co-variates referred to as a *risk factor* for a specified disease. An important epidemiological problem is to learn how the prevalence of the disease varies with the risk factor. Let $r = j$ and $r = k$ indicate two values of the risk factor. Let the presence or absence of the disease be indicated by a binary variable y, with $y = 1$ if a person is ill and $y = 0$ if healthy. The problem is to compare $P(y = 1 \mid w, r = k)$ and $P(y = 1 \mid w, r = j)$.

Epidemiologists compare these conditional disease probabilities through the *relative risk*

$$(6.1) \qquad RR \equiv P(y = 1 \mid w, r = k)/P(y = 1 \mid w, r = j)$$

and the *attributable risk*

$$(6.2) \qquad AR \equiv P(y = 1 \mid w, r = k) - P(y = 1 \mid w, r = j).$$

For example, let y indicate the occurrence of heart disease, let r indicate whether a person smokes cigarettes (yes $= k$, no $= j$), and let w give a person's age, sex, and occupation. For each value of w, RR gives the ratio of the probability of heart disease conditional on smoking to the probability of heart disease conditional on not smoking, while AR gives the difference between these probabilities.

Texts on epidemiology discuss both relative and attributable risk, but empirical research has focused on relative risk. This focus is hard to justify from the perspective of public health. The health impact of altering a risk factor presumably depends on the number of illnesses averted, that is, on the attributable risk times the size of the population. The relative risk statistic is uninformative about this quantity.

Example Consider two scenarios. In one, the probability of heart disease conditional on smoking is 0.12 and conditional on nonsmoking is

0.08. In the other, these probabilities are 0.00012 and 0.00008. The relative risk in both scenarios is 1.5. The attributable risk is 0.04 in the first scenario and 0.00004 in the second.   ❑

It seems odd that epidemiological research emphasizes relative risk rather than attributable risk. Indeed, the practice has long been criticized (see Berkson, 1958; Fleiss, 1981, sec. 6.3; and Hsieh, Manski, and McFadden, 1985). The rationale, such as it is, seems to rest on the widespread use in epidemiology of response-based sampling.

Random sampling of the population reveals the distribution $P(y, w, r)$, hence the response probabilities $P(y \mid w, r = k)$ and $P(y \mid w, r = j)$. Epidemiologists have, however, found that random sampling can be a costly way to gather data. So they have often turned to less expensive stratified sampling designs, especially to response-based designs. One divides the population into ill ($y = 1$) and healthy ($y = 0$) response strata and samples at random within each stratum. Response-based designs are considered to be particularly cost-effective in generating observations of serious diseases, as ill persons are clustered in hospitals and other treatment centers.

Cost-effectiveness in data collection is a virtue only if the sampling process reveals something useful to the researcher. Response-based sampling reveals the conditional distributions $P(w, r \mid y = 1)$ and $P(w, r \mid y = 0)$, which are not of direct interest to epidemiologists. How then have epidemiologists used response-based samples?

Bayes Theorem plays a large role in the analysis of response-based sampling, so it simplifies the exposition to assume that the covariates x have a discrete distribution. I shall maintain this assumption throughout the chapter, but the reader should understand that it is not essential. To apply the analysis to situations in which some components of x have continuous distributions, one need only replace probabilities of x-values by densities in the statement of Bayes Theorem.

The Rare-Disease Assumption

We begin with an important negative fact. Consider any value of (w, r) with $P(w, r \mid y = 1) > 0$ and $P(w, r \mid y = 0) > 0$. Response-based sampling data reveal nothing about the magnitude of the response probability $P(y = 1 \mid w, r)$.

To see this, use Bayes Theorem and the Law of Total Probability to write

$$P(y = 1 \mid w, r)$$

(6.3)
$$= \frac{P(w, r \mid y = 1)\, P(y = 1)}{P(w, r)}$$

$$= \frac{P(w, r \mid y = 1)\, P(y = 1)}{P(w, r \mid y = 1)\, P(y = 1) + P(w, r \mid y = 0)\, P(y = 0)}.$$

Response-based sampling reveals $P(w, r \mid y = 1)$ and $P(w, r \mid y = 0)$, but it is uninformative about $P(y = 1)$. The fact that $P(y = 1)$ can lie anywhere between zero and one implies that $P(y = 1 \mid w, r)$ can lie anywhere between zero and one.

Facing this situation, epidemiologists have commonly combined response-based sampling data with the assumption that the disease under study occurs rarely in the population. Formally, analysis under the *rare-disease assumption* is concerned with the limiting behavior of relative and attributable risk as $P(y = 1 \mid w)$ approaches zero.

The rare-disease assumption point-identifies both relative and attributable risk. To see this, rewrite equation (6.3) in the equivalent form

$$P(y = 1 \mid w, r)$$

(6.4)
$$= \frac{P(r \mid w, y = 1)\, P(y = 1 \mid w)}{P(r \mid w)}$$

$$= \frac{P(r \mid w, y = 1)\, P(y = 1 \mid w)}{P(r \mid w, y = 1)\, P(y = 1 \mid w) + P(r \mid w, y = 0)\, P(y = 0 \mid w)}.$$

Inserting the right-hand-side expression into the definitions of relative and attributable risk yields

(6.5)

$$RR = \frac{P(r = k \mid w, y = 1)}{P(r = j \mid w, y = 1)}$$

$$\times \frac{P(r = j \mid w, y = 1)\, P(y = 1 \mid w) + P(r = j \mid w, y = 0)\, P(y = 0 \mid w)}{P(r = k \mid w, y = 1)\, P(y = 1 \mid w) + P(r = k \mid w, y = 0)\, P(y = 0 \mid w)}$$

and

(6.6)

$$AR = \frac{P(r=k\mid w, y=1)\,P(y=1\mid w)}{P(r=k\mid w, y=1)\,P(y=1\mid w) + P(r=k\mid w, y=0)\,P(y=0\mid w)}$$
$$- \frac{P(r=j\mid w, y=1)\,P(y=1\mid w)}{P(r=j\mid w, y=1)\,P(y=1\mid w) + P(r=j\mid w, y=0)\,P(y=0\mid w)}.$$

Letting $P(y=1\mid w)$ approach zero, we obtain

(6.7) $$\lim_{P(y=1\mid w)\to 0} RR = \frac{P(r=k\mid w, y=1)}{P(r=j\mid w, y=1)}\ \frac{P(r=j\mid w, y=0)}{P(r=k\mid w, y=0)}$$

and

(6.8) $$\lim_{P(y=1\mid w)\to 0} AR = 0.$$

Cornfield (1951) showed that equation (6.7) is the relative risk under the rare-disease assumption. The expression on the right side of (6.7) is called the *odds ratio* and may also be written as a function of the response probabilities. That is,

(6.9)
$$OR \equiv \frac{P(y=1\mid w, r=k)}{P(y=0\mid w, r=k)}\ \frac{P(y=0\mid w, r=j)}{P(y=1\mid w, r=j)}$$
$$= \frac{P(r=k\mid w, y=1)}{P(r=j\mid w, y=1)}\ \frac{P(r=j\mid w, y=0)}{P(r=k\mid w, y=0)}.$$

Equality of these expressions follows from equation (6.4).

Cornfield's finding motivates the widespread epidemiological practice of using response-based samples to estimate the odds ratio and then invoking the rare-disease assumption to interpret the odds ratio as relative risk. Fleiss's statement that retrospective studies are "valid from the more general point of view of the advancement of knowledge" is an endorsement of this practice, despite its associated implication that attributable risk is zero. Fleiss's statement that retrospective studies are "useless from the point of view of public health" reflects the widespread belief that "retrospective studies are incapable of providing estimates" of attributable risk (Fleiss, 1981, p. 92). I show in the next section that this assessment is somewhat too pessimistic.

6.2 Bounds on Relative and Attributable Risk

Suppose that a pair of response-based samples is available, but no other information. Although response-based sampling reveals nothing about the magnitude of the response probability $P(y = 1 \mid w, r)$ at a fixed value of (w, r), the data are informative about the way that $P(y = 1 \mid w, r)$ varies with r. We already know that the odds ratio is point-identified. Inspection of equation (6.9) shows that the odds ratio reveals whether $P(y = 1 \mid w, r = k)$ is larger than $P(y = 1 \mid w, r = j)$. In particular,

(6.10a) $OR < 1 \Rightarrow P(y = 1 \mid w, r = k) < P(y = 1 \mid w, r = j),$

(6.10b) $OR = 1 \Rightarrow P(y = 1 \mid w, r = k) = P(y = 1 \mid w, r = j),$

(6.10c) $OR > 1 \Rightarrow P(y = 1 \mid w, r = k) > P(y = 1 \mid w, r = j).$

We can go beyond (6.10) to prove that response-based sampling implies informative lower and upper bounds on relative and attributable risks. These bounds are developed here.

I use a numerical example concerning smoking and heart disease to illustrate the findings. Among persons with specified covariates w, let the actual probabilities of heart disease conditional on smoking and nonsmoking be 0.12 and 0.08, and let the fraction of persons who smoke be 0.50. These values imply that the unconditional probability of heart disease is 0.10 and that the probabilities of smoking conditional on being ill and healthy are 0.60 and 0.49. The implied odds ratio is 1.57, relative risk is 1.50, and attributable risk is 0.04. Thus the parameters of the example are

$$P(y = 1 \mid w, r = k) = 0.12 \quad P(y = 1 \mid w, r = j) = 0.08$$
$$P(r = k \mid w) = P(r = j \mid w) = 0.50$$
$$P(y = 1 \mid w) = 0.10$$
$$P(r = k \mid w, y = 1) = 0.60 \quad P(r = k \mid w, y = 0) = 0.49$$
$$OR = 1.57 \quad RR = 1.50 \quad AR = 0.04.$$

Relative Risk

Examine the expression for relative risk given in equation (6.5). All the quantities on the right-hand side of this equation are revealed by response-based sampling, except for $P(y \mid w)$. All that is known is that $P(y = 1 \mid w)$ and $P(y - 0 \mid w)$ are nonnegative and sum to one. So we may determine the feasible values for RR by analyzing how the right-hand side of (6.5) varies across the logically possible values of $P(y \mid w)$. The result is that the relative risk must lie between the odds ratio and one. Formally, the identification region for RR is

(6.11a) $OR < 1 \Rightarrow H(RR) = [OR, 1]$,

(6.11b) $OR = 1 \Rightarrow RR - 1$,

(6.11c) $OR > 1 \Rightarrow H(RR) - [1, OR]$.

Proof of (6.11) Relative risk is a differentiable, monotone function of $P(y = 1 \mid w)$, the direction of change depending on whether OR is less than or greater than one. To see this, let $p \equiv P(y = 1 \mid w)$ and let $P_{im} \equiv P(r = i \mid w, y = m)$ for $i = j, k$, and $m = 0, 1$. Write the relative risk in (6.5) explicitly as a function of p. Thus define

$$RR_p = \frac{P_{k1}(P_{j1} - P_{j0})n + P_{j0}}{P_{j1}(P_{k1} - P_{k0})p + P_{k0}}.$$

The derivative of RR_p with respect to p is

$$\frac{P_{k1}}{P_{j1}} \times \frac{P_{j1}P_{k0} - P_{k1}P_{j0}}{[(P_{k1} - P_{k0})| + p + P_{k0}]^2}.$$

This derivative is positive if $OR < 1$, zero if $OR = 1$, and negative if $OR > 1$. Hence the extreme values of RR_p occur when p equals its extreme values of zero and one. Setting $p = 0$ makes $RR = OR$, and setting $p = 1$ makes $RR = 1$. Intermediate values are feasible because RR_p is continuous in p. ❑

In our example concerning smoking and heart disease, the odds ratio is 1.57. So we may conclude that the probability of heart disease conditional on smoking is at least as large as but no more than 1.57 times the probability conditional on nonsmoking.

Recall that the rare-disease assumption makes relative risk equal to the odds ratio. Thus this conventional epidemiological assumption always makes relative risks appear further from one than they actually are. The magnitude of the bias depends on the actual prevalence of the disease under study, the bias growing as $P(y = 1 \mid w)$ moves away from zero. This follows from the fact, shown in the above proof, that RR_p is monotone in p.

Attributable Risk

Examine the expression for attributable risk given in equation (6.6). Again, all the quantities on the right-hand side are revealed by response-based sampling except for $P(y \mid w)$. So we may determine the range of possible values for AR by analyzing how the right side of (6.6) varies across the logically possible values of $P(y \mid w)$.

Let AR_p denote the value that attributable risk would take if $P(y = 1 \mid w)$ were to equal any value p. That is, define

$$(6.12) \quad AR_p \equiv \frac{P(r = k \mid w, y = 1)p}{P(r = k \mid w, y = 1)p + P(r = k \mid w, y = 0)(1 - p)}$$
$$- \frac{P(r = j \mid w, y = 1)p}{P(r = j \mid w, y = 1)p + P(r = j \mid w, y = 0)(1 - p)}.$$

The result is that AR must lie between AR_π and zero, where

$$(6.13) \quad \pi \equiv \frac{\beta P(r = k \mid w, y = 0) - P(r = j \mid w, y = 0)}{[\beta P(r = k \mid w, y = 0) - P(r = j \mid w, y = 0)] - [\beta P(r = k \mid w, y = 1) - P(r = j \mid w, y = 1)]}$$

and where

$$(6.14) \quad \beta \equiv \left[\frac{P(r = j \mid w, y = 1) P(r = j \mid w, y = 0)}{P(r = k \mid w, y = 1) P(r = k \mid w, y = 0)} \right]^{1/2}.$$

Formally, the identification region for AR is

(6.15a) $OR < 1 \Rightarrow H(AR) = [AR_\pi, 0]$,

(6.15b) $OR = 1 \Rightarrow AR = 0$,

(6.15c) $OR > 1 \Rightarrow H(AR) = [0, AR_\pi]$.

Proof of (6.15) As $P(y = 1 \mid w)$ increases from zero to one, attributable risk changes parabolically, the orientation of the parabola depending on whether the odds ratio is less than or greater than one. To see this, again let $p = P(y - 1 \mid w)$ and $P_{im} \equiv P(r = i \mid w, y = m)$. Write attributable risk explicitly as a function of p, as in (6.12). Thus define

$$AR_p \equiv \frac{P_{k1}p}{(P_{k1} - P_{k0})p + P_{k0}} - \frac{P_{j1}p}{(P_{j1} - P_{j0})p + P_{j0}}.$$

The derivative of AR_p with respect to p is

$$\frac{P_{k1}P_{k0}}{[(P_{k1} - P_{k0})p + P_{k0}]^2} - \frac{P_{j1}P_{j0}}{[(P_{j1} - P_{j0})p + P_{j0}]^2}.$$

The derivative equals zero at

$$\pi = \frac{\beta P_{k0} - P_{j0}}{(\beta P_{k0} - P_{j0}) - (\beta P_{k1} - P_{j1})}$$

and at

$$\pi^* = \frac{\beta P_{k0} + P_{j0}}{(\beta P_{k0} + P_{j0}) - (\beta P_{k1} + P_{j1})},$$

where $\beta \equiv (P_{j1}P_{j0}/P_{k1}P_{k0})^{1/2}$ was defined in (6.14). Examination of the two roots reveals that π always lies between zero and one, but π^* always lies outside the unit interval; so π is the only relevant root. Thus AR_p varies parabolically as p rises from zero to one.

Observe that $AR_p = 0$ at $p = 0$ and at $p - 1$. Examination of the derivative of AR_p at $p = 0$ and at $p = 1$ shows that the orientation of the parabola depends on the magnitude of the odds ratio. If $OR < 1$, then as p rises from zero to one, AR_p falls continuously from zero to its minimum at π and then rises back to zero. If $OR > 1$, then AR_p rises continuously from zero to its maximum at π and then falls back to zero. In the borderline case where the odds ratio equals one, AR_p does not vary with p. $\square$

In our heart disease example, $\beta = 0.83$, $\pi = 0.51$, and $AR_\pi = 0.11$. Hence response-based sampling reveals that the attributable risk associated with smoking is between 0 and 0.11. (Recall that 0.04 is the actual value, which is unknown to the researcher.) This seems a useful finding from a public health perspective. After all, in the absence of empirical evidence, AR could take any value between -1 and 1.

6.3 Information on Marginal Distributions

The problem of inference from response-based samples is that this sampling process does not reveal the marginal response distribution $P(y)$. If $P(y)$ were known, then one would have all the information needed to point-identify the joint distribution $P(y, w, r)$; hence, the response probabilities $P(y \mid w, r)$ would be point-identified.

Beginning with Manski and Lerman (1977), the econometric literature on response-based sampling has emphasized that it is often possible to learn $P(y)$ from auxiliary data sources. Hsieh, Manski, and McFadden (1985) point out that published health statistics drawn from national household surveys or from hospital administrative records provide estimates of the population prevalence of many diseases. This article also calls attention to the fact that $P(y)$ may be inferred from information on the marginal distribution of the risk factor or of other covariates.

The marginal probability that the risk factor takes any value i is

$$
\begin{aligned}
P(r = i) = {} & P(r = i \mid y = 1)\, P(y = 1) \\
& + P(r = i \mid y = 0)[1 - P(y = 1)].
\end{aligned}
$$
(6.16)

Response-based sampling reveals $P(r = i \mid y = 1)$ and $P(r = i \mid y = 0)$. Suppose that $P(r = i)$ is known. Then (6.16) implies that $P(y)$ is point-identified, provided that $P(r = i \mid y = 1) \neq P(r = i \mid y = 0)$. For example, in a study of smoking and heart disease, national survey data may reveal the fraction of the population who are smokers. This information may then be combined with response-based sampling data to learn the fraction of the population with heart disease.

Similar reasoning shows that $P(y)$ may be inferred from knowledge of the expected value of a covariate. For example, let the first component of w be a person's age. Suppose that the average age $E(w_1)$ of the population is known. Observe that

$$(6.17) \quad E(w_1) = E(w_1 \mid y = 1) P(y = 1) + E(w_1 \mid y = 0)[1 - P(y = 1)].$$

Response-based sampling reveals $E(w_1 \mid y = 1)$ and $E(w_0 \mid y = 0)$. Hence knowledge of $E(w_1)$ implies knowledge of $P(y)$, provided that the average age $E(w_1 \mid y = 1)$ of ill people is not the same as the average age $E(w_1 \mid y = 0)$ of healthy ones.

6.4 Sampling from One Response Stratum

The literature on response-based sampling has mainly studied situations with sampling from both response strata. Sometimes it is only possible to sample from one response stratum, say, from the subpopulation with $y = 1$. For example, an epidemiologist studying the prevalence of a disease may use hospital records to learn the distribution of covariates among persons who are ill ($y = 1$), but may have no comparable data on persons who are healthy ($y = 0$). A social policy analyst studying participation in welfare programs may use the administrative records of the welfare system to learn the backgrounds of welfare recipients ($y = 1$), but may have no comparable information on nonrecipients ($y = 0$).

Sampling from one response stratum obviously reveals nothing about the magnitude of response probabilities. Nor does it reveal anything about relative and attributable risks. But inference becomes possible if other auxiliary data are available.

Recall equations (6.3) and (6.4), where Bayes Theorem was used to write the response probabilities in the equivalent forms

$$P(y = 1 \mid w, r) = \frac{P(w, r \mid y = 1) P(y = 1)}{P(w, r)}$$

$$= \frac{P(r \mid w, y = 1) P(y = 1 \mid w)}{P(r \mid w)}.$$

Sampling from the response stratum with $y = 1$ reveals $P(w, r \mid y = 1)$. Hsieh, Manski, and McFadden (1985) observed that the response probability $P(y = 1 \mid w, r)$ is point-identified if auxiliary data reveal the marginal response distribution $P(y)$ and the distribution $P(w, r)$ of covariates. This result also holds if auxiliary data reveal the conditional distributions $P(y \mid w)$ and $P(r \mid w)$. Manski (2003) studied settings in which auxiliary data reveal either $P(y)$ or $P(w, r)$, but not both. In these cases, the generic result is partial rather than point identification.

I illustrate below how auxiliary data sources may reveal $P(y \mid w)$ and $P(r \mid w)$.

Using Administrative Records to Infer AFDC Transition Rates

In the 1980s and 1990s, public concern with the perceived problem of "welfare dependence" in the United States stimulated considerable research on the dynamics of participation in the federal program of Aid for Families with Dependent Children (AFDC). Much of this work was described in the *Green Book,* an annual volume giving an overview of government entitlement programs, prepared by the Committee on Ways and Means of the U.S. House of Representatives (Committee on Ways and Means, 1993).

Empirical study of the dynamics of AFDC participation is conceptually straightforward if one can draw a random sample of the United States population and follow the respondents over their lives. Then one can, in principle, learn the complete time path of welfare participation of each respondent. Two surveys that approach this ideal are the Panel Study of Income Dynamics (PSID), begun in 1968 by the Institute of Social Research at the University of Michigan, and the National Longitudinal Survey of Youth (NLSY), begun in 1979 by the U.S. Department of Labor. Research on the dynamics of AFDC has been based primarily on PSID and NLSY data.

The high cost of administering longitudinal surveys such as the PSID and NLSY inhibits the drawing of samples large enough to reach precise statistical conclusions about welfare dynamics. So it makes sense to ask what may be learned from less costly response-based designs. Moffitt (1992) observed that the administrative records of the welfare system make it inexpensive to sample from the stratum of active AFDC recipients, but that it is much more costly to sample from the stratum of nonrecipients. Given this, he suggested studying the dynamics of AFDC participation by sampling from the former response stratum alone.

I shall formalize this suggestion and then apply the simple result pointed out by Hsieh, Manski, and McFadden (1985). Let T_0 be a specified date in time and let T_1 be a specified later date. Let w denote specified covariates. Let

$r = k$ if a family receives AFDC payments at date T_0,

$= j$ otherwise.

$y = 1$ if a family receives AFDC payments at date T_1,

$= 0$ otherwise.

The dynamics of AFDC participation between T_0 and T_1 are expressed by the *transition probabilities* $P(y = 1 \mid w, r = k)$ and $P(y = 1 \mid w, r = j)$.

Data on AFDC recipiency collected by the Administration for Children and Families of the U.S. Department of Health and Human Services and reported in the *1993 Green Book* provide the basis for "back-of-the-envelope" estimates of $P(r \mid w, y = 1)$, $P(y \mid w)$, and $P(r \mid w)$. Among the families receiving AFDC in some month of the year 1991, 64.7 percent had continuously received payments during the previous twelve months (Committee on Ways and Means, 1993, sec. 7, table 35, p. 705). Let T_1 be a date in 1991 and let T_0 be the same date twelve months earlier. Let the covariate w indicate a family with children under age 18 in the year 1991. Assume that all of the families receiving AFDC in 1990 or 1991 had children under age 18 in 1991. Also assume that any family receiving AFDC at both of the dates T_0 and T_1 received payments during the entire twelve-month interim period. Then the *Green Book* data reveal that $P(r = k \mid w, y = 1) = 0.647$.

The average monthly number of families receiving AFDC was 3,974,000 in 1990 and 4,375,000 in 1991 (Committee on Ways and Means, 1993, sec. 7, table 1, p. 616). There were 34,973,000 families with children under age 18 in 1991 (Committee on Ways and Means, 1993, app. G, table 4, p. 1117). So the *Green Book* data reveal that $P(r = k \mid w) = 3,974,000/34,973,000 = 0.114$ and that $P(y = 1 \mid w) = 4,375,000/34,973,000 = 0.125$.

Combining these findings yields

$$P(y = 1 \mid w, r = k) = \frac{P(r = k \mid w, y = 1)\, P(y = 1 \mid w)}{P(r = k \mid w)} = 0.709,$$

$$P(y = 1 \mid w, r = j) = \frac{P(r = j \mid w, y = 1)\, P(y = 1 \mid w)}{P(r = j \mid w)} = 0.050.$$

Thus a family receiving AFDC in 1990 had a 0.709 chance of receiving AFDC in 1991, but a family not receiving AFDC in 1990 had only a 0.050 chance of receiving AFDC in 1991.

6.5 General Binary Stratifications

Analysis of response-based sampling provides the foundation for study of more general stratified sampling processes in which a population is divided into two strata and random samples are drawn from one or both strata. The strata need not coincide with values of the outcome y. Nor need y be a binary variable.

To describe general binary stratifications, let each member of the population be described by values for (y, x, s). As before, (y, x) are the outcome and covariates. The new variable s indicates the stratum containing each person, with $s = 1$ if a person is a member of stratum 1 and $s = 0$ otherwise. Random sampling from stratum 1 reveals the distribution $P(y, x \mid s = 1)$, while random sampling from stratum 0 reveals $P(y, x \mid s = 0)$.

Our concern is to infer the conditional distribution $P(y \mid x)$. The analysis of relative and attributable risk in earlier sections of this chapter may be extended from response-based sampling to general binary stratified sampling. I, shall, however, examine only the problem of inference on $P(y \mid x)$ at a specified value of x. Hence we no longer need decompose x into the covariates w and the risk factor r.

Sampling from Both Strata

We first examine the situation in which samples are drawn from both strata. Use the Law of Total Probability to write $P(y \mid x)$ as

(6.18)
$$\begin{aligned}
P(y \mid x) = {} & P(y \mid x, s = 1)\, P(s = 1 \mid x) \\
& + P(y \mid x, s = 0)\, P(s = 0 \mid x).
\end{aligned}$$

The sampling process reveals $P(y \mid x, s = 1)$ and $P(y \mid x, s = 0)$. The sampling process does not restrict the stratum distribution $P(s \mid x)$, because inference on $P(s \mid x)$ is precisely the response-based sampling problem, with s here in the role of y earlier. So sampling from both strata reveals that $P(y \mid x)$ is an unrestricted mixture of the two distributions $P(y \mid x, s = 1)$ and $P(y \mid x, s = 0)$.

How informative is the sampling process about $P(y \mid x)$? The answer depends on how closely related the outcomes y and strata s are to one another, conditional on x. At one extreme, suppose the data show that y and s are statistically independent conditional on x; thus, $P(y \mid x, s = 1) = P(y \mid x, s = 0)$. Then equation (6.18) reduces to

$$(6.19) \quad P(y \mid x) = P(y \mid x, s = 1) = P(y \mid x, s = 0),$$

whatever $P(s \mid x)$ may be. So $P(y \mid x)$ is point-identified. Stratification is sometimes said to be *exogenous* when (6.19) holds.

At the other extreme, suppose that y is a binary response and that the sampling process is response based, so $s = y$. Then $P(y = 1 \mid x, s = 1) = 1$, $P(y = 1 \mid x, s = 0) = 0$, and equation (6.18) reduces to the identity

$$(6.20) \quad P(y \mid x) = P(s \mid x).$$

Thus, for inference on $P(y \mid x)$ at a specified value of x, response-based sampling is the least informative member of the class of binary stratified sampling processes.

This discussion has presumed that no information other than the stratified samples is available. The analysis of Section 6.3 shows that $P(s \mid x)$ is point-identified if auxiliary data reveal either the marginal stratum distribution $P(s)$ or the distribution $P(x)$ of covariates. Combining stratified samples with such auxiliary data point-identifies $P(y \mid x)$.

Sampling from One Stratum

Now suppose that observations are drawn from only one stratum, say, from the stratum with $s = 1$. Then the sampling process no longer reveals $P(y, x \mid s = 0)$. Inspection of equation (6.18) shows that there are no implied restrictions on $P(y \mid x)$. As $P(s = 1 \mid x)$ approaches zero, $P(y \mid x)$ approaches the unrestricted $P(y \mid x, s = 0)$.

Researchers sampling from one stratum commonly point-identify $P(y \mid x)$ by assuming that stratification is exogenous. An alternative is to bring to bear auxiliary data that, in the manner of Section 6.4, reveal the stratum distribution $P(s \mid x)$.

Suppose that auxiliary data reveal $P(s \mid x)$. Then $P(y \mid x, s = 1)$ and $P(s \mid x)$ are known, but $P(y \mid x, s = 0)$ is unrestricted. This is the same information as is available in the problem of missing outcome data examined in Chapters 2 through 4. Here, $P(y \mid x, s = 1)$ is the distribution of observed outcomes, $P(s = 0 \mid x)$ is the probability of missing data, and $P(y \mid x, s = 0)$ is the distribution of missing outcomes. Thus inference when a random sample drawn from one stratum is combined with knowledge of $P(s \mid x)$ is equivalent to inference with missing outcome data using the data alone.

II

Analysis of Treatment Response

7

The Selection Problem

Analysis of treatment response poses a pervasive and distinctive problem of prediction with missing outcomes. Studies of treatment response aim to predict the outcomes that would occur if alternative treatment rules were applied to a population. One cannot observe the outcomes that a person would experience under all treatments. At most, one can observe a person's *realized outcome;* that is, the one he experiences under the treatment he actually receives. The *counterfactual outcomes* that a person would have experienced under other treatments are logically unobservable.

For example, suppose that patients ill with a specified disease can be treated by drugs or surgery. The relevant outcome might be life span. One may want to predict the life spans that would occur if all patients of a certain type were to be treated by drugs. The available data may be observations of the realized life spans of patients in a study population, some of whom were treated by drugs and the rest by surgery.

Or, in the realm of economic policy, suppose that workers displaced by a plant closing can be retrained or given assistance in job search. The outcome of interest might be income. One may want to learn the incomes that would occur if all workers with specified backgrounds were retrained, and compare this with the incomes that would occur if these same workers were instead assisted in job search. The available data may be observations of the incomes realized by workers in a study population, some of whom were retrained and some of whom were given job assistance.

7.1 Anatomy of the Problem

To formalize the inferential problem, let the set T list all of the feasible treatments. Let each member j of a study population have covariates $x_j \in X$ and a *response function* $y_j(\cdot) : T \to Y$ that maps the mutually exclusive and exhaustive treatments $t \in T$ into outcomes $y_j(t) \in Y$. Thus $y_j(t)$ is the outcome that person j would realize if he were to receive treatment t; researchers variously call $y_j(t)$ a *potential, latent,* or *conjectural* outcome. The fact that $y_j(\cdot)$ is subscripted by j indicates that treatment response may be heterogeneous. The members of the population need not respond to treatment in the same way.

Concepts and Notation One might object to describing the treatments $t \in T$ as mutually exclusive, observing that a person might be given a combination of treatments. For example, an unemployed worker could first be retrained and then given help in job search. However, the combination (retraining followed by job search) constitutes a third treatment, which differs from (retraining without job search) and (job search without retraining). If a worker receives (retraining followed by job search), his outcomes under (retraining without job search) and (job search without retraining) are counterfactual.

The notation $y_j(\cdot)$ gives succinct expression to the idea that response functions may vary across the population. Econometric analysis has a long alternative tradition of expressing heterogeneity in treatment response as variation in outcomes with covariates. Let person j have a covariate vector $u_j \in U$. These covariates may include covariates that are observable to a researcher, but there is no need here to distinguish observable from unobservable covariates. A standard econometric response model expresses $y_j(\cdot)$ as $y_j(t) = y^*(t, u_j)$, where the function $y^*(\cdot, \cdot)$ is common to all persons j. In these terms, $y_j(t)$ is the outcome that person j would experience if he were to receive treatment t while holding his covariates fixed at their realized value u_j.

The notation $y_j(\cdot)$ also supposes that treatment response is individualistic. That is, the outcome experienced by person j depends only on the treatment that this person receives, not on the treatments received by other members of the population. This assumption will be maintained throughout our analysis. ❑

Let $z_j \in T$ denote the treatment actually received by person j. Then $y_j \equiv y_j(z_j)$ is the realized outcome, the one that person j actually experiences. The outcomes $[y_j(t), t \neq z_j]$ that he would have experienced under other treatments are counterfactual. Observation may reveal the population distribution $P(y, z \mid x)$ of realized outcomes and treatments for persons with covariates x. Observation cannot reveal the distribution of counterfactual outcomes.

Analysis of treatment response aims to predict the outcomes that would occur under alternatives to the realized treatment rule. In particular, researchers and policy makers often want to predict the outcomes that would occur if all persons with the same observed covariates were to receive the same treatment. Consider, for example, the medical setting described earlier. Let the relevant covariate be age. Then a treatment rule might mandate that all older patients receive drugs and all younger ones receive surgery.

By definition, $P[y(t) \mid x]$ is the distribution of outcomes that would occur if all persons with covariate value x were to receive a specified treatment t. Hence prediction of outcomes under a policy mandating treatment t for persons with covariates x requires inference on $P[y(t) \mid x]$. The problem of identification of this outcome distribution from knowledge of $P(y, z \mid x)$ is often called the *selection problem*. This expression refers to the fact that treatment selection determines which potential outcome is observable.

Prediction Using the Empirical Evidence Alone

The selection problem has the same structure as the missing outcomes problem of Chapter 2. To see this, write

$$P[y(t) \mid x] = P[y(t) \mid x, z = t] P(z = t \mid x)$$
$$+ P[y(t) \mid x, z \neq t] P(z \neq t \mid x)$$
(7.1)
$$= P(y \mid x, z = t) P(z = t \mid x)$$
$$+ P[y(t) \mid x, z \neq t] P(z \neq t \mid x).$$

The first equality is the Law of Total Probability. The second holds because $y(t)$ is the outcome experienced by persons who receive treatment t.

Observation of realized treatments and outcomes reveals $P(z \mid x)$. It reveals $P(y \mid x, z = t)$ when $P(z = t \mid x) > 0$. It reveals that $P(y \mid x, z = t) P(z = t \mid x) = 0$ when $P(z = t \mid x) = 0$; that is, when no one in the study population receives treatment t. The empirical evidence is uninformative about $P[y(t) \mid x, z \neq t]$. Hence the identification region for $P[y(t) \mid x]$ using the evidence alone is

(7.2)
$$H\{P[y(t) \mid x]\}$$
$$= \{P(y \mid x, z = t) P(z = t \mid x) + \gamma P(z \neq t \mid x), \gamma \in \Gamma_Y\}.$$

This set of distributions has the same form as the identification region for $P(y \mid x)$ given in (2.2) when outcome data are missing. Whereas the outcome there was y and the event $\{z = 1\}$ indicated observability of y, the outcome of interest here is $y(t)$ and $\{z = t\}$ indicates observability of $y(t)$. Thus all of the findings on identification of $P(y \mid x)$ with missing outcome data developed in Chapter 2 apply immediately to $P[y(t) \mid x]$.

Outcome Distributions One should be careful not to confuse the outcome distributions $P[y(t) \mid x]$ and $P(y \mid x, z = t)$. The former is the distribution of outcomes that would occur if all persons with covariates x were to receive treatment t. The latter is the distribution of outcomes that do occur within the subpopulation of persons who have covariates x and actually receive treatment t. These distributions are the same if treatment selection is random (see the discussion below), but they generally differ otherwise. ❑

Comparing Treatments

Studies of treatment response often aim to compare the outcomes that would occur if alternative treatment rules were applied to the population. A good practical reason is to provide decision makers with information useful in choosing treatments. We will study treatment choice in depth in Chapters 11 and 12. Complement 7A describes other perspectives on the comparison of treatments.

Suppose that one wants to compare policies mandating alternative treatments for persons with covariates x. Then one would like to learn the collection of potential outcome distributions $\{P[y(t) \mid x], t \in T\}$. Observation of realized treatments and outcomes is uninformative about all of the counterfactual outcome distributions $\{P[y(t) \mid x, z \neq t], t \in T\}$. Hence the joint identification region for $\{P[y(t) \mid x], t \in T\}$ using the empirical evidence alone is the Cartesian product of the component regions. That is,

$$(7.3) \qquad H\{P[y(t) \mid x], t \in T\} = \underset{t \in T}{\times} H\{P[y(t) \mid x]\}.$$

The structure of (7.3) shows that the empirical evidence is informative but that it reveals only so much. The evidence cannot jointly point-identify all of the outcome distributions $P[y(t) \mid x], t \in T$. This would require that the treatment selection probabilities $P(z = t \mid x), t \in T$ all equal one. However, these probabilities logically sum to one. There is thus an inevitable tension between identification of the outcome distributions for alternative treatments. The more often that a specified treatment t is selected in the study population, the more one learns about $P[y(t) \mid x]$ but the less one learns about $P[y(t') \mid x], t' \neq t$.

Indeed, observation alone cannot answer a basic question: Do outcomes vary with treatment? Counterfactual outcomes are unobservable. It is therefore possible that, for each person j, the potential outcomes $y_j(t), t \in T$ all equal the person's realized outcome y_j. Hence observation alone cannot refute the hypothesis that the outcome distributions $P[y(t) \mid x], t \in T$ are all the same.

Average Treatment Effects

A common research practice is to focus attention on two alternative treatments, say, t and t', and use observations of realized treatments and outcomes to test the null hypothesis that the *average treatment effect* is zero. That is,

$$(7.4) \qquad H_0 : E[y(t) \mid x] - E[y(t') \mid x] = 0.$$

Given that counterfactual outcomes are unobservable, it is possible that $y_j(t) = y_j(t')$ for every person j in the population. Hence the hypothesis of zero average treatment effect is not refutable using empirical evidence alone. The hypothesis is refutable only if the evidence is combined with sufficiently strong distributional assumptions.

The above reasoning shows that the value zero necessarily lies within the identification region for the average treatment effect $E[y(t) \mid x] - E[y(t') \mid x]$. The full form of the identification region can be obtained by emulation of the analysis of Section 2.3. In what follows, I suppose that the outcome space Y is bounded, with smallest and largest elements y_0 and y_1, respectively.

By the Law of Iterated Expectations and the observability of realized outcomes,

$$
\begin{aligned}
E[y(t) \mid x] &- E[y(t') \mid x] \\
&= E(y \mid x, z = t) P(z = t \mid x) \\
&\quad + E[y(t) \mid x, z \neq t] P(z \neq t \mid x) \\
&\quad - E(y \mid x, z = t') P(z = t' \mid x) \\
&\quad - E[y(t') \mid x, z \neq t'] P(z \neq t' \mid x).
\end{aligned}
$$

(7.5)

The empirical evidence reveals $E(y \mid x, z = t)$, $E(y \mid x, z = t')$, and $P(z \mid x)$. It is uninformative about $E[y(t) \mid x, z \neq t]$ and $E[y(t') \mid x, z \neq t']$, each of which can take any value in the interval $[y_0, y_1]$. Hence the identification region for the average treatment effect is the interval

$$
\begin{aligned}
\mathrm{H}\{E[y(t) \mid x] &- E[y(t') \mid x]\} \\
&= \big[E(y \mid x, z = t) P(z = t \mid x) + y_0 P(z \neq t \mid x) \\
&\qquad - E(y \mid x, z = t') P(z = t' \mid x) - y_1 P(z \neq t' \mid x), \\
&\qquad E(y \mid x, z = t) P(z = t \mid x) + y_1 P(z \neq t \mid x) \\
&\qquad - E(y \mid x, z = t') P(z = t' \mid x) - y_0 P(z \neq t' \mid x) \big].
\end{aligned}
$$

(7.6)

This interval necessarily contains the value zero. Its width is

$$
\begin{aligned}
(y_1 - y_0)\big[P(z \neq t \mid x) &+ P(z \neq t' \mid x) \big] \\
&= (y_1 - y_0)\big[2 - P(z = t \mid x) - P(z = t' \mid x) \big].
\end{aligned}
$$

(7.7)

Thus the width of the interval depends on the fractions of the study population receiving treatments t and t'. The sum of these fractions is between zero and one. Hence the width of the interval is at least $(y_1 - y_0)$ and no more than $2(y_1 - y_0)$.

The special case where t and t' are the only feasible treatments is particularly interesting. Then $P(z = t \mid x)$ and $P(z = t' \mid x)$ necessarily sum to one; hence, the interval has width $(y_1 - y_0)$. In the absence of empirical evidence, the average treatment effect could logically take any value in the interval $[y_0 - y_1, y_1 - y_0]$, which has width $2(y_1 - y_0)$. So the data alone confine the average treatment effect to exactly half its logically possible range. To learn more requires distributional assumptions.

Distributional Assumptions

The task ahead is to explore the identifying power of distributional assumptions. As always, the Law of Decreasing Credibility should be kept in mind. Inference using the evidence alone sacrifices strength of conclusions in order to maximize credibility. Inference with point-identifying assumptions sacrifices credibility in order to achieve strong conclusions. Between these poles, there are many assumptions with some identifying power.

Part I of this book showed how various distributional assumptions can help to identify an outcome distribution in the presence of missing outcome data. All of those findings apply here. Chapter 2 considered the assumption that outcomes are missing at random [equation (2.10)]. The selection-problem analog is

$$(7.8) \qquad P[y(t) \mid x, z = t] = P[y(t) \mid x, z \neq t].$$

This assumption, which point-identifies $P[y(t) \mid x]$, is credible in classical randomized experiments, where an explicit randomization mechanism has been used to assign treatments and all persons comply with their treatment assignments. However, the credibility of the assumption in other settings is almost invariably a matter of controversy. We will discuss randomized experiments at length in Sections 7.3 and 7.4 and in Chapter 10.

Chapter 3 studied identification with various assumptions that use instrumental variables. All of the findings reported there apply here immediately. One only needs to let $y(t)$ replace y and let the event $\{z = t\}$ replace $\{z = 1\}$.

Thus far, the selection problem is simply an instance of missing outcomes, whose study involves no new considerations beyond those studied in Part I. The selection problem takes on a distinctive character when one entertains assumptions that link outcomes across treatments, so observation of the realized outcome y_j becomes informative about the counterfactual outcomes $y_j(t)$, $t \neq z_j$. Linkage of outcomes across treatments occurs in models of treatment choice that assume persons use knowledge of potential outcomes to choose treatments; see Section 7.5. Linkage also occurs when one makes assumptions about the shape of the person-specific response functions $y_j(\cdot)$. We will study various such assumptions in Section 7.6 and in Chapters 8 and 9.

7.2 Sentencing and Recidivism

To illustrate the selection problem, consider how the sentencing of juvenile offenders may affect recidivism, that is, their future criminality. This question has long been of interest to criminologists, to the social planners who make sentencing policy, and to the public at large.

Ample data are available on the outcomes experienced by offenders given the sentences that they actually receive. However, researchers have long debated the counterfactual outcomes that offenders would experience if they were to receive other sentences. Moreover, the sentencing rules that judges actually use are largely unknown (see Manski and Nagin, 1998, secs. 2 and 4). Thus predicting the response of criminality to sentencing is a problem that might reasonably be studied using the empirical evidence alone.

Manski and Nagin (1998) analyzed data on the sentencing and recidivism of males in the state of Utah who were born from 1970 through 1974 and who were convicted of offenses before they reached age 16. We compared recidivism under the two main sentencing options available to judges: confinement in residential facilities ($t = b$) and sentences that do not involve residential confinement ($t = a$). The outcome of interest was taken to be a binary measure of recidivism, with $y = 1$ if an offender is not convicted of a subsequent crime in the two-year period following sentencing, and $y = 0$ if the offender is convicted of a subsequent crime. The distribution of realized treatments and outcomes in the study population was as follows:

Probability of residential treatment: $P(z = b) = 0.11$
Overall recidivism probability: $P(y = 0) = 0.61$
Recidivism probability in subpopulation receiving residential treatment: $P(y = 0 \mid z = b) = 0.77$
Recidivism probability in subpopulation receiving nonresidential treatment: $P(y = 0 \mid z = a) = 0.59$

These statistics reflect the sentencing policy actually used in Utah during the mid to late 1980s.

Now consider two alternative policies, one mandating residential treatment for all offenders and the other mandating nonresidential treatment. The recidivism probabilities under these policies are $P[y(b) = 0]$ and $P[y(a) = 0]$, respectively. If one were to assume that judges in Utah either purposefully or effectively sentence offenders at random to residential and nonresidential treatments, one would conclude that

$$P[y(b) = 0] = P(y = 0 \mid z = b) = 0.77,$$
$$P[y(a) = 0] = P(y = 0 \mid z = a) = 0.59.$$

In contrast, the identification regions for these potential recidivism probabilities using the empirical evidence alone are the intervals

$$H\{P[y(b) = 0]\} = [0.08, 0.97],$$
$$H\{P[y(a) = 0]\} = [0.53, 0.64].$$

These intervals are the worst-case bounds for event probabilities stated in Chapter 2 in (2.4). The calculations are as follows:

$$0.08 = (0.77)(0.11) \le P[y(b) = 0]$$
$$\le (0.77)(0.11) + 0.89 = 0.97;$$
$$0.53 = (0.59)(0.89) \le P[y(a) = 0]$$
$$\le (0.59)(0.89) + 0.11 = 0.64.$$

Observe how the widths of the two intervals differ. The region for $P[y(b) = 0]$ has width 0.89 because this is the fraction of the study population who received treatment a and who, therefore, have unobservable outcomes under treatment b. Symmetrically, the region for $P[y(a) = 0]$ has width 0.11.

The average treatment effect in this setting is the difference in recidivism probabilities under the two alternative policies; that is, $P[y(b) = 0] - P[y(a) = 0]$. Under the assumption of treatment at random, $P[y(b) = 0] - P[y(a) = 0] = 0.18$, indicating that nonresidential treatment is much better than residential treatment if the objective is to minimize recidivism. Using the data alone, application of (7.6) gives the identification region

$$H\{P[y(b) = 0] - P[y(a) = 0]\} = [-0.56, 0.44].$$

This interval necessarily includes the value zero and has width one.

7.3 Randomized Experiments

Many researchers argue that one particular distributional assumption should have primacy among all of the assumptions that might be brought to bear in analysis of treatment response. This assumption asserts statistical independence of the realized treatments z and the response functions $y(\cdot)$, conditional on the covariates x; that is,

$$(7.9) \qquad P[y(\cdot) \mid x, z] = P[y(\cdot) \mid x].$$

This assumption implies that (7.8) holds for all $t \in T$. Hence it point-identifies $P[y(t) \mid x]$ for all t such that $P(z = t \mid x) > 0$.

The rationale for giving (7.9) special status is the strong credibility that this assumption enjoys in classical randomized experiments. The classical argument for study of experiments with randomly assigned treatments is generally attributed to Fisher (1935) and can be paraphrased as follows:

> Let random samples of persons be drawn from the population of interest and formed into treatment groups. Let all members of a treatment group be assigned the same treatment and suppose that each subject complies with the assigned treatment. Then the distribution of outcomes experienced by the members of a treatment group will be the same (up to random sampling error) as would be observed if the treatment in question were received by all members of the population.

In principle, the argument applies both to *controlled experiments,* in which a researcher purposefully randomizes treatment assignments, and to so-called *natural experiments,* in which randomization is a consequence of some process external to the research project. From the perspective of inference, the randomization mechanism is irrelevant. What matters is that randomization makes it credible to assume that the realized treatments z are statistically independent of the response functions $y(\cdot)$.

The sentiment that randomized experiments provide the best empirical basis for analysis of treatment response is evident in a National Research Council report on the evaluation of AIDS prevention programs, which declares: "Well-executed randomized experiments require the fewest assumptions in estimating the effect of an intervention" (Coyle, Boruch, and Turner, 1989, p. 125). A *New York Times* article on the use of randomized experiments to evaluate social programs began with this lead: "Use of controls helps put the science into social science" (Passell, 1993, p. C1).

In the United States, the evidentiary primacy of randomized experiments has become so widely accepted that it is institutionalized in various laws and regulations of the federal government. The drug approval process of the Food and Drug Administration usually requires the effectiveness of a new drug to be shown in randomized clinical trials (Fisher and Moyé, 1999). The Education Sciences Reform Act of 2002 (Public Law 107-279) which provides for improvement of federal educational research, defines a scientifically valid educational evaluation to be one that "employs experimental designs using random assignment, when feasible, and other research methodologies that allow for the strongest possible causal inferences when random assignment is not feasible."

In the 1980s, randomized experiments came to dominate the evaluations of job training and welfare programs commissioned by the federal government and by major foundations. Dissatisfaction with evaluations of job training programs performed in the 1970s led the Department of Labor to commission an experimental evaluation of the Job Training Partnership Act in the mid-1980s (see Hotz, 1992). A set of experiments sponsored by the Ford Foundation and executed by the Manpower Demonstration Research Corporation (MDRC) influenced the federal government to choose experimental analysis as the preferred approach to evaluations of welfare reforms (see Greenberg and Wiseman, 1992).

By the early 1990s, experimentation had become so much the new orthodoxy of evaluation that Jo Anne Barnhart, an assistant secretary of the U.S. Department of Health and Human Services in the first Bush administration, could write this about the evaluation of training programs for welfare recipients:

> In fact, nonexperimental research of training programs has shown such methods to be so unreliable, that Congress and the Administration have both insisted on experimental designs for the Job Training Partnership Act (JTPA) and the Job Opportunities and Basic Skills (JOBS) programs. (Letter from Jo Anne B. Barnhart to Eleanor Chelimsky, reproduced as U.S. General Accounting Office [1992, appendix II])

Barnhart's reference to the unreliability of nonexperimental research reflects the view of some social scientists that the selection problem precludes credible inference on treatment response from nonexperimental data. Such authors as Bassi and Ashenfelter (1986), LaLonde (1986), and Coyle, Boruch, and Turner (1989) have recommended that study of treatment response should focus exclusively on the design and analysis of randomized experiments.

Experiments in Practice

The classical argument for randomized experiments has clear appeal, provided that the kind of experiment envisioned by Fisher can be performed. However, the classical argument rests on all sorts of assumptions that rarely hold in practice. Consider the following:

1. The classical argument supposes that subjects are drawn at random from the population of interest. Yet participation in experiments ordinarily cannot be mandated in democracies. Hence experiments in practice usually draw subjects at random from a pool of persons who volunteer to participate. So one learns about treatment response within the population of volunteers rather than within the population of interest.
2. The classical argument supposes that all participants in the experiment comply with their assigned treatments. In practice, subjects often do not comply. See Section 7.4 for further discussion.

3. The classical argument supposes that one observes the realized treatments, outcomes, and covariates of all participants in the experiment. In practice, experiments may have missing data. A particularly common problem is missing outcome data when researchers lose contact with participants before their outcomes can be recorded.

For these and other reasons, the experiments performed in practice often differ materially from the classical ideal.

Sensitivity to the problem was evident in Campbell and Stanley (1963), a book that has been something of a bible to many social scientists concerned with program evaluation. These authors discussed various "factors jeopardizing the validity" of experiments. In the economics literature, the validity of the classical argument was a prominent concern of researchers analyzing data from the income maintenance experiments of the 1970s (see Cain, 1986; Hausman and Wise, 1979; and Kurz and Spiegelman, 1973). Many of the contributors to the volumes edited by Hausman and Wise (1985) and Manski and Garfinkel (1992) concluded that the classical argument was not credible in the experimental evaluations of welfare, training, and other social programs performed in the 1980s.

What can experiments with randomly assigned treatments credibly reveal when the classical argument is not credible? Some researchers advocating experiments offer no guidance beyond the platitude that one should design them carefully. Many experimental evaluations of social programs are silent on the problem of extrapolating from the experiments performed to the programs of interest. For example, the influential analyses of welfare reform experiments reported in Gueron and Pauly (1991) only describe the mean outcomes experienced by the various treatment groups. One can use the reported experimental findings to predict program outcomes if one is willing to apply the classical argument. One is at a loss to interpret the findings if one does not think the classical argument credible.

A more constructive approach to the analysis of experiments in practice is to recognize the respects in which actual experiments may not adhere to the classical ideal and study identification in these circumstances. Section 7.4 shows how this approach can be applied to analysis of experiments having noncompliance with assigned treatments.

7.4 Compliance with Treatment Assignment

A participant in an experiment is said to comply with his assigned treatment if the treatment received coincides with the treatment assigned. In practice, noncompliance occurs often as a consequence of choices made by the participants in experiments. Consider, for example, the Illinois Unemployment Insurance (UI) Experiment carried out in 1984–1985. Newly unemployed persons were randomly assigned to conventional UI or to UI augmented by a wage subsidy paid to the employer if the unemployed person should find a full-time job within eleven weeks. Dubin and Rivers (1993) report that 32 percent of those assigned UI with the wage subsidy did not comply. These subjects chose instead to receive conventional UI.

In this section I suppose that a randomized experiment adheres to the classical ideal in all respects, except that some subjects may not comply with their assigned treatments. I also assume that a person's outcome depends only on the treatment that he receives, not on the one he is assigned. Treatment assignment may affect outcomes only indirectly, by making available an experimental treatment and encouraging a person to accept it. Chapter 10 studies the converse problem, in which all subjects in an experiment comply with their assigned treatments but some persons may not comply later on, when a treatment is mandated for the population at large.

To study noncompliance requires the introduction of new notation to distinguish the treatment received from the treatment assigned. We will continue to use z to denote the received treatment, and we will now use ζ to denote the assigned treatment. The classical argument supposes that $z_j = \zeta_j$ for each person j in the study population. Noncompliance occurs when $z_j \neq \zeta_j$.

Experiments without Crossover

We first examine the common case in which an experiment involves two treatments. One, labeled $t = b$, is an *innovation* that is not available to the general public. The other, labeled $t = a$, is a *status quo* treatment that is available outside of the experimental setting. Subjects who are randomly assigned to the innovation can refuse to comply and can choose the status quo treatment instead. However, subjects who are randomly assigned to the status quo treatment are not permitted to *cross over* to receive the innovation. These subjects must comply with their assignment. Researchers studying experiments of this type often refer to the former group of subjects as the *treatment group* and the latter as the *control group*.

The Illinois UI experiment illustrates an experiment without crossover. Subjects assigned to the version of UI with the wage subsidy were able to refuse their assignment and choose conventional UI instead. However, subjects assigned to conventional UI were not permitted to cross over and receive the version with the wage subsidy.

An experiment without crossover point-identifies the distribution $P[y(a) \mid x]$ of outcomes that would occur if all persons were to receive the status quo treatment. It is the case that

$$(7.10) \quad P[y(a) \mid x] = P[y(a) \mid x, \zeta = a] = P(y \mid x, \zeta = a).$$

Randomization of treatment assignment gives the first equality. This is a statistical independence assumption, the treatment assignment indicator ζ being an instrumental variable. Full compliance with treatment a gives the second equality. The sampling process reveals $P(y \mid x, \zeta - a)$.

If there is partial compliance with assignment to the innovation, the experiment partially identifies the distribution $P[y(b) \mid x]$ of outcomes that would occur if all persons were to receive the innovation. In the absence of crossover, outcomes under treatment b are observed only when $\zeta = b$ and $z = b$. It is the case that

$$
\begin{aligned}
P[y(b) \mid x] &= P[y(b) \mid x, \zeta = b] \\
&= P[y(b) \mid x, \zeta = b, z = b]\,P(z = b \mid x, \zeta = b) \\
&\quad + P[y(b) \mid x, \zeta = b, z \neq b]\,P(z \neq b \mid x, \zeta = b) \\
&= P(y \mid x, \zeta = b, z = b)\,P(z = b \mid x, \zeta = b) \\
&\quad + P[y(b) \mid x, \zeta = b, z \neq b]\,P(z \neq b \mid x, \zeta = b).
\end{aligned}
$$

(7.11)

Randomization of treatment assignment gives the first equality, the Law of Total Probability gives the second, and the observability of $y(b)$ when $z = b$ gives the third. The empirical evidence reveals $P(y \mid x, \zeta = b, z = b)$ and the compliance probabilities $P(z \mid x, \zeta = b)$. The evidence is uninformative about the outcome distribution $P[y(b) \mid x, \zeta = b, z \neq b]$

for those who do not comply with assignment to treatment b. Hence the identification region for $P[y(b) \mid x]$ is

$$
\begin{aligned}
& H\{P[y(b) \mid x]\} \\
(7.12) \quad & = \big[P(y \mid x, \zeta = b, z = b)\, P(z = b \mid x, \zeta = b) \\
& + \gamma P(z \neq b \mid x, \zeta = b), \, \gamma \in \Gamma_Y \big].
\end{aligned}
$$

This identification region has essentially the same structure as the one given in (7.2) using the data alone. The only difference from (7.2) is that here all of the distributions on the right-hand side are conditioned on the treatment assignment event $\{\zeta = b\}$.

Experiments with Crossover

Crossover sometimes occurs in experiments. Consider, for example, an educational experiment in which students are randomly assigned to classes with different attributes. The parents of a student who is assigned to one type of class might successfully lobby the school administration to change the assignment.

Experiments with crossover are more complex to analyze than are ones without crossover. Consider a general setting, with T being the set of feasible treatments. Randomization implies statistical independence of the assigned treatments ζ and the response functions $y(\cdot)$, conditional on the covariates x; that is,

$$
(7.13) \quad P[y(\cdot) \mid x, \zeta] = P[y(\cdot) \mid x].
$$

This is the same as the classical experimental assumption (7.9) if all persons comply, but it differs otherwise.

Characterization of the full identifying power of assumption (7.13) is a difficult task. Analysis to date has been limited to the special case in which outcomes are binary. In this case, Balke and Pearl (1997) showed that the identification region is the set of solutions to a certain linear programming problem. Unfortunately, a succinct interpretation of their finding has been elusive. The form of the identification region when outcomes are not binary remains entirely an open question.

A partial understanding of experiments with crossover can be obtained by focusing on a specified treatment t and replacing (7.13) with the weaker assumption

$$(7.14) \quad P[y(t) \mid x, \zeta] = P[y(t) \mid x].$$

This asserts only that ζ is independent of the t-component of the response function. The identifying power of (7.14) is known, because this assumption is an instance of the statistical independence assumption (3.6) studied in Section 3.3. Notationally, the covariates (x, ζ) here correspond to (u, v) there. Thus the treatment assignment indicator ζ is the instrumental variable.

Applying (3.8), the identification region for $P[y(t) \mid x]$ under assumption (7.14) is

$$H_1\{P[y(t) \mid x]\}$$

$$(7.15) \qquad = \bigcap_{t' \in T} \{P[y(t) \mid x, \zeta = t', z = t) \, P(z = t \mid x, \zeta = t')$$

$$+ \gamma_{t'} \cdot P(z \neq t \mid x, \zeta = t'), \gamma_{t'} \in \Gamma_Y\}.$$

In the absence of crossover, $P(z = t \mid x, \zeta = t') > 0$ only when $t' = t$. Then region (7.15) reduces to

$$H_1\{P[y(t) \mid x]\}$$

$$= \{P[y(t) \mid x, \zeta = t, z = t) \, P(z = t \mid x, \zeta = t)$$

$$(7.16) \qquad + \gamma_t \cdot P(z \neq t \mid x, \zeta = t), \gamma_t \in \Gamma_Y\},$$

which is the same as the region (7.12) derived earlier for experiments without crossover. In the presence of crossover, the intersection of sets taken in (7.15) becomes meaningful, as some persons who are assigned to treatments other than t actually receive treatment t and therefore yield observations of $y(t)$.

Given that assumption (7.13) is stronger than assumption (7.14), the identification region for $P[y(t) \mid x]$ under (7.13) must be a subset of region (7.15). Considering the case of binary outcomes, Balke and Pearl (1997) presented some numerical examples in which the identification

region under (7.13) is strictly smaller than region (7.15) and other examples in which the two regions coincide. Thus they found that assumption
(7.13) has identifying power beyond (7.14) for some configurations of
the experimental data but not for others.

Point Identification with Partial Compliance

The analysis above shows that randomized experiments with partial
compliance partially identify the potential outcome distributions
$P[y(t) \mid x]$, $t \in T$ rather than point-identify them. Nevertheless, researchers analyzing experiments with partial compliance routinely report point estimates of treatment response. How so?

Researchers sometimes assume that compliance is statistically independent of response functions. This assumption restores the classical
argument for randomized experimentation, but often without much credibility. Researchers sometimes model the decision to comply, supposing
that subjects comply when they perceive this to be in their self-interest.
For example, Hausman and Wise (1979) use a model of compliance decisions to predict the earnings outcomes that would occur if a tax schedule
offered in the Gary Income Maintenance Experiment were to be made
mandatory.

Rather than introduce assumptions, researchers sometimes define
the problem of interest to be inference on quantities that are point-
identified with partial compliance. Then they report point estimates of
these quantities rather than set estimates of $\{P[y(t) \mid x], t \in T\}$. Two such
approaches to the analysis of treatment response are discussed below.

Intention-to-Treat

Researchers analyzing experimental data sometimes define treatments
in a way that makes noncompliance logically impossible. Suppose one
defines t to be receipt of an offer of a specified treatment rather than
receipt of this treatment. Randomized assignment in an experiment
without compulsion essentially gives a subject an offer of treatment.
Hence z necessarily equals ζ. The term *intention-to-treat* is used to
describe an experimental offer of a treatment.

It is important to understand that redefining t to be an offer of treatment does not solve the selection problem but rather dismisses it by
redefining the objective of the research. The original objective was to

learn the outcome distribution that would occur if all members of the population were to actually receive a treatment. The redefined objective is to learn the outcome distribution that would occur if all members of the population were to receive an offer of the treatment, which they may either accept or reject.

To illustrate, consider again the Illinois Unemployment Insurance Experiment. Woodbury and Spiegelman (1987) describe the experiment as randomly assigning newly unemployed persons to conventional UI or to an offer of UI with a wage subsidy, allowing the unemployed person to choose between conventional UI and the wage-subsidy-augmented UI. Hence they view all subjects as complying with their assigned treatments, and they analyze the experimental data in the classical manner. This contrasts with the Dubin and Rivers (1993) study mentioned above, which pays considerable attention to noncompliance.

The findings reported by Woodbury and Spiegelman differ from those reported by Dubin and Rivers. In part, this is because the two sets of authors have different objectives. Woodbury and Spiegelman want to predict the outcomes that would occur if unemployed persons were permitted to choose between conventional UI and a program with a wage subsidy. Dubin and Rivers want to predict the outcomes that would occur if conventional UI were replaced by a program with a wage subsidy.

The Average Effect of Treatment on Compliers

Consider again an experiment without crossover, treatment b being the innovation and treatment a being the status quo. We have earlier shown that outcome distribution $P[y(b)]$ is partially identified, with identification region (7.12). Hence the average treatment effect $E[y(b)] - E[y(a)]$ is partially identified as well.

Bloom (1984) and Imbens and Angrist (1994) have studied inference on the average treatment effect within the subpopulation of persons who comply with assignment to the innovation; that is, the persons for whom $\{z = b, \zeta = b\}$. This *average effect of treatment on compliers* is $E[y(b) \mid \zeta = b, z = b] - E[y(a) \mid \zeta = b, z = b]$. In the absence of crossover, the subpopulation that complies with assignment b is the same as the group that actually receives treatment b. Hence the average effect of treatment on compliers is the same here as $E[y(b) \mid z = b] - E[y(a) \mid z = b]$, which is called the *average effect of treatment on the treated*. See Complement 7A for further discussion of the latter concept.

It turns out that this treatment effect is point-identified. Moreover, it has the simple form

$$
\begin{aligned}
(7.17) \quad & E\big[y(b) \mid \zeta = b, z = b\big] - E\big[y(a) \mid \zeta = b, z = b\big] \\
& = \big[E(y \mid \zeta = b) - E(y \mid \zeta = a)\big] \big/ P(z = b \mid \zeta = b).
\end{aligned}
$$

The quantity $E(y \mid \zeta = b) - E(y \mid \zeta = a)$ is the average effect of intention-to-treat. Thus the average effect of treatment on compliers is proportional to the average effect of intention-to-treat, the factor of proportionality being the reciprocal of the compliance probability $P(z = b \mid \zeta = b)$.

Proof of (7.17) To simplify the notation, I suppress the observable covariates x. The derivation holds conditioning on any specification of these covariates.

Consider the expressions $E[y(b) \mid \zeta = b, z = b]$ and $E[y(a) \mid \zeta = b, z = b]$. The former is point-identified, equaling the observable outcome distribution $E(y \mid \zeta = b, z = b)$. The surprising result is that the latter expression, which is the mean of a counterfactual outcome, is also point-identified.

To see how this is so, observe that

$$
\begin{aligned}
(7.18) \quad & E[y(a) \mid \zeta = b] \\
& = E[y(a) \mid \zeta = b, z = a]\, P(z = a \mid \zeta = b) \\
& \quad + E[y(a) \mid \zeta = b, z = b]\, P(z = b \mid \zeta = b) \\
& = E(y \mid \zeta = b, z = a)\, P(z = a \mid \zeta = b) \\
& \quad + E[y(a) \mid \zeta = b, z = b]\, P(z = b \mid \zeta = b).
\end{aligned}
$$

The first equality is the Law of Iterated Expectations, and the second holds because $y(a)$ is observed when $z = a$. Solving for $E[y(a) \mid \zeta = b, z = b]$ yields

$$
\begin{aligned}
(7.19) \quad & E[y(a) \mid \zeta = b, z = b] \\
& = \frac{E[y(a) \mid \zeta = b] - E(y \mid \zeta = b, z = a)\, P(z = a \mid \zeta = b)}{P(z = b \mid \zeta = b)}.
\end{aligned}
$$

Inspect the right-hand side of (7.19). The experiment reveals $E(y \mid \zeta = b, z = a)$ and $P(z \mid \zeta = b)$. Moreover,

$$(7.20) \quad E[y(a) \mid \zeta = b] = E[y(a) \mid \zeta = a] = E(y \mid \zeta = a).$$

The first equality holds because treatment assignment is randomized, and the second because there are no crossovers from the status quo treatment to the innovation. Thus $E[y(a) \mid z = b, \zeta = b]$ is point-identified, with

$$
(7.21) \quad
\begin{aligned}
&E[y(a) \mid \zeta = b, z = b] \\
&= \frac{E(y \mid \zeta = a) - E(y \mid \zeta = b, z = a)\, P(z = a \mid \zeta = b)}{P(z = b \mid \zeta = b)}.
\end{aligned}
$$

Application of (7.21) gives this expression for the effect of treatment on compliers:

$$
(7.22) \quad
\begin{aligned}
&E[y(b) \mid \zeta = b, z = b] - E[y(a) \mid \zeta = b, z = b] \\
&= E(y \mid \zeta = b, z = b) \\
&\quad - \frac{E(y \mid \zeta = a) - E(y \mid \zeta = b, z = a)\, P(z = a \mid \zeta = b)}{P(z = b \mid \zeta = b)}.
\end{aligned}
$$

Application of the Law of Iterated Expectations gives (7.17). □

It is intriguing that the average treatment effect on the subpopulation of compliers is point-identified even though the average treatment effect on the full population is only partially identified. And it is appealing that the treatment effect on compliers has a form as simple as (7.17). However, it is important to understand the special nature of the finding.

The original objective was to compare the outcomes of alternative treatments on the full population of interest. The average treatment effect on compliers compares outcomes only on the subpopulation of compliers. This is a special subpopulation whose response to treatment may, in principle, differ considerably from that of the complementary subpopulation of noncompliers. An experiment with partial compliance reveals nothing about response to treatment b within the latter subpopulation.

The finding is also special in that it is specific to settings with two feasible treatments where an experiment without crossover is performed. Imbens and Angrist (1994) and Angrist, Imbens, and Rubin (1996) have extended the original finding of Bloom (1984) to settings with two feasible treatments and an experiment with crossover. Their work on *local average treatment effects* defines a complier to be a person who would comply with his assigned treatment, whatever it may be. Compliance with an unassigned treatment is a counterfactual event, so it is not possible to observe whether any particular member of the population is or is not a complier. This makes the subpopulation of compliers even more special in settings with crossover than it is in ones without crossover.

7.5 Treatment by Choice

Discussion of compliance in randomized experiments leads naturally to consideration of treatment selection as a conscious choice made by or for members of the study population. Recall our earlier discussion of missingness by choice in Chapters 2 and 4. I emphasized there that choice behavior may make the observability of a behavioral outcome depend on the value of the outcome. The same possibility arises here. Whether the decision maker is person j or someone acting for him, the treatment z_j that this person receives may depend on the values $y_j(t)$, $t \in T$ of his potential outcomes. If so, assumptions about the treatment choice process can help to identify outcome distributions. The present discussion applies both to randomized experiments with partial compliance and to nonexperimental settings.

Outcome Optimization

The relationship between potential outcomes and treatment choice is particularly strong in economic models of outcome optimization with perfect foresight. Such models assume that person j (or someone acting for him) knows his potential outcomes $y_j(t)$, $t \in T$ and chooses a treatment that yields the best outcome.

A leading example in labor economics is the Roy (1951) model of occupation choice. There, the treatments are alternative occupations and the potential outcomes are the wages that a person would earn in these occupations. The person is assumed to know these wages and to choose the occupation with the highest wage.

Formally, the outcome-optimization model asserts that for each person j,

(7.23a) $\quad z_j = \underset{t \in T}{\operatorname{argmax}}\, y_j(t),$

(7.23b) $\quad y_j = \underset{t \in T}{\max}\, y_j(t).$

The model has identifying power because it provides an observable upper bound on the potential outcomes of all counterfactual treatments. All such outcomes must be no larger than the value y_j of the realized outcome.

To obtain the identification region for a potential outcome distribution $P[y(t) \mid x]$, we again examine equation (7.1), which is reproduced here:

$$P[y(t) \mid x] = P(y \mid x, z = t)\, P(z = t \mid x)$$
$$+ P[y(t) \mid x, z \neq t]\, P(z \neq t \mid x).$$

Recall that the empirical evidence alone is uninformative about the distribution $P[y(t) \mid x, z \neq t]$ of counterfactual outcomes. However, the evidence is partially informative about this distribution when combined with knowledge that $y_j(t) \leq y_j$ for all persons j. Then $P[y(t) \mid x, z \neq t]$ is known to be stochastically dominated by the observable outcome distribution $P(y \mid x, z \neq t)$. Hence the identification region for $P[y(t) \mid x]$ is

(7.24)
$$H_1\{P[y(t) \mid x]\}$$
$$= \{P(y \mid x, z = t)\, P(z = t \mid x) + \gamma P(z \neq t \mid x),\, \gamma \in \Gamma_{1Y}\},$$

where Γ_{1Y} is the set of all distributions on Y that are stochastically dominated by $P(y \mid x, z \neq t)$.

This identification region may seem abstract, but it gives a simple, sharp upper bound on any parameter of $P[y(t) \mid x]$ that respects stochastic dominance. Let $D(\cdot)$ be any such parameter. The sharp upper bound on $D\{P[y(t)\mid x]\}$ is $D[P(y\mid x)]$, the same parameter computed on the distribution of realized outcomes.

To see this, observe that the largest member of $H_1\{P[y(t)\mid x]\}$, in the sense of stochastic dominance, is obtained by setting $\gamma = P(y\mid x, z \neq t)$. By the Law of Total Probability,

$$
\begin{aligned}
(7.25) \quad & P(y\mid x, z = t)\, P(z = t\mid x) \\
& + P(y\mid x, z \neq t)\, P(z \neq t\mid x) = P(y\mid x).
\end{aligned}
$$

Hence the largest feasible value of $D\{P[y(t)\mid x]\}$ is $D[P(y\mid x)]$.

The Competing-Risks Model of Survival Analysis The outcome-optimization model of treatment choice has the same structure as the *competing-risks* model of survival analysis, with the maximization in (7.23) replaced by a minimization. The competing-risks model supposes that each person in a population faces multiple risks of death and succumbs to the risk that manifests itself first. The realized population distribution of causes of death and life span is observable. The inferential problem is to use this empirical evidence to learn the distribution of life span that would occur in a hypothetical environment where persons face only one specified risk. See Kalbfleisch and Prentice (1980) for an exposition.

Formally, let T be the set of risks. For $t \in T$, let $y_j(t)$ be the life span for person j if he were to face only risk t. Let $z_j \in T$ be the realized cause of death, and let y_j be the realized life span. The empirical evidence is the population distribution $P(y, z)$. The competing-risks model asserts that $y_j = \min_{t' \in T} y_j(t')$. The inferential problem is to learn the distribution $P[y(t)]$ of life spans that would occur if persons were to face only risk t.

Peterson (1976) showed that the empirical evidence and the competing-risk assumption partially identify single-risk life span distributions. However, empirical research has typically reported point estimates obtained by imposition of additional assumptions. ❑

Parametric Selection Models

The above shows that the outcome-optimization model of treatment choice has identifying power, but not enough to point-identify distributions of potential outcomes. Yet economists who use the model in empirical research routinely report point estimates of treatment response rather than set-valued ones. How so?

Point estimates are typically achieved by combining the assumption of outcome optimization with an assumption that restricts the distribution $P[y(\cdot) \mid x]$ of response functions to a specified parametric family. It is particularly common to assume that this distribution is multivariate normal with mean $(x\beta_t, t \in T)$ and variance matrix Σ. The inferential problem is then to learn the parameters $(\beta_t, t \in T)$ and Σ. Maddala (1983) provides an extensive exposition of such models, with explanation of conditions that are necessary and sufficient for point identification and consistent estimation of the parameters.

The issue here, as with the parametric selection models of Chapter 4, is that there usually is no substantive foundation underlying the assumption that $P[y(\cdot) \mid x]$ is a member of a specified parametric family of distributions. Hence point estimates obtained using such assumptions usually have little credibility.

Issues of credibility also afflict applications of the outcome-optimization model per se, even in the absence of accompanying parametric assumptions on response functions. It may be plausible to suppose in general terms that treatment choice is purposeful and dependent on decision makers' perceptions of potential outcomes. However, it may be less plausible to suppose that decision makers have perfect foresight about potential outcomes. Moreover, the outcomes of interest to the decision makers choosing treatments may not be the same as the ones of interest to a researcher studying treatment response. See Chapters 11, 13, and 14 for further discussion.

7.6 Treatment at Random in Nonexperimental Settings

Whereas economists have often sought to model treatment selection in nonexperimental settings as conscious choice behavior, statisticians have typically assumed that treatment selection is random conditional on specified covariates. See, for example, Rubin (1974) and Rosenbaum and Rubin (1983).

The idea is the same as was discussed in Section 3.2, under the heading "Missingness at Random." That is, a researcher who feels that assumption (7.8) is implausible when conditioning only on x may feel that the assumption is plausible when conditioning on x and other observable covariates w. Formally, the assumption is

(7.26) $P[y(t) \mid x, w, z = t] = P[y(t) \mid x, w, z \neq t].$

Assumption (7.26) is nonrefutable and point-identifies $P[y(t) \mid x]$. The reasoning is the same as in Section 3.2. The assumption is non-refutable because it directly restricts the distribution of counterfactual outcomes. It is point-identifying by the argument given in equations (3.2) and (3.3), with $y(t)$ replacing y and the event $\{z = t\}$ replacing $\{z = 1\}$.

To justify assumption (7.26), researchers often say that the covariates (x, w) "control for" treatment selection. However, use of the term "control for" here tends to be as vague as in the missing data context of Chapter 3. When researchers say that conditioning on certain covariates "controls for" treatment selection, they rarely give even a verbal explanation of what they have in mind, never mind a mathematical explanation.

Association and Causation

Instructors in statistics often caution their students that "association does not imply causation." What does this statement mean? In the language of analysis of treatment response, it cautions that assumption (7.26) may not be credible.

For specificity, let $t = a$ and $t = b$ be two treatments and consider the average treatment effect $E[y(b) \mid x, w] - E[y(a) \mid x, w]$. If (7.26) holds, then

(7.27)
$$E[y(b) \mid x, w] - E[y(a) \mid x, w]$$
$$= E(y \mid x, w, z = b) - E(y \mid x, w, z = a).$$

If (7.26) does not hold, equation (7.27) usually is incorrect.

The average treatment effect quantifies the relationship between conjectured treatments and potential outcomes—researchers sometimes refer to it as the average "causal effect." The right-hand side of (7.27) quantifies the association between realized treatments and outcomes— if it is positive (negative), persons who receive treatment b on average have larger (smaller) realized outcomes than do persons who receive treatment a. Thus association per se does not imply causation, but one might reasonably say that association combined with assumption (7.26) implies causation.

Sensitivity Analysis

Thinking that an assumption of form (7.26) may hold approximately but not exactly in practice, statisticians such as Rosenbaum (1995) and Rotnitzky, Robins, and Scharfstein (1998) have recommended performance of sensitivity analysis exploring the implications of moderate deviations from the assumption. The basic idea is to weaken the equality in (7.26) to an assumption that the distributions $P[y(t) \mid x, w, z = t]$ and $P[y(t) \mid x, w, z \neq t]$ are not too different from each other. The specific form of a sensitivity analysis depends on how one formally defines "not too different."

In general, sensitivity analysis yields partial rather than point identification of treatment response. The size and shape of the identification region for $P[y(t) \mid x]$ depends on the specific way that assumption (7.26) is weakened. In the limiting case, where $P[y(t) \mid x, w, z = t]$ and $P[y(t) \mid x, w, z \neq t]$ may differ arbitrarily from each other, sensitivity analysis yields the identification region for $P[y(t) \mid x]$ using the data alone.

7.7 Homogeneous Linear Response

The assumptions studied thus far in this chapter have focused on the process of treatment selection, with particular attention to treatment at random and treatment by choice. Excepting the brief discussion of parametric selection models in Section 7.5, we have placed no restrictions on the response functions $y(\cdot)$ of the population. There are also approaches to analysis of treatment response that rest heavily on assumptions about treatment response. I discuss an analytically simple case here, as a prelude to the material that will be covered in Chapters 8 and 9.

Suppose that treatments are real-valued, with t giving the magnitude of the treatment. In such situations, there is a long tradition of assuming that each person's response function is linear in t, with slope that is homogeneous across the population. Formally, the assumption is

(7.28) $y_j(t) = \beta t + \epsilon_j.$

This is a strong restriction. Not only do outcomes vary linearly with treatment magnitude, but a one-unit increase in treatment yields the same outcome change β for every member of the population. Equation (7.28) permits response functions to be heterogeneous only in their intercepts ϵ_j, which may vary with j.

Note If there are only two treatments, say, $t = 0$ and $t = 1$, linearity of treatment response is not per se a meaningful assumption. Without loss of generality, one can let $y_j(0) = \epsilon_j$ and $y_j(1) = \beta_j + \epsilon_j$, which is the same as the linear response model $y_j(t) = \beta_j t + \epsilon_j$. However, the constancy of β_j across the population expressed in (7.28) remains a strong assumption. This assumption implies that the treatment effect $y_j(1) - y_j(0)$ is constant across the population, with common value β. ❑

"The" Instrumental Variable Estimator

Although (7.28) is a strong assumption, combining it with the empirical evidence reveals nothing about the slope parameter β. The reason is the unobservability of counterfactual outcomes. For each person j, only the realized treatment and outcome (y_j, z_j) are observable. By (7.28), this observable pair satisfies the equation

$$(7.29) \quad y_j = \beta z_j + \epsilon_j.$$

Given any conjectured value for β, this equation is satisfied by setting the unobserved value of ϵ_j equal to $y_j - \beta z_j$. Hence the assumption and the empirical evidence are uninformative about β.

The situation changes dramatically when assumption (7.28) is accompanied by a suitable distributional assumption using an instrumental variable. Let v be a real-valued instrumental variable. In applied econometric research, there has been a long tradition of combining (7.28) with these covariance assumptions:

$$(7.30) \quad \text{Cov}(v, \epsilon) = 0,$$

$$(7.31) \quad \text{Cov}(v, z) \neq 0.$$

The empirical evidence makes assumption (7.31) refutable, but assumption (7.30) is not refutable.

Taken together, (7.29) and (7.30) yield the equation

$$0 = \text{Cov}(v, y - \beta z) = E[v(y - \beta z)] - E(v)E(y - \beta z)$$
$$(7.32) \quad = E(vy) - \beta E(vz) - E(v)E(y) + \beta E(v)E(z)$$
$$= \text{Cov}(v, y) - \beta \text{Cov}(v, z).$$

Given assumption (7.31), this equation point-identifies β, with

$$(7.33) \quad \beta = \text{Cov}(v, y)/\text{Cov}(v, z).$$

Finally, with β known, one may obtain each person j's intercept ϵ_j from (7.29). Thus the empirical evidence combined with assumptions (7.28), (7.30), and (7.31) point-identifies the response function $y_j(\cdot)$ of every member of the population.

Treatment at Random When treatments are selected at random, one may take the instrumental variable v to be the realized treatment z. Randomization implies that $\text{Cov}(z, \epsilon) = 0$, so (7.30) holds. It is the case that $\text{Cov}(v, z) = \text{Var}(z) > 0$, so (7.31) holds. Application of (7.33) yields $\beta = \text{Cov}(z, y)/\text{Var}(z)$. This expression is recognizable as the slope parameter of the best linear predictor of y given z, under square loss. ❑

Researchers sometimes refer to the sample analog of equation (7.33) as "the" instrumental variable estimator. This special designation has no compelling scientific basis. Chapter 3 emphasized that there are many distributional assumptions using instrumental variables. Moreover, each such assumption may be combined with a variety of restrictions on the shapes of response functions. For example, Section 9.4 combines an inequality-of-means assumption with the assumption that response functions are monotone.

The only reason one might give (7.33) and its sample analog particular attention is their historical status as the earliest use of instrumental variables. Goldberger (1972) traces (7.33) back to Wright (1928), who derived it in the context of a study of inference on supply and demand in competitive markets. This inferential problem will be examined in Chapter 8.

Mean Independence and Overidentification

Rather than assume covariance conditions (7.30) and (7.31), researchers sometimes assume the mean independence conditions

(7.34) $E(\epsilon \mid v) = E(\epsilon),$

(7.35) $E(z \mid v) \neq E(z).$

Assumption (7.34) implies (7.30). Assumptions (7.35) and (7.31) are not nested.

Taken together, (7.34) and (7.29) imply that the equation

(7.36) $E(y - \beta z \mid v = k) = E(y - \beta z)$

holds for every value of k on the support of $P(v)$. Given assumption (7.35), equation (7.36) point-identifies β, with

(7.37) $\beta = \dfrac{E(y \mid v = k) - E(y)}{E(z \mid v = k) - E(z)}$

for every value of k such that $E(z \mid v = k) \neq E(z)$.

When there exist more than two such values of k, β solves multiple nonredundant versions of equation (7.37). The parameter is then said to be *overidentified*. Overidentification is not a useful concept for identification analysis per se. Point identification means complete knowledge of a parameter, so it is superfluous to have multiple ways to determine the parameter's value. However, overidentification is useful for hypothesis testing and for finite-sample estimation of β.

Suppose that the right-hand side of (7.37) varies with the value of k. Then either the linear response model (7.29) or the mean independence assumption (7.34) must be incorrect. Thus overidentification implies that the joint hypothesis expressed in (7.29) and (7.34) is refutable.

Suppose that instead of testing the joint hypothesis, one wishes to use it as a maintained assumption. Then computation of the sample analog of (7.37) for different values of k offers alternate estimates of β. A statistically more precise estimate may be obtained by suitably combining these estimates. A large body of research in econometrics explores how to construct such estimates.

Complement 7A. Perspectives on Treatment Comparison

I wrote in Section 7.1 that studies of treatment response often aim to compare the outcomes that would occur if alternative treatment rules were applied to the population. This objective may seem straightforward when stated verbally, but formalization reveals two basic issues: How should the outcomes of alternative treatment rules be compared? What is the relevant population? The literature on analysis of treatment response does not give consensus answers to these questions.

Differences in Outcome Distributions or Distributions of Outcome Differences

Let there be two treatments, labeled a and b. Suppose that one wants to compare policies mandating treatment a or b for persons with covariates x. One way is to compare their outcome distributions $P[y(b) \mid x]$ and $P[y(a) \mid x]$. Another is to study the distribution $P[y(b) - y(a) \mid x]$ of the difference between the outcomes of the two treatments. To simplify the notation, I omit the covariates x in what follows.

The two approaches are logically distinct. Knowledge of $P[y(b) - y(a)]$ neither implies nor is implied by knowledge of $P[y(b)]$ and $P[y(a)]$. How should the two policies be compared, through $P[y(b)]$ and $P[y(a)]$, or through $P[y(b) - y(a)]$?

If the purpose of research is to improve social decisions, we might approach this question from the perspective of a social planner required to choose between the two policies. The standard prescription in welfare economics is for the planner to maximize a social welfare function $W(\cdot)$, whose argument is the distribution of outcomes under a specified policy. The planner should choose treatment b if $W\{P[y(b)]\} \geq W\{P[y(a)]\}$ and treatment a otherwise. Thus a planner maximizing a standard social welfare function wants to learn $P[y(b)]$ and $P[y(a)]$, not $P[y(b) - y(a)]$. This is the perspective that I have taken throughout the present chapter and that I will take more vigorously in Chapters 11 and 12.

Some researchers take a different perspective, in which treatment a is the status quo and treatment b is a proposed alternative. Their objective is inference on $P[y(b) - y(a)]$, which measures the distribution of outcome differences that would be experienced if treatment a were to be replaced by treatment b. Rubin (1974) and Rosenbaum (1984) refer to $y(b) - y(a)$ as the *causal effect* of treatment b. Heckman, Smith, and Clements (1997, p. 519) write: "Answers to a variety of important evaluation questions require knowledge of the distribution of programme impacts."

The distinction between these ways to compare treatments has been blurred for two reasons. First, empirical studies have mainly reported average treatment effects. It is the case that

(7A.1) $E[y(b) - y(a)] = E[y(b)] - E[y(a)]$.

Hence it does not matter in practice whether a researcher states that he is comparing $E[y(b)]$ and $E[y(a)]$ or studying $E[y(b) - y(a)]$.

Second, researchers sometimes impose assumption (7.28), which asserts that the treatment effect $y(b) - y(a)$ is constant across the population. Under this assumption, $P[y(b)]$ and $P[y(a)]$ are the same distribution up to a location shift of magnitude β, while $P[y(b) - y(a)]$ is a degenerate distribution with all its mass at β. Whichever way one wants to compare treatments, the problem is to learn β.

The conceptual distinction between the two perspectives becomes operationally meaningful if treatment response is heterogeneous and one does not use average treatment effects to compare treatments. Consider the idea of a *median treatment effect*. In general,

(7A.2) $\text{Med}[y(b) - y(a)] \neq \text{Med}[y(b)] - \text{Med}[y(a)]$.

Hence a researcher reporting a median treatment effect must be careful to state whether the object of interest is the left- or right-hand side of (7A.2).

The Population to Be Treated or the Subpopulation of the Treated

From the perspective of welfare economics, the relevant population for analysis of treatment response is the population that will be subjected to treatment. Nevertheless, researchers sometimes study treatment response within the subset of the study population that has received a specified treatment t. These researchers often report the *average effect of treatment on the treated:*

$$(7A.3) \quad \text{ATT}(t) \equiv E[y(b) \mid z = t] - E[y(a) \mid z = t],$$

where t may be treatment a or b.

Some studies reporting estimates of this treatment effect include Bloom (1984), Björklund and Moffitt (1987), Angrist (1990), Gueron and Pauly (1991), and Dubin and Rivers (1993). In Gueron and Pauly (1991), for example, treatment a was the then-current American social program of Aid to Families with Dependent Children (AFDC), and treatment b was a proposed alternative to AFDC. The analysis focused on $E[y(b) \mid z = a] - E[y(a) \mid z = a]$, the average effect on current AFDC recipients if these persons were to participate in the alternative instead.

Björklund and Moffitt (1987) stressed that, in general, the effect of treatment on the treated does not coincide with the average treatment effect for the population of welfare-economic interest. By the Law of Iterated Expectations, the relationship between these quantities is

$$
\begin{aligned}
E[y(b)] &- E[y(a)] \\
&= \big\{ E[y(b) \mid z = a] - E[y(a) \mid z = a] \big\} P(z = a) \\
&\quad + \big\{ E[y(b) \mid z = b] - E[y(a) \mid z = b] \big\} P(z = b) \\
&= \text{ATT}(a)\, P(z = a) + \text{ATT}(b)\, P(z = b).
\end{aligned}
$$

(7A.4)

Björklund and Moffitt used data on a Swedish manpower training program to illustrate that ATT(a) and ATT(b) may differ in sign in realistic situations.

Why do researchers analyze the effect of treatment on the treated? It is rare to find an explicit rationale. One study that tries to motivate the concept is Angrist (1990). Here, treatment b denotes being drafted into American military service during the period of the Vietnam War draft lottery, and treatment a denotes not being drafted. Taking the outcome to be a person's lifetime earnings, Angrist estimates $E[y(b) \mid z = b] - E[y(a) \mid z = b]$, the average effect of the draft on the lifetime earnings of those who were drafted. He motivates interest in this quantity by writing (p. 313): "A central question in the debate over military manpower policy is whether veterans are adequately compensated for their service."

Complement 7B. Word Problems

Problem 7.1

The authors of a study on the use of anti-inflammatory drugs to treat Alzheimer's disease have reported that

$M = 10,275$ persons aged fifty-five or older were asked to participate in the study;

$N = 6989$ of these persons actually participated in the study;

$M - N = 3286$ persons were contacted but did not participate.

Assume that all M persons are eligible for the study; thus the $M - N$ persons who do not participate are eligible persons who are not willing to participate. Assume that the M persons contacted are a random sample drawn from a population of potential study participants. Let t denote a possible treatment, with

$t = 0$ if a person never uses anti-inflammatory drugs,

$= 1$ if a person uses anti-inflammatory drugs for less than two years,

$= 2$ if a person uses anti-inflammatory drugs for at least two years.

Let z denote the treatment that a person actually receives; so $z = 0$, 1, or 2. Let $y(t)$ denote the outcome if the person were to receive treatment t, with $y(t) = 1$ if the person develops dementia during the study period and $y(t) = 0$ otherwise. Let $y \equiv y(z)$ denote the outcome that a person actually experiences. Let w denote willingness to participate in the study, with $w = 1$ if a person is willing to participate and $w = 0$ otherwise.

Let $N(y, z)$ denote the number of study participants who receive treatment z and experience outcome y. It is the case that

$$N(0, 0) = 2343 \quad N(0, 1) = 4123 \quad N(0, 2) = 230$$
$$N(1, 0) = 210 \quad \ \ N(1, 1) = 80 \quad \ \ \ N(1, 2) = 3.$$

Let $P[y(0), y(1), y(2), z, w]$ denote the joint population distribution of potential outcomes $[y(0), y(1), y(2)]$, received treatments z, and willingness to participate w. Let $P(y = 1 \mid z = t, w = 1)$ denote the probability of dementia among persons who receive t and are willing to participate in the study. Let $P_N(y - 1 \mid z = t, w = 1)$ be the sample estimate of this probability. Thus

$$P_N(y = 1 \mid z = t, w = 1) = N(1, t)/[N(0, t) + N(1, t)].$$

a. To compare treatments 0 and 2, the researchers who performed this study focused attention on the *realized relative risk* statistic, defined to be this ratio of outcome probabilities:

$$\theta \equiv P(y = 1 \mid z = 2, w = 1)/P(y = 1 \mid z = 0, w = 1).$$

A critic of the study complains that realized relative risk does not appropriately compare treatments 0 and 2. Instead, this critic recommends that attention should focus on the *potential relative risk* statistic, defined to be this ratio of outcome probabilities:

$$\beta \equiv P[y(2) = 1]/P[y(0) = 1].$$

Use the empirical evidence alone to estimate the identification region for β. Show your derivation clearly and give the numerical result.

b. Continue to assume that the objective is to learn β. Suppose that you are the researcher conducting the study and that you have research funds that can be spent in one of two ways:

Option 1. You can double the size of the random sample from $M = 10,275$ to $2M = 20,550$.

Option 2. You can provide participation incentives to the $M - N = 3286$ persons who originally did not participate in the study, and thereby persuade half of these nonparticipants (i.e., 1643 persons) to join the study.

Discuss how you would choose between these options. Explain your reasoning.

Problem 7.2
Suppose that a judge can sentence a convicted offender to either of two sentences: a year in prison or two years on probation. Suppose that the judge chooses sentences, denoted z, for 100 convicted offenders. The judge sentences 20 offenders to prison ($z = 1$) and the remaining 80 to probation ($z = 0$). You obtain data on these sentences and partially observe the number of crimes, denoted y, that each convicted offender commits in the five-year period after sentencing. Here are the data on the frequencies of different values of y.

	Sentence		
Crimes after sentencing	Prison ($z = 1$)	Probation ($z = 0$)	Total
$y = 0$	5	35	40
$y = 1$	12	43	55
$y = 2$ or more	3	2	5
Total	20	80	100

When answering parts a–c, consider the 100 offenders to be the population of interest, not a sample drawn from a larger population.

a. You are asked to predict y conditional on the event ($z = 1$). Given the data, what can be inferred about the best predictor of y conditional on ($z = 1$) under absolute loss? Under square loss?

b. Let $y(0)$ denote the numbers of crimes that an offender would commit if he were sentenced to probation. Given the available data, what can be inferred about $P[y(0) = 0]$? $E[y(0)]$? $M[y(0)]$?

c. Suppose that, at the time of sentencing, the judge somehow knows each offender's values of $[y(1), y(0)]$ and chooses sentences that minimize subsequent crime commission. Thus the judge chooses $z = 1$ if $y(1) < y(0)$ and $z = 0$ if $y(1) > y(0)$. Using this information and the available data, what can be inferred about the "status quo treatment effect" $P[y(1) = 0] - P(y = 0)$?

Problem 7.3
In a national health survey, a random sample is drawn from the population of American families. Complete and accurate information is

obtained about each sampled family's state of residence x, coverage under a private health insurance plan ($y = 1$ if yes, $y = 0$ if no), and coverage under the federal Medicaid health insurance plan ($z = b$ if yes, $z = a$ if no). Here are the findings for the residents of Wisconsin (WI) and Illinois (IL).

	$x = $ WI (sample size 1000)		$x = $ IL (sample size 1200)	
	$z = a$	$z = b$	$z = a$	$z = b$
$y = 0$	0.10	0.15	0.25	0.20
$y = 1$	0.70	0.05	0.50	0.05

For example, the top left entry (0.10) is the fraction of all Wisconsin families in the sample who have neither private health insurance nor Medicaid coverage.

A researcher is asked about the fraction of families in each state who would have private health insurance under two extreme policies. In one case, Medicaid would be extended to cover all families, not just those presently covered. In the other, the Medicaid program would be terminated. Formally, let treatment $t = b$ denote Medicaid coverage and $t = a$ denote no Medicaid coverage. Let $y(t) - 1$ if, under t, a family would have private health insurance; $y(t) = 0$ otherwise. Then the quantities of interest are $P[y(b) = 1 \mid x]$ and $P[y(a) = 1 \mid x]$. When answering the questions below, abstract from random sampling variation in the empirical evidence.

a. Suppose that the Medicaid program is terminated. Using only the empirical evidence, what can be inferred about the between-state outcome difference $P[y(a) = 1 \mid WI] - P[y(a) = 1 \mid IL]$?

b. Suppose that Medicaid coverage is extended to all families. Using only the empirical evidence, what can be inferred about the status quo treatment effect $P[y(b) = 1 \mid WI] - P(y = 1 \mid WI)$?

c. Suppose the researcher believes that $P[y(b) = 1 \mid WI] = P[y(b) = 1 \mid IL]$. Using this assumption and the empirical evidence, what can be inferred about $P[y(b) = 1 \mid WI] - P(y = 1 \mid WI)$?

Problem 7.4

Suppose that a physician can prescribe one of two drugs to patients newly diagnosed with lung cancer, drug a or b. Suppose that the physician chooses drugs, denoted z, for 100 patients. He prescribes drug a to 25 patients ($z = a$) and drug b to the remaining 75 ($z = b$). You obtain data on these treatment decisions and observe the number of years, denoted y, that each patient lives after the treatment decision. Here are the data on the frequencies of different values of y.

| | Treatment | | |
Years of life after treatment	($z = a$)	($z = b$)	Total
$y = 0$	5	20	25
$y = 1$	12	43	55
$y = 2$ or more	8	12	20
Total	25	75	100

When answering the questions below, consider the 100 patients to be the population of interest, not a sample drawn from a larger population.

a. You are asked to predict y conditional on the event ($z = a$). Given the available data, what can you deduce about the best predictor of y conditional on ($z = a$), under absolute loss?

b. Again you are asked to predict y conditional on the event ($z = a$). Given the available data, what can you deduce about the best predictor of y conditional on ($z = a$), under square loss?

c. Let $y(b)$ denote the numbers of years that a patient would live if he were prescribed drug b. Given the available data, what can you deduce about $E[y(b)]$?

d. What can you deduce about $M[y(b)]$?

e. Suppose that, at the time of treatment, the physician somehow knows each patient's values of $[y(a), y(b)]$ and chooses treatments that maximize subsequent length of life. Thus the physician chooses $z = a$ if $y(a) > y(b)$ and $z = b$ if $y(a) < y(b)$. Using this information and the available data, what can you deduce about $P[y(a) \geq 2]$?

f. As in part (e), suppose that the physician chooses treatments that maximize subsequent length of life. An observer asserts that the physician's effort is meaningless because, for any given patient, length of life is the same no matter which treatment is assigned. Discuss this assertion.

Problem 7.5

A survey firm conducting an election poll can contact voters by any of three modes: mail, telephone, or home interview. Let z denote the mode that the firm uses to contact a voter. Suppose that the firm contacts 1200 voters: 400 by mail ($z = 0$), 400 by telephone ($z = 1$), and 400 by home interview ($z = 2$). These voters are asked if they want the Republican party to regain control of Congress in the year 2008 election. The possible responses are no ($y = 0$), indifferent ($y = \frac{1}{2}$), and yes ($y = 1$). Suppose that all voters have a value of y, but some of them choose not to respond to the survey. Here are the data obtained.

	Contact mode		
	Mail	Telephone	Home interview
Response to survey question	($z = 0$)	($z = 1$)	($z = 2$)
$y = 0$	100	100	100
$y = \frac{1}{2}$	100	100	100
$y = 1$	100	100	100
No response	100	100	100

When answering the questions below, consider these 1200 voters to be the population of interest, not a sample drawn from a larger population.

a. You are asked to predict y conditional on the event ($z = 1$). Given the available data, what can you deduce about

(i) the best predictor of y conditional on ($z = 1$), under absolute loss?

(ii) the best predictor of y conditional on ($z = 1$), under square loss?

(iii) the best linear predictor of y given z under square loss, evaluated at ($z = 1$)?

b. Given the available data, what can you deduce about $P(z = 1 \mid y = 1)$? (*Hint:* The subpopulation with $y = 1$ may contain persons who do not respond to the survey.)

c. Let $y(t)$ denote the response that a voter would give if he or she were contacted by mode t, for $t = 0, 1, 2$. Given the available data, what can you deduce about the average treatment effect $E[y(1)] - E[y(0)]$ if

   (i) the data constitute the only information available?
   (ii) voters who do not respond to the survey have the same distribution of $[y(0), y(1), y(2)]$ as those who do respond?

Problem 7.6

Let the set of feasible treatments be $T = [0, \infty)$. Let $Y = [0, 1]$ be the logical domain of the outcomes. A researcher poses a homogeneous linear response model $y_j(t) = \beta t + \epsilon_j$. The researcher observes the realized distribution $P(y, z, v)$, where v is a covariate. He makes the covariance assumptions of Section 7.7, applies "the" instrumental variable estimator, and reports that $\beta = \text{Cov}(v, y)/\text{Cov}(v, z)$.

A critic of this research comments as follows: "If the reported value of β is nonzero, some part of the researcher's maintained assumptions must be wrong." Is the critic correct or not? Explain.

8

Linear Simultaneous Equations

This chapter examines traditional social science approaches to prediction of treatment response when realized treatments and outcomes are determined by equilibrium social interactions. By traditional approaches, I mean ones that posit models of homogeneous linear response and seek point identification of such models. The identification problem is commonly portrayed as one of solving a system of linear simultaneous equations.

Sections 8.1 and 8.2 consider the classical simultaneity problem of econometrics, where observations of market transactions are used to study the demand behavior of consumers and the supply behavior of firms in competitive markets. Section 8.3 discusses the analogous problem of inference on the reaction functions of the players in two-person games. Section 8.4 studies the reflection problem described in the opening pages of this book.

8.1 Simultaneity in Competitive Markets

A prominent concern of econometrics is to infer the structure of supply and demand from observations of transacted prices and quantities in competitive markets. The basic version of the problem supposes that there is a set of isolated markets for a given product, each market separated from the others in time or space. Each market j has a value for $[s_j(\cdot), d_j(\cdot), p_j, q_j, x_j]$. Here x_j are observed covariates characterizing market j, q_j is the quantity of product transacted, and p_j is the unit price at which these transactions take place. The market demand function $d_j(\cdot)$ gives the quantity that price-taking consumers would purchase if price were set at any level, so $d_j(t)$ is the quantity demanded if price is t. The market supply function $s_j(\cdot)$ gives the quantity that price-taking firms would offer if price were set at any level, so $s_j(t)$ is the quantity supplied if price is t.

The transaction (p_j, q_j) is assumed to be an equilibrium outcome. At price p_j, the quantity demanded and the quantity supplied both equal q_j. Thus (p_j, q_j) simultaneously solve the two equations

(8.1) $q_j = s_j(p_j)$,

(8.2) $q_j = d_j(p_j)$.

The value of $[s(\cdot), d(\cdot), p, q, x]$ may vary across markets. The probability distribution $P[s(\cdot), d(\cdot), p, q, x]$ expresses this variation. Econometric analysis may seek to learn the distribution $P[s(\cdot) \mid x]$ of supply functions among markets with covariates x, the distribution $P[d(\cdot) \mid x]$ of demand functions, or, more ambitiously, the joint distribution $P[s(\cdot), d(\cdot) \mid x]$. The data are observations of the transactions (p, q) in these markets. The *simultaneity problem* is the problem of inference on $P[s(\cdot), d(\cdot) \mid x]$ given knowledge of $P(p, q \mid x)$.

"The" Identification Problem in Econometrics

Analysis of simultaneity was so central to the early development of econometrics that it was long common for econometricians to think of identification and simultaneity as synonymous. Econometrics texts tended to discuss identification only in the context of simultaneity. Particularly revealing is the title chosen by Fisher (1966) for his monograph on the simultaneity problem. He titled the book *The Identification Problem in Econometrics* and justified this choice by writing in the preface (p. vii): "Because the simultaneous equation context is by far the most important one in which the identification problem is encountered, the treatment is restricted to that context."

From today's perspective, Fisher's judgment of the preeminence of simultaneity among all identification problems seems strained. Nevertheless, simultaneity certainly remains an important problem of econometrics.

Simultaneity Is Selection

Simultaneity is an instance of the selection problem. To see this, consider the distribution $P[d(t) \mid x]$ of the quantity demanded at price t in markets with covariates x. It is the case that

(8.3)
$$
\begin{aligned}
P[d(t) \mid x] &= P[d(t) \mid x, p = t]P(p = t \mid x) \\
&\quad + P[d(t) \mid x, p \neq t]P(p \neq t \mid x) \\
&= P(q \mid x, p = t)\, P(p = t \mid x) \\
&\quad + P[d(t) \mid x, p \neq t]P(p \neq t \mid x).
\end{aligned}
$$

The first equality is the Law of Total Probability, and the second holds by (8.2). Observation of market transactions reveals $P(q \mid x, p = t)$ and $P(p \mid x)$ but is uninformative about $P[d(t) \mid x, p \neq t]$. This is precisely the selection problem.

In the language of Chapter 7, price is a treatment and quantity demanded is an outcome. In each market j, the supply and demand functions $s_j(\cdot)$ and $d_j(\cdot)$ are two response functions, giving the quantities that would be supplied and demanded at alternative values for price. The notation t specifies a conjectural value for price, and p_j gives the realized price in market j. The observed outcome is q_j, which equals both $s_j(p_j)$ and $d_j(p_j)$. The quantities that would be supplied and demanded if price were to take values other than p_j are counterfactual outcomes.

Here, as in other instances of the selection problem, the inferences that may be drawn depend on the assumptions imposed. The most basic maintained assumption of econometric analysis has been that the transaction price p_j satisfies equations (8.1) and (8.2). In addition, econometricians have traditionally assumed homogeneous linear response models for supply and demand. Section 8.2 presents the traditional approach. Chapter 9 shows how the simultaneity problem may be partially addressed with weaker and more credible assumptions.

8.2 The Linear Market Model

Study of the linear market model was initiated in the 1920s and crystallized by the early 1950s (see Hood and Koopmans, 1953). Stripped to its essentials, the model is

$$(8.4a) \quad s_j(t) = \beta_1 t + \epsilon_{j1},$$

$$(8.4b) \quad d_j(t) = \beta_2 t + \epsilon_{j2}.$$

Equation (8.4a) states that supply $s_j(\cdot)$ is a linear function of price t, with the same slope β_1 in every market. The supply function varies across markets only in its intercept ϵ_{j1}. Equation (8.4b) imposes analogous restrictions on demand.

The analysis of Section 7.7 shows that the slope of the supply function is point-identified if an instrumental variable v_1 satisfies the covariance assumptions

$$(8.5) \quad \mathrm{Cov}(v_1, \epsilon_1) = 0,$$

$$(8.6) \quad \mathrm{Cov}(v_1, p) \neq 0.$$

Assumptions (8.4a), (8.5), and (8.6) imply that

$$(8.7) \quad \beta_1 = \mathrm{Cov}(v_1, q)/\mathrm{Cov}(v_1, p).$$

Equation (8.7) restates result (7.33), with (v_1, q, p) replacing (v, y, z).

With β_1 known, one may determine the intercept $\epsilon_{j1} = q_j - \beta_1 p_j$ of each market's supply function. Thus assumptions (8.4a), (8.5), and (8.6) point-identify the supply function in every market. There is no need to specify the form of the demand function or, for that matter, even to assume that consumers are price takers.

Analogously, the slope of the demand function is point-identified if an instrumental variable v_2 satisfies the covariance assumptions

$$(8.8) \quad \mathrm{Cov}(v_2, \epsilon_2) = 0,$$

$$(8.9) \quad \mathrm{Cov}(v_2, p) \neq 0.$$

Then

(8.10) $\beta_2 = \mathrm{Cov}(v_2, q)/\mathrm{Cov}(v_2, p).$

With β_2 known, one may determine the intercept $\epsilon_{j2} = q_j - \beta_2 p_j$ of each market's demand function. There is no need to specify the supply function or even to assume that firms are price takers.

Observe that these results are obtained without imposing the usual economic assumptions that supply functions are upward sloping (i.e., $\beta_1 \geq 0$) and demand functions are downward sloping (i.e., $\beta_2 \leq 0$). Chapter 9 studies the identifying power of these assumptions.

Credibility of the Assumptions

Results (8.7) and (8.10) are simple and powerful. The impediment to application is their questionable credibility. Why should supply and demand be linear functions of price? And why should the slope parameters be the same across markets? These assumptions have no foundation in economic theory, and researchers usually find it difficult to justify them.

And what of the covariance assumptions using instrumental variables? I will focus on assumptions (8.8) and (8.9), as assumptions (8.5) and (8.6) are analogous.

Economists often say that a covariate v_2 is a "valid instrument" if v_2 "does not affect demand but does affect supply." A reasonable way to formalize the phrase "does not affect demand" is to assert the statistical independence assumption $P[d(\cdot) \mid v_2] = P[d(\cdot)]$. When demand functions have the linear form (8.4b), this implies that $P(\epsilon_2 \mid v_2) = P(\epsilon_2)$, which in turn implies the zero covariance condition (8.8).

When economists say that an instrumental variable "does affect supply," they have in mind that $P[s(\cdot) \mid v_2] \neq P[s(\cdot)]$. This statistical dependence assumption, combined with the assumption that markets are in equilibrium, makes it plausible to suppose that observed prices and realizations of v_2 are statistically dependent; that is, $P(p \mid v_2) \neq P(p)$. From here, it is a short leap to suppose that equilibrium prices are correlated with v_2, as stated in (8.9).

Analysis of the Reduced Form

The above analysis of identification in the linear market model does not simultaneously use the market-equilibrium equations (8.1) and (8.2). The argument for point identification of the supply slope parameter uses only (8.1), not (8.2). Symmetrically, the argument for point identification of the demand slope parameter uses only (8.2), not (8.1).

Econometrics texts often present an alternative analysis that simultaneously uses (8.1) and (8.2) to derive the *reduced form* of the market model and then uses the reduced form to study identification. I explain here.

The usual exposition begins by restating the linear market model as

(8.11a) $s_j(t) = \beta_1 t + x_j'\alpha_1 + u_{j1},$

(8.11b) $d_j(t) = \beta_2 t + x_j'\alpha_2 + u_{j2},$

(8.11c) $E(u_1, u_2 \mid x) = 0.$

Equations (8.11a) and (8.11b) are (8.4a) and (8.4b) combined with the supposition that the intercepts ϵ_1 and ϵ_2 are linear functions of observed and unobserved covariates; thus, $\epsilon_{j1} = x_j'\alpha_1 + u_{j1}$ and $\epsilon_{j2} = x_j'\alpha_2 + u_{j2}$, where α_1 and α_2 are parameter vectors. Equation (8.11c) is equivalent to assuming that $E(\epsilon_1 \mid x) = x'\alpha_1$ and $E(\epsilon_2 \mid x) = x'\alpha_2$.

Assume that $\beta_1 \neq \beta_2$. When the linear model (8.11a)–(8.11b) is combined with the equilibrium equations (8.1) and (8.2), we find that the equilibrium quantity and price are

(8.12a) $q_j = x_j'\pi_1 + (\beta_1 u_{j2} - \beta_2 u_{j1})/(\beta_1 - \beta_2),$

(8.12b) $p_j = x_j'\pi_2 + (u_{j2} - u_{j1})/(\beta_1 - \beta_2),$

where

(8.13a) $\pi_1 \equiv (\beta_1\alpha_2 - \beta_2\alpha_1)/(\beta_1 - \beta_2),$

(8.13b) $\pi_2 \equiv (\alpha_2 - \alpha_1)/(\beta_1 - \beta_2).$

Thus the equilibrium quantity and price are linear functions of (x_j, u_{j1}, u_{j2}), with parameters that are functions of the supply and demand parameters $(\beta_1, \beta_2, \alpha_1, \alpha_2)$.

Equations (8.11a) and (8.11b) are called the *structural form* of the linear market model, while equations (8.12a) and (8.12b) are called its *reduced form*. The structural form specifies how the supply and demand functions vary with conjectured price and with covariates. The reduced form specifies how equilibrium (price, quantity) pairs vary with covariates.

It follows from equations (8.12) and (8.11c) that the mean regressions of equilibrium quantity and price on x have the linear form

(8.14a) $\quad E(q \mid x) = x' \pi_1,$

(8.14b) $\quad E(p \mid x) = x' \pi_2.$

The empirical evidence reveals $E(q \mid x)$ and $E(p \mid x)$. Hence the parameters π_1 and π_2 are point-identified if the support of $P(x)$ contains K linearly independent values of x, where K is the dimension of the x-vector.

The function (8.13) mapping the supply and demand parameters $(\beta_1, \alpha_1, \beta_2, \alpha_2)$ into the reduced-form parameters (π_1, π_2) is many-to-one rather than one to one. Hence knowledge of (π_1, π_2) does not point-identity $(\beta_1, \alpha_1, \beta_2, \alpha_2)$. These parameters become point-identified when knowledge of (π_1, π_2) is combined with suitable restrictions on $(\beta_1, \alpha_1, \beta_2, \alpha_2)$.

By far the most common practice is to invoke *exclusion restrictions,* asserting that some components of α_1 (or α_2) equal zero while the corresponding components of α_2 (or α_1) are nonzero. For example, assume that $\alpha_{1K} = 0$ but $\alpha_{2K} \neq 0$. Then $\pi_{1K}/\pi_{2K} = \beta_1$, so β_1 is point-identified. Moreover, $\pi_{1k} - \beta_1 \pi_{2k} = \alpha_{1k}$, for $k = 1, \dots, K$, so α_1 is identified. Similarly, exclusion of a component of α_2 point-identifies the demand function parameters.

It is natural to ask how point identification through an exclusion restriction relates to the approach that uses covariance assumptions (8.8) and (8.9). The answer is that an exclusion restriction implies multiple covariance assumptions and, hence, overidentifies the slope parameter.

Suppose again that $\alpha_{1K} = 0$ but $\alpha_{2K} \neq 0$. Recall that $E(\epsilon_1 \mid x) = x'\alpha_1$ and $E(\epsilon_2 \mid x) = x'\alpha_2$. Define $x_{-K} \equiv (x_1, \ldots, x_{K-1})$ to be the first $(K-1)$-components of x. The exclusion restriction implies that, conditional on x_{-K}, $E(\epsilon_1 \mid x)$ does not vary with x_K and $E(\epsilon_2 \mid x)$ varies linearly with x_K. Hence $\mathrm{Cov}(\epsilon_1, x_K \mid x_{-K}) = 0$ and $\mathrm{Cov}(\epsilon_2, x_K \mid x_{-K}) \neq 0$. Given this, the argument of Section 7.7 shows that

$$(8.15) \quad \beta_1 = \mathrm{Cov}(x_K, q \mid x_{-K})/\mathrm{Cov}(x_K, p \mid x_{-K})$$

for all values of x_{-K} on the support of $P(x)$.

8.3 Equilibrium in Games

Many social interactions, from divorce proceedings to union-management negotiations to superpower rivalry, can usefully be thought of as games. The basic two-person game imagines that each of two players must select an action. Player 1 chooses an action from a set of feasible choices, and player 2 chooses an action from his choice set.

It is common to assume that the players in game j have *reaction functions* $r_{j1}(\cdot)$ and $r_{j2}(\cdot)$ specifying the action that each would choose as a function of the action chosen by the other. Thus $r_{j1}(t_2)$ is the action that player 1 would choose if player 2 were to select action t_2. Similarly, $r_{j2}(t_1)$ is the action that player 2 would choose if player 1 were to select action t_1. An equilibrium of the game is a pair of mutually consistent actions. Thus (r_{j1}, r_{j2}) is an equilibrium pair of actions if

$$(8.16) \quad r_{j1} = r_{j1}(r_{j2})$$

and

$$(8.17) \quad r_{j2} = r_{j2}(r_{j1}).$$

The objective is to learn the distribution $P[r_1(\cdot), r_2(\cdot) \mid x]$ of reaction functions across games in which the players have specified covariates x. The simultaneity problem arises when one attempts to infer

$P[r_1(\cdot), r_2(\cdot) \mid x]$ from observations of equilibrium outcomes. Empirical researchers often assert the homogeneous linear response model

(8.18a) $\quad r_{j1}(t_2) = \beta_1 t_2 + \epsilon_{j1}$,

(8.18b) $\quad r_{j2}(t_1) = \beta_2 t_1 + \epsilon_{j2}$.

The analysis of Section 7.7 shows that the slope parameters of this model are point-identified if there are instrumental variables that satisfy appropriate covariance assumptions.

Ehrlich, the Supreme Court, and the National Research Council

A central problem of criminology is to learn the deterrent effect of sanctions on criminal behavior. In the early 1970s, it became common for criminologists to analyze observed crime rates and sanction levels as equilibrium outcomes of two-person games, where criminals (player 1) choose a crime rate, and society (player 2) chooses sanctions. Linear reaction functions were used to specify the crime rate that criminals would choose if sanctions were set at level t_2 and the sanctions that society would choose if the crime rate were t_1.

The simultaneity problem in inference on deterrence became a concern beyond the community of academic criminologists when the Solicitor General of the United States (Bork et al., 1974) argued to the Supreme Court that a study by Isaac Ehrlich provided credible findings on the deterrent effect of capital punishment. Ehrlich (1975) used annual data on murders and sanctions in the United States to estimate a "murder supply" function specifying the murder rate that would occur as a function of sanction levels, including the risk of capital punishment faced by a convicted murderer. He concluded (p. 398): "In fact, the empirical analysis suggests that on the average the tradeoff between the execution of an offender and the lives of potential victims it might have saved was of the order of 1 for 8 for the period 1933–1967 in the United States."

This finding, and its citation before the Supreme Court as evidence in support of capital punishment, generated considerable controversy. A constructive outcome was a series of critiques of the Ehrlich study by Passell and Taylor (1975), Bowers and Pierce (1975), and Klein, Forst, and Filatov (1978), among others. Moreover, a panel of the National

Research Council (NRC) was established to investigate in depth the problem of inference on deterrence (Blumstein, Cohen, and Nagin, 1978).

The NRC Panel on Research on Deterrent and Incapacitative Effects focused much of its attention on the simultaneity problem and stressed the difficulty of finding plausible exclusion restrictions to identify deterrent effects. The panel also examined in depth two other identification problems presenting obstacles to inference on deterrence: error in measuring crime rates and confounding of deterrence and incapacitation. In all, the panel report presents an exceptionally clearheaded portrayal of the difficulties inherent in the empirical study of deterrence.

Regarding the deterrent effect of capital punishment, the panel concluded (p. 62): "The current evidence on the deterrent effect of capital punishment is inadequate for drawing any substantive conclusion." Cautious scientific assessments of this sort are reasonably common in NRC studies and are usually followed by calls for more research. But this NRC panel went on to draw a more unusual conclusion (p. 63):

> In undertaking research on the deterrent effect of capital punishment, however, it should be recognized that the strong value content associated with decisions regarding capital punishment and the high risk associated with errors of commission make it likely that any policy use of scientific evidence on capital punishment will require extremely severe standards of proof. The nonexperimental research to which the study of the deterrent effects of capital punishment is necessarily limited almost certainly will be unable to meet those standards of proof. Thus, the Panel considers that research on this topic is not likely to produce findings that will or should have much influence on policymakers.

This conclusion is both admirable and distressing. It is admirable that a panel of distinguished social scientists was willing to declare that social science research likely cannot resolve a behavioral question of vital public concern. Powerful incentives induce many researchers to maintain strong assumptions in order to draw strong conclusions. The NRC panel rejected the temptation.

The conclusion is distressing for the vacuum it leaves. If research on the deterrent effect of capital punishment should not have much influence on policy makers, what should influence them? Should policy makers reach conclusions about deterrence based solely on their own observations and reasoning, unaided by research? If so, how should they cope with the inferential problems that stymie social scientists? Should they succumb to the temptation to maintain whatever assumptions are needed to reach conclusions? Or should they give no weight to deterrence and base policy only on their normative views of just punishment? Neither option is appealing.

8.4 The Reflection Problem

Endogenous, Contextual, and Correlated Effects

I began this book by calling attention to three hypotheses often advanced to explain the common observation that individuals belonging to the same group tend to behave similarly. These hypotheses are

endogenous effects, where the propensity of an individual to behave in some way varies with the prevalence of the behavior in the group;

contextual effects, where the propensity of an individual to behave in some way varies with the distribution of background characteristics in the group; and

correlated effects, where individuals in the same group tend to behave similarly because they face similar environments or have similar individual characteristics.

Endogenous and contextual effects express distinct ways that individuals might be influenced by their social environments, while correlated effects express a nonsocial phenomenon. For example, consider the high school achievement of a teenage youth. There is an endogenous effect if, all else equal, individual achievement tends to vary with the average achievement of the students in the youth's high school, ethnic group, or other reference group. There is a contextual effect if achievement tends to vary with, say, the socioeconomic composition of the reference group. There are correlated effects if youth in the same school tend to achieve similarly because they are taught by the same teachers or because they have similar family backgrounds.

Social scientists have long been concerned with reinforcing endogenous effects, where the propensity of an individual to behave in some way increases with the prevalence of the behavior in the reference group. A host of terms are commonly used to describe these effects: conformity, imitation, contagion, bandwagons, herd behavior, social norms, and keeping up with the Joneses. Economists have always been fundamentally concerned with a particular non-reinforcing endogenous effect: an individual's demand for a product varies with price, which is partly determined by aggregate demand in the relevant market.

Contextual effects became an important concern of sociologists in the 1960s, when substantial efforts were made to learn how youth are influenced by their school and neighborhood environment (Coleman et al., 1966; Sewell and Armer, 1966; Hauser, 1970). A more recent resurgence of interest in spatial concepts of the underclass spawned further empirical studies (e.g., Crane, 1991; Jencks and Mayer, 1989; and Mayer, 1991).

Distinguishing among endogenous, contextual, and correlated effects is important because these hypotheses have differing implications for prediction of policy impacts. For example, consider an educational intervention providing tutoring to some of the students in a school but not to the others. If individual achievement increases with the average achievement of the students in the school, then an effective tutoring program not only directly helps the tutored students but, as their achievement rises, indirectly helps all students in the school, with a feedback to further achievement gains by the tutored students. Contextual and correlated effects do not generate this *social multiplier.*

The Linear-in-Means Model

Empirical research seeking to distinguish endogenous, contextual, and correlated effects has often used a *linear-in-means* model. This model characterizes each member of the population by a value for the variables (y, x, w, u). Here y is an outcome, x are covariates characterizing an individual's presumed reference group, and (w, u) are other covariates. For example, y might measure a youth's achievement in high school and x might be a vector of indicator variables that name the youth's school within the set of schools attended by members of the population. The covariates (w, u) might measure the youth's socioeconomic status and ability.

Consider a researcher who observes a random sample of (y, x, w) but does not observe the associated realizations of u. The variables (x, w, u) are assumed to determine y through the linear model

(8.19a) $\quad y_j = \alpha + \beta E(y \mid x_j) + E(w \mid x_j)'\gamma + w_j'\lambda + u_j,$

(8.19b) $\quad E(u \mid x, w) = x'\delta,$

where $(\alpha, \beta, \gamma, \delta, \lambda)$ is a parameter vector. Given (8.19), the mean regression of y on (x, w) has the linear form

(8.20) $\quad E(y \mid x, w) = \alpha + \beta E(y \mid x) + E(w \mid x)'\gamma + x'\delta + w'\lambda.$

If $\beta \neq 0$, the linear regression (8.20) is said to express an endogenous effect: the response y varies with $E(y \mid x)$, the mean outcome among the members of the reference group. If $\gamma \neq 0$, the model is said to express a contextual effect: y varies with $E(w \mid x)$, the mean of the covariates w among the members of the reference group. If $\delta \neq 0$, the model is said to express correlated effects: persons in reference group x tend to have similar unobserved covariates, and, hence, similar outcomes. The parameter λ is said to express the direct effect of w on y.

What legitimates the use of the term "effect" to describe the parameters $(\beta, \gamma, \delta, \lambda)$? Researchers appear to have in mind, but do not state explicitly, a four-dimensional treatment (t_1, t_2, t_3, t_4), these being conjectural values of $[E(y \mid x), E(w \mid x), x, w]$, and a homogeneous linear response model

(8.21a) $\quad y_j(t_1, t_2, t_3, t_4) = \alpha + \beta t_1 + t_2'\gamma + t_3'\delta + t_4'\lambda + \epsilon_j,$

(8.21b) $\quad E(\epsilon \mid x, w) = 0.$

Thus parameters $(\beta, \gamma, \delta, \lambda)$ are treatment effects expressing how each person's outcome would change if any component of the treatment vector were to change by one unit, holding the other components fixed.

The realized treatment vector for person j is $[z_{j1} = E(y \mid x_j), z_{j2} = E(w \mid x_j), z_{j3} = x_j, z_{j4} = w_j]$. Hence equation (8.19a) holds with $u_j = x_j'\delta + \epsilon_j$. Equation (8.21b) implies (8.19b). We thus obtain the linear-in-means model.

Identification of the Parameters

The sampling process reveals $P(y, x, w)$. The inferential question is: What does knowledge of $P(y, x, w)$ reveal about $(\alpha, \beta, \gamma, \delta, \lambda)$? Let K denote the dimension of the vector $[1, E(y \mid x), E(w \mid x), x, w]$. Model (8.20) poses a set of linear equations in the parameters $(\alpha, \beta, \gamma, \delta, \lambda)$, one equation for each value of (x, w) in the population. If the model is correct, these equations have a unique solution if and only if the population contains K linearly independent values of $[1, E(y \mid x), E(w \mid x), x, w]$. However, Manski (1993) showed that these vectors are necessarily linearly dependent, as a consequence of the reflection problem.

The reflection problem arises out of the presence of $E(y \mid x)$ as a regressor in (8.20). Taking expectations of both sides of (8.20) with respect to w reveals that $E(y \mid x)$ solves the *social-equilibrium* equation

$$(8.22) \quad E(y \mid x) = \alpha + \beta E(y \mid x) + E(w \mid x)'\gamma + x'\delta + E(w \mid x)'\lambda.$$

Provided that $\beta \neq 1$, equation (8.22) has a unique solution, namely,

$$(8.23) \quad E(y \mid x) = [\alpha + E(w \mid x)'(\gamma + \lambda) + x'\delta]/(1 - \beta).$$

Thus model (8.20) implies that $E(y \mid x)$ is a linear function of $[1, E(w \mid x), x]$.

This derivation explains why the term *reflection problem* appropriately describes the inferential difficulty. On the one hand, the linear-in-means model posits that individual outcomes depend on the mean outcome of the reference group. On the other hand, the mean outcome in the group is itself determined by the outcomes of the individual members of the group. The social-equilibrium equation formally describes this bidirectional relationship between individual outcomes and their group means. The result is that we are unable to determine whether the mean group outcome affects individual outcomes or simply reflects them.

What conclusions can be drawn about the model parameters? Inserting (8.23) into (8.20) yields the linear reduced-form model

$$(8.24) \quad \begin{aligned} E(y \mid x, w) &= \alpha/(1 - \beta) + E(w \mid x)'[(\gamma + \lambda\beta)/(1 - \beta)] \\ &\quad + x'\delta/(1 - \beta) + w'\lambda. \end{aligned}$$

The reduced form is a set of linear equations in the vector of composite parameters $[\alpha/(1-\beta), (\gamma+\lambda\beta)/(1-\beta), \delta/(1-\beta), \lambda]$, one equation for each value of (x, w). Again supposing that the model is correct, these equations have a unique solution if and only if the population contains $K-1$ linearly independent values of the vector $[1, E(w \mid x), x, w]$. Then the composite parameters are point-identified.

Identification of the composite parameters does not enable one to distinguish between endogenous and contextual effects, but it does permit one to learn whether some social effect is present. If some element of the composite parameter vector $\gamma/(1-\beta)+\lambda\beta/(1-\beta)$ is nonzero, then either β or the relevant element of γ must be nonzero. So some social effect is present. Observe that β is point-identified if an element of $\gamma/(1-\beta)+\lambda\beta/(1-\beta)$ is nonzero and one assumes that the relevant component of γ equals zero.

The linear independence requirement for $[1, E(w \mid x), x, w]$ is satisfied in some empirical settings but not others. The requirement fails to hold if any of these conditions occurs:

(i) w is a function of x,
(ii) $E(w \mid x)$ does not vary with x,
(iii) $E(w \mid x)$ varies linearly with x.

Thus the feasibility of inferring the presence of some social effect depends on the manner in which w varies with x. Inference requires both within-group variation in w and nonlinear between-group variation in w.

Inferring the Composition of Reference Groups

Researchers studying social interactions rarely offer empirical evidence to support their specifications of reference groups. The prevailing practice is simply to assume that individuals are influenced by $E(y \mid x)$ and $E(w \mid x)$, for some specified x. Among the few studies that do bring empirical evidence to bear are Coleman, Katz, and Menzel (1957), Duncan, Haller, and Portes (1968), and Woittiez and Kapteyn (1991). These studies attempt to elicit reference group information from survey respondents.

Suppose that a researcher does not know the composition of reference groups. Can the researcher infer the composition of reference groups from the observed distribution of outcomes and covariates? The answer is negative.

To see this, let x be any hypothesized specification of reference groups and let w be any specified function of x, say, $w = w(x)$. Knowledge of x implies knowledge of $w(x)$. Hence the equality

$$(8.25) \quad E(y \mid x, w) = E(y \mid x)$$

holds tautologically. Comparing equations (8.25) and (8.20) shows that (8.25) is the special case of (8.20) in which $\beta = 1$ and $\alpha = \gamma = \delta = \lambda = 0$. Thus the hypothesis that mean group outcomes affect individual outcomes is not refutable.

9

Monotone Treatment Response

9.1 Shape Restrictions

Chapter 8 supposed that response to a real-valued treatment is linear in the treatment magnitude, all members of the population having the same slope parameter. This is a strong restriction on the response functions $y(\cdot)$. It has much identifying power when coupled with certain distributional assumptions, but it is hard to motivate.

Researchers sometimes have more credible information about the shape of response functions. In particular, one may have reason to believe that outcomes vary monotonically with the magnitude of the treatment. The assumption of *monotone treatment response* (MTR) asserts that, for all persons j and all treatment pairs (s, t),

$$(9.1) \qquad t \geq s \Rightarrow y_j(t) \geq y_j(s).$$

Assumption MTR permits each person to have a distinct response function. It only requires that all response functions be monotone.

It is easy to see that assumption MTR is not refutable. For each person j, only one point on the response function $y_j(\cdot)$ is observable, namely, $y_j \equiv y_j(z_j)$. Hence the empirical evidence is necessarily consistent with the hypothesis that $y_j(\cdot)$ is weakly increasing. For example, the evidence is consistent with the hypothesis that every response function is flat, with $\{y_j(t) = y_j, t \in T, \text{ all } j\}$.

This chapter studies the selection problem when response functions are assumed to be weakly increasing. With obvious modifications, the analysis also applies when response is weakly decreasing. The analysis to be presented originally appeared in Manski (1997a) and Manski and Pepper (2000). The former article also studies the related shape restrictions of semimonotonicity and concave monotonicity.

There are many settings in which one may be confident that response is monotone, semimonotone, or concave-monotone, but be wary of assuming anything else. Economic analysis of demand and production provide good illustrations.

Downward-Sloping Demand

The one relatively firm conclusion of the theory of demand is that market demand ordinarily is a downward-sloping function of price. This is not a universal prediction. Texts on consumer theory distinguish between the substitution and income effects of price changes. When income effects are sufficiently strong, consumer optimization implies the existence of *Giffen goods,* for which demand increases with price over some domain. The modern theory of markets with imperfect information emphasizes that price may convey information. If the informational content of price is sufficiently strong, demand functions need not always slope downward. These exceptions notwithstanding, the ordinary presumption of economists is that demand functions slope downward.

Economic theory does not yield other conclusions about the shape of demand functions. Nor does the theory of demand per se imply anything about price determination. Conclusions about price determination can be drawn only if assumptions about the structure of demand are combined with assumptions about the behavior of the firms that produce the product in question. Thus demand analysis offers a good example of an inferential problem in which an analyst can reasonably assert that response functions are monotone but may be wary of imposing other assumptions.

Oddly, the traditional linear market model of econometric analysis does not assume that market demand is downward-sloping. Instead, as we saw in Chapter 8, the traditional analysis assumes that demand is a linear function of price, with the same slope parameter in each market. Nothing is assumed about the sign or magnitude of the slope.

Production Analysis

Production analysis typically supposes that firms use inputs to produce a scalar output; thus, the input is the treatment and the output is the response. Firm j has a production function $y_j(\cdot)$ mapping inputs into output, so $y_j(t)$ is the output that firm j produces when t is the input vector. The most basic tenet of the economic theory of production is that output weakly increases with the magnitude of the inputs. If there is a single input (say, labor), this means that treatment response is monotone. If there is a vector of inputs (say, labor and capital), treatment response is semimonotone.

Formally, suppose that there are K inputs, and let $s \equiv (s_1, s_2, \ldots, s_K)$ and $t \equiv (t_1, t_2, \ldots, t_K)$ be two input vectors. Production theory predicts that $y_j(t) \geq y_j(s)$ if input vector t is at least as large, component by component, as input vector s; that is, if $t_k \geq s_k$, all $k = 1, \ldots, K$. Production theory does not predict the ordering of $y_j(t)$ and $y_j(s)$ when the input vectors t and s are unordered, each having some components larger than the other. Thus production functions are semimonotone.

Consider, for example, the production of corn. The inputs include land and seed. The output is bushels of corn. Production theory predicts that the quantity of corn produced by a farm weakly increases with its input of land and seed. Production theory does not predict the effect on corn production of increasing one input component and decreasing the other.

Economists typically assume more than that production functions are semimonotone. They often assume that production functions exhibit diminishing marginal returns, which means that the production function is concave in each input component, holding the other components fixed. In so-called *short-run* production analysis, researchers distinguish two types of inputs: variable inputs whose values can be changed and fixed inputs whose values cannot be changed. Short-run production analysis performs thought experiments in which the variable inputs are varied and the fixed inputs are held fixed at their realized values. Thus the variable inputs are considered to be treatments and the fixed inputs to be covariates, and the short-run production function maps variable inputs into output. Suppose that there is one variable input. Then it is common to assume that the short-run production function $y_j(\cdot)$ is concave-monotone in this input. In the short-run production of corn, for example, seed would usually be thought of as the variable input and land as the fixed input. A researcher might find it plausible to assume that, holding land fixed, output of corn rises with the input of seed but with diminishing returns.

Economists studying production often find it difficult to justify assumptions on the shapes of production functions beyond concave monotonicity. Researchers usually use tight parametric models of production, but they rarely can do more than assert on faith that such models are adequate "approximations" to actual production functions. Economists also often find it difficult to specify how firms choose their inputs, one reason being that optimal input decisions depend on the structure of the market within which firms compete. Thus production analysis offers another good example of an inferential problem in which an analyst can reasonably assert that response functions are monotone but may be wary of imposing other assumptions.

9.2 Bounds on Parameters That Respect Stochastic Dominance

The assumption of monotone treatment response has particular power to identify parameters of outcome distributions that respect stochastic dominance. I will first prove a general result giving sharp lower and upper bounds for any such parameter. I will then apply this result to means of increasing functions of outcomes.

In what follows, the outcome space Y is a closed subset of the extended real line, which is the ordinary real line $(-\infty, \infty)$ extended to include the limits $-\infty$ and ∞. The parameters of interest have the form $D\{P[y(t) \mid x]\}$, for a specified treatment t and covariates x. To simplify the notation, I suppress x below and shorten $D\{P[y(t)]\}$ to $D[y(t)]$.

The General Result

Let T be an ordered set of treatments and let assumption (9.1) hold. Let t be a specified treatment. Let y_0 and y_1 be the smallest and largest elements of Y. For each member j of the population, define the observable quantities

(9.2a)
$$y_{0j}(t) \equiv y_j \quad \text{if } t \geq z_j$$
$$\equiv y_0 \quad \text{otherwise,}$$

$$y_{1j}(t) \equiv y_j \quad \text{if } t \leq z_j$$

(9.2b)

$$\equiv y_1 \quad \text{otherwise.}$$

Here, $y_{0j}(t)$ is the smallest feasible value of $y_j(t)$ and $y_{1j}(t)$ is its largest feasible value. I will show that the sharp bounds on $D[y(t)]$ are

(9.3) $D[y_0(t)] \leq D[y(t)] \leq D[y_1(t)].$

Being sharp, these bounds are necessarily the endpoints of the identification region for $D[y(t)]$. However, the identification region need not be the entire interval connecting these endpoints. Here, as in other findings for parameters that respect stochastic dominance, the interior of the interval may contain nonfeasible values if $D(\cdot)$ is a quantile. See the end of Section 2.1.

Proof of (9.3) Monotonicity of $y_j(\cdot)$ implies this sharp bound on $y_j(t)$:

$$z_j > t \Rightarrow y_0 \leq y_j(t) < y_j,$$

(9.4) $z_j = t \Rightarrow y_j(t) = y_j,$

$$z_j < t \Rightarrow y_j < y_j(t) \leq y_1.$$

Equivalently,

(9.5) $y_{0j}(t) \leq y_j(t) \leq y_{1j}(t).$

There are no cross-person restrictions, so the sharp bound on $\{y_j(t),$ all $j\}$ is

(9.6) $y_{0j}(t) \leq y_j(t) \leq y_{1j}(t), \quad$ all $j.$

Hence the random variable $y_0(t)$ is stochastically dominated by $y(t)$, which in turn is stochastically dominated by $y_1(t)$. This shows that (9.3) is a bound on $D[y(t)]$.

Bound (9.3) is sharp because bound (9.6) is sharp. That is, the empirical evidence and assumption MTR are consistent with the hypothesis $\{y_j(t) = y_{0j}(t),$ all $j\}$ and also with the hypothesis $\{y_j(t) = y_{1j}(t),$ all $j\}$. □

This result shows that assumption MTR qualitatively reduces the severity of the selection problem. Using the empirical evidence alone, a realized outcome y_j is informative about potential outcome $y_j(t)$ only if the realized treatment z_j is t; then $y_j = y_j(t)$. Using the empirical evidence and assumption MTR, observation of y_j always yields an informative lower or upper bound on $y_j(t)$, as shown in equation (9.4).

Indeed, the bound on $D[y(t)]$ given in (9.3) is generally informative even if no member of the study population receives treatment t. Thus assumption MTR enables partial prediction of outcomes for proposed new treatments that have never been used in practice.

Means of Increasing Functions of the Outcome

Result (9.3) is simple to state and prove, but it is too abstract to give a clear sense of the identifying power of assumption MTR. The result becomes more transparent when applied to the means of increasing functions of the outcome $y(t)$.

Let $f(\cdot) : Y \to R$ be a weakly increasing function of the outcome. The expectation $E\{f[y(t)]\}$ is a parameter that respects stochastic dominance. Application of (9.3) gives

$$
\begin{aligned}
(9.7) \quad & f(y_0) P(z > t) + E[f(y) \mid z \le t] P(z \le t) \le E\{f[y(t)]\} \\
& \le f(y_1) P(z < t) + E[f(y) \mid z \ge t] P(z \ge t).
\end{aligned}
$$

The lower bound is the mean of the observable random variable $f[y_0(t)]$, and the upper bound is the mean of $f[y_1(t)]$.

It is revealing to compare (9.7), which exploits assumption MTR, with the bound on $E\{f[y(t)]\}$ using the data alone. The bound using the data alone is

$$
\begin{aligned}
(9.8) \quad & f(y_0) P(z \ne t) + E[f(y) \mid z = t] P(z = t) \le E\{f[y(t)]\} \\
& \le f(y_1) P(z \ne t) + E[f(y) \mid z = t] P(z = t).
\end{aligned}
$$

Whereas this bound draws information about $E\{f[y(t)]\}$ only from the (y, z) pairs with $z = t$, all (y, z) pairs are informative under assumption MTR. The lower bound in (9.7) draws information from the persons with $z \leq t$. The upper bound draws information from those with $z \geq t$.

Upper Tail Probabilities

Bound (9.7) has an interesting application to upper tail probabilities. Let $r \in (y_0, y_1]$. The indicator function $1[y(t) \geq r]$ is an increasing function of $y(t)$ and $E\{1[y(t) \geq r]\} = P[y(t) \geq r]$. Hence inequality (9.7) yields

$$(9.9) \qquad P(z \leq t \cap y \geq r) \leq P[y(t) \geq r] \leq P(z < t \cup y \geq r).$$

The informativeness of this bound depends on the distribution of realized treatments and outcomes. If $P(z \leq t \cap y \geq r) = 0$ and $P(z < t \cup y \geq r) = 1$, then (9.9) is the trivial bound $0 \leq P[y(t) \geq r] \leq 1$. If $P(z \leq t \cap y \geq r) = P(z < t \cup y \geq r)$, assumption MTR point-identifies $P[y(t) \geq r]$.

9.3 Bounds on Treatment Effects

There are two ways to define treatment effects in terms of a parameter that respects stochastic dominance, corresponding to the two perspectives on analysis of treatment response discussed in Complement 7A. Let $t \in T$ and $s \in T$ be two treatments, with $t > s$. One may compare these treatments through $D[y(t)] - D[y(s)]$ or $D[y(t) - y(s)]$. The two treatment effects coincide when $D(\cdot)$ is an expectation function but otherwise may differ.

Sharp bounds on both treatment effects are easily obtained from the sharp bound on $D[y(t)]$ given in (9.3). The bounds are

$$(9.10) \qquad 0 \leq D[y(t)] - D[y(s)] \leq D[y_1(t)] - D[y_0(s)],$$

$$(9.11) \qquad D(0) \leq D[y(t) - y(s)] \leq D[y_1(t) - y_0(s)].$$

The lower bounds in (9.10) and (9.11) are implied by assumption MTR and do not depend on the empirical evidence. Assumption MTR and the evidence together determine the upper bounds.

Proof of (9.10) Monotonicity of response implies that $y(t)$ stochastically dominates $y(s)$, so zero is a lower bound on $D[y(t)] - D[y(s)]$. Result (9.3) implies that $D[y_1(t)] - D[y_0(s)]$ is an upper bound. We need to prove that these bounds are sharp.

Consider person j. Monotonicity of $y_j(\cdot)$ gives this sharp bound on $\{y_j(t), y_j(s)\}$:

$$s < t < z_j \Rightarrow y_0 \leq y_j(s) \leq y_j(t) \leq y_j,$$

$$s < t = z_j \Rightarrow y_0 \leq y_j(s) \leq y_j(t) = y_j,$$

$$(9.12) \quad s < z_j < t \Rightarrow y_0 \leq y_j(s) \leq y_j \leq y_j(t) \leq y_1,$$

$$s = z_j < t \Rightarrow y_j = y_j(s) \leq y_j(t) \leq y_1,$$

$$z_j < s < t \Rightarrow y_j \leq y_j(s) \leq y_j(t) \leq y_1.$$

There are no cross-person restrictions, so the data and assumption MTR are consistent with the hypothesis $\{y_j(s) = y_j(t), \text{ all } j\}$ and also with $\{y_j(t) = y_{1j}(t), y_j(s) = y_{0j}(s), \text{ all } j\}$. Hence (9.10) is sharp.   ❏

Proof of (9.11) The proof to (9.10) showed that the sharp joint bound on $\{y_j(t) - y_j(s), \text{ all } j\}$ is

$$(9.13) \quad 0 \leq y_j(t) - y_j(s) \leq y_{1j}(t) - y_{0j}(s), \quad \text{all } j.$$

Hence the degenerate distribution with all mass at 0 is stochastically dominated by $y(t) - y(s)$, which in turn is dominated by $y_1(t) - y_0(s)$. Thus (9.11) is a bound on $D[y(t) - y(s)]$. This bound is sharp because bound (9.13) is sharp.   ❏

Average Treatment Effects

The average treatment effect is the same under both perspectives on treatment comparison. Hence bounds (9.10) and (9.11) coincide in this case. The bound is

$$
\begin{aligned}
0 \leq E[y(t)] - E[y(s)] &= E[y(t) - y(s)] \\
(9.14) \qquad &\leq y_1 \cdot P(z < t) + E(y \mid z \geq t) \cdot P(z \geq t) \\
&\quad - y_0 \cdot P(z > s) - E(y \mid z \leq s) \cdot P(z \leq s).
\end{aligned}
$$

This result takes a particularly simple form when outcomes are binary. Let Y be the two-element set $\{0, 1\}$. Then $y_0 = 0$, $y_1 = 1$, and (9.14) becomes

(9.15)
$$0 \leq P[y(t) = 1] - P[y(s) = 1] = P[y(t) - y(s) = 1]$$
$$\leq P(y = 0, z < t) + P(y = 1, z > s).$$

9.4 Monotone Response and Selection

Traditional econometric analysis of simultaneity combines a homogeneous linear response model with an exclusion restriction or a zero covariance assumption. Assumption MTR may similarly be combined with other assumptions. This section presents one interesting possibility, combining assumption MTR with the assumption of monotone treatment selection. Section 9.5 gives an empirical illustration.

The assumption of *monotone treatment selection* (MTS) asserts that for each $t \in T$,

(9.16) $s' \geq s \Rightarrow E[y(t) \mid z = s'] \geq E[y(t) \mid z = s].$

A version of this nonrefutable assumption was studied in Section 3.5, in the context of prediction with missing outcome data, under the name "means missing monotonically." The name "monotone treatment selection" is more descriptive in the present setting.

Interpreting the Statement "Wages Increase with Schooling"

Assumptions MTR and MTS express distinct restrictions on treatment response and selection. In principle, both assumptions could hold, or one, or neither. To understand more about how the assumptions differ, consider the variation of wages with schooling.

Labor economists studying the returns to schooling usually suppose that each person j has a human-capital production function $y_j(t)$, giving the wage that j would receive were he to have t years of schooling. Labor economists often say that "wages increase with schooling." Assumptions MTR and MTS interpret this statement in different ways.

The MTR interpretation is that each person's wage function is weakly increasing in conjectured years of schooling. This assumption expresses the standard economic view that education is a production process in which schooling is the input and wage is the output. Hence wages increase with conjectured schooling.

The MTS interpretation is that persons who select higher levels of schooling have weakly higher mean wage functions than do those who select lower levels of schooling. This assumption is consistent with economic models of schooling choice and wage determination that predict that persons with higher ability tend to have higher wage functions and tend to choose more schooling than do persons with lower ability.

Yet a third possible interpretation of "wages increase with schooling" is that observed wages increase with realized years of schooling; that is, $E(y \mid z = t)$ increases with t. This interpretation is not an assumption but rather a statement about the empirical pattern of realized wages and schooling.

Bounds on Mean Outcomes and Average Treatment Effects

Consider inference on a mean potential outcome $E[y(t)]$ and on an average treatment effect $E[y(t)] - E[y(s)]$. I report here several findings proved in Manski and Pepper (2000).

Assumption MTS alone implies this sharp bound on $E[y(t)]$:

$$y_0 P(z < t) + E(y \mid z = t) P(z \geq t) \leq E[y(t)]$$
$$\leq y_1 P(z > t) + E(y \mid z = t) P(z \leq t).$$

(9.17)

When assumptions MTR and MTS are combined, the sharp bound becomes

$$\sum_{s<t} E(y \mid z = s) P(z = s) + E(y \mid z = t) P(z \geq t) \leq E[y(t)]$$

(9.18)

$$\leq \sum_{s>t} E(y \mid z = s) P(z = s) + E(y \mid z = t) P(z \leq t).$$

Combining the two assumptions yields this bound on the average treatment effect:

$$0 \leq E[y(t)] - E[y(s)]$$
$$\leq \sum_{t'>t} E(y \mid z = t') P(z = t') + E(y \mid z = t) P(z \leq t)$$

(9.19)

$$- \sum_{s'<s} E(y \mid z = s') P(z = s') - E(y \mid z = s) P(z \geq s).$$

The bound (9.18) on $E[y(t)]$ achieved through combined use of assumptions MTR and MTS has an important feature that is not shared by the bounds (9.7) and (9.17) obtained using only one assumption or the other. The latter bounds are informative only when the outcome space Y is bounded. In contrast, the former bound is informative even when Y is unbounded. In this sense, the combination of assumptions MTR and MTS has qualitatively more identifying power than either assumption alone.

Another important fact is that the combined assumption is refutable. Manski and Pepper show that, when both assumptions hold, the observable mean $E(y \mid z = t)$ is a weakly increasing function of t. Hence an empirical finding that $E(y \mid z = t)$ does not increase with t implies that at least one of the two assumptions must be incorrect. In this sense as well, the combination of assumptions MTR and MTS is qualitatively more powerful than either assumption alone.

9.5 Bounding the Returns to Schooling

Labor economists studying schooling as a treatment commonly suppose that each individual j has a log(wage) function $y_j(t)$, giving the log(wage) that j would receive were he to obtain t years of schooling. In theories of schooling and labor supply, $y_j(\cdot)$ is interpreted as person j's production function for human capital. Observing realized covariates, schooling, and wages, labor economists seek to learn about these production func tions. In particular, many studies report estimates of the mean returns to completing t years of schooling relative to s years, for $s < t$. This is the average treatment effect

$$(9.20) \quad \Delta(s, t \mid x) \equiv E[y(t) \mid x] - E[y(s) \mid x].$$

Note Use of log(wage) rather than wage to measure the production of human capital follows the prevailing practice in labor economics. The reasons are not so much substantive as historical. Early studies of the returns to schooling, such as Mincer (1958), posed specific models for log(wages) that led to the establishment of conventions followed by later researchers. ❑

To infer the returns to schooling, researchers often assume, without compelling reason, that log(wage) varies linearly with conjectured schooling. They combine this homogeneous linear response model with a zero covariance assumption to achieve point identification. Card (1994) reviews the literature.

Manski and Pepper (2000) report an empirical analysis of the returns to schooling under assumptions MTR and MTS. As indicated in Section 9.4, both assumptions are consistent with economic thinking about human-capital accumulation. Even if these assumptions do not warrant unquestioned acceptance, they merit serious consideration.

Data

The analysis used data from the National Longitudinal Survey of Youth (NLSY). In its base year of 1979, the NLSY interviewed 12,686 persons who were between the ages of 14 and 22 at that time. Nearly half of the respondents were randomly sampled, the remainder being selected to overrepresent certain demographic groups. We restricted attention to the 1257 randomly sampled white males who reported in 1994 that they were full-time year-round workers with positive wages. The self-employed were excluded. Thus the empirical analysis concerned the subpopulation of persons with these observable covariates.

The NLSY provides data on respondents' realized years of schooling and hourly wage in 1994. Thus z is realized years of schooling, the response variable $y_j(t)$ is the log(wage) that person j would experience if he were to have t years of schooling, and y_j is the observed hourly log(wage). The object of interest is the average treatment effect $\Delta(s, t)$ for specified values of s and t.

Statistical Considerations

In this application, it was necessary only to estimate the upper bound on $\Delta(s, t)$ given in (9.19). Thus we had to estimate the probabilities $P(z)$ of realizing z years of schooling and the expectations $E(y \mid z)$ of log(wage) conditional on schooling. The empirical distribution of schooling was used to estimate $P(z)$, and the sample average log(wage) of respondents with z years of schooling was used to estimate $E(y \mid z)$.

Asymptotically valid confidence intervals for the bounds may be computed using the delta method or bootstrap approaches. We applied the percentile bootstrap method. The bootstrap sampling distribution of an estimate of the upper bound in (9.19) is its sampling distri-

Table 9.1 Empirical mean log(wage) and distribution of years of schooling

z	$E(y \mid z)$	$P(z)$	Sample size
8	2.249	0.014	18
9	2.302	0.018	22
10	2.195	0.018	23
11	2.346	0.025	32
12	2.496	0.413	519
13	2.658	0.074	93
14	2.639	0.083	104
15	2.693	0.035	44
16	2.870	0.189	238
17	2.775	0.038	48
18	3.006	0.051	64
19	3.009	0.020	25
20	2.936	0.021	27
Total			1257

bution under the assumption that the unknown distribution $P(y, z)$ equals the empirical distribution of these variables in the sample of 1257 randomly sampled NLSY respondents. The 0.95-quantile of the bootstrap sampling distribution is reported next to each upper-bound estimate.

Findings

Table 9.1 gives the estimates of $E(y \mid z)$ and $P(z)$ used to estimate the bounds. The table shows that 41 percent of the NLSY respondents have 12 years of schooling and 19 percent have 16 years, but the support of the schooling distribution stretches from 8 years to 20 years. Hence we were able to report findings on $\Delta(s, t)$ for $t = 9$ through 20 and $8 \leq s < t$.

Section 9.4 noted that assumption MTR-MTS is a testable hypothesis, which should be rejected if $E(y \mid z)$ is not weakly increasing in z. The estimate of $E(y \mid z)$ in Table 9.1 for the most part does increase with z, but there are occasional dips. Computing a uniform 95 percent confidence band for the estimate of $E(y \mid z)$, we found that the band contains everywhere monotone functions.

Table 9.2 MTR-MTS upper bounds on returns to schooling

s	t	Estimate	Bootstrap 0.95-quantile
8	9	0.390	0.531
9	10	0.334	0.408
10	11	0.445	0.525
11	12	0.313	0.416
12	13	0.253	0.307
13	14	0.159	0.226
14	15	0.202	0.288
15	16	0.304	0.369
16	17	0.165	0.256
17	18	0.386	0.485
18	19	0.368	0.539
19	20	0.296	0.486
12	16	0.397	0.450

Table 9.2 reports the estimates and bootstrap 0.95-quantiles of the upper bounds on $\Delta(t-1, t)$, $t = 9, \ldots, 20$, followed by the upper bound on $\Delta(12, 16)$, which compares high school completion with college completion. To provide context, it is useful to review the point estimates of $\Delta(t-1, t)$ reported in the literature on the returns to schooling. Most of the point estimates cited in the survey by Card (1994) are between 0.07 and 0.09. Card (1993) reports a point estimate of 0.132. Ashenfelter and Krueger (1994) report various estimates and conclude (p. 1171): "Our best estimate is that increased schooling increases average wage rates by about 12–16 percent per year completed."

None of the estimates of upper bounds on $\Delta(t-1, t)$ in Table 9.2 lies below the point estimates reported in the literature. The smallest of the upper bound estimates are 0.159 for $\Delta(13, 14)$ and 0.165 for $\Delta(16, 17)$. These are about equal to the largest of the available point estimates, namely, those in Ashenfelter and Krueger (1994). It may therefore appear that assumption MTR-MTS does not, in this application, have sufficient identifying power to affect current thinking about the magnitude of the returns to schooling.

A different conclusion emerges with consideration of the upper bound on $\Delta(12, 16)$. We estimate that completion of a four-year college yields at most an increase of 0.397 in mean log(wage) relative to completion of high school. This implies that the average value of the four year-by-year treatment effects $\Delta(12, 13)$, $\Delta(13, 14)$, $\Delta(14, 15)$, and $\Delta(15, 16)$ is at most 0.099, which is well below the point estimates of Card (1993) and Ashcnfelter and Krueger (1994). This conclusion continues in force if, acting conservatively, one uses the bootstrap 0.95-quantile of 0.450 to estimate the upper bound on $\Delta(12, 16)$. Then the implied upper bound on the average value of the year-by-year treatment effects is 0.113. Thus we found that, under assumption MTR-MTS, the returns to college-level schooling are smaller than some of the point estimates that have been reported.

10

The Mixing Problem

10.1 Extrapolation from Experiments to Rules with Treatment Variation

A broad concern of the analysis of treatment response is extrapolation from a realized treatment rule to alternative rules. Observing the outcomes y experienced when the members of a study population receive treatments z, one wants to predict the outcomes that would occur if some members of the population were to receive other treatments.

The selection problem studied in Chapters 7 through 9 concerns extrapolation to a treatment rule in which all persons with covariates x receive the same treatment. Thus these chapters studied identification of the potential outcome distributions $\{P[y(t) \mid x], t \in T\}$ and of treatment effects that compare specified alternative treatments.

This chapter studies extrapolation to rules in which treatment may vary systematically within the group of persons with covariates x. Such rules cannot be implemented by a planner who only observes x, but they can be implemented by decision makers who observe more than x. Within-group variation is particularly common when each member of the population selects his own treatment. For example, medical patients may choose among the treatment options that physicians propose, youth may choose among a range of schooling alternatives, and so on.

This chapter specifically studies extrapolation from classical randomized experiments. As described in Chapter 7, a classical experiment assigns treatments to random samples of the population, and all subjects comply with their assigned treatments. Hence a classical experiment point-identifies $P[y(t) \mid x]$, $t \in T$. However, an experiment does not point-identify the outcome distributions that would occur under rules in which treatment may vary systematically across persons with co-variates x. The task is to characterize what an experiment does reveal about outcomes under such treatment rules. This is called the *mixing problem*.

The mixing problem reverses the partial-compliance problem studied in Section 7.4. There one observed the outcomes of an experiment in which some subjects did not comply with their assigned treatments, and one wanted to predict the outcomes that would occur with full compliance. Here one observes the outcomes of an experiment with full compliance, and one wants to predict the outcomes that would occur in settings with partial compliance.

From Marginals to Mixtures

Stripped to its essentials, the mixing problem concerns inference on a probability mixture, given knowledge of its marginals. To formalize the problem, we need notation for a treatment rule and for the outcomes that would occur under this rule. A treatment rule specifies a treatment to be received by each member of a population. Let τ denote such a rule. The treatment that person j would receive under rule τ is denoted $z_{\tau j}$, and the resulting outcome is $y_{\tau j} \equiv y_j(z_{\tau j})$. The random variable y_τ describing population outcomes under rule t is

$$(10.1) \quad y_\tau \equiv \sum_{t \in T} y(t) \cdot 1[z_\tau = t].$$

Consider the group of persons with covariates x. It follows from (10.1) that the distribution $P(y_\tau \mid x)$ of y_τ conditional on x is

$$(10.2) \quad P(y_\tau \mid x) = \sum_{t \in T} P[y(t) \mid x, z_\tau = t] P(z_\tau = t \mid x).$$

A randomized experiment reveals the outcome distributions $P[y(t) \mid x]$, $t \in T$. For each value of t, the Law of Total Probability gives

$$(10.3) \quad \begin{aligned} P[y(t) \mid x] &= P[y(t) \mid x, z_\tau = t] P(z_\tau = t \mid x) \\ &\quad + P[y(t) \mid x, z_\tau \neq t] P(z_\tau \neq t \mid x). \end{aligned}$$

Thus $P[y(t) \mid x]$ is a mixture of the outcome distributions $P[y(t) \mid x, z_\tau = t]$ and $P[y(t) \mid x, z_\tau \neq t]$, with mixing probabilities $P(z_\tau = t \mid x)$ and $P(z_\tau \neq t \mid x)$.

If these mixing probabilities are known, identification of $P[y(t) \mid x, z_\tau = t]$ using knowledge of $P[y(t) \mid x]$ is the mixture decomposition problem of Chapter 5. To study identification of $P(y_\tau \mid x)$, one may first determine the identification regions for $P[y(t) \mid x, z_\tau = t]$, $t \in T$ and then apply the results to (10.2). If the mixing probabilities are unknown, study of the mixing problem requires other tools.

Section 10.2 uses a famous randomized experiment to illustrate the mixing problem and show the inferences that are possible with various assumptions. The remainder of the chapter presents the analysis underlying this illustration. To keep the analysis simple, I only consider identification of event probabilities in settings with two treatments and only provide proofs of sharp bounds rather than of identification regions. More general findings are presented in Manski (2003, chap. 10), which studies identification of parameters that respect stochastic dominance in settings with multiple treatments.

10.2 Extrapolation from the Perry Preschool Experiment

A notable early use of experiments with random assignment of treatments to evaluate antipoverty programs was the Perry Preschool Project begun in the early 1960s. Intensive educational and social services were provided to a random sample of about sixty black children, aged three and four, living in a low-income neighborhood of Ypsilanti, Michigan. No special services were provided to a second random sample of such children drawn to serve as a control group. The treatment and control groups were subsequently followed into adulthood. Among other things, it was found that 67 percent of the treatment group and 49 percent of the control group were high school graduates by age 19. This and similar findings for other outcomes have been cited widely as evidence that intensive early childhood educational interventions improve the outcomes of children at risk. See Berrueta-Clement et al. (1984) and Holden (1990).

Let $t = b$ be the educational and social services provided to children participating in the project, and let $t = a$ be the services available to children in the control group. Let $y(t)$ be a binary variable indicating high school graduation by age 19. For purposes of this illustration, consider the Perry Preschool Project to be a classical randomized experiment and ignore the fact that the sample sizes were small. With these idealizations, the data revealed that $P[y(b) = 1] = 0.67$ and $P[y(a) = 1] = 0.49$. Thus the high school graduation rate would be 0.67 if all children in the relevant population were to receive the services provided by the Perry Preschool Project and 0.49 if none of them were to receive these services.

The question is this: What does the experiment reveal about the high school graduation rate that would occur under a treatment rule in which some children receive the Perry Preschool services and the rest do not? For example, what would be the graduation rate if budget limitations were to require rationing of services? What would it be if some parents were to refuse to allow their children to receive the services?

Table 10.1 summarizes the inferences that can be made with the experimental evidence alone and with various assumptions. The remainder of this section discusses these findings.

Table 10.1   The Perry Preschool Project

Experimental evidence
$P[y(b) = 1 \mid x] = 0.67$ $P[y(a) = 1 \mid x] = 0.49$

Assumptions	Graduation rate
Experimental evidence alone	[0.16, 1]
Statistically independent outcomes	[0.33, 0.83]
Monotone treatment response	[0.49, 0.67]
Treatment at random	[0.49, 0.67]
Outcome maximization	[0.67, 1]
+ statistically independent outcomes	0.83
1/10 population receives treatment b	[0.39, 0.59]
5/10 population receives treatment b	[0.17, 0.99]
9/10 population receives treatment b	[0.57, 0.77]

Source: Manski (1997b), table 1.

Prediction Using the Empirical Evidence Alone

It might be conjectured that, if some children were to receive the Perry Preschool services and the rest were not, the high school graduation rate would necessarily lie between those observed in the Perry Preschool control and treatment groups, namely, 0.49 and 0.67. This conjecture is correct under certain assumptions but not in general.

The experiment alone reveals only that the graduation rate would lie between 0.16 and 1. To see why, observe that each member of the population has one of these four values for $[y(b), y(a)]$:

$$[y(b) = 0, y(a) = 0], \qquad [y(b) = 0, y(a) = 1],$$
$$[y(b) = 1, y(a) = 0], \qquad [y(b) = 1, y(a) = 1].$$

Treatment assignment has no impact on persons for whom $y(b) = y(a)$ but determines the outcomes of persons for whom $y(b) \neq y(a)$. The highest feasible graduation rate is attained by a treatment rule that always selects the treatment with the better graduation outcome, and so gives treatment b to each person with $[y(b) = 1, y(a) = 0]$ and treatment a to each person with $[y(b) = 0, y(a) = 1]$. Then the only persons who do not graduate are those with $[y(b) = 0, y(a) = 0]$, so the graduation rate is $1 - P[y(b) = 0, y(a) = 0]$. Symmetrically, the lowest feasible graduation rate is attained by a rule that, by design or error, gives treatment a to each person with $[y(b) = 1, y(a) = 0]$ and treatment b to each person with $[y(b) = 0, y(a) = 1]$. Then the only persons who graduate are those with $[y(b) = 1, y(a) = 1]$, so the graduation rate is $P[y(b) = 1, y(a) = 1]$.

The experiment does not reveal the joint probabilities $P[y(b) = 0, y(a) = 0]$ and $P[y(b) = 1, y(a) = 1]$, because treatments b and a are mutually exclusive. The experiment does reveal the marginal probabilities $P[y(b) = 1] = 0.67$ and $P[y(a) = 1] = 0.49$. It can be shown that among all joint distributions $P[y(b), y(a)]$ that are consistent with these marginals, there is one that minimizes both $P[y(b) = 0, y(a) = 0]$ and $P[y(b) = 1, y(a) = 1]$. This is

$$P[y(b) = 0, y(a) = 0] = 0, \qquad P[y(b) = 0, y(a) = 1] = 0.33,$$
$$P[y(b) = 1, y(a) = 0] = 0.51, \qquad P[y(b) = 1, y(a) = 1] = 0.16.$$

Hence the highest and lowest graduation rates consistent with the experimental evidence are 1 and 0.16. The above argument is formalized in Section 10.3.

Prediction with Assumptions

The interval [0.16, 1] is the worst-case bound on the graduation rate, obtained without any assumptions on treatment response or on the treatment rule that might be used in practice. Combining the evidence with assumptions can narrow the range of possible graduation rates.

Consider assumptions on treatment response. One might assume that being treated by the preschool intervention can never harm a child's schooling prospects; that is, treatment response is monotone, with $y(b) \geq y(a)$ for all children. If so, the graduation rate must lie between those observed in the control and treatment groups, namely, 0.49 and 0.67. A more neutral assumption might be that outcomes $y(b)$ and $y(a)$ are statistically independent of one another. This implies that the graduation rate must lie between 0.33 and 0.83. These results are proved in Section 10.4.

Consider assumptions on the treatment rule. Perhaps treatment decisions will be made by omniscient parents or social workers who choose for each child the treatment yielding the better outcome. This outcome-optimization assumption implies that the graduation rate must lie between 0.67 and 1. On the other hand suppose that treatments will be selected at random, with unknown selection probabilities. Then the graduation rate must lie between the 0.49 and 0.67 observed in the control and treatment groups.

It may be that resource constraints limit implementation of the intervention to part of the population. Suppose that one knows the fraction of the population receiving the intervention but does not know the composition of the treated and untreated subpopulations. As Table 10.1 shows, knowing that 1/10 or 5/10 or 9/10 of the population receives the intervention implies that the graduation rate must lie in the interval [0.39, 0.59] or [0.17, 0.99] or [0.57, 0.77], respectively. The first and third intervals are relatively narrow, but the second is rather wide, almost as wide as the interval found using the experimental evidence alone. This pattern of results reflects the fact that discretion in selecting treatments is much more constrained when the fraction of the population receiving the intervention is fixed at a value near zero or one than when it is fixed at 5/10. See Section 10.5.

The scenarios considered thus far bound the high school graduation rate but do not point-identify it. By combining assumptions, the graduation rate can be point-identified. For example, assume that $y(b)$ and $y(a)$ are statistically independent of one another and that each child receives the treatment yielding the better outcome. Then the implied graduation rate is 0.83. See Section 10.6.

The general lesson is that experimental evidence alone permits only weak conclusions to be drawn about the high school graduation rate when treatments vary. Experimental evidence combined with assumptions yields stronger conclusions. The nature of these stronger conclusions depends critically on the assumptions imposed.

10.3 Identification of Event Probabilities with the Experimental Evidence Alone

Let B be a subset of outcome space Y. I show here and in the sections that follow what experimental evidence and various assumptions imply about the event probability $P(y_\tau \in B \mid x)$ when there are two treatments, say, a and b. The analysis in this section makes no assumptions about the response functions $y(\cdot)$ or the treatment rule τ. To simplify the notation, I suppress the conditioning covariates x.

Define $C \equiv P[y(b) \in B] + P[y(a) \in B]$. Using the experimental evidence alone, the sharp bound on $P(y_\tau \in B)$ is

$$(10.4) \quad \max(0, C - 1) \le P(y_\tau \in B) \le \min(C, 1).$$

This result formalizes the reasoning in the Perry Preschool illustration. There $B = \{1\}$, $P[y(a) \in B] = 0.49$, $P[y(b) \in B] = 0.67$, and $C = 1.16$.

Proof of (10.4) The largest possible value of $P(y_\tau \in B)$ is $1 - P[y(b) \notin B \cap y(a) \notin B]$. This is achieved by a rule that always chooses a treatment whose outcome lies in B, when such a treatment exists. The smallest possible value of $P(y_\tau \in B)$ is $P[y(b) \in B \cap y(a) \in B]$. This is achieved by a rule that always chooses a treatment whose outcome lies in the complement of B, when such a treatment exists. Thus $P(y_\tau \in B)$ must lie in the interval

(10.5)
$$P[y(b) \in B \cap y(a) \in B] \leq P(y_\tau \in B)$$
$$\leq 1 - P[y(b) \notin B \cap y(a) \notin B].$$

If the joint distribution $P[y(a), y(b)]$ were known, (10.5) would be the sharp bound on $P(y_\tau \in B)$. We are concerned, however, with the situation in which only the marginals $P[y(b)]$ and $P[y(a)]$ are known. In this situation, the sharp lower bound on $P(y_\tau \in B)$ is the smallest value of $P[y(b) \in B \cap y(a) \in B]$ that is consistent with the known $P[y(b)]$ and $P[y(a)]$. The sharp upper bound is one minus the smallest feasible value of $P[y(b) \notin B \cap y(a) \notin B]$.

Let $A \subset Y$. It can be shown that knowledge of the marginals $P[y(b)]$ and $P[y(a)]$ implies this sharp bound on $P[y(b) \in A \cap y(a) \in A]$:

(10.6)
$$\max\{0, P[y(b) \in A] + P[y(a) \in A] - 1\}$$
$$\leq P[y(b) \in A \cap y(a) \in A]$$
$$\leq \min\{P[y(b) \in A], P[y(a) \in A]\}.$$

Application of the lower bound in (10.6) with $A = B$ yields the lower bound on $P(y_\tau \in B)$ in (10.4). Application of the lower bound in (10.6) with $A = Y - B$ yields the upper bound.

Inequality (10.6) was proved by Fréchet (1951); see Ord (1972) for an exposition. It is elementary to show that $P[y(b) \in A \cap y(a) \in A]$ must lie within the bound. The upper bound holds because the event $[y(b) \in A \cap y(a) \in A]$ implies each of its component events $[y(b) \in A]$ and $[y(a) \in A]$. The lower bound holds because

$$1 \geq P[y(b) \in A \cup y(a) \in A]$$
$$= P[y(b) \in A] + P[y(a) \in A] - P[y(b) \in A \cap y(a) \in A].$$

Fréchet's general analysis of the problem of inference on a joint distribution from knowledge of its marginals shows that bound (10.6) is sharp. ❏

Observe that the bound on $P(y_\tau \in B)$ is informative from the left or the right but not from both sides simultaneously. The width of the bound narrows toward 0 as C approaches 0 or 2, but it widens toward 1 as C approaches 1. Thus knowledge of the marginals may reveal a lot or a little about the magnitude of $P(y_\tau \in B)$, depending on the empirical value of C.

10.4 Treatment Response Assumptions

The proof of result (10.4) showed that, if the joint distribution $P[y(b), y(a)]$ is known, then inequality (10.5) gives the sharp bound on $P(y_\tau \in B)$. Treatment response assumptions can make this bound computable. This section presents two cases.

Statistically Independent Outcomes

Assume that outcomes $y(b)$ and $y(a)$ are statistically independent of one another; thus,

(10.7) $P[y(b), y(a)] = P[y(b)] P[y(a)].$

The experimental evidence reveals $P[y(b)]$ and $P[y(a)]$, so (10.5) gives the sharp bound on $P(y_\tau \in B)$. The bound is

(10.8)
$$P[y(b) \in B] P[y(a) \in B]$$
$$\leq P(y_\tau \in B) \leq 1 - P[y(b) \notin B] P[y(a) \notin B].$$

Application of this bound to the Perry Preschool illustration gives $0.33 \leq P(y_\tau = 1) \leq 0.83$.

Monotone Treatment Response

Assume now that treatment response is monotone, with $y_j(b) \geq y_j(a)$ for all persons j. Note that the knowledge of $P[y(b)]$ and $P[y(a)]$ obtained from a classical experiment makes this assumption a refutable hypothesis. If assumption MTR holds, distribution $P[y(b)]$ stochastically dominates $P[y(a)]$.

Let y_0 be the smallest feasible value of y and let the set B have the form $B = [y_0, r]$ for some real number r. Assumption MTR implies that

(10.9) $P[y(b) \le r \cap y(a) \le r] = P[y(b) \le r]$.

Thus the experimental evidence and assumption MTR together reveal $P[y(b) \le r \cap y(a) \le r]$. Hence the sharp bound on $P(y_\tau \le r)$ is again given by (10.5), which now takes the form

(10.10) $P[y(b) \le r] \le P(y_\tau \le r) \le P[y(a) \le r]$.

This result can be applied to the Perry Preschool illustration by setting $r = 0$ and observing that $P(y_\tau = 1) = 1 - P(y_\tau < 0)$ in that setting. The resulting bound is $0.49 \le P(y_\tau = 1) \le 0.67$.

10.5 Treatment Rule Assumptions

This section shows the identifying power of assumptions that restrict the treatment rule that might be used in practice. I first suppose that treatment is statistically independent of outcomes, as in a classical experiment. I then suppose that the treatment with the better outcome is chosen. The section also examines inference when the fraction of the population receiving each treatment is known but nothing is known about the composition of the subpopulations receiving each treatment.

Treatment at Random

Assume that, under rule τ, the treatment z_τ received by each person is statistically independent of the person's outcomes $[y(b), y(a)]$. That is,

(10.11) $P[y(b), y(a) \mid z_\tau] = P[y(b), y(a)]$.

Then equation (10.2) reduces to

(10.12) $P(y_\tau) = P[y(b)] P(z_\tau = b) + P[y(a)] P(z_\tau = a)$.

If the fractions $P(z_\tau)$ of the population receiving each treatment are known, then $P(y_\tau)$ is point-identified. If $P(z_\tau)$ is not known, (10.12)

implies that $P(y_\tau \in B)$ must lie between $P[y(b) \in B]$ and $P[y(a) \in B]$. Thus the sharp bound on $P(y_\tau \in B)$ is

$$
\min\{P[y(b) \in B], P[y(a) \in B]\}
$$
$$
\leq P(y_\tau \in B) \leq \max\{P[y(b) \in B], P[y(a) \in B]\}.
$$

(10.13)

In the Perry Preschool illustration, this bound is $0.49 \leq P(y_\tau = 1) \leq 0.67$.

Outcome Optimization

Assume now that rule τ selects the treatment with the better outcome, so $y_\tau = \max[y(b), y(a)]$. For any value of r, this rule implies that

$$(10.14) \quad P(y_\tau \leq r) = P[y(b) \leq r \cap y(a) \leq r].$$

The experimental evidence does not point-identify the right-hand side of (10.14), but the Fréchet bound (10.6) yields

$$
\max\{0, P[y(b) \leq r] + P[y(a) \leq r] - 1\}
$$
$$
\leq P[y(b) \leq r \cap y(a) \leq r]
$$
$$
\leq \min\{P[y(b) \leq r], P[y(a) \leq r]\}.
$$

(10.15)

Hence we obtain this sharp bound on $P(y_\tau \leq r)$:

$$
\max\{0, P[y(b) \leq r] + P[y(a) \leq r] - 1\}
$$
$$
\leq P(y_\tau \leq r) \leq \min\{P[y(b) \leq r], P[y(a) \leq r]\}.
$$

(10.16)

This finding can be applied to the Perry Preschool illustration by again setting $r = 0$ and observing that $P(y_\tau = 1) = 1 - P(y_\tau \leq 0)$ in that setting. The result is $0.67 \leq P(y_\tau = 1) \leq 1$.

Known Treatment Shares

The assumptions examined so far in this section specify the rule used to select treatments but do not directly constrain the fraction of the population receiving each treatment. It is also of interest to consider the reverse situation, where one knows the fraction receiving each treatment but does not know the treatment rule. For example, I noted earlier that resource constraints could limit implementation of the Perry Preschool treatment to part of the eligible population. Knowledge of the budget constraint and the cost of preschooling would suffice to determine the fraction of the population receiving the treatment. It may be more diffi-cult to learn how school officials, social workers, and parents interact to determine which children receive the treatment.

Suppose that a known fraction p of the population receive treatment a and that the remaining fraction $1 - p$ receive treatment b. So

(10.17) $\quad P(z_\tau = a) = p.$

By the Law of Total Probability,

(10.18)
$$P(y_\tau \in B) = P[y(b) \in B \mid z_\tau = b](1 - p)$$
$$+ P[y(a) \subset B \mid z_\tau = a]p.$$

The experimental evidence is informative about $P[y(b) \in B \mid z_\tau = b]$ and $P[y(a) \in B \mid z_\tau = a]$ because

(10.19)
$$P[y(b) \in B] = P[y(b) \in B \mid z_\tau = b](1 - p)$$
$$\mid P[y(b) \in B \mid z_\tau = a]p,$$

(10.20)
$$P[y(a) \in B] = P[y(a) \in B \mid z_\tau = b](1 - p)$$
$$+ P[y(a) \in B \mid z_\tau = a]p.$$

Analysis of the mixture decomposition problem in Section 5.2 shows that knowledge of $P[y(b)]$ and p places $P[y(b) \in B \mid z_\tau = b]$ in the iden-tification region

(10.21)
$$H\{P[y(b) \in B \mid z_\tau = b]\}$$
$$= [0, 1] \cap [\{P[y(b) \in B] - p\}/(1 - p), P[y(b) \in B]/(1 - p)],$$

which is an application of (5.10). Similarly,

(10.22)
$$H\{P[y(a) \in B \mid z_\tau = a]\}$$
$$= [0, 1] \cap [\{P[y(a) \in B] - (1 - p)\}/p, P[y(a) \in B]/p].$$

Application of these results to (10.18) yields

$$\max\{0, P[y(b) \in B] - p\} + \max\{0, P[y(a) \in B] - (1-p)\}$$
$$(10.23) \qquad \leq P(y_\tau \in B) \leq \min\{1-p, P[y(b) \in B]\}$$
$$+ \min\{p, P[y(a) \in B]\}.$$

Table 10.1 reports this bound in the Perry Preschool illustration for several values of p.

10.6 Combining Assumptions

Taken one at a time, the assumptions examined in Sections 10.4 and 10.5 improve the worst-case bound of Section 10.3 but are not strong enough to point-identify the outcome distribution under rule τ. Various combinations of these assumptions can point-identify $P(y_\tau)$. Here are two possibilities.

Suppose one knows that rule τ will make treatment selection random and one also knows the fraction p of the population who will receive treatment a. These two assumptions together imply that

$$(10.24) \quad P(y_\tau) = P[y(b)](1-p) + P[y(a)]p.$$

All the quantities on the right-hand side are known, so $P(y_\tau)$ is point-identified. In the Perry Preschool illustration, $P(y_\tau = 1) = (0.67)(1-p) + (0.49)p$.

Alternatively, assume that outcomes $y(b)$ and $y(a)$ are statistically independent of one another and also that the treatment with the larger outcome will always be selected. Then

$$(10.25) \quad P(y_\tau \leq r) = P[y(b) \leq r]P[y(a) \leq r]$$

for all values of r. In the Perry Preschool illustration, this gives $P(y_\tau = 1) = 0.83$.

11

Planning under Ambiguity

11.1 Studying Treatment Response to Inform Treatment Choice

An important practical objective of empirical studies of treatment response is to provide decision makers with information useful in choosing treatments. Often the decision maker is a planner who must choose treatments for a heterogeneous population. The planner may want to choose treatments whose outcomes maximize the welfare of this population.

Consider, for example, a physician choosing medical treatments for a population of patients. The physician may observe each patient's demographic attributes, medical history, and the results of diagnostic tests. He may then choose a treatment rule that makes treatment a function of these covariates. If the physician acts on behalf of his patients, the outcome of interest may measure patient health status, and welfare may measure health status minus the cost of treatment, in comparable units.

Or consider a judge choosing sentences for a population of convicted offenders. The judge may observe each offender's past criminal record, demeanor in court, and other attributes. Subject to legislated sentencing guidelines, she may consider these covariates when choosing sentences. If the judge acts on behalf of society, the outcome of interest may measure recidivism, and social welfare may decrease with recidivism and the cost of carrying out a sentence.

Variation in treatment with observed covariates is such a common planning practice that several terms are used to describe it. In public discourse, this practice may be described as *screening* or *profiling*. In the professional literature on the economics of information, it is often called *statistical discrimination*.

Empirical studies of treatment response are useful to planners to the extent that they reveal how outcomes vary with treatments and observable covariates. Identification problems and the necessity of statistical inference from sample data prevent attainment of complete knowledge of treatment response. Hence it is important to ask how a planner with partial knowledge of treatment response might reasonably make treatment choices. This chapter studies planning when the distribution of treatment response is partially identified. Chapter 12 examines planning with sample data.

It has been traditional in evaluation of social policy to distinguish between the researchers who analyze treatment response and the planners who make policy. To study treatment choice with partial knowledge of treatment response, it is productive to eliminate this distinction and consider a planner who performs his own research in service of treatment choice. Thus this chapter and the next take the perspective of a planner who observes a study population, combines the empirical evidence on treatment response with assumptions that he deems credible, and then chooses treatments for the population of interest.

Partial Identification and Ambiguity

Economists who study social planning generally regard treatment choice as an optimization problem. They assume that the planner knows the distribution of treatment response and chooses a treatment rule to maximize social welfare. For example, economists studying optimal income taxation assume the planner knows how the tax schedule affects the distribution of labor supply (e.g., Mirrlees, 1971). Those studying optimal criminal justice systems assume the planner knows how policing and sanctions affect offense rates (e.g., Polinsky and Shavell, 2000).

In these and other domains, an actual planner may have only partial knowledge of the distribution of treatment response. As a consequence, he may not be able to determine an optimal policy. Such a planner faces a problem of treatment choice under *ambiguity*.

Semantics A decision maker with a partially known objective function is said to face a problem of choice under ambiguity. The term *ambiguity* appears to have originated with Ellsberg (1961), who sought to understand choice behavior in situations where an objective function depends on an unknown probability distribution. In a famous thought experiment, he asked subjects to draw a ball from either of two urns, one with a known distribution of colors and the other with an unknown distribution of colors.

The term *ambiguity* is used widely in decision theory today; see, for example, Einhorn and Hogarth (1986) and Camerer and Weber (1992). However, this is not universal. Some authors have used *ignorance* as a synonym for ambiguity (e.g., Arrow and Hurwicz, 1972, and Maskin, 1979). Much earlier, Keynes (1921) and Knight (1921) used the word *uncertainty* to describe decision problems with completely unknown probability distributions. Referring to the latter author, some modern researchers use the expression *Knightian uncertainty*. ❏

Problems of partial identification that arise in the empirical analysis of treatment response can generate ambiguity about the identity of optimal treatment rules. This chapter shows how. Section 11.2 introduces basic concepts used to study choice under ambiguity. As an initial illustration, Section 11.3 considers treatment choice using data from a randomized experiment with partial compliance.

Section 11.4 lays out in broad terms an additive optimization problem that a planner might want to solve. Section 11.5 considers how the planner might approach this problem with partial knowledge of treatment response. To further illustrate ideas, Section 11.6 shows how the selection problem of Chapter 7 generates ambiguity and discusses how a planner might reasonably make treatment choices using the empirical evidence alone. Other illustrative case studies are reported in Brock (2006) and Manski (2006).

Some of the treatment rules studied in this chapter are *fractional* rules that allocate observational identical persons to different treatments. Section 11.7 discusses an ethical issue that arises in application of such rules. Finally, Section 11.8 discusses decentralized treatment choice as an alternative to social planning.

11.2 Criteria for Choice under Ambiguity

Here is the problem of choice under ambiguity, in abstraction. We begin with a choice set C and a decision maker who must choose an action from this set. The decision maker wants to maximize an objective function $f(\cdot): C \to R$ that maps actions into real-valued outcomes. The decision maker faces a standard optimization problem if he knows the choice set and the objective function. He faces a problem of choice under ambiguity if he knows the choice set but not the objective function. Instead, he knows only that $f(\cdot) \in F$, where F is some set of possible objective functions.

Dominance

How should the decision maker choose among the feasible actions? Clearly, he should not choose a *dominated* action. Action $d \in C$ is said to be dominated if there exists another feasible action, say, c, that is at least as good as d for all objective functions in F and strictly better for some function in F. Formally, d is dominated if there exists a c such that $g(d) \leq g(c)$ for all $g(\cdot) \in F$ and $g(d) < g(c)$ for some $g(\cdot) \in F$.

Let D denote the undominated subset of C. How should the decision maker choose among the elements of D? Let c and d be two undominated actions. Then either $[g(c) = g(d)$, all $g(\cdot) \in F]$ or there exist $g'(\cdot) \in F$ and $g''(\cdot) \in F$ such that $g'(c) > g'(d)$ and $g''(c) < g''(d)$. In the former case, c and d are equally good choices and the decision maker is indifferent between them. In the latter case, the decision maker cannot order the two actions. Action c may yield a better or worse outcome than action d; the decision maker cannot say which. Thus the normative question "How should the decision maker choose?" has no unambiguously correct answer.

Indeed, a basic tenet of optimization theory breaks down. Consider the effect on welfare of adding a new feasible action, say, e, to the choice set. In an optimization problem, expansion of the choice set from C

to $C \cup e$ cannot decrease welfare, because the decision maker will not choose e if C contains a better action c. Under ambiguity, expansion of the choice set may decrease welfare. Suppose that e neither dominates nor is dominated by any element of D, so the new set of undominated actions is $D \cup e$. Then the decision maker may choose e, yet it may be that $f(e) < f(c)$.

Although there is no optimal choice among undominated actions, decision theorists have not wanted to abandon the idea of optimization. So they have proposed various ways of transforming the unknown objective function $f(\cdot)$ into a known function, say, $h(\cdot)$, that can be maximized. In principle, one should maximize this function only over the undominated actions D. However, it often is difficult to determine which actions are undominated. Hence the usual practice is to perform the maximization over the full set C of feasible actions.

One leading idea is to average the elements of F and maximize the resulting function. This yields Bayes decision rules. Another is to seek an action that, in some well-defined sense, works uniformly well over all elements of F. This yields the maximin and minimax-regret criteria.

Bayes Decisions

Bayesian decision theorists suggest that a decision maker who knows only that $f(\cdot) \in F$ should choose an action that maximizes some average of the elements of F. Let π be a specified probability distribution over the elements of F. For each feasible action c, let $h(c)$ be the mean value of $g(c)$ across the feasible functions $g(\cdot)$, the mean being calculated with respect to π. Formally, this is the integral $h(c) \equiv \int g(c)d\pi$. The Bayes criterion with respect to π chooses an action that maximizes this $h(\cdot)$. Thus a Bayes decision with respect to π solves the optimization problem

$$(11.1) \quad \max_{c \in C} \int g(c)d\pi.$$

In general, Bayes decisions depend on the distribution π placed on F. Bayesian decision theorists recommend that π should express the decision maker's personal beliefs about where $f(\cdot)$ lies within F. For this reason, π is called a *subjective* probability distribution or a *prior* distribution.

Bayesians offer various rationality arguments for use of a Bayes criterion. The most basic of these is that Bayes decisions generally are undominated, provided that the expectations $\int g(\cdot)d\pi$ are finite (Berger, 1985, p. 253). This and other rationality arguments do not, however, answer the decision maker's bottom-line question: How well does the rule perform?

Consider, for example, the famous axiomatic approach of Savage (1954). Savage shows that a decision maker whose choices are consistent with certain axioms can be interpreted as using a Bayes decision rule. Many decision theorists consider the Savage axioms to be appealing. Acting in a manner that is consistent with these axioms does not, however, imply that chosen actions yield good outcomes. Berger (1985) calls attention to this, stating (p. 121): "A Bayesian analysis may be 'rational' in the weak axiomatic sense, yet be terrible in a practical sense if an inappropriate prior distribution is used."

A common practice is to act as if one knows $f(\cdot)$. One may admit to not knowing $f(\cdot)$ but nevertheless argue that pragmatism requires making some "reasonable," "plausible," or "convenient" assumption. Thus one somehow imputes the objective function and then chooses an action that is optimal under the imputed function. Formally, an *imputation rule* selects some $h(\cdot) \in F$ and chooses an action that maximizes this $h(\cdot)$. Imputation rules are special cases of Bayes rules that place probability one on a single element of F.

Maximin Criterion

The maximin criterion suggests that the decision maker choose an action that maximizes the minimum welfare attainable under the functions in F. For each feasible action c, let $h(c)$ be the minimum value of $g(c)$ across the feasible functions $g(\cdot)$. This is $h(c) \equiv min_{g(\cdot)\in F}g(c)$. A maximin rule chooses an action that maximizes this $h(\cdot)$. Thus a maximin rule solves the optimization problem

$$(11.2) \quad \max_{c\in C} \min_{g(\cdot)\in F} g(c).$$

The maximin criterion has a clear normative foundation in *competitive games*. In a competitive game, the decision maker chooses an action from C. Then a function from F is chosen by an opponent whose objective is to minimize the realized outcome. A decision maker who knows that he is a participant in a competitive game does not face ambiguity. He faces the problem of maximizing the known function $h(\cdot)$ specified in the maximin rule.

There is no compelling reason why the decision maker should or should not use a maximin rule when $f(\cdot)$ is a fixed but unknown objective function. In this setting, the appeal of the maximin criterion is a personal rather than normative matter. Some decision makers may deem it essential to protect against worst-case scenarios, while others may not. Wald (1950), who studied the maximin criterion in depth, did not contend that a maximin rule is optimal, only that it is "reasonable." Considering the case in which the objective is to minimize rather than maximize $f(\cdot)$, he wrote (p. 18): "a minimax solution seems, in general, to be a reasonable solution of the decision problem."

Minimax-Regret Criterion

The minimax-regret criterion suggests that the decision maker choose an action that minimizes the maximum loss to welfare that results from not knowing the objective function. The idea is simple in concept, but it requires a bit more work to describe formally than was the case with the Bayes and maximin criteria.

Imagine that the decision maker chooses some action c and that the objective function is some $g(\cdot)$. The loss in potential welfare resulting from choice of this action is $\max_{d \in C} g(d) - g(c)$. This loss, called *regret*, is the nonnegative difference between the maximum welfare attainable with objective function $g(\cdot)$ and the welfare attained by choice of c.

The true objective function is unknown, but we can compute the maximum regret of action c over all feasible functions $g(\cdot)$. This is $h(c) \equiv \max_{g(\cdot) \in F}[\max_{d \in C} g(d) - g(c)]$. A minimax-regret rule chooses an action that minimizes this $h(\cdot)$. Thus a minimax-regret rule solves the optimization problem

$$(11.3) \quad \min_{c \in C} \max_{g(\cdot) \in F} [\max_{d \in C} g(d) - g(c)].$$

The maximin and minimax-regret criteria are sometimes confused with one another. Comparison of (11.2) and (11.3) shows that they are generally distinct, and Section 11.3 will give a dramatic illustration of this. The two criteria are the same only in special cases. Suppose in particular that the quantity $\max_{d \in C} g(d)$ is constant for all feasible $g(\cdot)$, say, with value K. Then the maximum regret of action c is

$$\max_{g(\cdot) \in F} [\max_{d \in C} g(d) - g(c)] = \max_{g(\cdot) \in F} [K - g(c)] = K - \min_{g(\cdot) \in F} g(c).$$

The constant K does not affect the minimax-regret criterion, which requires choice of an action $c \in C$ that minimizes $- \min_{g(\cdot) \in F} g(c)$. This is the same as the maximin criterion.

11.3 Treatment Using Data from an Experiment with Partial Compliance

This section illustrates treatment choice under ambiguity in an instructive simple setting, before we go on to consider a broader class of choice problems.

Consider a partial-compliance situation of the type addressed in Section 7.4. There are two treatments, a status quo labeled $t = a$ and an innovation labeled $t = b$. The outcome of interest is binary, with $y(t) = 1$ denoting success of treatment t and $y(t) = 0$ denoting failure. There are no observed covariates.

A randomized experiment is performed on a study population. Subjects assigned to the innovation can refuse to comply and choose the status quo treatment instead. Those assigned to the status quo cannot cross over to receive the innovation. Section 7.4 showed that the empirical evidence point-identifies $P[y(a) = 1]$ but only partially identifies $P[y(b) = 1]$. By equation (7.12), its identification region is the interval

$$H\{P[y(b) = 1]\}$$

(11.4)
$$= \left[P(y = 1 \mid \zeta = b, z = b) \, P(z = b \mid \zeta = b), \right.$$
$$P(y = 1 \mid \zeta = b, z = b) \, P(z = b \mid \zeta = b)$$
$$\left. + P(z \neq b \mid \zeta = b) \right],$$

where ζ is the treatment that a subject is assigned and z is the treatment that he receives.

Consider a planner who must choose treatments for a new population known to be identical to the study population in its distribution of

treatment response. The planner's objective is to maximize the rate of treatment success. Suppose that the planner can mandate treatments in the new population, so noncompliance is not a concern there.

In this setting, one feasible treatment rule assigns the innovation to all members of the treatment population and another assigns everyone to the status quo. The feasible rules also include *fractional* treatment allocations, which randomly assign the innovation to a specified fraction of the population and the status quo to the remainder. Let $U(\delta, P)$ denote the social welfare attained by assigning a fraction δ of the population to the innovation and $1 - \delta$ to the status quo, P being the population distribution of treatment response. Let $\alpha \equiv P[y(a) = 1]$ and $\beta = P[y(b) = 1]$. Then

(11.5) $U(\delta, P) = \alpha(1 - \delta) + \beta\delta = \alpha + (\beta - \alpha)\delta.$

The planner would like to solve the optimization problem $\max_{\delta \in [0, 1]} U(\delta, P)$. An optimal rule assigns everyone to the innovation if $\beta > \alpha$ and everyone to the status quo if $\alpha > \beta$. All treatment allocations are equally good if $\beta = \alpha$. In any case, the maximum attainable value of social welfare is $\max(\alpha, \beta)$.

The problem of interest is treatment choice when the planner knows α but only knows that β lies in the interval $[\beta_L, \beta_U]$, where

(11.6a) $\beta_L \equiv P(y = 1 \mid \zeta = b, z = b) \, P(z = b \mid \zeta = b),$

(11.6b)
$\beta_U \equiv P(y = 1 \mid \zeta = b, z = b) \, P(z = b \mid \zeta = b)$
$\quad + P(z \neq b \mid \zeta = b)$

are the lower and upper bounds of the identification region for β. Rule $\delta = 1$ dominates all other treatment allocations if $\alpha \leq \beta_L$, and $\delta = 0$ dominates all other allocations if $\alpha \geq \beta_U$. In the former case, the planner knows that $\beta \geq \alpha$ even though he does not know the exact value of β. In the latter case, he knows that $\alpha \geq \beta$.

The planner faces a problem of treatment choice under ambiguity if $\beta_L < \alpha < \beta_U$. In this case the planner does not know the ordering of α and β, so all treatment allocations are undominated. To choose an allocation, the planner might apply a Bayes rule, the maximin criterion, or the minimax-regret criterion. These approaches yield different results, as follows.

Bayes Rules A Bayesian planner places a subjective probability distribution π on the interval $[\beta_L, \beta_U]$, computes the subjective mean value of social welfare, and chooses a treatment allocation that maximizes this subjective mean. Thus the planner solves the optimization problem

$$(11.7) \quad \max_{\delta \in [0, 1]} \alpha + [E_\pi(\beta) - \alpha]\delta,$$

where $E_\pi(\beta) = \int \beta d\pi$ is the subjective mean of β. Problem (11.7) is identical in form to the original problem $\max_{\delta \in [0, 1]} U(\delta, P)$, with $E_\pi(\beta)$ replacing β. The Bayes decision assigns everyone to the innovation if $E_\pi(\beta) > \alpha$ and everyone to the status quo if $\alpha > E_\pi(\beta)$. All treatment allocations are Bayes decisions if $E_\pi(\beta) = \alpha$.

Maximin Criterion A maximin planner acts as if β equals β_L, its smallest feasible value. Thus the planner solves the optimization problem

$$(11.8) \quad \max_{\delta \in [0, 1]} \alpha + (\beta_L - \alpha)\delta.$$

Problem (11.8) has the same form as $\max_{\delta \in [0, 1]} U(\delta, P)$, with β_L replacing β. We are considering cases with $\beta_L < \alpha < \beta_U$, so the maximin treatment allocation is $\delta = 0$, which assigns everyone to the status quo.

Minimax-Regret Criterion Suppose that the planner chooses allocation δ. The resulting regret at a specified value of β is

$$\max(\alpha, \beta) - [\alpha + (\beta - \alpha)\delta]$$
$$= (\alpha - \beta)\delta \cdot 1[\beta < \alpha] + (\beta - \alpha)(1 - \delta) \cdot 1[\beta > \alpha].$$

Maximum regret across all the feasible values of β is

$$\max_{\beta \in [\beta_L, \beta_U]} (\alpha - \beta)\delta \cdot 1[\beta < \alpha] + (\beta - \alpha)(1 - \delta) \cdot 1[\beta > \alpha]$$
$$= \max[(\alpha - \beta_L)\delta, (\beta_U - \alpha)(1 - \delta)].$$

Thus a minimax-regret rule solves the optimization problem

$$(11.9) \quad \min_{\delta \in [0,1]} \max \left[(\alpha - \beta_L)\delta, (\beta_U - \alpha)(1 - \delta) \right].$$

The quantity $(\alpha - \beta_L)\delta$ is increasing in δ, whereas $(\beta_U - \alpha)(1 - \delta)$ is decreasing in δ. The solution to (11.9) is obtained by choosing δ to equalize these two quantities. This gives the minimax-regret treatment allocation

$$(11.10) \quad \delta_{MR} = (\beta_U - \alpha)/(\beta_U - \beta_L).$$

Observe that the minimax-regret allocation is fractional. The fraction of the population assigned to the innovation depends on the location of α within the interval $[\beta_L, \beta_U]$, with δ_{MR} decreasing linearly from one to zero as α increases from β_L to β_U. Complement 11A shows that minimax-regret allocations are always fractional in planning problems with two undominated treatments.

The Illinois UI Experiment

To illustrate, recall the Illinois Unemployment Insurance (UI) Experiment discussed in Section 7.4. The status quo treatment is conventional UI, and the innovation is UI with a wage subsidy. Let $y(t) = 1$ if an unemployed person is rehired within 11 weeks and $y(t) = 0$ otherwise. Dubin and Rivers (1993, table 1) report that

$$\alpha = 0.35 \qquad P(y = 1 \mid \zeta = b, z = b) = 0.38$$
$$P(z = b \mid \zeta = b) = 0.68.$$

Hence $\beta_L = 0.26$ and $\beta_U = 0.58$.

Suppose that the objective is to maximize the fraction of unemployed persons who are rehired within 11 weeks. A Bayes rule assigns everyone to UI with the wage subsidy if $E_\pi(\beta) > 0.35$ and everyone to conventional UI if $E_\pi(\beta) < 0.35$. The maximin rule assigns everyone to conventional UI. The minimax-regret rule assigns 72 percent of all unemployed persons to UI with the wage subsidy and 28 percent to conventional UI.

11.4 An Additive Planning Problem

The treatment choice problem of Section 11.3 is an elementary member
of a broad class of additive planning problems with partial knowledge
of treatment response. The word "additive" here means that social welfare adds together individual welfare terms across the members of the
population. An important special case is *utilitarian* planning, where the
planner's perspective on individual welfare is the same as the perspective
that the members of the population hold for themselves.

I now develop this class of problems. Here I lay out the optimization
problem that the planner would like to solve. Section 11.5 considers
the planner's situation when the distribution of treatment response is
partially identified.

The Choice Set

Suppose that a planner must choose a treatment rule assigning a treatment to each member of a population. The planner observes certain
covariates $x_j \in X$ for each member j of the population. For simplicity, suppose that the covariate space X has finitely many elements and
that $P(x = \xi) > 0$ for all $\xi \in X$. The planner can differentiate persons
with different values of x, but he cannot distinguish among persons
with the same observed covariates. Hence a feasible treatment rule assigns all persons with the same observed covariates to one treatment
or fractionally allocates these persons across treatments in a random
manner.

Formally, let Δ denote the space of functions $\delta(\cdot, \cdot)$ that map $T \times X$
into the unit interval and whose values sum to one across the elements
of T; that is, $\sum_{t \in T} \delta(t, \xi) = 1$ for all $\xi \in X$. The feasible treatment rules
are the elements of Δ.

An important subclass of Δ are the *singleton rules* that assign all
persons with the same observed covariates to one treatment. Thus $\delta(\cdot, \cdot)$
is a singleton rule if, for each $\xi \in X$, $\delta(t, \xi) = 1$ for some $t \in T$ and
$\delta(s, \xi) = 0$ for all $s \neq t$. Nonsingleton fractional rules randomly allocate
persons with covariates ξ across multiple treatments, with assignment
shares $[\delta(t, \xi), t \in T]$.

In some settings, a planner may not be permitted to use certain
covariates (say, race or gender) to assign treatments. If so, the present
description of the choice set remains accurate if x is defined to be the

covariates that the planner is permitted to use, rather than the full vector of covariates that the planner observes.

Objective Function and Optimal Treatment Rule

Suppose that the planner wants to choose a feasible treatment rule that maximizes population mean welfare. The welfare from assigning treatment t to person j is $u_j(t) \equiv u[y_j(t), t, x_j]$. Thus welfare may depend on the treatment a person receives, the outcome of that treatment, and the person's covariates. The planner knows the form of the welfare function $u(\cdot, \cdot, \cdot)$ and he observes x_j. However, he does not observe the potential outcomes $[y_j(t), t \in T]$.

Example Economists often assume welfare to have the "benefit-cost" form $u[y(t), t, x] = y(t) - c(t, x)$, where $c(t, x)$ is the real-valued cost of assigning treatment t to a person with covariates x and $y(t)$ is the real-valued benefit of this treatment. In the case of a physician, $y_j(t)$ may measure the health status of patient j following receipt of treatment t, and $c(t, x_j)$ may be the cost of treatment. At the time of treatment choice, the physician may know the costs of alternative medical treatments but not their health outcomes. Similarly, in the case of a judge, $y_j(t)$ may measure the criminal behavior of offender j following receipt of sentence t, and $c(t, x_j)$ may be the cost of carrying out the sentence. Again, the judge may know the costs of alternative sentences but not their criminality outcomes. ❑

For each feasible treatment rule $\delta(\cdot, \cdot)$, the population mean welfare that would be realized if the planner were to choose rule $\delta(\cdot, \cdot)$ has the additive form

$$(11.11) \quad U(\delta, P) \equiv \sum_{\xi \in X} P(x = \xi) \sum_{t \in T} \delta(t, \xi) \cdot E[u(t) \mid x = \xi].$$

Here $U(\delta, P)$ is social welfare when treatment rule $\delta(\cdot, \cdot)$ is applied to a population with distribution of treatment response P. The expression $E[u(t) \mid x = \xi]$ is the mean welfare realized when persons with covariates ξ receive treatment t. The fraction of the population with covariates ξ and treatment t is $P(x = \xi)\delta(t, \xi)$. The double summation on the right-hand side of (11.11) aggregates welfare across persons with different values of ξ and t.

The planner wants to solve the problem

$$(11.12) \quad \max_{\delta \in \Delta} U(\delta, P).$$

Let S denote the unit simplex in $R^{|T|}$. The maximum in (11.12) is achieved if, for each $\xi \in X$, the planner chooses $\delta(\cdot, \xi)$ to solve the problem

$$(11.13) \quad \max_{\delta(\cdot, \xi) \in S} \sum_{t \in T} \delta(t, \xi) \cdot E[u(t) \mid x = \xi].$$

The maximum in (11.13) is achieved by a singleton rule that allocates all persons with covariates ξ to a treatment that solves the problem

$$(11.14) \quad \max_{t \in T} E[u(t) \mid x = \xi].$$

There is a unique optimal rule if problem (11.14) has a unique solution for every $\xi \in X$. There are multiple optimal rules if (11.14) has multiple solutions for some $\xi \in X$. In the latter case, all rules that randomly allocate persons with the same covariates among their optimal treatments are optimal. In any event, the population mean welfare achieved by an optimal rule is

$$(11.15) \quad U^*(P) \equiv \sum_{\xi \in X} P(x = \xi) \left\{ \max_{t \in T} E[u(t) \mid x = \xi] \right\}.$$

The Value of Covariate Information

The population welfare achievable by an optimal treatment rule depends on the observed covariates. The set of feasible treatment rules grows as the planner observes more covariates that differentiate members of the population. Hence optimal welfare cannot fall, and may rise, as more covariates are observed.

In particular, compare $U^*(P)$ with the welfare achievable when no covariates are observed. In that case, the optimal feasible treatment rule yields welfare $U^0(P) \equiv \max_{t \in T} E[u(t)]$. Hence the value of observing covariates x is the nonnegative quantity $U^*(P) - U^0(P)$. If observation of x is costly and welfare is measured in commensurate units,

$U^*(P) - U^0(P)$ is the amount that the planner should be willing to pay to observe x.

The value of observing x is positive whenever optimal treatments vary with x. It is zero if there exists a common optimal treatment t^* that solves (11.14) for all values of x. Thus observable heterogeneity in treatment response is relevant to treatment choice if and only if optimal treatments vary with the observed covariates.

Published studies of treatment response rarely report all of the covariate information that planners might like to have. Consider, for example, a physician who must choose treatments for a population of heterogeneous patients. Physicians observe many potentially treatment-relevant covariates for their patients. Physicians often know the outcomes of randomized clinical trials evaluating alternative treatments. However, the medical journal articles that report the findings of clinical trials usually describe outcomes only within broad risk-factor groups. Complement 11B discusses this reporting practice further.

Nonseparable Planning Problems

An important property of the optimal treatment rule derived above is its separability across covariate values. That is, the optimal rule for persons with covariates ξ is invariant with respect to the situations of persons with other values of x. This separability greatly simplifies analysis of treatment choice, but it does rest on our specification of the planning problem. Other planning problems of potential interest may yield nonseparable solutions. Here are two reasons why.

Equity-Conscious Objective Functions The idea of a planner with a social welfare function that adds up welfare across the population carries forward a long tradition in public economics. Nevertheless, this perspective may not be realistic in some settings. Equity-conscious objective functions make social welfare depend on the relative positions of different members of the population. Optimal rules for such welfare functions are not separable across covariate values.

Nonrectangular Sets of Feasible Treatment Rules I have assumed that the set of feasible treatment rules is rectangular; that is, each member of the population may receive any treatment in set T, regardless of the treatments assigned to other persons. Budgetary or technological constraints may render a treatment set nonrectangular, in which case optimal treatment rules generally are not separable.

Suppose, for example, that there is a budgetary upper bound on the total cost of treating the population. Then the feasible rules satisfy the inequality $\sum_{\xi \in X} P(x = \xi) \sum_{t \in T} \delta(t, \xi) c(t, \xi) \leq K$, where K is the budget and $c(t, \xi)$ is the cost of assigning treatment t to a person with covariates ξ. The budget constraint binds if the total cost of the optimal rules determined in (11.14) exceeds K. If so, application of (11.14) is infeasible.

11.5 Planning with Partial Knowledge of Treatment Response

A planner who knows the treatment response distributions $P[y(t) \mid x]$, $t \in T$ can determine an optimal treatment rule. Our concern is a planner who does not know the response distributions but who observes a study population in which treatments have been selected and outcomes realized. This section lays out general principles and Section 11.6 gives an application.

For simplicity, I consider throughout a two-period setting, the study population being observed in the first period and treatment decisions being made in the second. It clearly is important to also study more complex multiple-period settings, where treatment decisions each period are informed by all the treatment outcomes observed to date.

Study Population and Treatment Population

If observation of a study population is to yield information useful in treatment choice, a planner must be able to extrapolate from the study population to the population that will be treated. The treatment choice problem discussed in Section 11.3 and the ones studied in Sections 11.6 and 11.7 assume that the study population and the treatment population have the same distribution of treatment response. It often is optimistic to suppose that a planner can observe a study population that is distributionally identical to the treatment population. Nevertheless, this is a natural idealization, and treatment choice under ambiguity is a challenging task even in this benign setting.

Some research on treatment response downplays the importance of correspondence between the study population and the population to be treated. Donald Campbell and his collaborators have argued that studies of treatment effects should be judged primarily by their *internal validity* and only secondarily by their *external validity* (e.g., Campbell and Stanley, 1963; Cook and Campbell, 1979; Campbell, 1984). By internal validity, Campbell meant the credibility of findings within the study population, whatever it may be. By external validity, he meant the credibility of extrapolating findings from the study population to another population of interest.

Campbell's assertion of the primacy of internal validity led him to view classical randomized experiments as ideal for analysis of treatment response, even when the experiment is performed on a population that differs materially from the population of interest. When considering the use of nonexperimental data, Campbell and his collaborators have recommended that researchers aim to emulate as closely as possible the conditions of a classical experiment, again even if this requires study of a population that differs materially from the population of interest.

Taking Campbell's thinking to the extreme, researchers concerned with evaluation of social programs sometimes analyze treatment response in populations that differ fundamentally from the populations that planners must treat. As discussed in Complement 7A, researchers sometimes report the effect of treatment on the treated, where "the treated" are the members of a study population who actually received a specified treatment. As discussed in Section 7.4, researchers attempting to cope with noncompliance in randomized experiments sometimes report the effect of treatment on compliers, these being persons who would comply with their assigned experimental treatments, whatever they might be.

From the perspective of treatment choice, analysis of treatment response in populations that differ materially from the treatment population is sensible if one can credibly assume that treatment response is homogeneous. Then planners can be confident that research findings can be extrapolated to the populations they must treat. In human populations, however, homogeneity of treatment response may be the exception rather than the rule. Whether the context be medical or educational or social, persons may vary in their response to treatment. To the degree that treatment response is heterogeneous, a planner must take care when extrapolating research findings from a study population to a treatment population, as optimal treatments in the two may differ. Hence correspondence between the study population and the treatment population assumes considerable importance.

Criteria for Planning under Ambiguity

Whatever the empirical evidence and maintained assumptions may be, let Γ index the set of feasible *states of nature*. Thus $(P_\gamma, \gamma \in \Gamma)$ is the set of values that the planner deems feasible for the distribution of treatment response.

Let $\delta \in \Delta$ and $\delta' \in \Delta$ be any two feasible treatment rules. Rule δ dominates δ' if $U(\delta, P_\gamma) \geq U(\delta', P_\gamma)$ for all $\gamma \in \Gamma$ and $U(\delta, P_\gamma) > U(\delta', P_\gamma)$ for some $\gamma \in \Gamma$. The ranking of the two rules is ambiguous if $U(\delta, P_\gamma) > U(\delta', P_\gamma)$ for some $\gamma \in \Gamma$ and $U(\delta, P_\gamma) < U(\delta', P_\gamma)$ for other $\gamma \in \Gamma$.

Facing ambiguity, a Bayesian planner would place a subjective distribution π on Γ and solve the optimization problem

$$(11.16) \quad \max_{\delta \in \Delta} \int U(\delta, P_\gamma) d\pi.$$

The separable-in-covariates structure of $U(\delta, P_\gamma)$ implies that, for each covariate value ξ, a Bayes rule solves the problem $\max_{t \in T} \int E_\gamma[u(t) \mid x = \xi] d\pi$. Thus a Bayes rule has the same form as the optimal treatment rule (11.14), with the unknown $E[u(t) \mid x = \xi]$ replaced by its subjective mean.

A planner applying the maximin criterion would solve the problem

$$(11.17) \quad \max_{\delta \in \Delta} \min_{\gamma \in \Gamma} U(\delta, P_\gamma).$$

One applying the minimax-regret criterion would solve

$$(11.18) \quad \min_{\delta \in \Delta} \max_{\gamma \in \Gamma} U^*(P_\gamma) - U(\delta, P_\gamma).$$

Here, $U^*(P_\gamma)$ is the optimal population mean welfare that would be achievable if it were known that $P = P_\gamma$; that is, by (11.15),

$$(11.19) \quad U^*(P_\gamma) \equiv \sum_{\xi \in X} P(x = \xi)\left\{\max_{t \in T} E_\gamma[u(t) \mid x = \xi]\right\}.$$

The quantity $U^*(P_\gamma) - U(\delta, P_\gamma)$ is the regret of rule δ in state of nature γ.

11.6 Planning and the Selection Problem

This section applies the general ideas of Section 11.5 to a planner who faces the selection problem using the empirical evidence alone.

Recall Section 7.1, where we studied comparison of treatments using data on the realized treatments and outcomes in a study population. We found that data alone cannot refute the hypothesis that the outcome distributions $P[y(t) \mid x]$, $t \in T$ are all the same. This suggests that ambiguity in treatment choice is a generic phenomenon when a planner confronts the selection problem with the empirical evidence alone. Consideration of a simple setting makes the point.

Consider a planning problem with two treatments, where outcomes lie in the unit interval and the welfare of a treatment is its outcome. Thus $T = \{a, b\}$, $u[y(t), t, \xi] = y(t)$, and $Y = [0, 1]$. The treatment choice problem is separable in the covariates x, so we need not make them explicit.

Consider the treatment rules that assign all persons to $t = a$ or, contrariwise, all to $t = b$. In state of nature γ, these rules yield population welfare $E_\gamma[y(a)]$ and $E_\gamma[y(b)]$, respectively. For each person j in the study population and each treatment t, outcome $y_j(t)$ is observable if and only if $z_j = t$. This and the Law of Iterated Expectations imply that

$$
\begin{aligned}
E_\gamma[y(a)] &= E(y \mid z = a)\, P(z = a) \\
&\quad + E_\gamma[y(a) \mid z = b] P(z = b),
\end{aligned}
$$
(11.20a)

$$
\begin{aligned}
E_\gamma[y(b)] &= E(y \mid z = b)\, P(z = b) \\
&\quad + E_\gamma[y(b) \mid z = a] P(z = a).
\end{aligned}
$$
(11.20b)

The counterfactual quantities $\{E_\gamma[y(a) \mid z = b], E_\gamma[y(b) \mid z = a]\}$ can take any value in the unit square. Suppose that $0 < E(y \mid z = a) < 1$ and $0 < E(y \mid z = b) < 1$. Inspection of (11.20) shows that

$$
\{E_\gamma[y(a) \mid z = b] = 1,\ E_\gamma[y(b) \mid z = a] = 0\}
$$
$$
\Rightarrow E_\gamma[y(a)] > E_\gamma[y(b)],
$$
$$
\{E_\gamma[y(a) \mid z = b] = 0,\ E_\gamma[y(b) \mid z = a] = 1\}
$$
$$
\Rightarrow E_\gamma[y(a)] < E_\gamma[y(b)].
$$

Hence the ranking of these rules is ambiguous.

Although a planner confronting the selection problem with the empirical evidence alone typically cannot determine an optimal treatment rule, he can use a Bayes, maximin, or minimax-regret approach to choose treatments. We consider each in turn. To keep the exposition simple, I continue to focus on the two-treatment setting described above.

Bayes Rules

Problem (11.16) gave the Bayes criterion in the abstract. Consider the treatment rule assigning a fraction δ of the population to treatment b and the remaining $1 - \delta$ to treatment a. The subjective mean social welfare of this rule is

(11.21)
$$\int U(\delta, P_\gamma)d\pi$$
$$= (1 - \delta)[E(y \mid z = a)P(z = a) + q(a)P(z = b)]$$
$$+ \delta[E(y \mid z = b)P(z = b) + q(b)P(z = a)],$$

where $q(t) \equiv \int E_\gamma[y(t) \mid z \neq t]d\pi$ is the planner's subjective mean for the counterfactual value of mean welfare under treatment t. The Bayes criterion chooses δ to maximize the expression on the right-hand side of (11.21). The result is

(11.22)
$$\delta_{\text{Bayes}} = 1 \text{ if } E(y \mid z = b)P(z = b) + q(b)P(z = a)$$
$$> E(y \mid z = a)P(z = a) + q(a)P(z = b),$$
$$= 0 \text{ if } E(y \mid z = b)P(z = b) + q(b)P(z = a)$$
$$< E(y \mid z = a)P(z = a) + q(a)P(z = b),$$
$$= [0, 1] \text{ if } E(y \mid z = b)P(z = b) + q(b)P(z = a)$$
$$= E(y \mid z = a)P(z = a) + q(a)P(z = b).$$

Observe how the subjective distribution π affects Bayesian planning through the subjective means $q(\cdot)$. Varying π can make $[q(a), q(b)]$ take any value in the unit square. Thus the treatment choice resulting from Bayesian planning depends critically on the subjective distribution that the planner places on the feasible states of nature.

Maximin Criterion

Problem (11.17) gave the maximin criterion in the abstract. Consider the treatment rule assigning a fraction δ of the population to treatment b and the remaining $1 - \delta$ to treatment a. The minimum welfare attained by this rule across all states of nature is

$$\min_{\gamma \in \Gamma} U(\delta, P_\gamma)$$

$$(11.23) \quad = \min_{(k_a, k_b) \subset [0, 1]^2} (1 - \delta)[E(y \mid z = a) \, P(z = a) + k_a P(z = b)]$$

$$+ \delta[E(y \mid z = b) \, P(z = b) + k_b P(z = a)]$$

$$= (1 - \delta) \cdot E(y \mid z = a) \, P(z = a) + \delta \cdot E(y \mid z = b) \, P(z = b).$$

The maximin criterion chooses δ to maximize the expression on the right-hand side of (11.23). The result is

$$\delta_M = 1 \text{ if } E(y \mid z = b) \, P(z - b) > E(y \mid z = a) \, P(z = a),$$

$$(11.24) \quad = 0 \text{ if } E(y \mid z = b) \, P(z = b) < E(y \mid z = a) \, P(z = a),$$

$$= [0, 1] \text{ if } E(y \mid z = b) \, P(z = b) = E(y \mid z = a) \, P(z = a).$$

The maximin criterion is simple to apply and to comprehend. From the maximin perspective, the desirability of treatment t increases with the mean welfare $E(y \mid z = t)$ realized by persons in the study population who received the treatment and with the fraction $P(z = t)$ of persons who received the treatment. The second factor gives form to the conservatism of the maximin criterion. All else equal, the more prevalent a treatment was in the study population, the more expedient it is to choose this treatment in the population of interest.

Minimax-Regret Criterion

Problem (11.18) gave the minimax-regret criterion in the abstract. This criterion is not as transparent as are the Bayes and maximin ones, but the minimax-regret rule has a simple form in the two-treatment setting considered here. This is

$$(11.25) \quad \delta_{MR} = [1 - E(y \mid z = a)] P(z = a) + E(y \mid z = b) \, P(z = b).$$

This rule is generically fractional, with the fraction of persons allocated to treatment b increasing linearly with $E(y \mid z = b)$ and decreasing linearly with $E(y \mid z = a)$.

Proof To shorten the notation, let $e_t \equiv E(y \mid z = t)$ and $p_t \equiv P(z = t)$. Consider the treatment rule assigning a fraction δ of the population to treatment b and the remaining $1 - \delta$ to treatment a. In any state of nature γ, the Law of Iterated Expectations and knowledge of the distribution of realized treatments and outcomes in the study population give

$$E_\gamma[y(t)] = e_t p_t + E_\gamma[y(t) \mid z \neq t](1 - p_t).$$

All quantities on the right-hand side are known except for $E_\gamma[y(t) \mid z \neq t]$. Hence the regret of rule δ in state of nature γ is

$$U^*(P_\gamma) - U(\delta, P_\gamma)$$
$$= \max[e_a p_a + k_{\gamma a} p_b, e_b p_b + k_{\gamma b} p_a]$$
$$- (1 - \delta)(e_a p_a + k_{\gamma a} p_b) - \delta(e_b p_b + k_{\gamma b} p_a),$$

where $k_{\gamma t} \in [0, 1]$ is a possible value of $E_\gamma[y(t) \mid z \neq t]$. Maximum regret over all states of nature is

$$\max[(1 - \delta)(e_b p_b + p_a - e_a p_a), \delta(e_a p_a + p_b - e_b p_b)].$$

The quantity $\delta(e_a p_a + p_b - e_b p_b)$ is increasing in δ, whereas $(1 - \delta)(e_b p_b + p_a - e_a p_a)$ is decreasing in δ. The minimax-regret treatment allocation is obtained by choosing δ to equalize these two quantities. This gives (11.25). ☐

Sentencing Juvenile Offenders

To illustrate treatment choice using the empirical evidence alone, recall our discussion of sentencing and recidivism in Section 7.2. Consider a judge who observes the treatments and outcomes of the study population and who must choose sentences for a new cohort of convicted offenders. The judge believes that the study population and the new cohort have the same distribution of treatment response. The judge does not feel that any other assumptions are credible.

This is an instance of the two-treatment problem, so the results obtained above apply here. The distribution of realized treatments and outcomes in the study population is

$$P(z = b) = 0.11 \quad P(y = 1 \mid z = b) = 0.23 \quad P(y = 1 \mid z = a) = 0.41.$$

The task is to use this empirical evidence to choose treatments for an analogous population of offenders who have not yet been sentenced.

Here are the results if the judge applies a Bayes rule, the maximin criterion, or the minimax-regret criterion: A Bayes rule assigns all offenders to treatment b if $0.03 + (0.89)q(b) > 0.36 + (0.11)q(a)$, and all to treatment a if the inequality is reversed. The maximin rule assigns all offenders to treatment a. The minimax-regret rule assigns 0.55 of all offenders to treatment b and 0.45 to treatment a.

11.7 The Ethics of Fractional Treatment Rules

The standard practice in research on social planning has been to consider only singleton rules, which treat observationally identical people identically. Section 11.4 showed that restriction of attention to singleton rules is inconsequential in additive planning problems where the planner knows the distribution of treatment response. Then there always exists an optimal singleton rule, this being (11.14).

Considering only singleton rules is consequential in settings with partial knowledge of treatment response. We have found that the minimax-regret rule is fractional in the partial-compliance setting of Section 11.3 and the selection-problem setting of Section 11.6. Indeed, Complement 11A shows that the minimax-regret rule is always fractional when there are two undominated treatments.

Implementation of a fractional minimax-regret rule is appealing because it enables society to diversify a risk that is privately indivisible. An individual cannot diversify; a person receives either treatment a or b. Yet society can diversify by having positive fractions of the population receive each treatment.

A possible ethical objection to fractional rules is that they violate the normative principle calling for "equal treatment of equals." Fractional rules are consistent with this principle in the *ex ante* sense that all observationally identical people have the same probability of receiving a particular treatment. Fractional rules violate the principle in the *ex post* sense that observationally identical persons ultimately receive different treatments.

Societies sometimes implement the ex ante sense of "equal treatment" in the design of major policies. Examples include random drug testing, calls for jury service, and the American green card and Vietnam draft lotteries. Experiments with randomized assignment of treatments also provide equal treatment in the ex ante sense. Indeed, the prevailing standard of medical ethics permits randomized clinical trials only when partial knowledge of treatment response prevents a determination that one treatment is superior to another.

Here is a simple, dramatic illustration of the difference between the ex ante and ex post senses of equal treatment.

Choosing Treatments for X-Pox

Suppose that a new viral disease called X-pox is sweeping the world. Medical researchers have proposed two mutually exclusive treatments, $t = a$ and $t = b$, which reflect alternative hypotheses, say, H_a and H_b, about the nature of the virus. If H_t is correct, all persons who receive treatment t survive and all others die. It is known that one of the two hypotheses is correct, but it is not known which one; thus, there are two states of natures, $\gamma = H_a$ and $\gamma = H_b$. Suppose that the objective is to maximize the survival rate of the population.

There are two singleton rules in this setting, one giving treatment a to the entire population and the other giving b. Each rule provides equal treatment of equals in the ex post sense. Each also equalizes realized outcomes. The entire population either survives or dies.

Consider the rule in which a fraction $\delta \in [0, 1]$ of the population receives treatment b and the remaining $1 - \delta$ receives treatment a. Under this rule, the fraction who survive is

$$\delta \cdot 1[\gamma = H_b] + (1 - \delta) \cdot 1[\gamma = H_a].$$

The maximin and minimax-regret rules both set $\delta = \frac{1}{2}$. These rules treat everyone equally ex ante, each person having a 50 percent chance of receiving each treatment. They do not treat people equally ex post. Nor do they equalize outcomes. To the contrary, half the population lives and half dies.

11.8 Decentralized Treatment Choice

This chapter has considered a planner who chooses treatments on behalf of a population. Economists often ask when it is desirable to decentralize treatment choice, leaving it to each member of the population to choose his own treatment. Decentralization is not sensible when public and private objectives diverge sharply. We would not want to have convicted offenders choose their own sentences or households choose their own income tax schedules. Decentralization may be appealing when public and private objectives are reasonably congruent. Then the relative merits of planning and decentralized treatment choice depend on the relative effectiveness of society and private persons in achieving their common objectives.

The Informational Argument for Decentralization

To make the strongest case for decentralization, suppose that social and private objectives are fully congruent, with society and each person j wanting to choose an action that maximizes the welfare function $u_j(\cdot)$ over $t \in T$. In settings of this type, economists often assert that individuals tend to be better informed than planners and, hence, better able to make choices for themselves. Let us scrutinize this informational argument.

An extreme form of the assertion is the assumption of *perfect foresight* maintained in some studies; an example is the outcome-optimization assumption discussed in Section 7.5. Perfect foresight means that person j knows his own response function $y_j(\cdot)$. With perfect foresight and congruent objectives, decentralized treatment choice maximizes social welfare over all treatment rules. Thus decentralization yields the best possible result from the social perspective.

Somewhat less extreme is the prevalent three-part assumption that individuals (i) observe more covariates than planners do, (ii) know the distribution of treatment response conditional on their observed covariates, and (iii) choose actions that maximize their expected outcomes. Formally, suppose that person j

(i) observes certain covariates (x_j, w_j),
(ii) knows the treatment response distribution $P[y(\cdot) \mid x_j, w_j]$,
(iii) chooses an action that maximizes $E[u(t) \mid x_j, w_j]$ on $t \in T$.

Then decentralized treatment choice achieves social welfare $E\{\max_{t \in T} E[u(t) \mid x, w]\}$. This is at least as large as the maximum social welfare attainable by a planner who observes only covariates x, namely, $E\{\max_{t \in T} E[u(t) \mid x]\}$. Hence decentralized choice is superior to planning.

The problem with the above assumptions is that economists typically make them without offering any evidence of their realism. Do individuals actually observe more covariates than do planners? Consider, for example, the situation of medical patients. Do patients know more about their own health status than do examining physicians? In this and many other treatment settings, it may be more reasonable to think that individuals and planners observe overlapping but nonnested covariates.

Do individuals know the distribution of treatment response conditional on their observed covariates? I have stressed that planners usually have only partial knowledge of treatment response. Individuals, like planners, confront identification problems and statistical difficulties as they seek to draw inferences. Hence it cannot be realistic to routinely assume that person j knows the response distribution $P[y(\cdot) \mid x_j, w_j]$. See Chapter 13 for further discussion.

If individuals have only partial knowledge of treatment response, they cannot solve the optimization problems that economists assume they solve. As with planners, individuals choose treatments under ambiguity. Thus the third part of the three-part assumption is suspect as well.

The bottom line is that one should be skeptical of broad assertions that individuals are better informed than planners and, hence, make better choices. Of course, skepticism of such assertions does not imply that one should endorse planning. In a world replete with ambiguity, credible comparison of planning and decentralization may not be feasible.

Decentralized Treatment of X-Pox

To illustrate how ambiguity complicates comparison of planning and decentralization, consider again the X-pox scenario of Section 11.7. Assume that all persons want to survive, so social and private objectives are congruent. Also assume that everyone has the same information, this being that the possible states of nature are $\gamma = H_a$ and $\gamma = H_b$.

We saw earlier that a planner who uses the maximin or minimax-regret criterion gives each treatment to 50 percent of the population. The result is that 50 percent survive and the remainder die. What will happen if treatment choice is decentralized?

The answer depends on how individuals make choices under ambiguity. Although individuals might use randomizing devices to make decisions, they cannot implement personal fractional allocations—each person must ultimately choose treatment a or b. When only singleton rules are available, the maximin and minimax-regret criteria do not deliver determinate choices. If persons use Bayes rules, treatment choices depend on the subjective distributions held by the population.

It is not known how individuals would actually behave in a scenario of the X-pox type. Hence it is not possible to credibly predict what would happen if treatment choice were decentralized.

Complement 11A. Minimax-Regret Rules for Two Treatments Are Fractional

This complement shows that the minimax-regret rule is always fractional in problems with two undominated treatments. For simplicity, I suppress the covariates x.

Let $T = \{a, b\}$ and suppose that both treatments are undominated. Thus there exist states of nature γ and γ' such that $E_\gamma[u(a)] > E_\gamma[u(b)]$ and $E_{\gamma'}[u(a)] < E_{\gamma'}[u(b)]$. The minimax-regret criterion is

(11A.1)
$$\min_{\delta \in [0,1]} \max_{\gamma \in \Gamma} \max\{E_\gamma[u(a)], E_\gamma[u(b)]\}$$
$$- \{(1-\delta)E_\gamma[u(a)] + \delta E_\gamma[u(b)]\}.$$

This problem always has a unique fractional solution.

Proof Let $\Gamma(a)$ and $\Gamma(b)$ be the subsets of Γ on which treatments a and b are superior. That is, let $\Gamma(a) \equiv \{\gamma \in \Gamma : E_\gamma[u(a)] \geq E_\gamma[u(b)]\}$ and $\Gamma(b) \equiv \{\gamma \in \Gamma : E_\gamma[u(b)] \geq E_\gamma[u(a)]\}$. The maximum regret of rule δ on all of Γ is $\max[R(\delta, a), R(\delta, b)]$, where

$$R(\delta, a) \equiv \max_{\gamma \in \Gamma(a)} E_\gamma[u(a)] - \{(1 - \delta)E_\gamma[u(a)] + \delta E_\gamma[u(b)]\}$$

(11A.2)
$$= \max_{\gamma \in \Gamma(a)} \delta\{E_\gamma[u(a)] - E_\gamma[u(b)]\}$$

$$= \delta \max_{\gamma \in \Gamma(a)} \{E_\gamma[u(a)] - E_\gamma[u(b)]\}$$

is the maximum regret on $\Gamma(a)$ and

$$R(\delta, b) \equiv \max_{\gamma \in \Gamma(b)} E_\gamma[u(b)] - \{(1 - \delta)E_\gamma[u(a)] + \delta E_\gamma[u(b)]\}$$

(11A.3)
$$= \max_{\gamma \in \Gamma(b)} (1 - \delta)\{E_\gamma[u(b)] - E_\gamma[u(a)]\}$$

$$= (1 - \delta) \max_{\gamma \in \Gamma(b)} \{E_\gamma[u(b)] - E_\gamma[u(a)]\}$$

is the maximum regret on $\Gamma(b)$. As δ increases from 0 to 1, $R(\cdot, a)$ increases linearly from 0 to $R(1, a)$ and $R(\cdot, b)$ decreases linearly from $R(0, b)$ to 0. The fact that both treatments are undominated implies that $R(1, a) > 0$ and $R(0, b) > 0$. Hence the minimax-regret rule is the unique $\delta \in (0, 1)$ such that $R(\delta, a) = R(\delta, b)$. This is

$$\delta_{MR} = \frac{\max\limits_{\gamma \in \Gamma(b)} \{E_\gamma[u(b)] - E_\gamma[u(a)]\}}{\max\limits_{\gamma \in \Gamma(a)} \{E_\gamma[u(a)] - E_\gamma[u(b)]\} + \max\limits_{\gamma \in \Gamma(b)} \{E_\gamma[u(b)] - E_\gamma[u(a)]\}.}$$

(11A.4)   ❑

The basic idea underlying this result is that singleton and fractional treatment rules have different extremum properties across states of nature. Each singleton rule is the best rule in some states of nature and the worst in the others. In contrast, fractional rules yield intermediate social welfare in all states of nature. These facts suggest that the minimax-regret rule is fractional rather than singleton.

Complement 11B. Reporting Observable Variation
in Treatment Response

I have emphasized that, to inform treatment choice, research on treatment response should aim to learn how treatment response varies with covariates that planners can observe. If all persons respond to treatment in the same known manner, then it is best to treat all persons uniformly. However, if treatment response varies with observable covariates, then planners can do better by implementing treatment rules in which treatment varies appropriately with these covariates. For example, judges may be able to lower recidivism among criminal offenders by sentencing some offenders to prison and others to probation. Social workers may be able to increase the life-cycle earnings of welfare recipients by placing some in job training and others in basic skills classes. In these and many other cases, the key to success is to determine which persons should receive which treatments.

Nevertheless, the prevalent research practice has been to report treatment response in the population as a whole or within broad sub-populations, rather than conditional on the covariates that planners may observe. An article reviewing evaluations of training programs for the economically disadvantaged exemplifies this practice (Friedlander, Greenberg, and Robins, 1997). Throughout their extended discussion of inferential problems that arise in evaluating training programs, the authors assume that all potential trainees respond uniformly to treatment. Their subsequent discussion of empirical findings presents separate estimates of treatment effects only for the very broad demographic groups of adult men, adult women, and youth. The authors do not, even in their concluding "Agenda for Future Evaluations," ask how response to training may vary with schooling, work experience, or other covariates that the administrators of training programs may observe.

The Friedlander et al. article faithfully portrays the literature that it reviews, so I do not intend to single it out for criticism. Similar inattention to observable heterogeneity in treatment response is prevalent in other major literatures. Consider the vast body of medical research through clinical trials. Physicians commonly have much information—medical histories, diagnostic test findings, and demographic attributes—about the patients they treat. Yet the medical journal articles that report on clinical trials typically present estimates of treatment effects aggregated to broad demographic groups.

An article on a clinical trial comparing alternative psychosocial treatments for cocaine dependence provides an apt illustration. Crits-Christoph et al. (1999) report on a National Institute on Drug Abuse study randomly placing 487 cocaine-dependent patients in one of four treatment groups, each designated treatment combining group drug counseling (GDC) with another form of therapy. In some respects, the article is attentive to the possibility of heterogeneity in treatment response. The authors call attention to the fact that previous findings on the relative merits of psychotherapy and drug counseling for treatment of opiate-dependent patients do not hold up in the context of cocaine dependence. They provide much descriptive information on the characteristics of the subjects, including measures of race, sex, age, education, employment status, type and severity of drug use, psychiatric state, and personality. They test hypotheses that treatment effects do not vary with patient psychiatric state or personality. However, the article does not report outcomes conditional on any of the patient covariates observed by the researchers. Indeed, its formal conclusion section makes no reference to the possibility that treatment response might vary with observable covariates, stating simply (p. 493): "Compared with professional psychotherapy, a manual-guided combination of intensive individual drug counseling and GDC has promise for the treatment of cocaine dependence."

Why have researchers done so little to analyze observable heterogeneity in treatment response? Concern for the confidentiality of subjects' identities may inhibit reporting some covariate data. Editorial restrictions on the lengths of journal articles may prevent researchers from reporting useful findings.

Some researchers may firmly believe that, in their study settings, treatment response is homogeneous across the population. If so, then covariate information has no value. However, it is difficult to imagine many cases in which it is credible to assume homogeneous treatment response, without empirical investigation.

I conjecture that a prevalent reason why researchers neglect to analyze observable heterogeneity in treatment response is concern for the statistical precision of their estimates of treatment effects. Conventional ideas about what constitutes adequate statistical precision for an empirical finding to be of interest have been strongly influenced by the theory of hypothesis testing. Conditioning on covariates generally reduces the statistical precision of estimates of treatment effects, to the point where findings become "statistically insignificant" by conventional criteria. Hence researchers often restrict their attention to population-wide average treatment effects, or effects within large subpopulations.

If researchers want to inform treatment choice, they should not view statistical insignificance as a reason to refrain from studying observable heterogeneity in treatment response. A planner must be concerned with the quantitative variation of outcomes with treatments and covariates. Hypothesis tests do not address this question.

Complement 11C. Word Problems

Problem 11.1
Consider choice between a status quo treatment $t = a$ and an innovation $t = b$ using data from a randomized experiment with partial compliance. The outcome is binary, $\alpha = P[y(a) = 1]$ and $\beta = P[y(b) = 1]$. The objective is to choose a treatment allocation $\delta \in [0, 1]$ that maximizes the population rate of treatment success.

Suppose that two experiments are performed. In both, subjects assigned to treatment a must comply, but those assigned to treatment b can choose not to comply. The experiments are identical except that, in the second one, subjects assigned to treatment b are paid \$100 if they comply with the assigned treatment. The analogous subjects in the first experiment do not receive this payment. The findings are as follows:

$$\text{Experiment 1: } \alpha = 0.35 \qquad P(y = 1 \mid \zeta = b, z = b) - 0.38$$
$$P(z = b \mid \zeta = b) = 0.68.$$
$$\text{Experiment 2: } \alpha = 0.35 \qquad P(y = 1 \mid \zeta = b, z = b) = 0.30$$
$$P(z = b \mid \zeta = b) = 0.80.$$

Assume that offering \$100 for compliance has no effect on the population distribution of treatment response $P[y(\cdot)]$. Consider a planner who observes the findings of both experiments.

a. What is (are) the Bayes treatment rule(s) for a planner who places a uniform subjective distribution on the identification region for β?

b. What is (are) the minimax-regret treatment rule(s)?

Problem 11.2

Suppose that each member of a population makes a binary choice, whether or not to purchase one unit of a specified product. Let $d(\cdot)$ denote the population demand function; thus, $d(t) \in [0, 1]$ is the fraction of the population who would make the purchase if price equals t. Let the realized price be p and the realized demand be $d \equiv d(p)$.

You observe the realized (p, d), which satisfy $0 < p < 1$ and $0 < d < 1$. You know that $d(t) \in [0, 1]$ for all t and that $d(\cdot)$ is a weakly downward-sloping function of t. You have no other information. Your objective is to maximize revenue. That is, you want to choose t to solve the problem $\max_{t \geq 0} t \cdot d(t)$. Answer these questions, giving your reasoning:

  a. What are the feasible states of nature?

  b. What prices are dominated?

  c. What is (are) the maximin price(s)?

12

Planning with Sample Data

12.1 Statistical Induction

The ambiguity in treatment choice studied in Chapter 11 arose purely out of identification problems. In practice, a planner may observe only a random sample of the study population. This generates further ambiguity. As burdensome as identification problems may be, they at least have the analytical clarity of exercises in deductive logic. Statistical inference is a murky matter of induction from samples to populations.

The standard practice is to estimate point-identified population features by their sample analogs. Statisticians and econometricians regularly appeal to asymptotic theory to justify the practice. In this manner, I have several times pointed out that identification regions can be estimated consistently by their sample analogs. Similarly, the Bayes, maximin, and minimax-regret treatment rules developed in Chapter 11 can be estimated consistently by their sample analogs.

Consider, for example, treatment using data from an experiment with partial compliance. Our analysis of this problem in Section 11.3 supposed that the quantities $(\alpha, \beta_L, \beta_U)$ are known. If the experiment is performed on a random sample of size N from the study population, the planner may estimate these quantities by their sample analogs $(\alpha_N, \beta_{LN}, \beta_{UN})$. These estimates may be used to produce consistent estimates of the Bayes, maximin, and minimax-regret rules given in (11.7), (11.8), and (11.9), respectively.

Appealing to asymptotic theory is convenient, but it gives at most approximate guidance to a planner who must make treatment choices using sample data. The limit theorems of asymptotic theory describe the behavior of estimates as sample size increases to infinity. They do not reveal how estimates perform in specific finite-sample settings. A planner's objective is not to obtain estimates with good asymptotic properties but rather to choose a good treatment rule with the data available. Using a consistency theorem to guide treatment choice with sample data requires a leap of faith that the empirical distribution of the sample data approximates the population distribution "well enough."

The Wald (1950) development of statistical decision theory addresses treatment choice with sample data directly, without recourse to asymptotic approximations. It seamlessly integrates the study of identification and statistical inference. These nice properties make statistical decision theory warrant attention.

This chapter presents Wald's general principles in Section 12.2 and gives an illustrative case study in Section 12.3. Section 12.2 is on the abstract side. Some readers may prefer to skim it first, next read Section 12.3 in detail, and then return to Section 12.2 for a second reading.

The brevity of the chapter is due to the dearth of accessible material to present. Wald developed the principles of statistical decision theory in the 1930s and 1940s. A surge of important extensions and applications followed in the 1950s, but this period of rapid development came to a close by the 1960s.

Why did statistical decision theory lose momentum long ago? One reason may have been the technical difficulty of the subject. Wald's ideas are fairly easy to describe in the abstract, but applying them tends to be analytically and numerically demanding. Another reason may have been diminishing interest in decision making as the motivation for statistical analysis. Modern statisticians and econometricians tend to view their objectives as estimation and hypothesis testing rather than decision making. A third contributing factor may have been the criticism of Wald's thinking put forward by those decision theorists who espouse the *conditionality principle* as a sine qua non of statistical decision making. I will explain this matter in Section 12.2.

I cannot be sure what role each of the above reasons played in the vanishing of statistical decision theory from statistics and econometrics in the latter part of the twentieth century, but the near absence of the subject in mainstream journals and textbooks of the period is indisputable. I think this unfortunate; hence, this chapter.

12.2 Wald's Development of Statistical Decision Theory

Wald considered the broad problem of using sample data to make a decision. His worldview eliminates the common separation of activities between empirical research and decision making. Thus the researcher and the decision maker are one and the same person.

Wald posed the task as choice of a *statistical decision function*, which maps the available data into a choice among the feasible actions. In a treatment choice setting, a statistical decision function is a rule for using the data to choose a treatment allocation. I will call such a rule a *statistical treatment rule.*

In general, no statistical decision function that makes nontrivial use of sample data can perform best in every realization of a sampling process. Hence Wald recommended evaluation of statistical decision functions as *procedures* applied as the sampling process is engaged repeatedly to draw independent data samples. The idea of a procedure transforms the original statistical problem of induction from a single sample into the deductive problem of assessing the probabilistic performance of a statistical decision function across realizations of the sampling process.

Perspectives on Evaluation of Procedures Thinking of statistical analysis as the evaluation of procedures was not original to Wald. It is at the heart of the frequentist perspective on statistics and is central to the standard theories of estimation and hypothesis testing. It is this basic tenet of frequentist statistics that so rankles decision theorists of the conditional Bayes school. They argue that statistical inference should be conditioned on the observed data alone and not rest on thought experiments that contemplate how a procedure would perform in repeated sampling; see, for example, Berger (1985, chap. 1). I will have more to say about this later in this section. ❑

How might one evaluate statistical decision functions as procedures? Wald suggested comparison of alternative statistical decision functions by their mean performance across realizations of the sampling process. Wald, who formalized the decision maker's goal as minimization of an objective function, termed this criterion *risk*. Here, where the goal is maximization of a social welfare function, I call it *expected welfare*. Let us now formalize these ideas, in the context of treatment choice.

Expected Welfare of a Statistical Treatment Rule

Chapter 11 considered treatment rules that map observed covariates into treatment allocations. Extending this idea, statistical treatment rules map covariates and sample data into treatment allocations.

Let Q denote the sampling process generating data from the study population. A leading case is random sampling, but we need not be this specific. Let Ψ denote the sample space; that is, Ψ is the set of data samples that may potentially be drawn under Q. Let $\psi \in \Omega$ denote a possible data sample. For example, in the case of random sampling of the study population, ψ would be the sample realizations of outcomes y, treatments z, and covariates x.

Extending the notation for treatment rules in Chapter 11 to encompass statistical treatment rules, let Δ henceforth denote the space of functions that map $T \times X \times \Psi$ into the unit interval and that satisfy the adding-up conditions:

$$\delta \in \Delta \Rightarrow \sum_{t \in T} \delta(t, \xi, \psi) = 1 \text{ for all } (\xi, \psi) \in X \times \Psi.$$

Each function $\delta \in \Delta$ is a feasible statistical treatment rule.

Let δ be any such rule. Repeated engagement of the sampling process to draw independent samples makes social welfare a random variable. The expected welfare yielded by δ in repeated samples, denoted $W(\delta, P, Q)$, depends on the population distribution of treatment response and on the sampling process generating the data.

In an additive planning problem,

$$W(\delta, P, Q)$$

(12.1)
$$\equiv \int \left\{ \sum_{\xi \in X} P(x = \xi) \sum_{t \in T} \delta(t, \xi, \psi) \cdot E[u(t) \mid x = \xi] \right\} dQ$$

$$= \sum_{\xi \in X} P(x = \xi) \sum_{t \in T} E[\delta(t, \xi, \psi)] \cdot E[u(t) \mid x = \xi].$$

In the first equality, the expression in brackets gives the social welfare that is realized if the sample data are ψ. The integral with respect to Q gives the expected value of welfare across repeated samples. The second equality is a simplified version of the first one, obtained by observing that $E[\delta(t, \xi, \psi)] \equiv \int \delta(t, \xi, \psi)dQ$ is the expected (across repeated samples) fraction of persons with covariates ξ who are assigned to treatment t.

States of Nature

Choosing δ to maximize expected welfare yields the optimal treatment rule, but performance of this maximization requires knowledge of P. To develop implementable criteria for treatment choice, let Γ again index the feasible states of nature. Thus $[(P_\gamma, Q_\gamma), \gamma \in \Gamma]$ is the set of (P, Q) pairs that the planner deems possible.

The present set Γ is generically larger than the one considered in Chapter 11. One reason is that the planner may not have full knowledge of the sampling process Q. Another is that features of P that were assumed known in Chapter 11 no longer are known here.

For specificity, recall our examination of planning and the selection problem in Section 11.6. We supposed there that the planner knows the distribution $P(y, z, x)$ of realized outcomes, treatments, and covariates in the study population. Hence the feasible states of nature were restricted to ones with the known value of this distribution. Here, the planner observes only a random sample of the study population and, hence, does not know $P(y, z, x)$. Thus the present specification of Γ includes all feasible values of this distribution.

I will continue to assume that the planner knows the distribution $P(x)$ of covariate values. This is realistic because, from the beginning, I have presumed that the planner observes x for each member of the treatment population.

Admissibility

The most basic prescription of Wald's development of statistical decision theory is that a decision maker should not choose an action that is dominated in risk. Such an action is called *inadmissible*. An action that is not dominated in risk is called *admissible*.

In the treatment choice setting, a statistical treatment rule is inadmissible if there exists another feasible rule that yields at least the same expected welfare in all feasible states of nature and larger expected welfare in some state of nature. Thus rule δ is inadmissible if there exists another rule, say, δ', such that $W(\delta', P_\gamma, Q_\gamma) \geq W(\delta, P_\gamma, Q_\gamma)$ for all $\gamma \in \Gamma$ and $W(\delta', P_\gamma, Q_\gamma) > W(\delta, P_\gamma, Q_\gamma)$ for some $\gamma \in \Gamma$. Rule δ is admissible if there does not exist a rule δ' that dominates it in risk.

Admissibility is widely accepted as a desirable property for a statistical decision function. However, its operational implications are limited for two main reasons. First, in those settings where it is possible to determine which statistical decision functions are admissible, there often turn out to be many such functions; Section 12.3 illustrates this. Second, there are many settings of practical interest where analysis of admissibility poses an unsolved technical challenge, so it is unknown which decision functions are and are not admissible. This is the general case today in problems with partial identification of treatment response.

Implementable Criteria for Treatment Choice

To develop implementable criteria for decision making with sample data, statistical decision theorists have studied the same three broad ideas that were discussed in Chapter 11. The Bayesian prescription is to use a statistical decision function that works well on average across the feasible states of nature. The maximin and minimax-regret prescriptions are to use a decision function that, in one of two senses, works well uniformly over Γ.

In the context of treatment choice, a Bayesian planner places a subjective probability measure π on Γ and solves the optimization problem

$$(12.2) \quad \max_{\delta \in \Delta} \int W(\delta, P_\gamma, Q_\gamma) d\pi.$$

The maximin criterion is

$$(12.3) \quad \max_{\delta \in \Delta} \min_{\gamma \in \Gamma} W(\delta, P_\gamma, Q_\gamma).$$

The minimax-regret criterion is

$$(12.4) \quad \min_{\delta \in \Delta} \max_{\gamma \in \Gamma} U^*(P_\gamma) - W(\delta, P_\gamma, Q_\gamma).$$

Here, as in Chapter 11, $U^*(P_\gamma)$ is the maximum social welfare that would be achievable if it were known that $P = P_\gamma$.

Conditional Bayesian Planning The Bayes criterion (12.2), which views treatment rules as procedures, differs in concept but agrees in practice with the conditional Bayes prescription for decision making. The latter calls on the planner to combine π and the sample data ψ to form a *posterior* subjective distribution π_ψ, conditional on ψ. The planner then chooses δ to maximize the expected value of $U(\delta, P)$ with respect to π_ψ. It turns out that the solution of this problem at all points in the sample space yields the solution to (12.2). See Berger (1985, sec. 4.4.1). This mathematical fact enables Bayesian decision theorists to assert that Bayesian planning fits within the Wald framework and also adheres to the conditionality principle. ❏

Unification of Identification, Statistical Inference, and Sample Design

Wald's statistical decision theory may be applied whenever the expected welfare function W is well defined. Subject to this regularity condition, the theory has breathtaking generality. It enables comparison of all feasible statistical treatment rules. It applies whatever the sampling process may be, whatever the sample size may be, and whatever information the planner may have about the population and the sampling process.

The set Γ of feasible states of nature expresses whatever assumptions about treatment response and the sampling process that the planner is willing to maintain. This set may be finite-dimensional (parametric) or infinite-dimensional (nonparametric). The maintained assumptions may point-identify or partially identify the distribution of treatment response. Thus statistical decision theory unifies the study of identification and statistical inference, in the service of decision making.

Wald's theory also enables comparison of alternative sampling processes. Throughout this book, I have taken as given the sampling process generating data from the study population. Sometimes a planner can jointly choose a sampling process and a treatment rule that uses the data generated by this process. Viewing the matter in abstraction, let $C(Q)$ denote the cost of conducting sampling process Q, with cost measured in the same units as welfare. Then the expected welfare of (treatment rule, sampling process) pair (δ, Q) is $W(\delta, P, Q) - C(Q)$. The planner can, in principle, use a Bayes, maximin, or minimax-regret criterion to jointly choose Q and δ.

12.3 Using a Randomized Experiment to Evaluate an Innovation

To illustrate the above abstract ideas, this section examines what may be the simplest nontrivial case of treatment choice using sample data. Outcomes are binary, there are no observed covariates, and there are two treatments, one being the status quo and the other being an innovation. The planner knows the response distribution of the status quo treatment, but not that of the innovation. To learn about the innovation, a classical randomized experiment is performed. The problem is to use the experimental data to inform treatment choice.

A theorem of Karlin and Rubin (1956) shows that, in this setting, the admissible treatment rules coincide with the *monotone treatment rules*. These are rules that assign all persons to the status quo treatment if the experimental success rate is below some threshold and all to the innovation if the success rate is above the threshold. After explaining this important result, I give several examples of monotone rules. The minimax-regret rule is particularly appealing. This rule solves a sensible optimization problem and makes judicious use of sample data.

Several recent papers extend the analysis discussed here to settings with observed covariates, bounded rather than binary outcomes, and more general welfare functions. The interested reader is directed to Manski (2004b), Manski and Tetenov (2007), Schlag (2006), and Stoye (2006).

The Setting

Let $t = a$ be the status quo treatment and $t = b$ be the innovation. Suppose that the planner knows the success probability $\alpha \equiv P[y(a) = 1]$ of the status quo treatment but does not know the success probability $\beta \equiv P[y(b) = 1]$ of the innovation. The planner wants to choose treatments to maximize the success probability.

An experiment is performed to learn about outcomes under the innovation, with N subjects randomly drawn from the population and assigned to treatment b. There is full compliance with the assigned treatment. Of the subjects, a number n realize outcome $y = 1$ and the remaining $N - n$ realize outcome $y = 0$. The outcomes of all subjects are observed. Thus the experiment point-identifies β. The planner only faces a problem of statistical inference.

In this setting, the sample size N indexes the sampling process, and the number n of experimental successes is a sufficient statistic for the sample data. The feasible statistical treatment rules are functions $\delta(\cdot)$: $[0, \ldots, N] \to [0, 1]$ that map the number of experimental successes into a treatment allocation. That is, for each value of n, rule $\delta(\cdot)$ randomly allocates a fraction $\delta(n)$ of the population to treatment b and the remaining $1 - \delta(n)$ to treatment a.

The expected welfare of rule δ is

$$W(\delta, P, N) = \alpha \cdot E[1 - \delta(n)] + \beta \cdot E[\delta(n)]$$
(12.5)
$$= \alpha + (\beta - \alpha) \cdot E[\delta(n)].$$

The number of experimental successes is distributed binomial $B[\beta, N]$, so

(12.6) $$E[\delta(n)] = \sum_{i=0}^{N} \delta(i) \cdot f(n = i; \beta, N),$$

where $f(n - i; \beta, N) = N![i! \cdot (N - i)!]^{-1} \beta^i (1 - \beta)^{N-i}$ is the binomial probability of i successes.

The only unknown determinant of expected welfare is β. Hence Γ indexes the feasible values of β. Let $\beta_\gamma \equiv P_\gamma[y(b) = 1]$. I presume that $(\beta_\gamma, \gamma \in \Gamma)$ contains values that are smaller and larger than α; otherwise, the choice problem is trivial.

The Admissible Treatment Rules

In this setting, larger values of n are evidence for larger values of β. Hence it is reasonable to conjecture that admissible treatment rules should be ones in which the fraction of the population allocated to treatment b increases with n. In fact, the admissible treatment rules are a simple subclass of these rules.

Following Karlin and Rubin (1956), define a *monotone treatment rule* to be one of the form

$$\delta(n) = 0 \quad \text{for } n < n_0,$$
$$(12.7) \quad \delta(n) = \lambda \quad \text{for } n = n_0,$$
$$\delta(n) = 1 \quad \text{for } n > n_0,$$

where $0 \leq n_0 \leq N$ and $0 \leq \lambda \leq 1$ are constants specified by the planner. Thus a monotone rule allocates all persons to treatment a if n is smaller than the threshold n_0, a fraction λ to treatment b if $n = n_0$, and all persons to treatment b if n is larger than n_0. Observe that monotone rules have simple expressions for the expected treatment allocation, namely,

$$(12.8) \quad E[\delta(n)] = f(n > n_0; \beta, N) + \lambda \cdot f(n = n_0; \beta, N).$$

Suppose that $0 < \alpha < 1$ and let the feasible set $(\beta_\gamma, \gamma \in \Gamma)$ exclude the values 0 and 1. Karlin and Rubin (1956, theorem 4) show that the collection of monotone treatment rules is the set of admissible rules.

Some Monotone Rules

The collection of monotone treatment rules is a mathematically "small" subset of the space of all feasible treatment rules, as it excludes all functions $\delta(\cdot)$ that do not have form (12.7). Nevertheless, it still contains a broad range of rules. Here are some of them.

Data-Invariant Rules These are the rules $\delta(\cdot) = 0$ and $\delta(\cdot) = 1$, which assign all persons to treatment a or b, respectively, whatever the realization of n may be.

Empirical Success Rules An optimal treatment rule allocates all persons to treatment a if $\beta < \alpha$ and all to treatment b if $\beta > \alpha$. An empirical success rule emulates the optimal rule by replacing β with its sample analog, the empirical success rate n/N. Thus, an empirical success rule has the form

$$\delta(n) = 0 \quad \text{for } n < \alpha N,$$
$$(12.9) \quad \delta(n) = \lambda \quad \text{for } n = \alpha N, \qquad \text{where } 0 \leq \lambda \leq 1,$$
$$\delta(n) = 1 \quad \text{for } n > \alpha N.$$

Bayes Rules A Bayesian planner has enormous discretion because the form of the Bayes rule depends critically on the prior subjective distribution placed on β. To see this, consider the class of beta priors, which form the conjugate family for a binomial likelihood. Let $(\beta_\gamma, \gamma \in \Gamma) = (0, 1)$ and let the prior be beta with parameters (c, d). Then the posterior mean for β is $(c + n)/(c + d + N)$; see, for example, DeGroot (1970, sec. 9.2, theorem 1). The resulting Bayes rule is

$$\delta(n) = 0 \quad \text{for } (c + n)/(c + d + N) < \alpha,$$
$$(12.10) \quad \delta(n) = \lambda \quad \text{for } (c + n)/(c + d + N) = \alpha, \quad \text{where } 0 \leq \lambda \leq 1,$$
$$\delta(n) = 1 \quad \text{for } (c + n)/(c + d + N) > \alpha.$$

As (c, d) tend to zero, the Bayes rule approaches an empirical success rule. Moreover, the class of Bayes rules includes the data-invariant rules $\delta(\cdot) = 0$ and $\delta(\cdot) = 1$. The former occurs if the parameters (c, d) of the beta prior distribution satisfy $(c + N)/(c + d + N) < \alpha$. The latter occurs if $c/(c + d + N) > \alpha$.

Statistical Significance Rules These rules use a one-sided hypothesis test to choose between the status quo treatment and the innovation. The null hypothesis is that both treatments yield the same social welfare; that is, $\beta = \alpha$. The alternative is that treatment b is superior to treatment a; that is, $\beta > \alpha$. Treatment b is chosen if the null is rejected and treatment a otherwise. Thus the rule is

$$\delta(n) = 0 \quad \text{for } n \leq d(\alpha, s, N),$$
$$(12.11)$$
$$\delta(n) = 1 \quad \text{for } n > d(\alpha, s, N),$$

where s is the specified size of the test and $d(\alpha, s, N)$ is the associated critical value. Given that n is binomial, $d(\alpha, s, N) = \min i : f(n > i; \alpha, N) \leq s$.

The use of one-sided hypothesis tests to make treatment choices is institutionalized in the U.S. Food and Drug Administration premarket drug approval process, which calls for comparison of a new drug under study $(t = b)$ with an approved treatment if one exists or a placebo otherwise $(t = a)$. Approval of the new treatment normally requires a one-sided rejection of the null hypothesis in two independent randomized clinical trials (see Fisher and Moyé, 1999).

Although statistical significance rules are monotone treatment rules, the conventional practice of hypothesis testing is remote from the problem of treatment choice with sample data. If the null hypothesis $[\beta = \alpha]$ is correct, all feasible treatment rules yield the same expected welfare. If not, alternative rules may yield different expected welfare. A statistical test indicates only whether the sample data are inconsistent (in the usual sense of having low probability of being realized under the null) with the hypothesis that all feasible rules yield the same expected welfare.

Maximin Rule The minimum expected welfare for rule δ is

$$(12.12) \quad \min_{\gamma \in \Gamma} W(\delta, P_\gamma, N) = \alpha + \min_{\gamma \in \Gamma} (\beta_\gamma - \alpha) E_\gamma [\delta(n)],$$

where $E_\gamma[\delta(n)]$ is the expression in (12.8) with β_γ replacing β. By assumption, $(\beta_\gamma, \gamma \in \Gamma)$ contains values that are smaller than α. Moreover, $E_\gamma[\delta(n)] > 0$ for all $\beta_\gamma > 0$ and all monotone treatment rules except for $\delta(\cdot) = 0$, the rule that always chooses treatment a. Hence the maximin rule is the data-invariant rule $\delta(\cdot) = 0$.

Minimax-Regret Rule The regret of rule δ in state of nature γ is

$$U^*(P_\gamma) - W(\delta, P_\gamma, N)$$

$$(12.13) \quad \begin{aligned} &= \max(\alpha, \beta_\gamma) - \{\alpha + (\beta_\gamma - \alpha) \cdot E_\gamma[\delta(n)]\} \\ &= (\beta_\gamma - \alpha)\{1 - E_\gamma[\delta(n)]\} \cdot 1[\beta_\gamma \geq \alpha] \\ &\quad + (\alpha - \beta_\gamma) E_\gamma[\delta(n)] \cdot 1[\alpha \geq \beta_\gamma]. \end{aligned}$$

Thus regret is the mean welfare loss when a member of the population is assigned the inferior treatment, multiplied by the expected fraction of the population assigned this treatment.

The minimax-regret rule does not have an analytical solution, but it can be determined numerically. Table 12.1 reports the minimax-regret rule for specified values of α and N when all values of β are feasible; that is, when $(\beta_\gamma, \gamma \in \Gamma) = [0, 1]$. The top two panels display the value of (n_0, λ) for this rule. The third panel displays the value of minimax regret.

The top panel of the table shows that the threshold n_0 of experimental successes for allocation of persons to treatment b increases with the

Table 12.1 Minimax-regret treatment rules

	$N=0$	$N=1$	$N=2$	$N=3$	$N=4$	$N=5$	$N=6$	$N=7$	$N=8$	$N=9$	$N=10$
n_0: threshold sample size											
$\alpha = 0.10$	0	0	0	0	0	0	0	0	0	1	1
$\alpha = 0.25$	0	0	0	1	1	1	1	2	2	2	2
$\alpha = 0.50$	0	1	1	2	2	3	3	4	4	5	5
$\alpha = 0.75$	0	1	2	2	3	4	5	5	6	7	8
$\alpha = 0.90$	0	1	2	3	4	5	6	7	8	8	9
λ: threshold allocation											
$\alpha = 0.10$	0.9	0.67	0.52	0.41	0.32	0.26	0.18	0.09	0	0.89	0.78
$\alpha = 0.25$	0.75	0.36	0.17	0.93	0.67	0.42	0.18	0.93	0.67	0.43	0.18
$\alpha = 0.50$	0.5	1	0.5	1	0.5	1	0.5	1	0.5	1	0.5
$\alpha = 0.75$	0.25	0.64	0.83	0.07	0.33	0.58	0.82	0.07	0.33	0.57	0.82
$\alpha = 0.90$	0.1	0.33	0.48	0.59	0.68	0.74	0.82	0.91	1	0.11	0.22
R: minimax-regret value											
$\alpha = 0.10$	0.09	0.067	0.052	0.041	0.033	0.027	0.022	0.019	0.017	0.017	0.017
$\alpha = 0.25$	0.19	0.09	0.052	0.039	0.038	0.035	0.03	0.027	0.027	0.025	0.023
$\alpha = 0.50$	0.25	0.063	0.063	0.044	0.044	0.035	0.035	0.03	0.03	0.027	0.027
$\alpha = 0.75$	0.19	0.09	0.052	0.039	0.038	0.035	0.03	0.027	0.027	0.025	0.023
$\alpha = 0.90$	0.09	0.067	0.052	0.041	0.033	0.027	0.022	0.019	0.017	0.017	0.016

sample size and with the success probability of treatment a. The inequality $|n_0 - \alpha N| \leq 1$ holds everywhere in the table. Thus the minimax-regret rule is well approximated by an empirical success rule.

The third panel shows that the value of minimax regret decreases by roughly an order of magnitude as the sample size increases from 0 to 10. The specific pattern of decrease varies markedly with the value of α. A curiosity is that R is a step function when $\alpha = 0.5$, with decreases occurring at odd values of N but not at even values.

Savage on the Maximin and Minimax–Regret Criteria

The findings in Table 12.1 make plain that treatment choice using the minimax-regret rule can differ fundamentally from treatment choice using the maximin rule. Savage (1951), whose review of Wald (1950) first explicitly distinguished between these criteria for decision making, argued strongly against application of the minimax (here maximin) criterion, writing (p. 63): "Application of the minimax rule . . . is indeed ultra-pessimistic; no serious justification for it has ever been suggested, and it can lead to the absurd conclusion in some cases that no amount of relevant experimentation should deter the actor from behaving as though he were in complete ignorance." Our finding that the maximin treatment rule is data-invariant illustrates this "absurd conclusion." Savage emphasized that although the minimax (here maximin) criterion is "ultra-pessimistic," the minimax-regret criterion is not. Our finding that the minimax-regret rule approximates the empirical success rule illustrates that the minimax-regret criterion is not particularly pessimistic.

The generic difference between the maximin and minimax-regret criteria may not have been apparent when Savage wrote the above passage, because the literature of the time focused on special cases in which the two criteria are equivalent. These are the cases, noted at the end of Section 11.2, in which maximum welfare is constant across all states of natures.

III

Predicting Choice Behavior

13

Revealed Preference Analysis

We have throughout this book found many reasons why researchers and planners may want to study choice behavior. Chapter 2 emphasized that outcome data are often missing by choice, and Chapter 4 discussed how economists use selection models to point-identify outcome distributions. In Chapter 7 we observed that noncompliance with assigned treatments in randomized experiments is a choice made by experimental subjects. Chapters 10 and 11 considered prediction of outcomes and evaluation of welfare when treatment choice is decentralized.

Chapters 13 through 15 study prediction of choice behavior as a problem of predicting treatment response. In these chapters, a treatment is a choice set—a set of feasible actions among which a person must choose. A potential outcome is the action that a person would choose if he were to face a specified choice set.

As elsewhere in the analysis of treatment response, the conclusions that may be drawn about choice behavior depend on the available data and on the assumptions brought to bear. This opening chapter scrutinizes the prevalent economic practice of *revealed preference analysis,* which combines data on the choices actually made by a study population with assumptions about their decision processes. Revealed preference analysis can be a powerful predictive tool, but only if one is willing to maintain strong assumptions that can be difficult to motivate. Thus the Law of Decreasing Credibility asserts itself again.

13.1 Revealing the Preferences of an Individual

The original form of revealed preference analysis introduced by Samuelson (1938, 1948) considered the classical economic problem of predicting the commodity demands of a person with a given income when commodities have given prices. Samuelson supposed that a researcher observes the consumption bundles that a person chooses in various income-price settings. He showed that the observed consumption outcomes, when combined with standard assumptions of consumer theory, enable some predictions regarding the consumption bundles that this person would choose in other income-price scenarios.

Observation of One Choice Setting

Suppose first that one observes a person's consumption in a single choice setting. Let there be K commodities, with realized price vector $p \equiv (p_k, k = 1, \dots, K)$. Suppose that the person has income m and that he chooses the commodity bundle $c \equiv (c_k, k = 1, \dots, K)$; thus, the person purchases c_k units of commodity k. Let $d \equiv (d_k, k = 1, \dots, K)$ denote any nonchosen commodity bundle that costs strictly less than m to purchase at the prevailing prices.

Now consider a counterfactual scenario in which the price vector and the person's income are (p^0, m^0) rather than (p, m). Suppose that commodity bundles c and d both remain feasible in this scenario; that is, both bundles cost no more than m^0 to purchase when the price vector is p^0. Might the person choose bundle d in this scenario?

This prediction question calls for extrapolation from an observed choice setting to a counterfactual scenario, so one's ability to answer depends on what one is willing to assume. Standard consumer theory assumes that persons are rational and that their preferences do not exhibit satiation. *Rationality* means that a person orders all commodity bundles in terms of preference and chooses one that is ranked highest among those that are feasible. *Nonsatiation* means that a person strictly prefers a larger commodity bundle to a smaller one. (Bundle d' is larger than d if $d'_k \geq d_k$ for all commodities k and $d'_k > d_k$ for some k.)

These assumptions and the datum that the person chooses bundle c in the observed income-price setting imply that the person strictly prefers c to d. Rationality and the choice datum imply that d is not strictly preferred to c, but leave open the possibility of indifference between c and d. Nonsatiation and the presumption that d costs less than m eliminates the possibility of indifference. Thus revealed preference analysis predicts that the person would not choose d in any scenario where both c and d are feasible choices.

The nonsatiation assumption enables further predictions as well. Consider any bundle c' that is larger than c and any bundle d' that is smaller than d. Nonsatiation, combined with preference of c over d, implies that the person strictly prefers c' to d'.

Observation of Multiple Choice Settings

With observation of only one choice setting, one can only perform extrapolations of the above kind. More powerful applications of revealed preference analysis are possible if one observes the consumption bundles that a person chooses in multiple income-price settings. The key is application of the *transitivity property* of preferences.

Consider three commodity bundles, say, c, d, and e. Suppose that observation of behavior in one income-price setting shows that a person strictly prefers bundle c to d, while observation of another setting shows that this person strictly prefers bundle d to e. Transitivity of preferences implies that this person strictly prefers bundle c to e. Thus transitivity enables one to form chains of inference across choice settings. Economists such as Afriat (1967) and Varian (1982) have characterized these chains of inference.

Application to General Choice Problems

Although Samuelson developed revealed preference analysis for prediction of consumer demand, the basic ideas apply to general choice problems. Let (c, d, e) be alternatives of any kind, not necessarily commodity bundles, and assume that a person has a strict preference ordering over these alternatives.

Suppose that the person is observed to choose c when all three alternatives are feasible. Then we may conclude that he would continue to choose c over d if alternative e were not available.

Suppose that observation of behavior in one choice setting shows that the person strictly prefers c to d, while observation of another setting shows that he strictly prefers d to e. Then transitivity implies that he strictly prefers c to e.

The only part of Samuelson's revealed preference approach that is not entirely general is the nonsatiation assumption, which presumes that alternatives can be partially ordered from small to large. Even this assumption is applicable in many contexts other than consumer demand.

Thought Experiment or Practical Prescription for Prediction?

Samuelsonian revealed preference analysis is admirable for its objective of predicting choice behavior with weak assumptions. The assumptions of rationality and nonsatiation enjoy high credibility among economists. (Some researchers do not find these assumptions credible, but I will defer discussion of this matter until Chapter 15.) Varian (1982) emphasizes credibility when he compares conventional parametric demand analysis with the Samuelson approach. He states that parametric analysis will be satisfactory "only when the postulated parametric forms are good approximations to the 'true' demand functions." He then writes approvingly that revealed preference analysis "is *nonparametric* in that it requires no *ad hoc* specifications of functional forms for demand equations" (p. 945).

A severe practical problem with Samuelsonian revealed preference analysis is its presumption that one can observe individual behavior in multiple choice settings. The mutual exclusivity of treatments makes this a logical impossibility. If a person is observed to have income m and face prices p, then this person does not have another income or face other prices. Thus the literal form of Samuelsonian analysis is more a thought experiment than a practical prescription for prediction. (Research in axiomatic decision theory considers an extreme version of this thought experiment. See Complement 13B.)

To apply revealed preference analysis, empirical researchers obtain multiple choice observations in various ways. Some researchers use choice data for multiple persons who face different choice sets and assume that these persons share the same preferences. This assumption enables a researcher to act as if he observes multiple choices by one person. However, the ensuing analysis rests critically on the maintained assumption of preference homogeneity, which often has no foundation.

Another approach is to ask a person to state the action he would choose in multiple counterfactual settings. This practice, called *hypothetical choice, stated preference,* or *intentions* analysis, has merit to the extent that persons are willing and able to accurately predict their own behavior in the scenarios that researchers pose to them. See Chapter 14 for further discussion.

13.2 Random Utility Models of Population Choice Behavior

Whereas Samuelsonian revealed preference analysis aims to predict the choice behavior of an individual, the form of revealed preference analysis developed by McFadden (1974) seeks to predict the distribution of choices made by the members of a population. The McFadden approach supposes that a researcher observes the decisions made by a population of heterogeneous persons, each of whom faces one discrete choice problem. McFadden showed that these data, combined with assumptions on the population distribution of preferences, enable estimation of parametric probabilistic choice models. He then showed how probabilistic choice models may be used to predict population choice behavior in other settings.

McFadden's vision of discrete choice analysis had four essential features:

(a) Econometric analysis of behavior should be fully consistent with utility theory. In particular, it should be formally interpretable as describing the behavior of a population of heterogeneous decision makers, each of whom chooses the best available alternative.

(b) Econometric analysis should enable the researcher to predict choice behavior in counterfactual settings. In particular, it should enable the researcher to predict population behavior if new alternatives were to become available or existing ones were to become unavailable. To achieve this, alternatives and decision makers should be characterized in terms of their attributes.

(c) Econometric analysis should recognize that empirical researchers typically possess incomplete data on the attributes of the decision makers that compose the population and the alternatives available to them.

(d) Econometric analysis should be computationally practical.

I describe his approach here and give an illustration in Section 13.3.

Consistency with Utility Theory

Applying basic utility theory to the problem of discrete choice, Mc-Fadden assumed that each member of a study population faces a finite choice set and selects an action that maximizes utility. I will suppose here that all members of the population face the same choice set, denoted C, which is a finite subset of a universe of potential alternatives, denoted A. The assumption of a common choice set simplifies the exposition and is maintained in much of the literature, but it is not critical to what follows.

Formally, let person j have a utility function $u_j(\cdot)$ that assigns a utility value to each alternative in A. Suppose that this person is observed to choose some action $c \in C$. Then the standard revealed preference argument holds that person j ranks c highest among the feasible alternatives. Thus $u_j(c) \geq u_j(d)$, all $d \in C$.

Terminology Research on discrete choice typically has not used the language and notation of the analysis of treatment response, but it is easy enough to define concepts in those terms. The set T of potential treatments is the set of all nonempty finite subsets of A, each of which is a possible choice set. For any $D \subset A$, potential outcome $y_j(D)$ is the action that person j would choose if he were to face choice set D. The realized outcome for person j is $y_j \equiv y_j(C)$. This is the action that person j chooses when facing the realized choice set C.   ❏

Assume that indifference between alternatives occurs with probability zero. Then the fraction of the population who choose c equals the fraction of the population for whom c is the utility-maximizing action. Thus the *choice probability* for alternative c is

(13.1) $P(y = c) = P[u(\cdot): u(c) \geq u(d), \text{ all } d \in C]$.

Equation (13.1) is a *random-utility-model* description of observed choices. In psychology, random utility models date back to Thurstone (1927) as a way of conceptualizing semirational behavior. The psychological interpretation, exposited in Luce and Suppes (1965), assumes that each decision maker carries a distribution of utility functions internally and selects one at random whenever a decision must be made. McFadden reinterpreted the randomness as arising from variation in utility functions across the population rather than variation within an individual.

Prediction Using Attributes of Alternatives and Decision Makers

Suppose that one could learn the population distribution of utility functions. Then a random utility model would not only describe observed population behavior but would enable prediction of behavior in counterfactual scenarios where members of the population face choice sets other than C. Suppose, for example, that all persons were to face choice set D. The counterfactual choice probability for each $c \in D$ is

(13.2) $P[y(D) = c] = P[u(\cdot): u(c) \geq u(d), \text{ all } d \subset D]$.

However, learning the distribution of utility functions from choice data is no small problem. Observation of the study population only yields equation (13.1), or the analogous equation conditional on observed covariates of decision makers. Clearly, many distributions of utility functions can solve this equation. Complement 13A discusses the inferences that are possible using only (13.1) and no other maintained assumptions.

McFadden reasoned that the researcher should bring to bear assumptions that restrict the distribution of utility functions. His central idea was to transform the hitherto qualitative distinctions among alternatives and decision makers into quantitative differences in their attributes. Thus the second step in the development of discrete choice analysis was to assume that each alternative d can be characterized through a vector of attributes, say, w_d, and that each decision maker j can be characterized through a vector of attributes, say, x_j. Then the utility of alternative d to person j has the form

(13.3) $u_j(d) = u(w_d, x_j)$,

where $u(\cdot, \cdot)$ maps the attributes of alternatives and decision makers into utility values. With knowledge of these attributes and the form of $u(\cdot, \cdot)$, a researcher can determine the utility of any alternative to any decision maker and, hence, can predict the decision maker's choice behavior. For example, a transportation researcher can predict how commuters with specified income and job attributes would choose among travel modes with specified travel-time and travel-cost attributes.

Characterization of alternatives and decision makers as attribute vectors marked a sharp departure from prevailing economic practice. In classical consumer theory, goods are qualitatively distinct and so are consumers. There is no way to predict the demand for a new good. Nor is there any way to predict the behavior of new consumers.

Incomplete Data and Conditional Choice Probabilities

One more conceptual step was needed to yield a viable approach to discrete choice analysis. It is not realistic to think that an empirical researcher will have complete data on the attributes of alternatives and decision makers. Nor is it realistic to think that the researcher fully knows the form of the function $u(\cdot, \cdot)$ mapping attributes into utility values.

A viable approach emerges if the researcher has enough partial knowledge of $u(\cdot, \cdot)$ and of the population distribution of unobserved attributes. In particular, McFadden assumed that $u(\cdot, \cdot)$ has the linear form

$$(13.4) \quad u(w_d, x_j) = v(w_{do}, x_{jo})\beta + \epsilon_{jd}.$$

Here $v(\cdot, \cdot)$ is a known vector-valued function of the components of w_d and x_j that the researcher can observe, labeled w_{do} and x_{jo}, while β is a commensurate parameter vector. The unobserved variables $\epsilon_j \equiv (\epsilon_{jd}, d \in C)$ express the contribution of unobserved attributes to utility.

With this setup, McFadden derived choice probabilities conditional on the observed attributes. Let $W_{Co} \equiv (w_{do}, d \in C)$. Consider the subpopulation of persons with observed covariates x_o. Assume that the researcher knows the distribution $P(\epsilon \mid x_o, W_{Co})$ up to the value of a parameter vector α. Let this parametrized distribution be denoted F_α. Then the random utility model implies that the choice probability for alternative c conditional on (x_o, W_{Co}) is

$$P(y = c \mid x_o, W_{Co})$$

$$(13.5) \qquad = F_\alpha\big[\epsilon: v(w_{co}, x_o)\beta + \epsilon_c \geq v(w_{do}, x_o)\beta + \epsilon_d,$$

$$\text{all } d \in C \mid x_o, W_{Co}\big].$$

These conditional choice probabilities provide the basis for inference on the parameters (β, α) using data on the choices and attributes of a random sample of decision makers. Observation of the study population reveals the conditional choice probabilities on the left-hand side of equation (13.5). Hence the identification region for (β, α) is the set of parameter values that make (13.5) hold for all alternatives c and for all values of x_o in the support of $P(x_o)$. The parameters are point-identified if these equations have a unique solution. If no parameter value solves (13.5) for all values of c and x_o, the model does not correctly portray choice behavior.

Practicality through the Conditional Logit Model

At this point the conceptual development of modern discrete choice analysis was complete. The remaining question was practicality, a matter whose interpretation must depend on the computational power of the day.

McFadden was concerned that estimation of the parameters (β, α) be tractable. He judged that, with the computational technology available at the time of his work, discrete choice analysis would be practical only if the conditional choice probabilities have a quite simple form. With this in mind, he searched for a convenient assumption to impose on the distribution of the unobserved variables ϵ.

He found what he was looking for in the earlier work of Marschak (1960) and Holman and Marley (cited in Luce and Suppes, 1965) on psychological random utility models. Adapting results proved by these authors, he assumed that ϵ is statistically independent of (x_o, W_{Co}) and that the components of $(\epsilon_d, d \in C)$ are independent and identically distributed, each according to the Type I extreme-value distribution. These assumptions imply that the conditional choice probabilities have the *multinomial logit* form

$$(13.6) \quad P(y = c \mid x_o, W_{Co}) = \frac{\exp[v(w_{co}, x_o)\beta]}{\sum\limits_{d \in C} \exp[v(w_{do}, x_o)\beta]}.$$

The distribution of ϵ having been fully specified, there are no α parameters to be estimated here, only the β parameters.

The binary logit model had been prominent in biostatistics since its introduction by Berkson (1944). In the 1960s, versions of the multinomial logit model had been independently investigated by a number of

researchers in different disciplines, including Theil (1971) in econometrics. McFadden's derivation of the model as a description of population
behavior consistent with utility theory was new and more general than
had appeared earlier. For these reasons, McFadden did not use the name
"multinomial logit" to describe his innovation. Instead, he called it the
conditional logit model.

Necessary and sufficient conditions for point identification of β are
easily obtained by expressing (13.6) in the equivalent form

$$(13.7) \quad \log \frac{P(y = c \mid x_o, W_{Co})}{P(y = d \mid x_o, W_{Co})} = [v(w_{co}, x_o) - v(w_{do}, x_o)]\beta.$$

Let β have dimension K. The empirical evidence reveals the choice
probabilities on the left-hand side of (13.7). This linear equation in β
holds for all $(c, d) \in C \times C$ and for all support values of x_o. Hence
β is point-identified if there exist K linearly independent values of
$v(w_{co}, x_o) - v(w_{do}, x_o)$.

Other Distributional Assumptions

Since the 1970s, the econometric analysis of discrete choice has retained the basic aspects of McFadden's original work—the random
utility model framework, the attribute characterization of alternatives and decision makers, and the resulting conditional choice probabilities. However, the particular distributional assumptions of the
conditional logit model have been subjected to close examination, and
models making many alternative assumptions have been studied. The
idea has been to make distributional assumptions that yield computationally tractable conditional choice probabilities, retain point identification
of model parameters, and yet are reasonably flexible in their behavioral
implications.

Many researchers have studied *multinomial probit* models, which
assume that $(\epsilon_d, d \in C)$ are distributed multivariate normal (e.g., Daganzo, Bouthelier, and Sheffi, 1977; Hausman and Wise, 1978; Lerman
and Manski, 1981; Berry, Levinsohn, and Pakes, 1994). Some such
models have a *random coefficients* feature, allowing the parameters β
to vary randomly across persons rather than be fixed across the population. And McFadden has generalized the conditional logit model in
various ways. In one stream of research, he retained the assumption that

each ϵ_d has an extreme-value distribution but relaxed the assumption that the variables $(\epsilon_d, d \in C)$ are mutually independent. This yielded the *generalized extreme-value* model introduced in McFadden (1978) and studied in more depth in McFadden (1981). In another stream, he studied random coefficient versions of the logit model (McFadden and Train, 2000).

The models described above aim to weaken the assumptions of the conditional logit model, but they all assume that the distribution of ϵ is known up to some parameters. Concern with the restrictiveness of any parametric model has led to the development of a branch of discrete choice analysis that imposes nonparametric distributional assumptions. In the first work of this type, Manski (1975) assumed that the unobserved $(\epsilon_d, d \in C)$ are independent and identically distributed conditional on (x_o, W_{Co}). Thus $P(\epsilon_d, d \in C \mid x_o, W_{Co})$ has the product form

$$(13.8) \quad P(\epsilon_d, d \in C \mid x_o, W_{Co}) = \prod_{d \in C} F(\epsilon_d \mid x_o, W_{Co}).$$

The distribution $F(\cdot \mid x_o, W_{Co})$ is assumed to be continuous and strictly increasing but otherwise is unspecified. These assumptions imply the following inequality relationship between choice probabilities and utility values:

$$
\begin{aligned}
(13.9) \quad & P(y = c \mid x_o, W_{Co}) > P(y = d \mid x_o, W_{Co}) \\
& \Leftrightarrow v(w_{co}, x_o)\beta > v(w_{do}, x_o)\beta.
\end{aligned}
$$

The identification region for β is the set of parameter values that make (13.9) hold for all alternatives (c, d) and all values of x_o in the support of $P(x_o)$.

Many researchers have subsequently focused on binary choice settings and studied various assumptions that place some restriction on the unobserved ϵ without confining it to a parametric family of distributions. Manski (1988b) and Horowitz (1998) review this literature.

Extrapolation

A primary objective of discrete choice analysis is to enable prediction of choice behavior in scenarios where members of the population face counterfactual choice sets. How is this done?

For concreteness, suppose that all members of the study population were to face choice set D rather than C. Let $W_{Do} \equiv (w_{do}, d \in D)$ denote the observable attributes of the elements of D. Then, for each $c \in D$, repetition of the derivation leading to (13.5) yields the counterfactual conditional choice probability

$$P[y(D) = c \mid x_o, W_{Do}]$$

(13.10) $$= P\big[\epsilon: v(w_{co}, x_o)\beta + \epsilon_c \geq v(w_{do}, x_o)\beta + \epsilon_d,$$

$$\text{all } d \in C \mid x_o, W_{Do}\big].$$

If β and the distribution $P[\epsilon_d, d \in C \mid x_o, W_o]$ are known, the right-hand side of (13.10) is computable.

Extrapolation using the conditional logit model is particularly simple. Extending the distributional assumption made for $(\epsilon_d, d \in C)$, assume that the unobserved variables $P(\epsilon_d, d \in D)$ are independent and identically distributed, each with the Type I extreme-value distribution. Then the counterfactual choice probability (13.10) has the form

(13.11) $$P[y(D) = c \mid x_o, W_{Do}] = \frac{\exp[v(w_{co}, x_o)\beta]}{\sum\limits_{d \in D} \exp[v(w_{do}, x_o)\beta]}.$$

13.3 College Choice in America

I shall use my own analysis of college-going behavior, performed with David Wise, to describe the main features of econometric practice. Manski and Wise (1983, chaps. 6 and 7) used observations from the National Longitudinal Study of the High School Class of 1972 (NLS72) to estimate a random utility model of college enrollment. We then used the estimated model to predict the enrollment impacts of the Pell Grant program, the major federal college scholarship program.

The NLS72 survey, commissioned by the National Center for Educational Statistics, provides schooling, work, and background data on almost 23,000 high school seniors drawn from over 1300 high schools in the United States in spring 1972. Data were obtained through a series of questionnaires distributed to the respondents and to their high schools and through periodic follow-up surveys.

The starting point for our analysis was to assume that the patterns of college enrollment and labor force participation observed among the NLS72 respondents are the consequence of decisions made by these students, by colleges, and by employers. Colleges and employers make admissions decisions and job offers that determine the options available to each high school senior upon graduation. Each senior selects among the available options.

An Idealized Binary Choice Setting

What do the NLS72 data reveal about the decision processes generating postsecondary activities? If we assume that a student chooses the most preferred alternative from the available options, observations of chosen activities partially reveal student preferences. For simplicity, assume that after high school graduation a student has two alternatives: $d = 1$ is college enrollment and $d = 0$ is work. (The estimated model actually posed multiple alternatives.) If we observe that NLS72 respondent j chose to go to college, we may infer that $u_j(1) \geq u_j(0)$. If person j chose to work, then $u_j(0) \geq u_j(1)$. The NLS72 data provide a large set of these inequalities, one for each respondent.

The preference inequalities implied by observation of these activity choices do not provide sufficient information to allow us to predict how a student not in the sample would select between college and work or how a student in the sample would have behaved if conditions had differed. To extrapolate behavior, we must combine the NLS72 data with assumptions restricting the form of preferences.

For example, we might assume that the utility of college enrollment to student j depends on his ability v_{1j} and his parents' income v_{2j}, on the quality v_{3j} and cost v_{4j} of his best college option, and on an unobserved variable ϵ_{j1}. Similarly, the utility of working might depend on his best potential wage v_{5j} and on an unobserved variable ϵ_{j0}. In particular, suppose that the utilities have the linear form

$$(13.12a) \quad u_j(1) = \beta_1 v_{1j} + \beta_2 v_{2j} + \beta_3 v_{3j} + \beta_4 v_{4j} + \epsilon_{j1}$$

and

$$(13.12b) \quad u_j(0) = \beta_5 v_{5j} + \epsilon_{j0}.$$

Then the preference inequalities revealed by the NLS72 data are

(13.13)
$$y_j = 1 \Rightarrow \beta_1 v_{1j} + \beta_2 v_{2j} + \beta_3 v_{3j} + \beta_4 v_{4j} - \beta_5 v_{5j} + \epsilon_j \geq 0,$$
$$y_j = 0 \Rightarrow \beta_1 v_{1j} + \beta_2 v_{2j} + \beta_3 v_{3j} + \beta_4 v_{4j} - \beta_5 v_{5j} + \epsilon_j \leq 0,$$

where $\epsilon_j \equiv \epsilon_{j1} - \epsilon_{j0}$.

Assuming that the distribution of ϵ is continuous, the probability that a student with observed characteristics v chooses to enroll in college is

$$(13.14) \quad P(y = 1 \mid v) = P(v\beta + \epsilon \geq 0 \mid v),$$

where $v \equiv (v_1, v_2, v_3, v_4, -v_5)$ and $\beta \equiv (\beta_1, \ldots, \beta_5)$. If ϵ_1 and ϵ_0 are assumed to be independent and identically distributed with the Type I extreme-value distribution, then ϵ has the standard logistic distribution and the choice probabilities have the binary logit form

$$(13.15) \quad P(y = 1 \mid v) = \frac{e^{v\beta}}{1 + e^{v\beta}}.$$

Predicting the Enrollment Effects of Student Aid Policy

Manski and Wise (1983) estimated a random utility model that is more complex than the one described above, but not qualitatively different. The estimated model was used to study the impact on freshman college enrollments of the Basic Educational Opportunity Grant program, later renamed the Pell Grant program. This federal scholarship program was initiated in 1973, so the NLS72 respondents were not eligible at the time of their initial postsecondary schooling decisions.

In the context of our random utility model, the Pell Grant program influences behavior by changing the college costs v_4 that students face. Given knowledge of the program eligibility criteria and award formula, we can estimate the cost of college to any given student in the presence of the program. This done, we can predict how students would behave in the presence and absence of the program. We can then aggregate these predictions to generate predictions of aggregate freshman college enrollments in the United States.

Table 13.1 presents some of the findings concerning the version of the program that was in effect in 1979. The predictions indicate that the Pell

Table 13.1   Predicted enrollments in 1979, with and without the Pell Grant program
(thousands of students)

Income group	All schools		Four-year college		Two-year college		Voc.-tech. school	
	With Pell	Without Pell	With Pell	Without Pell	With Pell	Without Pell	With Pell	Without Pell
Lower	590	370	128	137	349	210	113	23
Middle	398	354	162	164	202	168	34	22
Upper	615	600	377	378	210	198	28	24
Total	1603	1324	668	679	761	576	174	69

Note: Lower income — below $16,900. Upper income = above $21,700.
Source: Manski and Wise (1983), table 7.4.

Grant program was responsible for a substantial increase (59 percent) in the college enrollment rate of low-income students, a moderate increase (12 percent) in middle-income enrollments, and a minor increase (3 percent) in the rate for upper-income students.

Overall, we predicted that 1,603,000 of the 3,300,000 persons who were high school seniors in 1979 would enroll in full-time postsecondary education in 1979–80. In contrast, only 1,324,000 would have enrolled had the Pell Grant program not been in operation. The table indicates that the enrollment increases induced by the existence of the program were totally concentrated at two-year colleges and vocational-technical schools. Enrollments at four-year schools were essentially unaffected.

Power and Price of the Analysis

Federal scholarship programs with varying eligibility criteria and award formulas have been proposed, but only a few programs have actually been implemented. Revealed preference analysis of college enrollments makes it possible to predict the impacts of a wide variety of proposed and actual programs. This ability to extrapolate is very powerful.

The price of extrapolation is the set of assumptions imposed. The assumption of rationality alone yields very limited ability to extrapolate; see Complement 13A. The power of revealed preference analysis emerges only when strong restrictions of the type discussed in Section 13.2 are placed on the form of preferences. This analysis of college choice illustrates the kinds of preference assumptions that have typically been imposed in empirical studies.

13.4 Random Expected–Utility Models

Our scrutiny of revealed preference analysis has thus far supposed that decision makers have complete knowledge of their choice environments. Complete knowledge is a maintained assumption of the classical consumer demand problem studied by Samuelson. McFadden's development of discrete choice analysis does not necessarily assume complete knowledge. However, applications of the approach when decision makers act with partial knowledge must come to grips with a severe complication that we have not yet addressed. I begin to address the issue here and continue through Chapters 14 and 15.

Economists commonly assume that persons form probabilistic expectations for unknown quantities and that they maximize expected utility. Presuming this description of behavior to be accurate, the inferential problem is to use choice data to learn the subjective probability distributions that express expectations and the utility functions that embody preferences over outcomes. (The realism of expected utility maximization as a description of choice behavior is a subject of much controversy, both among economists and between economists and others. This is an important question, but I leave it aside for now and will return to it in Chapter 15.)

Formally, let Γ be the set of feasible states of nature and, for $\gamma \in \Gamma$, let $u_j(c, \gamma)$ be the utility of action c to person j in state of nature γ. The usual economic assumption is that person j places a subjective probability distribution on Γ, say, π_j, and chooses an action that maximizes expected utility. Thus, if j faces choice set C and chooses action c, the standard revealed preference argument implies that $\int u_j(c, \gamma)d\pi_j \geq \int u_j(d, \gamma)d\pi_j$, all $d \in C$.

Suppose that indifference between alternatives occurs with probability zero. Then the fraction of the population who choose alternative c is the fraction of the population who have preferences and expectations such that c maximizes expected utility. Thus the conditional choice probability for alternative c is

$$P(y = c \mid x_o, W_{Co}) = P[u(\cdot, \cdot), \pi : \int u(c, \gamma)d\pi$$

(13.16)

$$\geq \int u(d, \gamma)d\pi, \text{ all } d \in C \mid x_o, W_{Co}].$$

Equation (13.16) gives a random expected-utility model description of choice behavior.

The complication relative to choice settings with complete knowledge is clear. The earlier task was to infer the population distribution of utility functions. The problem now is to infer the joint distribution of utility functions and subjective probability distributions. The identification problem in the earlier context was difficult enough. It is all the more difficult now.

Identification of the Decision Rules of Proposers in Ultimatum Games

Here is an illustration, drawn from Manski (2002b). The behavior of subjects playing the ultimatum game has been of considerable interest to experimental economists. The ultimatum game is a game of proposal-response in which the proposer offers a division of a specified amount of money. The responder either accepts the offer, in which case the division is realized, or rejects it, in which case both players receive nothing. Roth (1995, chap. 4) reviews the empirical findings. A common finding has been that proposers often offer responders an even division of the money. Experimental economists have taken this as evidence of a prevalent preference for *fairness*. However, the decision to offer an even division can also arise when a proposer who wants to maximize private utility has appropriate expectations about the behavior of responders.

Suppose that a proposer is given K dollars and that $C = [0, K]$ is the set of offers he can make to the responder. For $c \in C$, let $d(c) = 1$ if the responder would accept an offer of size c and let $d(c) = 0$ if he would reject the offer. Then the payoffs to proposer and responder are $f(1, c, d) = (K - c)d(c)$ and $f(2, c, d) = cd(c)$, respectively.

Assume that subjects playing the role of proposer are of six types, each having one of two utility functions and one of three forms of expectations. The two utility functions are

$$u_1[f(1, c, d), f(2, c, d)] = f(1, c, d) = (K - c)d(c),$$
$$u_2[f(1, c, d), f(2, c, d)] = f(1, c, d)f(2, c, d)$$
$$= [(K - c)d(c)]cd(c).$$

Subjects with the first utility function aim to maximize their own payoff. Those with the second exhibit a strong form of fairness in which they care equally about their own payoff and that of the other player.

The three forms of expectations are

$$\pi_1[d(c) = 1] = \tfrac{1}{2} + \min(c/K, \tfrac{1}{2}),$$
$$\pi_2[d(c) = 1] = \min[c/(K - c), 1],$$
$$\pi_3[d(c) = 1] = \min(c/K, 1).$$

Subjects with expectations π_1 believe that the probability with which a responder would accept a proposal rises from $\tfrac{1}{2}$ to 1 as the size of the offer rises from 0 to $K/2$. Those with π_2 believe that the chance of acceptance rises from 0 to 1 as the offer rises from 0 to $K/2$. Those with π_3 believe that the chance of acceptance rises from 0 to 1 as the offer rises from 0 to K.

Let $c(i, j)$ be the action chosen by a proposer who has the ith utility function and the jth expectations. Maximization of expected utility by the six types of subjects yields these chosen actions:

$$c(1, 1) = K/4 \qquad c(1, 2) = K/2 \qquad c(1, 3) = K/2$$
$$c(2, 1) = K/2 \qquad c(2, 2) = K/2 \qquad c(2, 3) = 2K/3$$

Observe how preferences and expectations combine to determine the chosen actions. Fully four of the six types offer the responder an even division of the money. Subjects with both utility functions offer an even division if they have the second form of expectations. Thus choice data do not reveal the preferences of subjects playing proposer in the ultimatum game. They reveal only that preferences and expectations combine to yield the observed offers.

Rational Expectations Assumptions

Point identification of random expected-utility models plainly requires strong maintained assumptions. A common practice has been to assume that decision makers have specific expectations and to suppose that these expectations are "rational" in the sense of being objectively correct. We have previously discussed perfect foresight, which is the extreme form of rational expectations; see Sections 7.5 and 11.8.

Imposition of expectations assumptions reduces the task of empirical inference to revelation of preferences alone, but at a high cost in credibility. Researchers performing econometric analysis of choice data often have enormous difficulty defending the expectations assumptions they maintain. As a consequence, they have similar difficulty justifying the findings they report.

Parts I and II of this book send a clear message of skepticism about the realism of rational expectations assumptions. Decision makers face the same identification problems as researchers. It is not credible to suppose, without substantiation, that expectations are either literally or approximately rational.

Even if the assumption of rational expectations were plausible, this assumption by itself does not pin down the specific expectations that persons hold. The assumption only asserts that persons hold objectively correct expectations conditional on the information they possess. A researcher must still ask what information decision makers possess and what constitutes objectively correct expectations conditional on this information. The standard practice has been for a researcher to pose a point-identified model of the economy, to assert that this model is correct, and also to assert knowledge of the information on which persons condition their expectations.

Why do economists regularly assume that they and the decision makers they study share rational expectations? One reason may be the elegant manner in which these assumptions close a model. A researcher specifies his own vision of how the economy works, and he assumes that the persons who populate the economy share this vision. This is tidy and self-gratifying.

Another reason may be the convenience of convention. Choice data do not enable one to infer the expectations that decision makers hold. Hence researchers who are uncomfortable with rational expectations assumptions can do no better than invoke some other unsubstantiated assumption. Rather than speculate in an unorthodox manner, they follow convention and assume rational expectations.

How Do Youth Infer the Returns to Schooling?

To illustrate the implausibility of rational expectations assumptions, consider again the returns to schooling, which we have discussed in Section 9.5 and elsewhere. Labor economists have performed many empirical studies of the returns to schooling. Reading this large literature reveals that researchers vary greatly in their assumptions and findings.

Now consider youth making schooling decisions. Labor economists regularly assume that youth form rational expectations for the returns to schooling and that they use these expectations to choose between schooling and other options. However, youth confront the same inferential problems as do labor economists studying the returns to schooling. If economists have not been able to reach consensus on the returns to schooling, is it plausible that youth have rational expectations? I think not.

I would particularly stress that youth and labor economists alike must contend with the logical unobservability of counterfactual outcomes. Much as economists attempt to infer the returns to schooling from data on schooling choices and outcomes, youth may attempt to learn through observation of the outcomes experienced by family, friends, and others who have made their own past schooling decisions. However, youth cannot observe the outcomes that these people would have experienced had they made other decisions. The possibilities for inference, and the implications for decision making, depend fundamentally on the assumptions that youth maintain about these counterfactual outcomes.

Complement 13A. Prediction Assuming Strict Preferences

As discussed in Section 13.2, econometric analysis of discrete choice rests on rather strong maintained assumptions. The prevailing practice asserts that the population distribution of utility functions belongs to a specified parametric family of distributions. The branch of the literature that makes nonparametric distributional assumptions studies models that are somewhat less restrictive but that still embody much structure.

This book has emphasized inference with weak assumptions, so we should want to explore the possibilities. Suppose one assumes only that each member of the population maximizes utility. With no restrictions placed on the population distribution of utility functions, what predictions about choice behavior are possible?

The immediate answer is that no predictions are possible. The reason is that each person could have a flat utility function, making him indifferent among all alternatives. Then rationality is a vacuous assumption that carries no implications for choice behavior.

The situation changes if one makes the minimal assumption, which we have maintained throughout our discussion of random utility models, that indifference between alternatives occurs with probability zero; thus, preferences almost always are strict rather than weak. Now the predictive possibilities depend on the choice sets faced by the study population. We have so far assumed that all members of the study population face the same choice set. Instead, suppose now that persons may differ in the choice sets they face. Moreover, suppose that choice sets are randomly assigned, whether through purposeful randomization or through some natural process. Then the feasible predictions depend on the choice sets the population faces.

I will show this in the simplest interesting context, where the universe A of alternatives contains three elements, say, (c, d, e). Analysis of this type was undertaken in the psychological literature on random utility models a half-century ago. See Marschak (1960)

There are six distinct strict preference orderings: $(c \succ d \succ e)$, $(c \succ e \succ d)$, $(d \succ c \succ e)$, $(d \succ e \succ c)$, $(e \succ c \succ d)$, $(e \succ d \succ c)$. There are four nontrivial choice sets: (c, d, e), (c, d), (c, e), (d, e). The relationship between choice probabilities and the distribution of preferences is as follows:

$$
\text{(13A.1a)} \quad
\begin{aligned}
&P[y = c \mid z = (c, d, e)] \\
&\quad = P[y(c, d, e) = c] = P(c \succ d \succ e) + P(c \succ e \succ d),
\end{aligned}
$$

$$
\text{(13A.1b)} \quad
\begin{aligned}
&P[y = d \mid z = (c, d, e)] \\
&\quad = P[y(c, d, e) = d] = P(d \succ c \succ e) + P(d \succ e \succ c),
\end{aligned}
$$

$$
\text{(13A.1c)} \quad
\begin{aligned}
&P[y = e \mid z = (c, d, e)] \\
&\quad = P[y(c, d, e) = e] = P(e \succ c \succ d) + P(e \succ d \succ c).
\end{aligned}
$$

$$P[y = c \mid z = (c, d)]$$

(13A.2a) $= P[y(c, d) = c]$

$$= P(c \succ d \succ e) + P(c \succ e \succ d) + P(e \succ c \succ d),$$

$$P[y = d \mid z = (c, d)]$$

(13A.2b) $= P[y(c, d) = d]$

$$= P(d \succ c \succ e) + P(d \succ e \succ c) + P(e \succ d \succ c).$$

$$P[y = c \mid z = (c, e)]$$

(13A.3a) $= P[y(c, e) = c]$

$$= P(c \succ d \succ e) + P(c \succ e \succ d) + P(d \succ c \succ e),$$

$$P[y = e \mid z = (c, e)]$$

(13A.3b) $= P[y(c, e) = e]$

$$= P(e \succ d \succ c) + P(e \succ c \succ d) + P(d \succ e \succ c).$$

$$P[y = d \mid z = (d, e)]$$

(13A.4a) $= P[y(d, e) = d]$

$$= P(c \succ d \succ e) + P(d \succ e \succ c) + P(d \succ c \succ e),$$

$$P[y = e \mid z = (d, e)]$$

(13A.4b) $= P[y(d, e) = e]$

$$= P(c \succ e \succ d) + P(e \succ d \succ c) + P(e \succ c \succ d).$$

As in Part II, z denotes the realized treatment, which is a choice set here. In each case, the first equality holds due to random assignment of choice sets. The second equality expresses the assumption that almost all members of the population have strict preferences.

   With this as background, we can study the predictions that are possible with observation of choice behavior from different choice sets. I consider three illustrative cases.

All Persons Face Set (c, d) The empirical evidence reveals $P[y \mid z = (c, d)]$; hence, (13A.2) restricts the distribution of preferences. Consider prediction of behavior in the counterfactual scenario where the choice set is (c, d, e). By (13A.1a) and (13A.2a),

(13A.5) $P[y(c, d, e) = c] = P[y = c \mid z = (c, d)] - P(e \succ c \succ d).$

Equation (13A.2a) shows that $0 \leq P(e \succ c \succ d) \leq P[y = c \mid z = (c, d)]$. Hence

(13A.6) $0 \leq P[y(c, d, e) = c] \leq P[y = c \mid z = (c, d)]$.

In words, adding alternative e to choice set (c, d) cannot increase the choice probability for c and could lower it to zero.

All Persons Face Set (c, d, e) The empirical evidence reveals $P[y \mid z = (c, d, e)]$; hence, (13A.1) restricts the distribution of preferences. Consider prediction of behavior in the counterfactual scenario where the choice set is (c, d). By (13A.1a) and (13A.2a),

(13A.7) $P[y(c, d) = c] = P[y = c \mid z = (c, d, e)] + P(e \succ c \succ d).$

Equation (13A.1c) shows that $0 \leq P(e \succ c \succ d) \leq P[y = e \mid z = (c, d, e)]$. Hence

$$
\begin{aligned}
& P[y = c \mid z = (c, d, e)] \\
(13\text{A}.8) \quad & \leq P[y(c, d) = c] \\
& \leq P[y = c \mid z = (c, d, e)] + P[y = e \mid z = (c, d, e)].
\end{aligned}
$$

In words, if alternative e is eliminated from choice set (c, d, e), the persons who chose c or d would not change their behavior. The persons who chose e now must choose either c or d. The lower bound on $P[y(c, d) = c]$ occurs if they all choose d and the upper bound if they all choose c.

Some Persons Face Set (c, d) and Some Face (d, e) The empirical evidence reveals $P[y \mid z = (c, d)]$ and $P[y \mid z = (d, e)]$; hence, (13A.2) and (13A.4) restrict the distribution of preferences. Consider prediction of behavior in the counterfactual scenario where the choice set is (c, e). By (13A.2a) and (13A.3a),

$$
\begin{aligned}
(13\text{A}.9) \quad & P[y(c, e) = c] \\
& = P[y = c \mid z = (c, d)] - P(e \succ c \succ d) + P(d \succ c \succ e).
\end{aligned}
$$

Equation (13A.4a) shows that $0 \leq P(d \succ c \succ e) \leq P[y = d \mid z = (d, e)]$.
Equation (13A.4b) shows that $0 \leq P(e \succ c \succ d) \leq P[y = e \mid z = (d, e)]$.
Hence

$$
\begin{aligned}
\text{(13A.10)} \quad & P[y = c \mid z = (c, d)] - P[y = e \mid z = (d, e)] \leq P[y(c, e) = c] \\
& \leq P[y = c \mid z = (c, d)] + P[y = d \mid z = (d, e)].
\end{aligned}
$$

This bound can be written in the equivalent form

$$
\begin{aligned}
& \max\{0, P[y = c \mid z = (c, d)] + P[y = d \mid z = (d, e)] - 1\} \\
\text{(13A.10')} \quad & \leq P[y(c, e) = c] \\
& \leq \min\{1, P[y = c \mid z = (c, d)] + P[y = d \mid z = (d, e)]\}.
\end{aligned}
$$

Marschak (1960) called this the *triangular condition*. Observe that the lower bound is informative when the sum $P[y = c \mid z = (c, d)] + P[y = d \mid z = (d, e)]$ is greater than one, and the upper bound is informative when this sum is less than one. The identification region for $P[y(c, e) = c]$ shrinks toward zero as the sum approaches zero and shrinks toward one as the sum approaches two.

Interestingly, we previously derived a bound of form (13A.10') in Chapter 10. There, in equation (10.4), it was the mixing-problem bound on event probabilities with the experimental evidence alone.

Complement 13B. Axiomatic Decision Theory

I have emphasized the severe difficulty of joint inference on preferences and expectations from choice data. Nonetheless, Savage (1954) developed a seminal theorem showing that choice data reveal the utility function and subjective probability distribution of a person whose behavior is consistent with maximization of expected utility. There is no contradiction, because our discussion and the Savage theorem envision having different choice data available. This complement explains.

Let person j be a member of the study population. Our discussion of inference on random expected-utility models supposes that a researcher observes one chosen action, this being the choice that person j makes from the choice set he actually faces. In contrast, the Savage theorem supposes that the researcher observes the actions that j would choose from all possible choice sets. Thus we assume that the researcher observes $y_j = y_j(C_j)$, where C_j is the realized choice set. Savage assumes that the researcher observes $y_j(D)$ for all nonempty sets $D \subset A$.

The choice data envisioned by Savage cannot be available in practice, so the Savage theorem does not yield a practical form of revealed preference analysis. Rather, it studies an extreme form of the thought experiment envisioned in Samuelsonian revealed preference analysis. A researcher equipped with the Savage data observes the choice that person j would make in every conceivable choice setting. Thus this researcher confronts no prediction problem requiring extrapolation from observed choices to counterfactual ones.

The Savage theorem is a leading example of research in *axiomatic decision theory*. Studies of this type typically suppose that one can observe $y_j(D)$ for all $D \subset A$. They assume that these choices satisfy specified properties, termed *axioms,* that are deemed to be "reasonable" or otherwise interesting from some perspective. The researcher then proves a *representation theorem* showing that the decision maker's choice behavior can be represented, or rationalized, as the behavior of a person who solves some optimization problem. For example, if choices obey Savage's axioms, behavior can be represented as that of a person who maximizes expected utility with a specific utility function over outcomes and subjective probability distribution over states of nature.

Axiomatic decision theory has the formal structure of revealed preference analysis, but its objectives are entirely different. Revealed preference analysis aims to be a practical tool enabling prediction of choice behavior in counterfactual scenarios. Axiomatic decision theory proves representation theorems for hypothetical patterns of choices.

14

Measuring Expectations

Chapter 13 ended with an indictment of the unsubstantiated rational expectations assumptions made in applications of random expected-utility models. To better cope with the difficulty of joint inference on preferences and expectations, one might anticipate that economists would use surveys or other means to measure the expectations that persons hold. However, economists have been deeply skeptical of subjective statements—they often assert that one should believe only what people do, not what they say. As a result, the profession for many years enforced something of a prohibition on the collection of expectations data. This professional prohibition has begun to break down in recent years. I describe here the history of research measuring expectations and its present status. The exposition draws on Manski (2004c).

This chapter, like those that have preceded it, addresses an identification problem created by missing data. In this case, the problem is inference on choice behavior in the absence of expectations data. This chapter differs from the others in its approach to the identification problem. We have until now studied inference when specified data are combined with various assumptions. Here we have the opportunity to mitigate the identification problem through collection of new data.

In common usage, the word "expectations" connotes beliefs about possible future events. The main part of this chapter discusses measurement of such expectations. Persons also form beliefs/expectations about past events and other facts that are relevant to choice behavior. Complement 14B discusses measurement of these expectations.

14.1 Elicitation of Expectations from Survey Respondents

This section describes some of the history of research on expectations, as a prelude to discussion of recent progress. I first critique the verbal questions posed in attitudinal research. I next discuss elicitation of probabilistic expectations in cognitive psychology. I then turn to economics.

Attitudinal Research

Attitudinal researchers have long used verbal questions to measure expectations. When asked to predict some outcome, respondents may be asked to report whether they "think" or "expect" that the event will occur. Sometimes they are asked to report the strength of this belief by reporting whether it is "very likely," "fairly likely," "not too likely," or "not at all likely" that the event will occur. A prominent example is this Michigan Survey of Consumers question on business conditions, the responses to which have been used since the 1950s to measure consumer confidence (Curtin, 1982):

> *Survey of Consumers Business-Conditions Question:* Now turning to business conditions in the country as a whole—do you think that during the next 12 months we'll have good times financially, or bad times, or what?

Another is this question on job loss in the General Social Survey, a pivotal sociological survey in the United States (Davis and Smith, 1994):

> *General Social Survey Job-Loss Question:* Thinking about the next twelve months, how likely do you think it is that you will lose your job or be laid off—very likely, fairly likely, not too likely, or not at all likely?

These questions illustrate a persistent problem that researchers face in interpreting verbal expectations data—assessment of the interpersonal comparability of responses. How do respondents to the Michigan survey interpret the phrases "business conditions" and "good times financially?" Do different respondents to the General Social Survey interpret the phrases "very likely, fairly likely, not too likely, or not at all likely" in the same way? Cognitive research does not give reason to think that responses should be or are comparable. Indeed, the available empirical evidence indicates that interpretation of verbal expectations questions varies substantially between persons (Lichtenstein and Newman, 1967; Beyth-Marom, 1982; Wallsten et al., 1986). One may also question whether responses are intrapersonally comparable; that is, a given respondent may interpret verbal phrases in different ways when asked about different events.

A second persistent problem is that the coarseness of the response options limits the information contained in the responses. Consider, for example, the fertility question asked female respondents in the annual June supplement to the Current Population Survey of the U.S. Bureau of the Census (U.S. Bureau of the Census, 1988):

> *Current Population Survey Fertility Question*: Looking ahead, do you expect to have any (more) children?   Yes   No   Uncertain

The three response options do not enable respondents to express the degree of uncertainty they perceive about their future childbearing.

Probabilistic Expectations in Cognitive Psychology

If persons can express their expectations in probabilistic form, elicitation of subjective probability distributions should have compelling advantages relative to verbal questioning. Perhaps the most basic attraction is that probability provides a well-defined absolute numerical scale for responses; hence, there is reason to think that responses may be interpersonally comparable. Another attraction is that empirical assessment of the internal consistency of respondents' expectations is possible. A researcher can use the algebra of probability (Bayes Theorem, the Law of Total Probability, etc.) to examine the internal consistency of a respondent's expectations about different events.

When probability has a frequentist interpretation, a researcher can compare elicited subjective probabilities with known event frequencies and reach conclusions about the correspondence between subjective beliefs and frequentist realities. Such *calibration studies* have a long history in cognitive psychology. Lichtenstein, Fischhoff, and Phillips (1982) review findings from 1906 on, and McClelland and Bolger (1994) update the review with findings from 1980 through 1994. Whereas the older studies mostly examined the accuracy of experts (e.g., weather forecasters' reported probabilities of precipitation), much recent research analyzes the expectations of nonexperts, especially students in a cognitive laboratory.

Within cognitive psychology, there has been controversy about the way in which humans internally represent their beliefs, and their ability and willingness to express their beliefs as numerical probabilities. Koriat, Lichtenstein, and Fischhoff (1980) and Ferrell and McGoey (1980) posed models in which individuals may have some difficulty expressing beliefs as numerical probabilities, but they nevertheless concluded that elicitation of numerical subjective probabilities is feasible. However, Zimmer (1983, 1984) argued that humans process information using verbal rather than numerical modes of thinking, and he concluded that expectations should be elicited in verbal rather than numerical forms.

Erev and Cohen (1990) and Wallsten et al. (1993) have reported that a majority of respondents prefer to communicate their own beliefs verbally and to receive the beliefs of others in the form of numerical probabilities. This asymmetry is intriguing but only marginally relevant to the design of expectations questions. The relevant question is not what communication mode respondents prefer to use, but rather what modes they are willing and able to use. Wallsten et al. (1993) report that virtually all of their respondents were willing to communicate their beliefs numerically, should the situation warrant it.

Another ongoing controversy concerns the manner in which persons process objective probabilistic information. In an influential article, Tversky and Kahneman (1974) summarized some experiments in which subjects were presented with statistics of various forms and were asked for probabilistic predictions of specified events. They interpreted the findings as showing that persons tend to use certain heuristic rules to process data, rather than Bayes Theorem.

To the extent that the Tversky and Kahneman experiments shed light on expectations formation in real life, they cast doubt on the assumption of rational expectations, not on the representation of expectations through subjective probability distributions. Indeed, Tversky and Kahneman argued for the psychological realism of subjective probabilities. Considering the propensity of axiomatic decision theorists to view subjective probabilities as constructs that may be inferred from choices, they wrote (p. 1130):

> It should perhaps be noted that, while subjective probabilities can sometimes be inferred from preferences among bets, they are normally not

formed in this fashion. A person bets on team A rather than on team B because he believes that team A is more likely to win; he does not infer this belief from his betting preferences. Thus, in reality, subjective probabilities determine preferences among bets and are not derived from them, as in the axiomatic theory of rational decision.

The controversy about the Tversky-Kahneman experiments concerns the degree to which they do shed light on subjects' use of Bayes Theorem to process data. Gigerenzer (1991) argued that the reported empirical regularities result not from respondents' use of heuristics but from the manner in which statistical information was presented to them. Here and elsewhere (e.g., Hoffrage et al., 2000), Gigerenzer and his colleagues have reported experimental evidence indicating that respondents perform much better in applying probability theory when statistics are presented in the form of natural frequencies rather than objective probabilities (e.g., "30 out of 10,000 cases," rather than "0.3 percent of cases").

Probabilistic Expectations in Economics

It is reasonable to ask whether the conventional economic wisdom against collection of subjective data is well grounded. It turns out that the scientific basis for hostility to measurement of expectations is meager. One influential event appears to have been the Machlup (1946) criticism of then ongoing efforts by economists to interview businessmen about their cost and revenue expectations. He argued that businessmen may not consciously think in terms of these economic concepts but, nonetheless, act in accordance with economic theory. Another important part of the story occurred in the 1950s and early 1960s, when economists reported negative evidence on the usefulness in predicting consumer purchase behavior of verbal assessments of expected household finances (National Bureau of Economic Research, 1960; Juster, 1964).

Among economists, the idea that survey measurement of probabilistic expectations might improve on the verbal approaches of attitudinal research appears to have originated with Juster (1966). Considering the case in which the behavior of interest is a binary purchase decision (buy or not buy), Juster considered how responses to traditional yes/no buying intentions questions should properly be interpreted. He wrote (p. 664): "Consumers reporting that they 'intend to buy A within X months' can be thought of as saying that the probability of their purchasing A within X months is high enough so that some form of 'yes' answer is more accurate than a 'no' answer." Thus he hypothesized that a consumer facing a yes/no intentions question responds as would a decision maker asked to make a best point prediction of a future random event. Working from this hypothesis, Juster concluded that it would be more informative to ask consumers for their purchase probabilities than for their buying intentions. In particular, he proposed questions that associate verbal expressions of likelihood with numerical probabilities to elicit purchase expectations for automobiles and other household appliances:

> *Juster Purchase Probability Questions:* Taking everything into account, what are the prospects that some member of your family will buy a _____ sometime during the next _____ months, between now and _____?
> Certainly, Practically Certain (99 in 100); Almost Sure (9 in 10); Very Probably (8 in 10); Probably (7 in 10); Good Possibility (6 in 10); Fairly Good Possibility (5 in 10); Fair Possibility (4 in 10); Some Possibility (3 in 10); Slight Possibility (2 in 10); Very Slight Possibility (1 in 10); No Chance, Almost No Chance (1 in 100).

He went on to collect data and concluded that elicited purchase probabilities are better predictors of subsequent individual purchase behavior than are yes/no intentions data. See Section 14.3 and Complement 14A for further discussion.

Market researchers were attracted to Juster's proposal (e.g., Morrison, 1979). The idea that expectations might be elicited probabilistically from survey respondents did not, however, draw the immediate attention of economists. By the time Juster's article was published, economists were preaching that empirical research on decision making should be based on choice data alone. A quarter century passed before economists began to systematically collect and analyze probabilistic expectations data.

The conventional economic wisdom finally unraveled in the 1990s. Numerous large-scale surveys now use probabilistic formats to elicit expectations, and a new field of empirical research on expectations has emerged. The major platforms for methodological exploration and substantive research include the Health and Retirement Study (Juster and Suzman, 1995; Hurd and McGarry, 1995), the Bank of Italy's Survey of

Household Income and Wealth (Guiso, Jappelli, and Terlizzese, 1992; Guiso, Jappelli, and Pistaferri, 2002), the Survey of Economic Expectations (Dominitz and Manski, 1997a, 1997b), the Dutch VSB Panel Survey (Das and Donkers, 1999), and the 1997 cohort of the National Longitudinal Survey of Youth (Fischhoff et al., 2000; Dominitz, Manski, and Fischhoff, 2001; Walker, 2001). Even the venerable Michigan Survey of Consumers now includes probabilistic questions along with its traditional verbal questions (Dominitz and Manski, 2004).

14.2 Illustrative Findings

This section describes some of what I have learned from my collaborative research, with Jeff Dominitz, eliciting probabilistic expectations from respondents to surveys in the United States. This work has mainly sought to answer basic empirical questions: How willing and able are respondents to reply to the questions posed? What expectations do persons hold for their futures?

Response Rates and Use of the Percent-Chance Scale

Although a long-term objective is to use expectations data to predict behavior, it has been natural to focus first on elementary matters. Showing that respondents are willing and able to respond to probabilistic questions is an obvious prerequisite for substantive interpretation of the data. When we began to collect expectations data in the early 1990s, we encountered considerable skepticism from researchers who asserted that probabilistic questioning would not "work."

One common assertion was that respondents would either refuse to answer the questions or would only give the responses 0, 50, and 100 percent. This concern has largely been laid to rest as empirical evidence has accumulated. We and other researchers have repeatedly found that respondents are as willing to respond to probabilistic questions as they are to traditional attitudinal questions on the same subjects. Respondents tend to report values at one percent intervals at the extremes (i.e., 0, 1, 2, and 98, 99, 100) and at five percent intervals elsewhere (i.e., 5, 10, . . . , 90, 95). Responses tend to be more bunched at 50 percent than at adjacent round values (40, 45, 55, 60). I discuss this phenomenon in Section 14.4.

To encourage full use of the percent-chance scale, it helps to familiarize respondents with the scale before commencing substantive questioning. The Survey of Economic Expectations (SEE), discussed below, used this introductory statement and opening question about the weather:

SEE Introduction and Opening Question: Now I will ask you some questions about future, uncertain outcomes. In each case, try to think about the whole range of possible outcomes and think about how likely they are to occur during the next 12 months. In some of the questions, I will ask you about the percent chance of something happening. The percent chance must be a number from 0 to 100. Numbers like 2 or 5 percent may be 'almost no chance,' 20 percent or so may mean 'not much chance,' a 45 or 55 percent chance may be a 'pretty even chance,' 80 percent or so may mean a 'very good chance,' and a 95 or 98 percent chance may be 'almost certain.' The percent chance can also be thought of as the number of chances out of 100.

Let's start with the weather where you live. What do you think is the percent chance (what are the chances out of 100) that it will rain tomorrow?

Another common assertion, especially from economists, was that responses to expectations questions might not reveal what persons "really think." To date, it is not possible to directly observe respondents' thinking; hence, this assertion is not directly refutable. However, it is possible to judge the *face validity* of responses. That is, one can examine the degree to which persons give responses that are consistent with the laws of probability and that are substantively reasonable. Recent empirical studies mainly, although not always, conclude that responses do possess face validity when the questions concern well-defined events that are relevant to respondents' lives.

One-Year-Ahead Income Expectations

To illustrate measurement of probabilistic expectations, I first discuss the questions on income expectations that Jeff Dominitz and I placed on an early version of our Survey of Economic Expectations. See Dominitz and Manski (1997a) for the details.

Economic analysis of household behavior assigns a central role to income expectations as a determinant of consumption/savings decisions.

Not having data on income expectations, economists studying consumption/saving have made assumptions. Consider, for example, Hall and Mishkin (1982), Skinner (1988), Zeldes (1989), Caballero (1990), and Carroll (1992). Each study assumes that persons use their own past incomes to forecast their future incomes. Perhaps so, but how do persons form expectations of future income conditional on past income? Each study assumes that persons know the actual stochastic process generating their income streams; that is, each assumes rational expectations. Each study specifies some parametric model of the income process and uses available data on income realizations to estimate the parameters.

In principle, expectations for a continuous variable such as income could be elicited in various ways. Respondents might be asked to report quantiles of their subjective distributions, moments of the distribution, or points on the cumulative distribution function. Morgan and Henrion (1990) discuss the practical pros and cons of different procedures for eliciting subjective distributions. Their recommendations formed the basis for our approach, with some tailoring of the procedures to fit the survey medium (telephone interview) and subject matter. In a telephone survey, it is infeasible to present visual aids that may help respondents to understand questions and to think probabilistically. Use of the telephone medium led us to reject elicitation of quantiles or moments of the subjective income distribution in favor of eliciting points on the distribution function.

Respondents were first asked to report the lowest and highest levels of income that they think possible in the year ahead. We did not interpret the answers to the preliminary questions literally as minimum and maximum incomes; the phrases "lowest possible" and "highest possible" are too vague to warrant this formal interpretation. Instead, we used the responses to suggest the support of the respondent's subjective distribution. Our reasoning was that responses to questions about a range of thresholds spanning the support of a respondent's subjective distribution should yield more information about the shape of the distribution than would the same number of questions asked about a narrower or wider range of thresholds.

Morgan and Henrion (1990) offer two additional, psychological, reasons for asking such preliminary questions. One is to decrease overconfidence problems where respondents focus too heavily on central tendencies, downweighting their uncertainty about outcomes. Another is to decrease anchoring problems where respondents' beliefs are influenced by the questions that interviewers pose. Suppose, for example, that a respondent expects his income to be no less than $30,000. If the first question asked concerns the probability that income will be less than $20,000, the respondent may perhaps be influenced to think that this amount is objectively reasonable. Thus asking respondents to provide their own minimum and maximum income levels, and basing subsequent thresholds on these values, replaces interviewer-induced anchoring with respondent self-anchoring. See Complement 14B for further discussion of anchoring.

The responses to the preliminary questions were used to set thresholds for a series of four probabilistic questions, of this form:

SEE Household Income Expectations Questions: What do you think is the percent chance (or what are the chances out of 100) that your total household income, before taxes, will be less than [insert threshold] over the next 12 months?

After division by 100, the responses give four points on a person's subjective distribution for household income in the year ahead. Thus, for each respondent j, we observe $F_{jk} \equiv P(y < y_{jk} \mid \Psi_j), k = 1, 2, 3, 4$, where y denotes future income, Ψ_j is the information available to respondent j, and $(y_{j1}, y_{j2}, y_{j3}, y_{j4})$ are the income thresholds about which this respondent is queried.

The subjective probabilities $(F_{jk}, k = 1, \ldots, 4)$ elicited from respondent j imply bounds on his subjective income distribution, but they do not point-identify the distribution. To facilitate analysis, we used the expectations data to fit a respondent-specific parametric distribution. Let $F(\cdot; m, q)$ denote the log-normal distribution function with median m and interquartile range (IQR) q, evaluated at any point. Let (m_j, q_j) solve the least-squares problem

$$\min_{m,q} \sum_{k=1}^{4} [F_{jk} - F(y_{jk}; m, q)]^2.$$

We used m_j and q_j to approximate respondent j's subjective median and IQR for income in the year ahead.

Supposing that actual subjective distributions are reasonably well approximated as log-normal, analysis of the cross-sectional distribution of (m, q) enables assessment of the expectations assumptions made in research on consumption/savings behavior. It has been common to assume a fixed relationship between the spread and central tendency of income expectations; some authors assume that spread does not vary with central tendency and others that spread is proportional to central tendency. We found that q tends to rise with m, but more slowly than proportionately. We also found substantial variation in q among respondents with the same value of m.

Many authors studying consumption/savings behavior have sought to explain the substantial cross-sectional variation in savings, conditional on observable attributes, documented by Avery and Kennickell (1991) and others. Hubbard, Skinner, and Zeldes (1995), for example, argue that some cross-sectional variation in savings reflects the incentive effects of asset-based, means-tested social insurance programs on precautionary savings. Other studies attribute cross-sectional variation in savings to heterogeneous preferences or to liquidity constraints. Our empirical finding of substantial variation in q among persons with the same m suggests that cross-sectional variation in the spread of income expectations may account for at least some of the observed cross-sectional variation in savings.

Social Security Expectations

Americans may be uncertain of their future Social Security retirement benefits for several reasons, including uncertainty about their future labor earnings, the formula now determining benefits, and the future structure of the Social Security system. Research aiming to understand the impact of Social Security policy on labor supply, retirement savings, and other household decisions has long been hampered by a dearth of empirical evidence on Social Security expectations. Respondents to the Health and Retirement Study (HRS) have provided point predictions of their future benefits, but uncertainty about benefits has not been measured.

Probabilistic expectations of Social Security retirement benefits were elicited from respondents to the Survey of Economic Expectations from 1999 through 2002. Respondents of ages 18–69 were read a brief description of the Social Security program and were then asked to predict their eligibility for benefits when 70 years old, as follows:

> *SEE Social Security Eligibility Question:* Politicians and the news media have been talking recently about the future of the Social Security retirement system, the federal program providing benefits to retired workers. The amount of benefits for which someone is eligible is currently determined by the person's retirement age and by earnings prior to retirement. There has been much discussion of changing the form of the Social Security system, so the future shape of the system is not certain. With this in mind, I would like you to think about what kind of Social Security retirement benefits will be available when you are older. In particular, think ahead to when you are about to turn 70 years old and suppose that you are not working at that time. What is the percent chance that you will be eligible to collect any Social Security retirement benefits at that time?

Dominitz and Manski (2006) study the responses to this question, which was posed to 2457 SEE respondents. Of the 2384 who reported a valid probability of eligibility for benefits at age 70, the mean subjective probability of eligibility was 0.57 and the median was 0.60. We found a striking age pattern in the responses, with older respondents tending to report much higher probabilities of eligibility than younger ones. For example, the estimated median subjective probability of eligibility was 0.40 at age 30, 0.50 at age 40, 0.70 at age 50, 0.90 at age 60, and 1.00 at age 65. Thus older Americans tended to be almost certain that, in one form or another, the Social Security system would survive at least ten more years. However, younger Americans had no such confidence in the continuation of the system until their retirement.

14.3 Using Expectations Data to Predict Choice Behavior

Let us return now to the prediction of choice behavior, which motivates measurement of expectations. Expectations data may be used to predict behavior in two different ways. Persons may be questioned about the choices that they would make in specified scenarios, and the responses used directly to predict their behavior. Or persons may be asked to report their expectations for unknown states of nature, and the responses combined with choice data to estimate random expected-utility models. I discuss both approaches here.

Choice Expectations

A common practice in market research and psychology, and an occasional one in economics, has been to pose choice scenarios and ask respondents to state their *intentions;* that is, to give a point prediction of the actions they would choose if they were to face these scenarios. I have cautioned (Manski, 1990b, 1999) that, even if persons have rational expectations, stated intentions may differ from eventual choices if researchers provide respondents with different information than they would have when facing actual choice problems. The norm has been to pose *incomplete scenarios*, where respondents are given only a subset of the information they would have in actual choice settings. When scenarios are incomplete, stated intentions are point predictions of uncertain choices, as Juster (1966) recognized long ago. See Complement 14A for some analysis.

Elicitation of probabilistic choice expectations overcomes the inadequacy of intentions data by permitting respondents to express uncertainty about their choice behavior in incomplete scenarios. The original Juster (1966) proposal was to elicit consumer subjective probabilities for future purchases and use the responses to predict actual purchases. One could also ask respondents to report choice expectations in scenarios that specify some conditioning event; for example, purchase probabilities supposing that some new product were available.

Use of choice expectations to predict actual choice behavior has two noteworthy features, one disadvantageous and the other advantageous. The disadvantageous feature is that if this approach is to yield accurate predictions, persons should have rational (or at least unbiased) choice expectations and realized choices should be statistically independent (or at least not strongly dependent) across the population (see Manski, 1999). The advantageous feature is that the approach does not require the researcher to assume anything about the decision rules that persons use.

Both features are apparent in a set of exploratory questions on hypothetical changes in Medicare policy posed in two waves of SEE. Respondents of age 50 to 64 were asked to report choice expectations in two scenarios. The first scenario supposed that Medicare policy remains unchanged in the future:

> *SEE Medicare Scenario:* Politicians and the news media have been talking recently about changes in Medicare, the federal health insurance program

for senior citizens. Currently, individuals 65 or older receive free insurance coverage, called Medicare Part A, which covers the cost of inpatient hospital care, home health care, hospice care, and some other services. In addition, these individuals may choose to purchase Medicare Part B, an insurance program that covers the costs of doctor's services, medical tests, and other health services not covered by Medicare Part A. The basic premium paid for Medicare Part B coverage is currently about $45 per month.

Think ahead to when you are about to turn 66 years old. Suppose that Medicare premiums stay as they currently are (about $45 per month for Part B). In this scenario, what do you think is the percent chance (what are the chances out of 100) that you would choose to purchase Medicare Part B coverage when you turn 66?

The second scenario supposed that premiums double to $90 per month, and posed the same question about purchase of Medicare Part B coverage at age 66.

Responses to these questions provide empirical evidence on a policy question of some interest. It is enticing to think that one may be able to predict the impact of Medicare policy in such a straightforward manner, without knowledge of how persons make decisions about insurance coverage. However, this presumes that the elicited choice expectations are accurate predictions of behavior.

Using Expectations and Choice Data to Estimate Random Expected-Utility Models

Researchers who use random expected-utility models to predict choice behavior envision using expectations data to relax assumptions about expectations for states of nature. Consider, for example, a labor economist studying schooling behavior. A researcher who observes only the choices that youth make confronts the inferential problem discussed in Section 13.4. Measurement of youths' expectations of the returns to schooling would solve this problem. Elicitation of entire distributions of life-cycle earnings may be impractical. Nevertheless, a researcher may use the available expectations data to lessen the dependence of inference on assumptions about expectations.

The advantages and disadvantages of this use of expectations data reverse those of the approach discussed above. The advantageous feature is that persons need not have rational expectations; it is enough to assume that elicited expectations faithfully describe persons' perceptions of their environments. The disadvantageous feature is that, given expectations and choice data, econometric analysis of behavior still requires assumptions about the distribution of preferences in the population of interest, as discussed in Chapter 13.

A notable article using probabilistic expectations data in econometric analysis of choice behavior is Nyarko and Schotter (2002), who elicited expectations of opponent behavior from experimental subjects playing a certain two-person game. Their analysis shows how probabilistic expectations data can help experimental economists to interpret subject behavior in settings such as the ultimatum game discussed in Section 13.4.

Several recent studies use expectations data to analyze the actual decision making of respondents to sample surveys. Delavande (2005) surveyed a small sample of sexually active young women in Chicago regarding their contraceptive choices and elicited their expectations for the effectiveness and side effects of alternative contraceptive methods. She combined the data on expectations and choices to estimate a random expected-utility model of contraception behavior. Lochner (2007) combined NLSY97 data on arrest expectations and crime commission to estimate a random expected-utility model of criminal behavior. Hurd, Smith, and Zissimopoulos (2004) investigated how the subjective survival probabilities elicited from HRS respondents are related to the times when they choose to retire and begin collecting Social Security benefits. Van der Klaauw and Wolpin (2002) used the HRS data on survival expectations and retirement expectations to help estimate a model of retirement behavior. These studies are a start, but economists have hardly begun to use probabilistic expectations data in econometric analysis of decision making.

14.4 Measuring Ambiguity

By and large, the discussion in Sections 14.2 and 14.3 accepted the psychological realism of probabilistic expectations and the idea that measured expectations faithfully describe persons' internal beliefs. There is by now ample empirical evidence that survey respondents are willing and able to report expectations in probabilistic form. Nevertheless, one should be careful before concluding that persons actually think probabilistically and use subjective probability distributions to make decisions.

After all, survey respondents also respond to questions seeking point predictions of uncertain events or verbal assessments of likelihood. Yet persons need not use point predictions or verbal assessments of likelihood to make decisions. What the empirical evidence does show is that, however they think and act, people are willing and able to report their beliefs in multiple forms—as point predictions, verbal assessments of likelihood, or probabilistic expectations.

With all the attention that this book has given to partial identification of probability distributions, it is natural to ask whether a person's expectations may take the form of a set of probability distributions. If so, then the single distributions that surveys now elicit from respondents are probabilistic summaries of ambiguity, much as point predictions are single-valued summaries of uncertainty. To enable persons to express ambiguity, survey researchers could elicit ranges of probabilities rather than precise probabilities for events of interest. This should be straightforward in the case of binary events, for which one could pose questions such as

> What do you think is the percent chance that event A will occur? Please respond with a particular value or a range of values, as you see fit

This format enables respondents to express whatever uncertainty or ambiguity they may feel. A respondent can express complete ignorance by reporting "0 to 100 percent," bounded ambiguity by reporting "30 to 70 percent," uncertainty by reporting "60 percent," or certainty by reporting "100 percent."

Elicitation of ranges of probabilities could help researchers eliciting probabilistic expectations to interpret the response "50 percent." Bruine de Bruin et al. (2000) and Fischhoff and Bruine de Bruin (1999) suggest that some respondents may state "fifty-fifty" to express *epistemic uncertainty;* that is, to signal an inability to place a precise probability on a future event. Elicitation of ranges would enable respondents to express ambiguity directly, rather than indirectly by saying "fifty-fifty." Presumably, respondents who continue to report 50 when permitted to state a range of values really mean 50 as a precise probability.

Complement 14A. The Predictive Power of Intentions Data: A Best-Case Analysis

This complement considers the potential power of intentions data to predict choice behavior. To begin, recall the Current Population Survey (CPS) question on fertility expectations cited in Section 14.1:

> *Current Population Survey Fertility Question:* Looking ahead, do you expect to have any (more) children?   Yes   No   Uncertain

Social scientists have long asked survey respondents to answer such *unconditional intentions* questions and have used the responses to predict actual behavior. Responses to fertility questions like that in the CPS have been used to predict fertility (Hendershot and Placek, 1981). Data on voting intentions have been used to predict American election outcomes (Turner and Martin, 1984). Surveys of buying intentions have been used to predict consumer purchase behavior (Juster, 1964).

Researchers also sometimes ask survey respondents to answer *conditional intentions* questions posing hypothetical scenarios. For example, a conditional intentions version of the CPS fertility question might be as follows:

> *Conditional Fertility Question:* Suppose that the government were to enact a child-allowance program providing families with five thousand dollars per year for each dependent child. If this program were in operation, would you expect to have any (more) children?   Yes   No   Uncertain

What is the predictive power of the responses to such questions? Just as revealed preference analysis requires assumptions about the structure of preferences, interpretation of stated intentions requires assumptions about how people respond to the questions posed and how they actually behave.

The worst case obviously is that stated intentions may reveal nothing about future behavior. To determine the best case, let us imagine ideal survey respondents who are fully aware of the process determining their behavior and who are fully willing to communicate their thinking to survey researchers. We can then ask how such ideal respondents would respond to intentions questions. I have studied this best-case scenario in the simple context of intentions questions calling for yes/no predictions of binary outcomes (Manski, 1990b). The analysis is described here.

Rational Expectations Responses to Intentions Questions

Let i and y be binary variables denoting the survey response and subsequent behavior, respectively. Thus $i = 1$ if a person responds "yes" to the intentions question, and $y = 1$ if behavior turns out to satisfy the property of interest.

Suppose that a researcher observes the intentions responses i and covariates x of a random sample of a study population, and is thus able to infer the distribution $P(i, x)$. The researcher, who does not observe persons' subsequent behavior y, wants to learn the choice probabilities $P(y \mid x, i)$ and $P(y \mid x)$; the former choice probability conditions on stated intentions and the latter does not. The inferential question is: What does knowledge of $P(i, x)$ reveal about $P(y \mid x, i)$ and $P(y \mid x)$?

I address this question under the best-case assumptions that (a) survey respondents are aware of the actual process determining their future behavior and (b) given the information they possess at the time of the survey, respondents offer their best predictions of their behavior, in the sense of minimizing expected loss (see Section 1.2). When these optimistic conditions hold, intentions data provide rational expectations point predictions of future behavior.

A person giving a rational expectations response to an intentions question recognizes that future behavior will depend in part on conditions known at the time of the survey and in part on events that have not yet occurred. For example, a woman responding to the CPS fertility question would recognize that her future childbearing will depend not only on her current family and work conditions, which are known to her at the time of the survey, but also on the future evolution of these conditions, which she cannot predict with certainty.

Let s denote the information possessed by a respondent at the time that an intentions question is posed. (In the case of a conditional intentions question, s includes the information provided in the statement of the hypothetical scenario.) Let u represent uncertainty that will be resolved between the time of the survey and the time at which the behavior y is determined. Then y is necessarily a function of (s, u), and so may be written $y(s, u)$. I shall not impose any restrictions on the form of the function $y(s, u)$.

Let $P_u \mid s$ denote the actual probability distribution of u conditional on s. Let $P(y \mid s)$ denote the actual distribution of y conditional on s. The event $y = 1$ occurs if and only if the realization of u is such that $y(s, u) = 1$. Hence, conditional on s, the probability that $y = 1$ is

(14A.1) $P(y = 1 \mid s) = P_u[y(s, u) = 1 \mid s]$.

A respondent with rational expectations knows $y(s, \cdot)$ and $P_u \mid s$ at the time of the survey; hence, she knows $P(y = 1 \mid s)$.

The respondent gives her best point prediction of her future behavior, in the sense of minimizing expected loss. The best prediction depends on the losses the respondent associates with the two possible prediction errors, $(i = 0, y = 1)$ and $(i = 1, y = 0)$. Whatever the loss function, the best prediction will satisfy the condition

(14A.2)
$$i = 1 \Rightarrow P(y = 1 \mid s) \geq p$$
$$i = 0 \Rightarrow P(y = 1 \mid s) \leq p,$$

for some threshold value $p \in (0, 1)$ that depends on the loss function. This formalizes the idea originally stated by Juster (1966) and discussed in Section 14.1. An alternative statement of (14A.2) that will be used below is

(14A.2′) $P(y = 1 \mid s, i = 0) \leq p \leq P(y = 1 \mid s, i = 1)$.

Prediction of Behavior Conditional on Intentions

Consider a researcher who wants to predict a respondent's future behavior y, conditional on her stated intention i and covariates x. Thus the researcher wants to learn $P(y \mid x, i)$. The researcher does not know the stochastic process $P_u \mid s$ generating future events nor the function $y(s, u)$ determining behavior.

A researcher who only knows that intentions are rational expectations predictions can draw no conclusions about $P(y \mid x, i)$. There are two reasons. First, if the respondent's threshold value p is unknown, equation (14A.2′) implies no restrictions on $P(y = 1 \mid s, i)$. Second, if the information s possessed by the respondent is unknown, knowledge of $P(y = 1 \mid s, i)$ yields no information about $P(y = 1 \mid x, i)$.

Conclusions can be drawn if (a) the researcher knows p and includes p among the variables x and (b) respondents know the attributes x, so s subsumes x. Then stated intentions reveal whether $P(y = 1 \mid x, i)$ is below or above p. To see this, observe that if condition (b) holds, the Law of Iterated Expectations implies that

(14A.3) $P(y = 1 \mid x, i) = E\big[P(y = 1 \mid s, i) \mid x, i\big].$

If condition (a) holds, all persons with the same value of x share the same threshold value p. So (14A.2) and (14A.3) together imply that

(14A.4) $P(y = 1 \mid x, i = 0) \leq p \leq P(y = 1 \mid x, i = 1).$

Prediction Not Conditional on Intentions

Researchers often want to predict the behavior of nonsampled members of the population from which the survey respondents were drawn. Intentions data are available only for the sampled persons, so the predictions cannot condition on i. Instead, the quantity of interest is $P(y = 1 \mid x)$.

Given conditions (a) and (b), the bound (14A.4) on $P(y = 1 \mid x, i)$ yields a bound on $P(y = 1 \mid x)$. By the Law of Total Probability,

(14A.5)
$$P(y = 1 \mid x) = P(y = 1 \mid x, i = 0)P(i = 0 \mid x)$$
$$+ P(y = 1 \mid x, i = 1)P(i = 1 \mid x).$$

The empirical evidence reveals the intentions probabilities $P(i \mid x)$, but we only know that the choice probabilities $P(y = 1 \mid x, i = 0)$ and $P(y = 1 \mid x, i = 1)$ lie in the intervals $[0, p]$ and $[p, 1]$, respectively. Hence (14A.5) implies this sharp bound on $P(y = 1 \mid x)$:

(14A.6) $pP(i = 1 \mid x) \leq P(y = 1 \mid x) \leq pP(i = 0 \mid x) + P(i = 1 \mid x).$

Observe that the bound width is $pP(i = 0 \mid x) + (1 - p)P(i = 1 \mid x)$. If $p = 1/2$, the bound width is $1/2$ for all values of $P(i \mid x)$.

Interpreting Fertility Intentions

It has long been known that intentions probabilities need not equal choice probabilities. That is, the relationship

(14A.7) $P(i = 1 \mid x) = P(y = 1 \mid x)$

need not hold (see Juster, 1966, p. 665). Nevertheless, some of the literature on fertility intentions has considered deviations from this equality as "inconsistencies" in need of explanation. Westoff and Ryder (1977, p. 449) state:

> The question with which we began this work was whether reproductive intentions are useful for prediction. The basic finding was that 40.5 percent intended more, as of the end of 1970, and 34.0 percent had more in the subsequent five years . . . . In other words, acceptance of 1970 intentions at face value would have led to a substantial overshooting of the ultimate outcome.

That is, the authors found that $P(i = 1 \mid x) = 0.405$, and subsequent data collection showed that $P(y = 1 \mid x) = 0.340$. Seeking to explain the observed "overshooting," the authors state:

> One interpretation of our finding would be that the respondents failed to anticipate the extent to which the times would be unpropitious for childbearing, that they made the understandable but frequently invalid assumption that the future would resemble the present—the same kind of forecasting error that demographers have often made.

Other demographic studies similarly presume that deviations from (14A.7) require explanation. See, for example, Davidson and Beach (1981) and O'Connell and Rogers (1983).

Rational expectations prediction does imply (14A.7) if future behavior depends only on the information s available at the time of the survey. Then a survey respondent can predict her future behavior with certainty. So i must equal y. However, we have shown that (14A.7) need not hold if events u not known at the time of the survey partially determine future behavior. A simple example makes the point forcefully.

Suppose that respondents to the CPS fertility question report that they expect to have more children when childbirth is more likely than not; that is, $p = 1/2$. Suppose that the probability of having more children is 0.51 for all women. Then all women report that they intend to have more children. This very substantial divergence between intentions and choice probabilities is consistent with the hypothesis that women report rational expectations predictions of their future fertility. By (14A.6), the rational expectations hypothesis implies only that $P(y = 1 \mid s)$ lies between 0.50 and 1.

Complement 14B. Measuring Expectations of Facts

An important special case of a rational expectations assumption is the presumption that persons have full knowledge of past events and other facts that are relevant to choice behavior. If persons have partial knowledge of facts, or incorrect perceptions, the rational expectations assumption is wrong.

Survey researchers routinely ask respondents to report point estimates for facts. For example, persons may be asked to report their pension types, the length of a past spell of unemployment, or details of their medical histories. Respondents who are uncertain about these matters sometimes choose not to respond to the questions posed. When they do respond, their self-reports may differ from actual values.

Modifying survey research practices to permit respondents to express uncertainty about facts can potentially reduce nonresponse and mis-reporting. Constructive steps in this direction have been taken by the Health and Retirement Study, which has used *unfolding bracket* questions to enable respondents to flexibly provide interval data on their income and assets. Respondents who are willing to provide point responses can do so. Those who are unwilling to respond to questions eliciting point responses are asked whether the quantity of interest lies above or below a sequence of specified thresholds. See Juster and Suzman (1995) and Hurd (1999).

Probabilistic elicitation of facts offers another route for improvement of survey research practices. When the fact of interest is real-valued, such as income or assets, the method used by Dominitz and Manski (1997a) to elicit income expectations may be applied. When the fact is

categorical, respondents can be asked to report their subjective probabilities of membership in each category.

For example, consider the reporting of pension type, which may be
defined-benefit or defined-contribution. A respondent who knows that
he holds a defined-benefit pension can report that his pension is of this
type with probability one. Someone who is unsure can place positive
probability on both types of pensions.

Probabilistic elicitation of facts has not been used as a tool of survey
research, but the idea has long had proponents in educational testing.
Shuford, Albert, and Massengill (1966) argued that requiring a student
to choose one answer to a true-false, multiple-choice, or fill-in-the-blank
question reveals (p. 125) "only a very small fraction of the information
potentially available from each query." They proposed that students
instead be asked to state subjective probabilities for the correctness
of alternative answers to a question. Moreover, they advocated use
of *reproducing scoring systems* to grade examinations. These scoring
systems make it optimal for a student to honestly reveal his beliefs,
provided that his objective is to maximize his expected test score.

Anchoring

A further potential advantage of probabilistic elicitation of facts is that
it may mitigate the anchoring problem encountered when persons are
asked to give point estimates. Psychologists have performed many randomized experiments showing that when subjects are told the value of
some real variable (say, A) and are then asked to provide a point estimate
of another real variable (say, B), estimates of B often vary monotonically
with the specified value of A. Tversky and Kahneman (1974) named this
phenomenon *anchoring*.

In the experiments showing the most substantial anchoring, B is a
fact about which most respondents are not well informed. For example, Tversky and Kahneman (1974) report an experiment in which B is
the percentage of African countries in the United Nations, Jacowitz and
Kahneman (1995) report ones in which B is the length of the Amazon
River or the height of the tallest redwood tree, and Wilson et al. (1996) report one in which B is the number of physicians and surgeons listed in the
local phone book. Several researchers have found that anchoring is less
pronounced when persons report themselves to be, or are conjectured to

be, more knowledgeable about *B*. Wilson et al. (1996) ask subjects to classify themselves as less or more knowledgeable about variable *B*, and they find less anchoring among those who classify themselves as more knowledgeable. Hurd (1999) reports that HRS respondents answering unfolding bracket questions exhibit less anchoring when, in Hurd's judgment, they are more knowledgeable about *B*.

The apparent relationship between anchoring and respondent knowledge suggests that elicitation of probabilistic expectations for *B* may mitigate anchoring problems by permitting persons to express uncertainty. Probabilistic questioning may be particularly effective when the method of elicitation enables respondents to self-anchor, as recommended by Morgan and Henrion (1990).

15

Studying Human Decision Processes

Except for criticism of rational expectations assumptions, Chapters 13 and 14 did not question the standard assumptions that modern economists maintain when studying choice behavior. I supposed that behavior is rational; that is, a person orders alternatives in terms of preference and chooses one that is ranked highest among those that are feasible. I also supposed that a person who has partial knowledge of his choice environment forms probabilistic expectations for unknown quantities and chooses an action that maximizes expected utility.

These standard assumptions have long been controversial outside the community of orthodox economists. Psychologists and neuroscientists, as well some economists who today call themselves *behavioral economists,* have stressed that humans are organisms with limited perceptual and cognitive powers. This being so, they assert that humans can no more than approximate the maximizing behavior assumed in economic models. The dispute concerns the nature and quality of the approximation.

This closing chapter considers the history and present status of the dispute from the perspective of this book. I focus more on the arguments that have been made and the kinds of research performed than on the specific findings reported. To organize the discussion, I find it useful to begin in the middle of the twentieth century and delineate three periods of research and debate, these being roughly 1950–1970, 1970–2000, and 2000–present. These periods are discussed in Sections 15.1 through 15.3.

15.1 As-If Rationality and Bounded Rationality

The As-If Argument of Friedman and Savage

Orthodox economists have long asserted that economic models of maximizing behavior are successful "as-if" approximations, even if not literal descriptions of decision processes. This assertion was made particularly strongly by Friedman and Savage (1948) and Friedman (1953), in defense not just of the basic idea of rationality but of the specific assumption that persons maximize expected utility and have rational expectations. Their argument, which uses an expert pool player as a metaphor, is so forceful and has been so controversial that I think it useful to quote it in full:

Friedman and Savage (1948, p. 298) "The hypothesis does not assert that individuals explicitly or consciously calculate and compare expected utilities. Indeed, it is not at all clear what such an assertion would mean or how it could be tested. The hypothesis asserts rather that, in making a particular class of decisions, individuals behave *as if* they calculated and compared expected utility and *as if* they knew the odds. The validity of this assertion does not depend on whether individuals know the precise odds, much less on whether they say that they calculate and compare expected utilities or think that they do, or whether it appears to others that they do, or whether psychologists can uncover any evidence that they do, but solely on whether it yields sufficiently accurate predictions about the class of decisions with which the hypothesis deals. Stated differently, the test by results is the only possible method of determining whether the *as if* statement is or is not a sufficiently good approximation to reality for the purpose at hand.

A simple example may help to clarify the point at issue. Consider the problem of predicting, before each shot, the direction of travel of a billiard ball hit by an expert billiard player. It would be possible to construct one or more mathematical formulas that would give the directions of travel that would score points and, among these, would indicate the one (or more) that would leave the balls in the best positions. The formulas might, of course, be extremely complicated, since they would necessarily take account of the location of the balls in relation to one another and to the cushions and of the complicated phenomena introduced by "english." Nonetheless, it seems not at all unreasonable that excellent predictions would be yielded by the hypothesis that the billiard player made his shots *as if* he knew the formulas, could estimate accurately by eye the angles, etc., describing the location of the balls, could make lightning calculations from the formulas, and could then make the ball travel in the direction indicated by the formulas. It would in no way disprove or contradict the hypothesis, or weaken our confidence in it, if it should turn out that the billiard player had never studied any branch of mathematics and was utterly incapable of making the necessary calculations: unless he was capable in some way of reaching approximately the same result as that obtained from the formulas, he would not in fact be likely to be an expert billiard player.

The same considerations are relevant to our utility hypothesis. Whatever the psychological mechanism whereby individuals make choices, these choices appear to display some consistency, which can apparently be described by our utility hypothesis. This hypothesis enables predictions to be made about phenomena on which there is not yet reliable evidence. The hypothesis cannot be declared invalid for a particular class of behavior until a prediction about that class proves false. No other test of its validity is decisive."   ❏

The last paragraph of this passage is admirable for its emphasis on prediction of choice behavior in counterfactual scenarios. However, I find it much less agreeable when Friedman and Savage propose that their "utility hypothesis" (that is, expected utility maximization and rational expectations) should be used to predict behavior until observation of behavior is able to refute the hypothesis. The broad lesson of Chapter 13 was that many models of behavior may be consistent with available choice data. A specific lesson was that the assumption of rational expectations is often suspect.

Why then do Friedman and Savage put forward one hypothesis, to the exclusion of all others? The reader may recall Friedman's own answer to this question, which I quoted in the Introduction and repeat here (Friedman, 1953, p. 10): "The choice among alternative hypotheses equally consistent with the available evidence must to some extent be arbitrary, though there is general agreement that relevant considerations are suggested by the criteria 'simplicity' and 'fruitfulness,' themselves notions that defy completely objective specification." I found this answer unsatisfactory in the Introduction and reiterate here. I see no reason why a scientist should choose to make predictions under a single hypothesis, dismissing others that are plausible and consistent with the available evidence. Doing so gives an impression of predictive power that one does not really have.

Simon and Bounded Rationality

Although many economists have found as-if rationality a compelling rationale for the assumptions they maintain, many other researchers have, with equal fervor, dismissed the notion out of hand. Simon (1955) put it this way in the article that spawned the modern literature in behavioral economics (p. 101):

> Because of the psychological limits of the organism (particularly with respect to computational and predictive ability), actual human rationality-striving can at best be an extremely crude and simplified approximation to the kind of global rationality that is implied, for example, by game-theoretical models.

This notion has come to be called *bounded rationality*. Simon put forward this mission for research on behavior (p. 99):

> Broadly stated, the task is to replace the global rationality of economic man with a kind of rational behavior that is compatible with the access to information and the computational capacities that are actually possessed by organisms, including man, in the kinds of environments in which such organisms exist

He went on to suggest that humans suffice with a coarse delineation between satisfactory and unsatisfactory outcomes, an idea that has come to be called *satisficing*.

A striking aspect of Simon's article is that it neither reports nor cites empirical evidence on actual human decision processes, save for a footnote briefly describing a personal observation. Instead, Simon relies on his own interpretation of "common experience," stating (p. 100):

> Lacking the kinds of empirical knowledge of the decisional processes that will be required for a definitive theory, the hard facts of the actual world can, at the present stage, enter the theory only in a relatively unsystematic and unrigorous way. But none of us is completely innocent

of acquaintance with the gross characteristics of human choice, or of the broad features of the environment in which this choice takes place. I shall feel free to call on this common experience as a source of the hypotheses needed for the theory about the nature of man and his world.

Thus, although the articles of Simon and Friedman-Savage put forward sharply contrasting hypotheses about human behavior, both articles are essentially speculative.

15.2 Choice Experiments

In the absence of empirical evidence, researchers with worldviews as divergent as Simon and Friedman-Savage might argue forever without any prospect for convergence. After a slow beginning in the 1950s and 1960s, a substantial body of empirical research has accumulated since the 1970s. The dominant mode of research has been that of experimental psychology, which has been adopted as well by experimental economics.

Research on choice behavior in experimental psychology usually means the design and performance of experiments that give subjects specified information and require them to choose among specified actions. The subjects typically are a convenience sample of persons, often students at a specific college, rather than a random sample drawn from a broad population. The proximate objective of the research usually is to test or demonstrate hypotheses about human perception, cognition, and decision processes. Prediction of choice behavior in counterfactual scenarios hardly ever forms part of the explicit agenda, although it may be an implicit reason for performing a study.

The research program of Kahneman and Tversky has been particularly influential, both within and beyond the discipline of psychology. It has also been controversial. I explain below.

Heuristics and Biases

In work on judgment under uncertainty, discussed earlier in Section 14.1, Tversky and Kahneman (1974) reported experiments on subjective assessments of probability before and after the provision of sample data. They observed some systematic inconsistencies with Bayes Theorem, which they termed *biases*. One of these is the anchoring phenomenon discussed in Complement 14B. The authors concluded that persons tend to use certain heuristics to process sample data rather than perform the algebra needed to apply Bayes Theorem. They wrote (p. 1124): "In general, these heuristics are quite useful, but sometimes they lead to severe and systematic errors." This statement is much in the spirit of Simon's bounded rationality.

Kahneman and Tversky (1979) reported experiments on decision making under risk that showed some systematic inconsistencies with the predictions of expected utility theory. They interpreted the observed choice behavior as demonstrating that persons evaluate actions in terms of gains and losses relative to a predetermined reference point, rather than in terms of absolute outcomes as in expected utility theory. They also interpreted observed behavior as demonstrating that persons evaluate gains and losses assymetrically, being risk averse with respect to gains and risk taking with respect to losses. They went on to embody these and other behavioral features in a model that they called *prospect theory*. As presented in the 1979 article, prospect theory presumes that decision makers solve well-defined maximization problems cast in terms of gains and losses. Thus it is not a wholesale rejection of economic thinking but rather a revision to expected utility theory to render what the authors believed to be a more accurate description of behavior.

Tversky and Kahneman (1981, 1986) reported further experiments on decision making that explore how choice behavior depends on the *framing* of the decision problem; that is, on the language that the researcher uses to describe the risks associated with alternative actions. These experiments had striking results. I quote here the statement and interpretation of the first experiment reported in the former article, which has drawn particular attention. In what follows, problem 1 and problem 2 are two alternative framings of the decision problem. The sample sizes and fractions of subjects making each choice are in brackets.

Tversky and Kahneman (1981, p. 453)

"Problem 1 [N = 152]: Imagine that the U.S. is preparing for the outbreak of an unusual Asian disease, which is expected to kill 600 people. Two alternative programs to combat the disease have been proposed. Assume that the exact scientific estimate of the consequences of the programs are as follows:

If Program A is adopted, 200 people will be saved. [72 percent]

If Program B is adopted, there is 1/3 probability that 600 people will be
saved, and 2/3 probability that no people will be saved. [28 percent]

Which of the two programs would you favor?

The majority choice in this problem is risk averse: the prospect of
certainly saving 200 lives is more attractive than a risky prospect of equal
expected value, that is, a one-in-three chance of saving 600 lives.

A second group of respondents was given the cover story of problem
1 with a different formulation of the alternative programs, as follows:

Problem 2 [N = 155]:

If Program C is adopted, 400 people will die. [22 percent]
If Program D is adopted, there is 1/3 probability that nobody will die,
and 2/3 probability that 600 people will die. [78 percent]

Which of the two programs would you favor?

The majority choice in problem 2 is risk taking: the certain death of
400 people is less acceptable than the two-in-three chance that 600 will
die. The preferences in problems 1 and 2 illustrate a common pattern:
choices involving gains are often risk averse and choices involving losses
are often risk taking. However, it is easy to see that the two problems
are effectively identical. The only difference between them is that the
outcomes are described in problem 1 by the number of lives saved and
in problem 2 by the number of lives lost." ❏

Tversky and Kahneman drew strong inferences from this and similar
findings in other framing experiments. They concluded not only that expected utility theory is unrealistic but that human behavior is inconsistent
with the basic *invariance* tenet of rationality, this being that "different
representations of the same choice problem should yield the same preferences" (Tversky and Kahneman, 1986, p. S253). Dismissing the basic
economic idea that persons have stable preference orderings over actions, they ultimately declared that "the normative and the descriptive
analyses of choice should be viewed as separate enterprises" (Tversky
and Kahneman, 1986, p. S275). This statement abandons the Simon view

of human behavior as a boundedly rational approximation to a rational ideal. It suggests that psychology should go its own way as a descriptive science of human behavior, no longer concerned with the way that economists conceptualize and study choice behavior.

Widespread Irrationality or Occasional Cognitive Illusions?

The specific experimental findings reported by Kahneman and Tversky during the course of their research program are not in serious question. The experiments described above have been replicated often, with broadly similar results. However, acceptance of the findings does not imply that one should accept the inferences that Kahneman and Tversky draw from them. Their conclusions that the experiments reveal general features of human behavior are huge extrapolations.

Consider, for example, the Asian-disease framing experiment cited above. In the passage describing the experiment, Tversky and Kahneman give their prospect-theory interpretation of the findings; that is, persons are risk averse when considering gains and risk taking when considering losses. They do not entertain other interpretations that are consistent with the findings. One such is that the subject pool contains many persons who are risk neutral. All of the treatment programs posed in the experiment yield the same expected result, namely, that 200 people will live and 400 will die. Thus, a risk-neutral person is indifferent among the programs. If the choice behavior of such a person is affected by the framing of problems 1 and 2, this is not evidence for prospect theory and does not imply failure of the invariance tenet of rationality.

While some psychologists have joined Kahneman and Tversky in extrapolating from particular laboratory experiments to general human behavior, others have not. In Chapter 14, I noted the response of Gigerenzer (1991) and his colleagues to the conclusions of Tversky and Kahneman (1974). Review articles by Shantcau (1989), Stanovich and West (2000), and Kühberger (2002) describe the variation in perspective across psychologists. Lopes (1991) deconstructs the rhetoric that Kahneman and Tversky have used in reporting their research.

An important reason why it is difficult to assess the external validity of the Kahneman-Tversky experiments is that these experiments reflect a purposeful search for choice tasks in which errors in judgment and decision making are prominent. Kahneman and Tversky (1982) have argued that purposeful search for errors is a useful methodological approach. They write (p. 123):

> Much of the recent literature on judgment and inductive reasoning has been concerned with errors, biases and fallacies in a variety of mental tasks . . . The emphasis on the study of errors is characteristic of research in human judgment, but is not unique to this domain: we use illusions to understand the principles of normal perception and we learn about memory by studying forgetting.

They later elaborate, stating (p. 124):

> There are three related reasons for the focus on systematic errors and inferential biases in the study of reasoning. First, they expose some of our intellectual limitations and suggest ways of improving the quality of our thinking. Second, errors and biases often reveal the psychological processes and the heuristic procedures that govern judgment and inference. Third, mistakes and fallacies help the mapping of human intuitions by indicating which principles of statistics or logic are non-intuitive or counter-intuitive.

This methodological approach may have scientific merit. However, the Kahneman-Tversky emphasis on the study of errors and biases creates a severe inferential problem for a reader of their published research. One learns the findings of the experiments that they report, which invariably show that errors and biases are commonplace. However, one learns nothing about the findings that would occur in experiments that they either do not report or did not perform.

Consider, for example, the Asian-disease framing experiment. How would subjects behave if the stated numbers of deaths and lives saved were changed, so that a risk-neutral person would not be indifferent between treatment programs (A, B, C, D)? Would the strong framing effect persist, or would it diminish as the welfare consequence of the decision becomes larger?

One could, of course, perform and report experiments that answer these questions. The Kahneman and Tversky articles on framing do not indicate whether such experiments were performed and, if so, what the findings were. Thus one cannot know whether the published findings demonstrate that humans are prone to widespread irrationality or only occasional cognitive illusions.

15.3 Prospects for a Neuroscientific Synthesis

A curious feature of behavioral research in experimental psychology has been its abstraction from the physiology of the human organism. For example, the Kahneman and Tversky articles discussed above do not tie the hypothesized heuristics and biases to the operation of the brain. The ideas of anchoring, evaluation of gains and losses, and framing are as much disembodied concepts as are the economist's concepts of preferences and expected utility.

The research tradition in neuroscience is different. To a neuroscientist, studying human choice behavior means research seeking to discover how the brain actually functions when it perceives, processes, and reacts to inputs from its environment. The proximate scientific objective is to understand behavior in physiological terms. A more distant applied objective is to learn facts about brain structure and operations that may prove useful in predicting or influencing behavior.

Until recently, research in neuroscience focused on the abnormalities in behavior created by injuries to the brain, chemical imbalances, and so on. Study of normal brain functioning while performing tasks of judgment and decision was infeasible in the absence of instruments capable of measuring the subtle electrical transmissions and chemical reactions that occur as the brain goes about its everyday operations. However, the recent invention of increasingly sophisticated instrumentation for brain imaging and related physiological measurements is now making it feasible to observe aspects of the biological processes that accompany judgment and decision making. As a result, we are seeing some convergence of experimental psychology with neuroscience, as well as the beginnings of a field of *neuroeconomics*. For example, McCabe et al. (2001) measure aspects of brain activity while subjects play a two-person game. Hsu et al. (2005) measure brain activity when subjects make decisions with different degrees of knowledge of the choice environment. De Martino et al. (2006) report on brain activity as subjects deal with choice problems that are framed in different ways. Camerer, Loewenstein, and Prelec (2005) review the emerging literature.

As I write this in 2006, neuroscientific research on judgment and decision making is in its infancy. Current instrumentation, while impressive, is much too primitive for researchers to assert that they can observe what subjects are thinking. At most, one can now measure some gross biological correlates of thinking. Nevertheless, the recent and ongoing research may already be having an important effect on the study of choice behavior by relating it to the physical properties of the human organism, as Simon sought to do over fifty years ago.

References

Afriat, S. 1967. "The Construction of Utility Functions from Expenditure Data." *International Economic Review*, 8:67–77.

Ahn, H., and J. Powell. 1993. "Semiparametric Estimation of Censored Selection Models with a Nonparametric Selection Mechanism." *Journal of Econometrics*, 58:3–29.

Andrews, D., S. Berry, and P. Jia. 2004. "Confidence Regions for Parameters in Discrete Games with Multiple Equilibria, with an Application to Discount Chain Store Location." Department of Economics, Yale University

Angrist, J. 1990. "Lifetime Earnings and the Vietnam Era Draft Lottery: Evidence from Social Security Administrative Records." *American Economic Review*, 80: 313–336.

Angrist, J., G. Imbens, and D. Rubin. 1996. "Identification of Causal Effects Using Instrumental Variables." *Journal of the American Statistical Association*, 91: 444–455.

Arrow. K., and L. Hurwicz. 1972. "An Optimality Criterion for Decision-Making Under Ignorance." In D. Carter and J. Ford, eds., *Uncertainty and Expectations in Economics*. Oxford: Blackwell.

Ashenfelter, O., and A. Krueger. 1994. "Estimates of the Economic Returns to Schooling from a New Sample of Twins." *American Economic Review*, 84: 1157–1173.

Avery, R., and A. Kennickell. 1991. "Household Saving in the U.S." *Review of Income and Wealth*, 37: 409–432.

Balke, A., and J. Pearl. 1997. "Bounds on Treatment Effects from Studies with Imperfect Compliance." *Journal of the American Statistical Association*, 92: 1171–1177.

Bassi, L., and O. Ashenfelter. 1986. "The Effect of Direct Job Creation and Training Programs on Low-Skilled Workers." In S. Danziger and D. Weinberg, eds., *Fighting Poverty*. Cambridge, Mass.: Harvard University Press.

Bedford, T., and I. Meilijson. 1997. "A Characterization of Marginal Distributions of (Possibly Dependent) Lifetime Variables Which Right Censor Each Other." *Annals of Statistics*, 25: 1622–1645.

Beresteanu, A., and F. Molinari. 2006. "Asymptotic Properties for a Class of Partially Identified Models." Department of Economics, Cornell University.

Berger, J. 1985. *Statistical Decision Theory and Bayesian Analysis*. New York: Springer-Verlag.

Berkson, J. 1944. "Application of the Logistic Function to Bioassay." *Journal of the American Statistical Association*, 39: 357–365.

Berkson, J. 1958. "Smoking and Lung Cancer: Some Observations on Two Recent Reports." *Journal of the American Statistical Association*, 53: 28–38.

Berrueta-Clement, J., L. Schweinhart, W. Barnett, A. Epstein, and D. Weikart. 1984. *Changed Lives: The Effects of the Perry Preschool Program on Youths through Age 19*. Ypsilanti, Mich.: High/Scope Press.

Berry, S., J. Levinsohn, and A. Pakes. 1994. "Automobile Prices in Market Equilibrium." *Econometrica*, 63: 841–890.

Beyth-Marom, R. 1982. "How Probable Is Probable? A Numerical Translation of Verbal Probability Expressions." *Journal of Forecasting*, 1: 257–269.

Bhattacharya, J., V. Shaikh, and E. Vytlacil. 2005. "Treatment Effect Bounds: An Application to Swan-Ganz Catherization." Department of Economics, Stanford University.

Björklund, A., and R. Moffitt. 1987. "Estimation of Wage Gains and Welfare Gains in Self-Selection Models." *Review of Economics and Statistics*, 69: 42–49.

Blackmore, J., and J. Welsh. 1983. "Selective Incapacitation: Sentencing According to Risk." *Crime and Deliquency*, 29: 504–528.

Bloom, H. 1984. "Accounting for No-Shows in Experimental Evaluation Designs." *Evaluation Review*, 8: 225–246.

Blumstein, A., J. Cohen, and D. Nagin, eds. 1978. *Deterrence and Incapacitation: Estimating the Effects of Criminal Sanctions on Crime Rates*. Washington, D.C.: National Academy Press.

Blumstein, A., J. Cohen, J. Roth, and C. Visher, eds. 1986. *Criminal Careers and Career Criminals*. Washington, D.C.: National Academy Press.

Blundell, R., A. Gosling, H. Ichimura, and C. Meghir. 2007. "Changes in the Distribution of Male and Female Wages Accounting for Employment Composition Using Bounds." *Econometrica*, 75: 323–363.

Bollinger, C. 1996. "Bounding Mean Regressions When a Binary Regressor Is Mismeasured." *Journal of Econometrics*, 73: 387–399.

Bork, R. (Solicitor General), et al. 1974. *Fowler v. North Carolina*, U.S. Supreme Court case no. 73-7031. Brief for U.S. as amicus curiae: 32–39.

Bowers, W., and G. Pierce. 1975. "The Illusion of Deterrence in Isaac Ehrlich's Research on Capital Punishment." *Yale Law Journal*, 85: 187–208.

Brock, W. 2006. "Profiling Problems with Partially Identified Structure." *Economic Journal*, 116: F427–F440.

Bruine de Bruin, W., B. Fischhoff, B. Halpern-Felsher, and S. Millstein. 2000. "Expressing Epistemic Uncertainty: It's a Fifty-Fifty Chance." *Organizational Behavior and Human Decision Processes*, 81: 115–131.

Caballero, R. 1990. "Consumption Puzzles and Precautionary Savings." *Journal of Monetary Economics*, 25: 113–136.

Cain, G. 1986. "The Issues of Marital Stability and Family Composition and the Income Maintenance Experiments." In A. Munnell, ed., *Lessons from the Income Maintenance Experiments*. Boston: Federal Reserve Bank of Boston.

Camerer, C., and M. Weber. 1992. "Recent Developments in Modeling Preferences: Uncertainty and Ambiguity." *Journal of Risk and Uncertainty*, 5: 325–370.

Camerer, C., G. Loewenstein, and D. Prelec. 2005. "Neuroeconomics: How Neuroscience Can Inform Economics." *Journal of Economic Literature*, 43: 9–64.

Campbell, D. 1984. "Can We Be Scientific in Applied Social Science?" *Evaluation Studies Review Annual*, 9: 26–48.

Campbell, D., and J. Stanley 1963, *Experimental and Quasi-Experimental Designs for Research*. Chicago: Rand McNally.

Card, D. 1993. "Using Geographic Variation in College Proximity to Estimate the Return to Schooling." Working Paper 4483, Cambridge, Mass.: National Bureau of Economic Research.

Card, D. 1994. "Earnings, Schooling, and Ability Revisited." Working Paper 4832, Cambridge, Mass.: National Bureau of Economic Research.

Carroll, C. 1992. "The Buffer-Stock Theory of Saving: Some Macroeconomic Evidence." *Brookings Papers on Economic Activity*, 2: 61–156.

Center for Human Resource Research. 1992. *NLS Handbook 1992. The National Longitudinal Surveys of Labor Market Experience*. Columbus, Ohio: Ohio State University.

Chaiken, J., and M. Chaiken. 1982. *Varieties of Criminal Behavior*. Report R-2814-NIJ, Santa Monica, Calif.: RAND Corporation.

Chernozhukov, V., H. Hong, and E. Tamer. 2007. "Estimation and Confidence Regions for Parameter Sets in Econometric Models." *Econometrica*, forthcoming.

Ciliberto, F., and E. Tamer. 2004. "Market Structure and Multiple Equilibria in Airline Markets." Department of Economics, Northwestern University.

Cochran, W. 1977. *Sampling Techniques*, third edition. New York: Wiley.

Cochran, W., F. Mosteller, and J. Tukey. 1954. *Statistical Problems of the Kinsey Report on Sexual Behavior in the Human Male*. Washington, D.C.: American Statistical Association.

Coleman, J., E. Campbell, C. Hobson, J. McPartland, A. Mood, F. Weinfeld, and R. York. 1966. *Equality of Educational Opportunity*. Washington, D.C.: U.S. Government Printing Office.

Coleman, J., E. Katz, and H. Menzel. 1957. "The Diffusion of an Innovation among Physicians." *Sociometry*, 20: 253–270.

Committee on Ways and Means, U.S. House of Representatives. 1993. *1993 Green Book*. Washington D.C.: U.S. Government Printing Office.

Cook, T., and D. Campbell. 1979. *Quasi-Experimentation: Design and Analysis Issues for Field Settings*. New York: Houghton-Mifflin.

Cornfield, J. 1951. "A Method of Estimating Comparative Rates from Clinical Data. Applications to Cancer of the Lung, Breast, and Cervix." *Journal of the National Cancer Institute*, 11: 1269–1275.

Coyle, S., R. Boruch, and C. Turner, eds. 1989. *Evaluating AIDS Prevention Programs*. Washington, D.C.: National Academy Press.

Crane, J. 1991. "The Epidemic Theory of Ghettos and Neighborhood Effects on Dropping Out and Teenage Childbearing." *American Journal of Sociology*, 96: 1226–1259.

Crits-Christoph, P., L. Siqueland, J. Blaine, and A. Frank. 1999. "Psychosocial Treatments for Cocaine Dependence." *Archives of General Psychiatry*, 56: 493–502.

Cross, P., and C. Manski. 2002. "Regressions, Short and Long." *Econometrica*, 70: 357–368.

Crowder, M. 1991. "On the Identifiability Crisis in Competing Risks Analysis." *Scandinavian Journal of Statistics*, 18: 223–233.

Curtin, R. 1982. "Indicators of Consumer Behavior: The University of Michigan Surveys of Consumers." *Public Opinion Quarterly*, 46: 340–352.

Daganzo, C., F. Bouthelier, and Y. Sheffi. 1977. "Multinomial Probit and Qualitative Choice: A Computationally Efficient Algorithm." *Transportation Science*, 11: 338–358.

Das, M., and B. Donkers. 1999. "How Certain Are Dutch Households about Future Income? An Empirical Analysis." *Review of Income and Wealth*, 45: 325–338.

Davidson, A., and L. Beach. 1981. "Error Patterns in the Prediction of Fertility Behavior." *Journal of Applied Social Psychology*, 11: 475–488.

Davis, J., and T. Smith. 1994. *The General Social Surveys, 1972–1994, Cumulative File.* Chicago: National Opinion Research Center.

DeGroot, M. 1970. *Optimal Statistical Decisions.* New York: McGraw-Hill.

Delavande, A. 2005. "Pill, Patch, or Shot? Subjective Expectations and Birth Control Choice." Discussion Paper 4856, Center for Economic Policy Research.

De Martino, B., D. Kumaran, B. Seymour, and R. Dolan. 2006. "Frames, Biases, and Rational Decision-Making in the Human Brain." *Science*, 313: 684–687.

Dominitz, J., and C. Manski. 1997a. "Using Expectations Data to Study Subjective Income Expectations." *Journal of the American Statistical Association*, 92: 855–867.

Dominitz, J., and C. Manski. 1997b. "Perceptions of Economic Insecurity: Evidence from the Survey of Economic Expectations." *Public Opinion Quarterly*, 61: 261–287.

Dominitz, J., and C. Manski. 2004. "How Should We Measure Consumer Confidence?" *Journal of Economic Perspectives*, 18: 51–66.

Dominitz, J., and C. Manski. 2006. "Measuring Pension-Benefit Expectations Probabilistically." *Labour*, 20: 201–236.

Dominitz, J., C. Manski, and B. Fischhoff. 2001. "Who Are Youth *At-Risk*?: Expectations Evidence in the NLSY-97." In R. Michael, ed., *Social Awakenings: Adolescents' Behavior as Adulthood Approaches.* New York: Russell Sage Foundation.

Dominitz, J., and R. Sherman. 2004. "Sharp Bounds under Contaminated or Corrupted Sampling with Verification, with an Application to Environmental Pollutant Data." *Journal of Agricultural, Biological, and Environmental Statistics*, 9: 319–338.

Dominitz, J., and R. Sherman. 2006. "Identification and Estimation of Bounds on School Performance Measures: A Nonparametric Analysis of a Mixture Model with Verification." *Journal of Applied Econometrics*, 21: 1295–1326.

Dubin, J., and D. Rivers. 1993. "Experimental Estimates of the Impact of Wage Subsidies." *Journal of Econometrics*, 56: 219–242.

Duncan, O., and B. Davis. 1953. "An Alternative to Ecological Correlation." *American Sociological Review*, 18: 665–666.

Duncan, O., A. Haller, and A. Portes. 1968. "Peer Influences on Aspirations: A Reinterpretation." *American Journal of Sociology*, 74: 119–137.

Ehrlich, I. 1975. "The Deterrent Effect of Capital Punishment: A Question of Life and Death." *American Economic Review*, 65: 397–417.

Einhorn, H., and R. Hogarth. 1986. "Decision Making under Ambiguity." In R. Hogarth and M. Reder, eds., *Rational Choice.* Chicago: University of Chicago Press.

Ellsberg, D. 1961. "Risk, Ambiguity, and the Savage Axioms." *Quarterly Journal of Economics*, 75: 643–669.

Erev, I., and B. Cohen. 1990. "Verbal versus Numerical Probabilities: Efficiency, Biases, and the Preference Paradox." *Organizational Behavior and Human Decision Processes*, 45: 1–18.

Ferguson, T. 1967. *Mathematical Statistics: A Decision-Theoretic Approach*. New York: Academic Press.

Ferrell, W., and P. McGoey. 1980. "A Model of Calibration for Subjective Probabilities." *Organizational Behavior and Human Performance*, 26: 32–53.

Fischhoff, B., and W. Bruine de Bruin. 1999. "Fifty-Fifty = 50%?" *Journal of Behavioral Decision Making*, 12: 149–163.

Fischhoff, B., A. Parker, W. Bruine de Bruin, J. Downs, C. Palmgren, R. Dawes, and C. Manski. 2000. "Teen Expectations for Significant Life Events." *Public Opinion Quarterly*, 64: 189–205.

Fisher, F. 1966. *The Identification Problem in Econometrics*. New York: McGraw-Hill.

Fisher, L., and L. Moyé. 1999. "Carvedilol and the Food and Drug Administration Approval Process: An Introduction." *Controlled Clinical Trials*, 20: 1–15.

Fisher, R. 1935. *The Design of Experiments*. London: Oliver and Boyd.

Fitzgerald, J., P. Gottschalk, and R. Moffitt. 1998. "An Analysis of Sample Attrition in Panel Data." *Journal of Human Resources*, 33: 251–299.

Fleiss, J. 1981. *Statistical Methods for Rates and Proportions*. New York: Wiley.

Fréchet, M. 1951. "Sur Les Tableaux de Correlation Donte les Marges Sont Donnees." *Annals de l'Universite de Lyon A*, Series 3, 14: 53–77.

Friedlander, D., D. Greenberg, and P. Robins. 1997. "Evaluating Government Training Programs for the Economically Disadvantaged." *Journal of Economic Literature*, 35: 1809–1855.

Friedman, M. 1953. *Essays in Positive Economics*. Chicago: University of Chicago Press.

Friedman, M., and L. Savage. 1948. "The Utility Analysis of Choices Involving Risk." *Journal of Political Economy*, 56: 279–304.

Frisch, R. 1934. *Statistical Confluence Analysis by Means of Complete Regression Systems*. Oslo, Norway: University Institute for Economics.

Galichon, A., and M. Henry. 2006. "Inference in Incomplete Models." Department of Economics, Columbia University.

Gigerenzer, G. 1991. "How to Make Cognitive Illusions Disappear: Beyond Heuristics and Biases." *European Review of Social Psychology*, 2: 83–115.

Ginther, D. 2002. "Alternative Estimates of the Effect of Schooling on Earnings." *Review of Economics and Statistics*, 82: 103–116.

Goldberger, A. 1972. "Structural Equation Methods in the Social Sciences." *Econometrica*, 40: 979–1001.

Goodman, L. 1953. "Ecological Regressions and Behavior of Individuals." *American Sociological Review*, 18: 663–664.

Greenberg, D., and M. Wiseman. 1992. "What Did the OBRA Demonstrations Do?" In C. Manski and I. Garfinkel, eds., *Evaluating Welfare and Training Programs*. Cambridge, Mass.: Harvard University Press.

Greenwood, P., and A. Abrahamse. 1982. *Selective Incapacitation*. Report R-2815-NIJ, Santa Monica, Calif.: RAND Corporation.

Gronau, R. 1974. "Wage Comparisons—A Selectivity Bias." *Journal of Political Economy*, 82: 1119–1143.

Gueron, J., and E. Pauly. 1991. *From Welfare to Work*. New York: Russell Sage Foundation.

Guiso, L., T. Jappelli, and L. Pistaferri. 2002. "An Empirical Analysis of Earnings and Employment Risk." *Journal of Business and Economic Statistics*, 20: 241–253.

Guiso, L., T. Jappelli, and D. Terlizzese. 1992. "Earnings Uncertainty and Precautionary Saving." *Journal of Monetary Economics*, 30: 307–337.

Haile, P., and E. Tamer. 2003. "Inference with an Incomplete Model of English Auctions." *Journal of Political Economy*, 111: 1–51.

Hall, R., and F. Mishkin. 1982. "The Sensitivity of Consumption to Transitory Income: Estimates from Panel Data on Households." *Econometrica*, 50: 461–477.

Härdle, W. 1990. *Applied Nonparametric Regression*. Cambridge: Cambridge University Press.

Hauser, R. 1970. "Context and Consex: A Cautionary Tale." *American Journal of Sociology*, 75: 645–664.

Hausman, J., and D. Wise. 1978. "A Conditional Probit Model for Qualitative Choice: Discrete Decisions Recognizing Interdependence and Heterogeneous Preferences." *Econometrica*, 46: 403–426.

Hausman, J., and D. Wise. 1979. "Attrition Bias in Experimental and Panel Data: The Gary Income Maintenance Experiment." *Econometrica*, 47: 455–473.

Hausman, J., and D. Wise, eds. 1985. *Social Experimentation*. Chicago: University of Chicago Press.

Heckman, J. 1976. "The Common Structure of Statistical Models of Truncation, Sample Selection, and Limited Dependent Variables and a Simple Estimator for Such Models." *Annals of Economic and Social Measurement*, 5: 479–492.

Heckman, J., J. Smith, and N. Clements. 1997. "Making the Most Out of Programme Evaluations and Social Experiments: Accounting for Heterogeneity in Programme Impacts." *Review of Economic Studies*, 64: 487–535.

Heckman, J., and E. Vytlacil. 2001. "Local Instrumental Variables." In C. Hsiao, K. Morimune, and J. Powell, eds., *Nonlinear Statistical Inference: Essays in Honor of Takeshi Amemiya.* Cambridge: Cambridge University Press.

Hendershot, G., and P. Placek, eds. 1981. *Predicting Fertility.* Lexingon, Mass.: D.C. Heath.

Hoffrage, U., S. Lindsey, R. Hertwig, and G. Gigerenzer. 2000. "Communicating Statistical Information." *Science*, 290: 2261–2262.

Holden, C. (1990). "Head Start Enters Adulthood." *Science*, 247: 1400–1402.

Honoré, B., and A. Lleras-Muney. 2006. "Bounds in Competing Risks Models and the War on Cancer." *Econometrica*, 74: 1675–1698.

Honoré, B., and E. Tamer. 2006. "Bounds on Parameters in Panel Dynamic Discrete Choice Models." *Econometrica*, 74: 611–629.

Hood, W., and T. Koopmans, eds. 1953. *Studies in Econometric Method.* New York: Wiley.

Horowitz, J. 1998. *Semiparametric Methods in Econometrics*, New York: Springer-Verlag.

Horowitz, J., and C. Manski. 1995. "Identification and Robustness with Contaminated and Corrupted Data." *Econometrica*, 63: 281–302.

Horowitz, J., and C. Manski. 1998. "Censoring of Outcomes and Regressors Due to Survey Nonresponse: Identification and Estimation Using Weights and Imputations." *Journal of Econometrics*, 84: 37–58.

Horowitz, J., and C. Manski. 2000. "Nonparametric Analysis of Randomized Experiments with Missing Covariate and Outcome Data." *Journal of the American Statistical Association*, 95: 77–84.

Horowitz, J., and C. Manski. 2006. "Identification and Estimation of Statistical Functionals Using Incomplete Data." *Journal of Econometrics*, 132: 445–459.

Horowitz, J., C. Manski, M. Ponomareva, and J. Stoye. 2003. "Computation of Bounds on Population Parameters When the Data Are Incomplete." *Reliable Computing*, 9: 419–440.

Hotz, J. 1992. "Designing an Evaluation of the Job Training Partnership Act." In C. Manski and I. Garfinkel, eds., *Evaluating Welfare and Training Programs*. Cambridge, Mass.: Harvard University Press.

Hotz, J., C. Mullin, and S. Sanders. 1997. "Bounding Causal Effects Using Data from a Contaminated Natural Experiment: Analyzing the Effects of Teenage Childbearing." *Review of Economic Studies*, 64: 575–603.

Hsieh, D., C. Manski, and D. McFadden. 1985. "Estimation of Response Probabilities from Augmented Retrospective Observations." *Journal of the American Statistical Association*, 80: 651–662.

Hsu, M., M. Bhatt, R. Adolphs, D. Tranel, and C. Camerer. 2005. "Neural Systems Responding to Degrees of Uncertainty in Human Decision-Making." *Science*, 310: 1680–1683.

Hubbard, G., J. Skinner, and S. Zeldes. 1995. "Precautionary Saving and Social Insurance." *Journal of Political Economy*, 103: 360–399.

Huber, P. 1981. *Robust Statistics*. New York: Wiley.

Hurd, M. 1999. "Anchoring and Acquiescence Bias in Measuring Assets in Household Surveys." *Journal of Risk and Uncertainty*, 19: 111–136.

Hurd, M., and K. McGarry. 1995. "Evaluation of the Subjective Probabilities of Survival in the Health and Retirement Study." *Journal of Human Resources*, 30: S268–S292.

Hurd, M., J. Smith, and J. Zissimopoulos. 2004. "The Effects of Subjective Survival on Retirement and Social Security Claiming." *Journal of Applied Econometrics*, 19: 761–775.

Imbens, G. 2004. "Nonparametric Estimation of Average Treatment Effects under Exogeneity: A Review." *Review of Economics and Statistics*, 86:4–29.

Imbens, G., and J. Angrist. 1994. "Identification and Estimation of Local Average Treatment Effects." *Econometrica*, 62: 467–476.

Imbens, G., and C. Manski. 2004. "Confidence Intervals for Partially Identified Parameters." *Econometrica*, 72: 1845–1857.

Jacowitz, K., and D. Kahneman. 1995. "Measures of Anchoring in Estimation Tasks." *Personality and Social Psychology Bulletin*, 21: 1161–1166.

Jencks, C., and S. Mayer. 1989. "Growing Up in Poor Neighborhoods: How Much Does It Matter?" *Science*, 243: 1441–1445.

Juster, T. 1964. *Anticipations and Purchases: An Analysis of Consumer Behavior.* Princeton: Princeton University Press.

Juster T. 1966. "Consumer Buying Intentions and Purchase Probability. An Experiment in Survey Design." *Journal of the American Statistical Association*, 61: 658–696.

Juster, T., and R. Suzman. 1995. "An Overview of the Health and Retirement Study." *Journal of Human Resources*, 30: S7–S56.

Kahneman, D., and A. Tversky. 1979. "Prospect Theory: An Analysis of Decision under Risk." *Econometrica*, 47: 263–291.

Kahneman, D., and A. Tversky. 1982. "On the Study of Statistical Intuitions." *Cognition*, 11: 123–141.

Kalbfleisch, J., and R. Prentice. 1980. *The Statistical Analysis of Failure Time Data*. New York: Wiley.

Karlin, S., and H. Rubin. 1956. "The Theory of Decision Procedures for Distributions with Monotone Likelihood Ratio." *Annals of Mathematical Statistics*, 27: 272–299.

Keynes, J. 1921. *A Treatise on Probability*. London: MacMillan.

King, G. 1997. *A Solution to the Ecological Inference Problem: Reconstructing Individual Behavior from Aggregate Data*. Princeton: Princeton University Press.

King, G., and L. Zeng. 2002. "Estimating Risk and Rate Levels, Ratios and Differences in Case-Control Studies." *Statistics in Medicine*, 21: 1409–1427.

Klein, L., B. Forst, and V. Filatov. 1978. "The Deterrent Effect of Capital Punishment: An Assessment of the Estimates." In A. Blumstein, J. Cohen, and D. Nagin, eds., *Deterrence and Incapacitation: Estimating the Effects of Criminal Sanctions on Crime Rates*. Washington, D.C.: National Academy Press.

Klepper, S., and E. Leamer. 1984. "Consistent Sets of Estimates for Regressions with Errors in All Variables." *Econometrica*, 52: 163–183.

Knight, F. 1921. *Risk, Uncertainty, and Profit*. Boston: Houghton-Mifflin.

Koenker, R., and G. Bassett. 1978. "Regression Quantiles." *Econometrica*, 46: 33–50.

Koopmans, T. 1949. "Identification Problems in Economic Model Construction." *Econometrica*, 17: 125–144.

Koriat, A., S. Lichtenstein, and B. Fischhoff. 1980. "Reasons for Confidence." *Journal of Experimental Psychology: Human Learning and Memory*, 6: 107–118.

Kreider, B., and J. Pepper. 2007. "Disability and Employment: Reevaluating the Evidence in Light of Reporting Errors." *Journal of the American Statistical Association*, forthcoming.

Kühberger, A. 2002. "The Rationality of Risky Decisions." *Theory and Psychology*, 12: 427–452.

Kurz, M., and R. Spiegelman. 1973. "Social Experimentation: A New Tool in Economics and Policy Research." Research Memorandum 22, Stanford Research Institute.

LaLonde, R. 1986. "Evaluating the Econometric Evaluations of Training Programs with Experimental Data." *American Economic Review*, 76: 604–620.

Lerman, S., and C. Manski. 1981. "On the Use of Simulated Frequencies to Approximate Choice Probabilities." In C. Manski and D. McFadden, eds., *Structural Analysis of Discrete Data with Econometric Applications*. Cambridge, Mass.: M.I.T. Press.

Lichtenstein, S., B. Fischhoff, and L. Phillips. 1982. "Calibration of Probabilities: The State of the Art to 1980." In D. Kahneman, P. Slovic, and A. Tversky, eds., *Judgment under Uncertainty: Heuristics and Biases*. New York: Cambridge University Press.

Lichtenstein, S., and R. Newman. 1967. "Empirical Scaling of Common Verbal Phrases Associated with Numerical Probabilities." *Psychonomic Science*, 9: 563–564.

Lochner, L. 2007. "Individual Perceptions of the Criminal Justice System." *American Economic Review*, 97: 444–460.

Lopes, L. 1991. "The Rhetoric of Irrationality." *Theory and Psychology*, 1: 65–82.

Luce, R., and P. Suppes. 1965. "Preference, Utility, and Subjective Probability." In R. Luce, R. Bush, and E. Galanter, eds., *Handbook of Mathematical Psychology*, vol. 3. New York: Wiley.

Machlup, F. 1946. "Marginal Analysis and Empirical Research." *American Economic Review*, 36: 519–554.

Maddala, G. S. 1983. *Limited-Dependent and Qualitative Variables in Econometrics*. Cambridge: Cambridge University Press.

Manski, C. 1975. "Maximum Score Estimation of the Stochastic Utility Model of Choice." *Journal of Econometrics*, 3: 205–228.

Manski, C. 1988a. "Ordinal Utility Models of Decision Making under Uncertainty." *Theory and Decision, 25*: 79–104.

Manski, C. 1988b. "Identification of Binary Response Models." *Journal of the American Statistical Association*, 83: 729–738.

Manski, C. 1989. "Anatomy of the Selection Problem." *Journal of Human Resources*, 24: 343–360.

Manski, C. 1990a. "Nonparametric Bounds on Treatment Effects." *American Economic Review Papers and Proceedings*, 80: 319–323.

Manski, C. 1990b. "The Use of Intentions Data to Predict Behavior: A Best Case Analysis." *Journal of the American Statistical Association*, 85: 934–940.

Manski, C. 1993. "Identification of Endogenous Social Effects: The Reflection Problem." *Review of Economic Studies*, 60: 531–542.

Manski, C. 1994. "The Selection Problem." In C. Sims, ed., *Advances in Econometrics, Sixth World Congress*. Cambridge: Cambridge University Press.

Manski, C. 1995. *Identification Problems in the Social Sciences*. Cambridge, Mass.: Harvard University Press.

Manski, C. 1997a. "Monotone Treatment Response." *Econometrica*, 65: 1311–1334.

Manski, C. 1997b. "The Mixing Problem in Programme Evaluation." *Review of Economic Studies*, 64: 537–553.

Manski, C. 1999. "Analysis of Choice Expectations in Incomplete Scenarios." *Journal of Risk and Uncertainty*, 19: 49–66.

Manski, C. 2000. "Identification Problems and Decisions under Ambiguity: Empirical Analysis of Treatment Response and Normative Analysis of Treatment Choice." *Journal of Econometrics*, 95: 415–442.

Manski, C. 2001. "Nonparametric Identification under Response-Based Sampling." In C. Hsiao, K. Morimune, and J. Powell, eds., *Nonlinear Statistical Inference: Essays in Honor of Takeshi Amemiya*. New York: Cambridge University Press.

Manski, C. 2002a. "Treatment Choice under Ambiguity Induced by Inferential Problems." *Journal of Statistical Planning and Inference*, 105: 67–82.

Manski, C. 2002b. "Identification of Decision Rules in Experiments on Simple Games of Proposal and Response." *European Economic Review*, 46: 880–891.

Manski, C. 2003. *Partial Identification of Probability Distributions*. New York: Springer-Verlag.

Manski, C. 2004a. "Social Learning from Private Experiences: The Dynamics of the Selection Problem." *Review of Economic Studies*, 71: 443–458.

Manski, C. 2004b. "Statistical Treatment Rules for Heterogeneous Populations," *Econometrica*, 72: 1221–1246.

Manski, C. 2004c. "Measuring Expectations." *Econometrica*, 72: 1329–1376.

Manski, C. 2005. *Social Choice with Partial Knowledge of Treatment Response*. Princeton: Princeton University Press.

Manski, C. 2006. "Search Profiling with Partial Knowledge of Deterrence." *Economic Journal*, 116: F385–F401.

Manski, C. 2007. "Minimax-Regret Treatment Choice with Missing Outcome Data." *Journal of Econometrics*, 139: 105–115.

Manski, C., and I. Garfinkel, eds. 1992. *Evaluating Welfare and Training Programs*. Cambridge, Mass.: Harvard University Press.

Manski, C., and S. Lerman. 1977. "The Estimation of Choice Probabilities from Choice-Based Samples." *Econometrica*, 45: 1977–1988.

Manski, C., and D. Nagin. 1998. "Bounding Disagreements about Treatment Effects: A Case Study of Sentencing and Recidivism." *Sociological Methodology*, 28: 99–137.

Manski, C., and J. Pepper. 2000. "Monotone Instrumental Variables: With an Application to the Returns to Schooling." *Econometrica*, 68: 997–1010.

Manski, C., G. Sandefur, S. McLanahan, and D. Powers. 1992. "Alternative Estimates of the Effect of Family Structure during Adolescence on High School Graduation." *Journal of the American Statistical Association*, 87: 25–37.

Manski, C., and E. Tamer. 2002. "Inference on Regressions with Interval Data on a Regressor or Outcome." *Econometrica*, 70: 519–546.

Manski, C., and A. Tetenov. 2007. "Admissible Treatment Rules for a Risk-Averse Planner with Experimental Data on an Innovation." *Journal of Statistical Planning and Inference*, 137: 1998–2010.

Manski, C., and D. Wise. 1983. *College Choice in America*. Cambridge, Mass.: Harvard University Press.

Marschak, J. 1960. "Binary Choice Constraints on Random Utility Indicators." In K. Arrow, ed., *Stanford Symposium on Mathematical Methods in the Social Sciences*. Palo Alto, Calif.: Stanford University Press.

Maskin, E. 1979. "Decision-Making under Ignorance with Implications for Social Choice." *Theory and Decision*, 11: 319–337.

Mayer, S. 1991. "How Much Does a High School's Racial and Socioeconomic Mix Affect Graduation and Teenage Fertility Rates?" In C. Jencks and P. Peterson, eds., *The Urban Underclass*. Washington, D.C.: The Brookings Institution.

McCabe, D., L. Houser, L. Ryan, V. Smith, and T. Trouard. 2001. "A Functional Imaging Study of Cooperation in Two-Person Reciprocal Exchange." *Proceedings of the National Academy of Sciences*, 98: 11832–11835.

McClelland, A., and F. Bolger. 1994. "The Calibration of Subjective Probabilities: Theories and Models 1980–94." In G. Wright and P. Ayton, eds., *Subjective Probability*. New York: Wiley.

McFadden, D. 1974. "Conditional Logit Analysis of Qualitative Choice Behavior." In P. Zarembka, ed., *Frontiers in Econometrics*. New York: Academic Press.

McFadden, D. 1978. "Modelling the Choice of Residential Location." In A. Karlqvist, L. Lundqvist, F. Snickars, and J. Weibull, eds., *Spatial Interaction Theory and Planning Models*. Amsterdam: North-Holland.

McFadden, D. 1981. "Econometric Models of Probabilistic Choice." In C. Manski and D. McFadden, eds., *Structural Analysis of Discrete Data with Econometric Applications*. Cambridge, Mass.: M.I.T. Press.

McFadden, D., and K. Train. 2000. "Mixed MNL Models for Discrete Response." *Journal of Applied Econometrics*, 15: 447–470.

Mincer, J. 1958. "Investment in Human Capital and Personal Income Distribution." *Journal of Political Economy*, 66:281–302.

Mirrlees, J. 1971. "An Exploration in the Theory of Optimal Income Taxation." *Review of Economic Studies*, 38; 175–208.

Moffitt, R. 1992. "Evaluation Methods for Program Entry Effects." In C. Manski and I. Garfinkel, eds., *Evaluating Welfare and Training Programs*. Cambridge, Mass.: Harvard University Press.

Molinari, F. 2002. "Missing Treatments." Department of Economics, Cornell University.

Molinari, F. 2007. "Partial Identification of Probability Distributions with Misclassified Data." *Journal of Econometrics*, forthcoming.

Morgan, G., and M. Henrion. 1990. *Uncertainty: A Guide to Dealing with Uncertainty in Quantitative Risk and Policy Analysis*. New York: Cambridge University Press.

Morrison, D. 1979. "Purchase Intentions and Purchase Behavior." *Journal of Marketing*, 43: 65–74.

National Bureau of Economic Research. 1960. *The Quality and Economic Significance of Anticipations Data*. Special Conference Series. Princeton: Princeton University Press.

Nyarko, Y., and A. Schotter. 2002. "An Experimental Study of Belief Learning Using Elicited Beliefs." *Econometrica*, 70: 971–1005.

O'Connell, M., and C. Rogers. 1983. "Assessing Cohort Birth Expectations Data from the Current Population Survey, 1971–1981." *Demography*, 20: 369–383.

Ord, J. 1972. *Families of Frequency Distributions.* Griffin's Statistical Monographs & Courses No. 30. New York: Hafner.

Passell, P. "Like a New Drug, Social Programs Are Put to the Test." *New York Times*, March 9, 1993, p. C1.

Passell, P., and J. Taylor. 1975. "The Deterrent Effect of Capital Punishment: Another View." Discussion Paper 74-7509, Department of Economics, Columbia University.

Pepper, J. 2000. "The Intergenerational Transmission of Welfare Receipt: A Nonparametric Bounds Analysis." *Review of Economics and Statistics*, 82: 472–88.

Pepper, J. 2003. "Using Experiments to Evaluate Performance Standards: What Do Welfare-to-Work Demonstrations Reveal to Welfare Reformers?" *Journal of Human Resources*, 38: 860–880.

Peterson, A. 1976. "Bounds for a Joint Distribution Function with Fixed Subdistribution Functions: Application to Competing Risks." *Proceedings of the National Academy of Sciences*, 73: 11–13.

Piliavin, I., and M. Sosin. 1988. "Exiting Homelessness: Some Recent Empirical Findings." Institute for Research on Poverty, University of Wisconsin–Madison.

Polinsky, M., and S. Shavell. 2000. "The Economic Theory of Public Enforcement of Law." *Journal of Economic Literature*, 38: 45–76.

Reiersol, O. 1941. "Confluence Analysis by Means of Lag Moments and Other Methods of Confluence Analysis." *Econometrica*, 9: 1–24.

Reiersol, O. 1945. "Confluence Analysis by Means of Instrumental Sets of Variables." *Arkiv fur Matematik, Astronomi Och Fysik*, 32A, No.4, 1–119.

Robins, J. 1989. "The Analysis of Randomized and Non-randomized AIDS Treatment Trials Using a New Approach to Causal Inference in Longitudinal Studies." In L. Sechrest, H. Freeman, and A. Mulley, eds., *Health Service Research Methodology: A Focus on AIDS*. Washington, D.C.: NCHSR, U.S. Public Health Service.

Robinson, W. 1950. "Ecological Correlation and the Behavior of Individuals." *American Sociological Review*, 15: 351–357.

Rosen, A. 2006. "Confidence Sets for Partially Identified Parameters That Satisfy a Finite Number of Moment Inequalities." Department of Economics, University College London.

Rosenbaum, P. 1984. "From Association to Causation in Observational Studies: The Role of Tests of Strongly Ignorable Treatment Assignment." *Journal of the American Statistical Association*, 79: 41–48.

Rosenbaum, P. 1995. *Observational Studies*. New York: Springer-Verlag.

Rosenbaum, P., and D. Rubin, 1983. "The Central Role of the Propensity Score in Observational Studies for Causal Effects." *Biometrika*, 70: 41–55.

Roth, A. 1995. "Bargaining Experiments." In J. Kagel and A. Roth, eds., *The Handbook of Experimental Economics*. Princeton: Princeton University Press.

Rotnitzky, A., J. Robins, and D. Scharfstein. 1998. "Semiparametric Regression for Repeated Outcomes with Nonignorable Nonresponse." *Journal of the American Statistical Association*, 93: 1321–1339.

Roy, A. 1951. "Some Thoughts on the Distribution of Earnings." *Oxford Economic Papers*, 3: 135–146.

Rubin, D. 1974. "Estimating Causal Effects of Treatments in Randomized and Nonrandomized Studies." *Journal of Educational Psychology*, 66: 688–701.

Rubin, D. 1976. "Inference and Missing Data." *Biometrika*, 63: 581–590.

Rubin, D. 1987. *Multiple Imputation for Nonresponse in Surveys*. New York: John Wiley & Sons.

Ruschendorf, L. 1981. "Sharpness of Fréchet-Bounds." *Zeitschrift fur Wahrscheinlichkeitstheorie und Verwandte Gebiete*, 57: 293–302.

Samuelson, P. 1938. "A Note on the Pure Theory of Consumer Behavior." *Economica*, 5: 61–71.

Samuelson, P. 1948. "Consumption Theory in Terms of Revealed Preferences." *Economica*, 15: 243–253.

Savage, L. 1951. "The Theory of Statistical Decision." *Journal of the American Statistical Association*, 46: 55–67.

Savage, L. 1954. *The Foundations of Statistics*. New York: Wiley.

Scharfstein, J., C. Manski, and J. Anthony. 2004. "On the Construction of Bounds in Prospective Studies with Missing Ordinal Outcomes: Application to the Good Behavior Game Trial." *Biometrics*, 60: 154–164.

Schlag, K. 2006. "ELEVEN-Tests Needed for a Recommendation." Working Paper ECO 2006–2, European University Institute.

Sewell, W., and J. Armer. 1966. "Neighborhood Context and College Plans." *American Sociological Review*, 31: 159–168.

Shaikh, V. 2005. "Inference for Partially Identified Econometric Models." Department of Economics, Stanford University.

Shaikh, V., and E. Vytlacil. 2005. "Threshold-Crossing Models and Bounds on Treatment Effects: A Nonparametric Approach." Department of Economics, Stanford University.

Shanteau, J. 1989. "Cognitive Heuristics and Biases in Behavioral Auditing: Review, Comments, and Observations." *Accounting, Organizations and Society*, 14: 165–177.

Shuford, E., A. Albert, and H. Massengill. 1966. "Admissible Probability Measurement Procedures." *Psychometrika*, 31: 125–145.

Simon, H. 1955. "A Behavioral Model of Rational Choice." *Quarterly Journal of Economics*, 69: 99–118.

Skinner, J. 1988. "Risky Income, Life Cycle Consumption and Precautionary Savings." *Journal of Monetary Economics*, 22: 217–255.

Stanovich, K., and R. West. 2000. "Individual Differences in Reasoning: Implications for the Rationality Debate?" *Behavioral and Brain Sciences*, 23: 645–726.

Stoye, J. 2004. "Partial Identification of Spread Parameters When Some Data Are Missing." Department of Economics, New York University.

Stoye, J. 2006. "Minimax-Regret Treatment Choice with Finite Samples." Department of Economics, New York University.

Theil, H. 1971. *Principles of Econometrics*. New York: Wiley.

Thurstone, L. 1927. "A Law of Comparative Judgment." *Psychological Review*, 34: 273–286.

Turner, C., and E. Martin, eds. 1984. *Surveying Subjective Phenomena*. New York: Russell Sage Foundation.

Tversky, A., and D. Kahneman. 1974. "Judgment under Uncertainty: Heuristics and Biases." *Science*, 185: 1124–1131.

Tversky, A., and D. Kahneman. 1981. "The Framing of Decisions and the Psychology of Choice." *Science*, 211: 453–458.

Tversky, A., and D. Kahneman. 1986. "Rational Choice and the Framing of Decisions." *Journal of Business*, 59: S251–S278.

U.S. Bureau of the Census. 1988. "Fertility of American Women: June 1987." In *Current Population Reports*, Series P-20, No. 427. Washington, D.C.: U.S. Government Printing Office.

U.S. Bureau of the Census. 1991. "Money Income of Households, Families, and Persons in the United States: 1988 and 1989." In *Current Population Reports*, Series P-60, No. 172. Washington, D.C.: U.S. Government Printing Office.

U.S. General Accounting Office. 1992. *Unemployed Parents*. GAO/PEMD-92–19BR, Gaithersburg, Md.: U.S. General Accounting Office.

Van der Klaauw, W., and K. Wolpin. 2002. "Social Security, Pensions, and the Savings and Retirement Behavior of Households," Department of Economics, University of Pennsylvania.

Varian, H. 1982. "The Nonparametric Approach to Demand Analysis." *Econometrica*, 50: 945–973.

Wald, A. 1950. *Statistical Decision Functions*. New York: Wiley.

Walker, J. 2001. "Adolescents' Expectations Regarding Birth Outcomes: A Comparison of the NLSY79 and NLSY97 Cohorts." In R. Michael, ed., *Social Awakenings: Adolescents' Behavior as Adulthood Approaches*, New York: Russell Sage Foundation.

Wallsten, T., D. Budescu, A. Rapoport, R. Zwick, and B. Forsyth. 1986. "Measuring the Vague Meanings of Probability Terms." *Journal of Experimental Psychology: General*, 115: 348–365.

Wallsten T., D. Budescu, R. Zwick, and S. Kemp. 1993. "Preferences and Reasons for Communicating Probabilistic Information in Verbal or Numerical Terms." *Bulletin of the Psychonomic Society*, 31: 135–138.

Westoff, C., and N. Ryder. 1977. "The Predictive Validity of Reproductive Intentions." *Demography*, 14: 431–453.

Willis, R., and S. Rosen. 1979. "Education and Self-Selection." *Journal of Political Economy*, 87: S7–S36.

Wilson, T., C. Houston, K. Etling, and N. Brekke. 1996. "A New Look at Anchoring Effects: Basic Anchoring and Its Antecedents." *Journal of Experimental Psychology: General*, 125: 387–402.

Woittiez, I., and A. Kapteyn. 1991. "Social Interactions and Habit Formation in a Labor Supply Model." Department of Economics, University of Leiden, the Netherlands.

Woodbury, S., and R. Spiegelman. 1987. "Bonuses to Workers and Employers to Reduce Unemployment: Randomized Trials in Illinois." *American Economic Review*, 77: 513–530.

Wright, S. 1928. Appendix B to Wright, P., *The Tariff on Animal and Vegetable Oils*. New York: McMillan.

Zaffalon, M. 2002. "Exact Credal Treatment of Missing Data." *Journal of Statistical Planning and Inference*, 105: 105–122.

Zeldes, S. 1989. "Optimal Consumption with Stochastic Income: Deviations from Certainty Equivalence." *Quarterly Journal of Economics*, 104: 275–298.

Zimmer, A. 1983. "Verbal vs. Numerical Processing of Subjective Probabilities." In R. Scholz, ed., *Decision Making under Uncertainty*, Amsterdam: North-Holland.

Zimmer, A. 1984. "A Model for the Interpretation of Verbal Predictions." *International Journal of Man-Machine Studies*, 20: 121–134.

Author Index

This index includes page references to authors where they are mentioned in the chapters, but not where they appear in the Reference section.

Subject Index

Absolute loss, 20–22, 31
Admissibility, 247–248
Admissible, 248, 250–252
Aid to Families with Dependent Children
(AFDC), 120–122, 159
Ambiguity, coping with, 6–10; and planning,
212–242; measuring, 288–299
Anchoring, 293, 306–307, 312, 317
As-if rationality, 309–311
Association and causation, 152
Asymptotic, 33, 37, 43, 53, 64, 72, 193,
243–244
Attitudinal research, 285, 288
Attributable risk, 110–119, 122
Attrition, 13, 36, 40–42
Average treatment effect (ATE), 131–133, 136,
145, 147–148, 152, 158–159, 166, 190,
192–194, 241
Axiomatic decision theory, 162, 282–283

Bandwidth, 24–25, 32–34
Barnhart, Jo Anne, 138
Basic Educational Opportunity Grant (BEOG).
See Pell Grant
Bayes decision or rule, 215–216, 219–221,
228, 230, 233, 237, 253
Bayes Theorem, 8, 23, 57, 65, 111–112, 119,
286–288, 312–313
Benefit-cost, 223
Best predictor, introduced, 19–21; estimation

from random samples, 22–24; parametric
models for, 89–91. *See also* Absolute loss,
Loss functions, Square loss
Binary outcome, 67, 71, 143, 250, 301
Bounded random variable, 43
Bounded rationality, 309–313

Calibration studies, 286
Case-control sampling, 9, 109. *See also*
Response-based sampling
Causal effect, 152, 158
Causation, 27, 152–153
Choice-based sampling, 9, 109. *See also*
Response-based sampling
Choice expectations, 296–297
Choice experiment, 312–317
Choice probability, 264–266, 270, 275, 281,
301
Choice under ambiguity, 213–219, 226
Clinical trial, 13, 137, 225, 234, 239–240, 253
Cognitive illusion, 315–317
Combining multiple surveys, 68–69
Comparing treatments, 130–131
Competing risks model, 11, 150
Competitive game, 216–217
Competitive market, 10, 155, 167–170
Compliance, 139–148, 199, 213, 218–219,
221, 227, 233, 241, 243, 251, 259
Complier, 145–148, 227
Conditional Bayes, 245, 249